Crossing Cultures

Readings for Composition

FOURTH EDITION

Henry Knepler

Illinois Institute of Technology

Myrna Knepler

Northeastern Illinois University

Kathleen Kane

Hostos Community College of the City University of New York

Macmillan College Publishing Company

NEW YORK

Editor: Barbara A. Heinssen
Production Supervisor: Bert Yaeger
Production Manager: Su Levine
Text Designer: Robert Freese
Cover Designer: Robert Freese
Cover illustration: Nicholas Hill
Photo Researcher: Robert Schatz

This book was set in Garamond Light by Carlisle Communications, Ltd. and was printed and bound by Arcata Fairfield. The cover was printed by New England Book Components, Inc. The color insert was printed by Princeton Polychrome Press.

Macmillan College Publishing Company
866 Third Avenue, New York, New York 10022

Macmillan College Publishing Company is part of
the Maxwell Communication Group of Companies.

Maxwell Macmillan Canada, Inc.
1200 Eglinton Avenue East
Suite 200
Don Mills, Ontario M3C 3N1

Library of Congress Cataloging-in-Publication Data

Crossing cultures : readings for composition / [compiled by Henry
   Knepler, Myrna Knepler, Kathleen Kane].
      p.   cm.
   Includes index.
   ISBN 0-02-365250-0 (pbk.)
   1. College readers.   2. English language—Rhetoric.   3. Cross-cultural
studies.   I. Knepler, Henry W.   II. Knepler, Myrna.
III. Kane, Kathleen, [date]
PE1417.C75   1994
808'.0427—dc20   93-2278
                                                                           CIP

Printing: 1 2 3 4 5 6 7   Year: 4 5 6 7 8 9 0

PREFACE

For this fourth edition of *Crossing Cultures* it is no longer necessary to explain why a reader designed for composition classes should deal with cross-cultural and inter-ethnic themes. When the book first made its appearance in the early 1980s, it was the only composition reader of its kind to do so exclusively. Now there are many—a reflection of the realization that the culture of the United States at the end of the twentieth century can best be seen a mosaic—a whole made of many parts.

Using Cross-cultural Themes

The success of this book has established the fact that cross-cultural subjects work well in a composition course. They have a strong impact on students: they challenge accepted beliefs by asking students to consider the lives, ideas, aspirations—and prejudices—of people who are very different from them. At the same time, reading, and having one's classmates read, selections related to one's own culture is likely to heighten students' self-assurance and cause them to reflect on the meaning of their own experience. This reflection and reaction to the readings and class discussion can often be the starting point for writing that "belongs" to the student yet extends beyond his or her own (perhaps limited) experience of the world.

Each selection has been chosen because it is "a good read" whose subject and style will engage college students and provide material for student–student and student–teacher discussions.

Crossing Cultures *as a Composition Text*

Content that is thematically interesting and challenging is not enough, however, for a reader to be useful in a class whose main goal is the improvement of student writing. *Crossing Cultures* provides many tools to aid in writing development. Arranged thematically, the selections also represent the major patterns of organization usually taught in a writing class. A supplementary Rhetorical Table of Contents points to those patterns.

Each selection, except for the poems, is followed by a set of exercises. "Some Important Words" singles out terms that may not be familiar to students. "Some of the Issues" aids students in careful reading.

"The Way We Are Told" leads them to an examination of the author's strategies. Each exercise section concludes with "Some Subjects for Writing." Asterisks indicate questions or writing topics that refer to more than one selection, often giving students the chance to compare and contrast two different views of the same subject.

All editions of *Crossing Cultures* have included headnotes to help the student prepare for reading and to point out other works by the same author. Many of these headnotes have been expanded in the fourth edition. The new *Instructor's Manual,* in addition to providing sample answers, contains additional background information about the author or setting of the selection.

Organization

Crossing Cultures contains eight thematically organized chapters introducing students to a wide variety of cultures in the United States. Because we need to look at other cultures in order to define our own, one chapter, "Other Worlds," places its emphasis on cultures elsewhere.

All editions of *Crossing Cultures* have contained selections of varying length and difficulty. Users of previous editions have told us that they appreciate this range and have found suitable material for both less experienced and more sophisticated student readers and writers. In this edition we have made the level of difficulty more transparent. Each of the eight chapters begins with accessible pieces, usually short, often personal and in some cases written by young writers in college or recently out of it. The selections that follow are of increasing complexity. All eight chapters now end with a short story and a poem.

New in the Fourth Edition

Eighteen selections are new to this edition, further extending the cultural range of the book. New pieces include work by Mike Rose (Italian-American), Amy Tan (Chinese-American), Anton Shammas (Palestinian), Sandra Cisneros (Latina) and Eva Hoffman (Polish-American). We have increased the number of women writers to twenty-seven.

A photo essay entitled "Rites of Passage in America" celebrates the diversity of the American experience. Accompanying it are questions designed to develop student visual and critical thinking skills.

Acknowledgments

Several reviewers have given us good advice on choice of selections as well as other features. We thank Donna Hicks, DeVry Institute of Technology; Ane Ipsen, California State University at Fullerton; James MacDonald, University of Southwestern Louisiana; Lori Miller, University of California at Irvine; Carol Serevino, University of Iowa; Donna Thomsen, Johnson and Wales; Bernadette Wikowski, Seton Hall University; Mark Wood, Portland Community College.

Anne Knepler worked long, hard, and skillfully at securing permissions for new and old pieces. Elinor Knepler provided invaluable help throughout the preparation of this edition, particularly during the final stages of editing and proofreading the manuscript. We are grateful for her patience, knowledge, and good judgment.

We want to thank the staff at Macmillan: Chris Migdol and his assistant, Robert Schatz, for finding photos that are both beautiful and appropriate; Bert Yaeger for overseeing the production; Cindy Branthoover for careful editing. Michelle Warren, the editorial assistant assigned to the book, was on hand to answer many questions.

Special thanks go to our editor, Barbara Heinssen, whose knowledge, ability, and hard work we have counted upon in this edition as well as previous ones.

CONTENTS

PART ONE   Growing Up   1

Elizabeth Wong   **The Struggle to Be an All-American Girl**   3

"... my brother and I had to go to Chinese school. No amount of kicking, screaming, or pleading could dissuade my mother, who was solidly determined to have us learn the language of our heritage."

Maya Angelou   **Graduation**   7

"Days before, we had made a sign for the Store, and as we turned out the lights Momma hung the cardboard over the doorknob. It read clearly: CLOSED. GRADUATION."

Maxine Hong Kingston   **Girlhood Among Ghosts**   19

"When I went to kindergarten and had to speak English for the first time, I became silent."

Jack Agueros   **Halfway to Dick and Jane: A Puerto Rican Pilgrimage**   25

"When you got to the top of the hill, something strange happened: America began, because from the hill south was where the 'Americans' lived. Dick and Jane were not dead; they were alive and well in a better neighborhood."

Lindsy Van Gelder   **The Importance of Being Eleven: Carol Gilligan Takes on Adolescence**   39

"Instead of living comfortably inside their own skin, they measure themselves against an idealized, perfect girl."

Mike Rose   **I Just Wanna Be Average**   45

"It's popular these days to claim you grew up on the streets."

Grace Paley   **The Loudest Voice**   60

"We learned 'Holy Night' without an error. 'How wonderful!' said Miss Glacé, the student teacher. 'To think that some of you don't even speak the language!' "

Countee Cullen   **Incident**   68

"Now I was eight and very small."

PART TWO   **Heritage**   69

John Tarkov   **Fitting In**   71
"Every father has a vision of what he'd like his son to be.
Every son has a vision in kind of his father."

Toni Morrison   **A Slow Walk of Trees**   76
"His name was John Solomon Willis, and when at age 5 he
heard from the old folks that 'the Emancipation Proclamation
was coming,' he crawled under the bed."

Michael Novak   **In Ethnic America**   82
"We did not feel this country belonged to us. We felt fierce
pride in it, more loyalty than anyone could know. But we
felt blocked at every turn."

Arthur L. Campa   **Anglo vs. Chicano: Why?**   90
"A century of association has inevitably acculturated both
Hispanos and Anglo-Americans to some extent, but there
still persist a number of culture traits that neither group has
relinquished altogether."

Anton Shammas   **Amérka, Amérka: A Palestinian
Abroad in the Land of the Free**   96
"We travel light, empty-pocketed, with the vanity of those
who think home is a portable idea, something that dwells
mainly in the mind or within a text."

Harry Mark Petrakis   **Barba Nikos**   106
"One of our untamed games was to seek out the owner of a
pushcart or a store, unmistakably an immigrant, and bedevil
him with a chorus of insults and jeers. To prove allegiance
to the gang it was necessary to reserve our fiercest
malevolence for a storekeeper or peddler belonging to our
own ethnic background."

Wendy Rose   **Three Thousand Dollar Death Song**   112
"From this distant point we watch our bones/auctioned with
our careful beadwork. . . ."

PART THREE   **Families**   115

Sun Park   **Don't Expect Me to Be Perfect**   116
"If I were a genius, I would not mind being treated like one.
But since I am not, I do."

Alfred Kazin **The Kitchen**   119

"All my memories of that kitchen are dominated by the
nearness of my mother sitting all day long at her sewing
machine, by the clacking of the treadle against the linoleum
floor, by the patient twist of her right shoulder as she
automatically pushed at the wheel with one hand. . . ."

Jane Howard **Families**   123

"Good families are much to all their members, but
everything to none."

Susan Chira **The Good Mother: Searching
for an Ideal**   129

"Caught between a fictional ideal, changing expectations of
women's roles and the reality that many mothers now work
because they must, women around the country are groping
for a new definition of the good mother."

Arlene Skolnick **The Paradox of Perfection**   139

"The image of the perfect, happy family makes ordinary
families seem like failures."

Amy Tan **Two Kinds**   148

" 'Only two kinds of daughters,' she shouted in Chinese. 'Those
who are obedient and those who follow their own mind!' "

Theodore Roethke **My Papa's Waltz**   160

"You . . . waltzed me off to bed/Still clinging to your shirt."

PART FOUR **Identities**   161

Marcus Mabry **Living in Two Worlds**   163

"In mid-December I was at Stanford, among the palm trees
and weighty chores of academe. . . . Once I got home to
New Jersey, reality returned."

Maria L. Muñiz **Back, but Not Home**   167

"I want to return because the journey back will also mean a
journey within. Only then will I see the missing piece."

Eva Hoffman **Lost in Translation**   171

". . . as I hear my choked-up voice straining to assert itself,
as I hear myself missing every beat and rhythm that would
say "funny" and "punch line," I feel a hot flush of
embarrassment."

Norman Podhoretz   **The Brutal Bargain**   177

"One of the longest journeys in the world is the journey
from Brooklyn to Manhattan."

Malcolm X   **Hair**   187

"I took the little list of ingredients . . . to a grocery store,
where I got a can of Red Devil lye, two eggs, and two
medium-sized white potatoes."

Gerald Early   **Their Malcolm, My Problem**   190

"Malcolm, frozen in time, stands before us as the lonely
outsider, a kind of bespectacled prince, estranged and
embattled, holding a high-noon posture of startling and
doomed confrontation."

Sandra Cisneros   **Barbie-Q**   203

"Yours is the one with mean eyes and a ponytail. Striped
swimsuit, stilettos, sunglasses, and gold hoop earrings."

Gwendolyn Brooks   **We Real Cool**   206

"We real cool. We/Left School."

PHOTO ESSAY   **Rites of Passage in America**   207

PART FIVE   **Encounters**   215

Brent Staples   **Night Walker**   217

". . . I soon gathered that being perceived as dangerous is a
hazard in itself."

Walter White   **I Learn What I Am**   222

"In the flickering light the mob swayed, paused, and began
to flow toward us. In that instant there opened up within
me a great awareness; I knew then who I was. I was a
Negro, . . ."

Jeanne Wakatsuki Houston and James D. Houston
Arrival at Manzanar   229

"Mama took out another dinner plate and hurled it at the
floor, then another and another, never moving, never
opening her mouth, just quivering and glaring at the
retreating dealer, with tears streaming down her cheeks."

Michael Dorris   **For the Indians, No Thanksgiving   236**

"Only good Indians are admitted into this tableau, of course:
those who accept the manifest destiny of a European
presence and are prepared to adopt English dining customs
and, by inference, English everything else."

Piri Thomas   **Alien Turf   240**

"This crap kept up for a month. They tried to shake me up.
Every time they threw something at me, it was just to see
me jump."

Dwight Okita   **In Response to Executive Order 9066:
All Americans of Japanese Descent Must Report
to Relocation Centers   252**

"My best friend is a white girl named Denise—/we look at
boys together."

PART SIX   **New Worlds   255**

Bette Bao Lord   **Walking in Lucky Shoes   257**

". . . shoes that took me up a road cleared by the footfalls of
millions of immigrants before me—to a room of my own."

Christopher Columbus   **Journal of Discovery,
October 10th to 12th, 1492   261**

"I was on the poop deck at ten o'clock in the evening when
I saw a light."

David Gates   **Who Was Columbus?   266**

"Like heroes from Julius Caesar to John Kennedy,
Christopher Columbus has mostly been who people wanted
him to be."

Michel Guillaume St. Jean de Crèvecoeur
What Is an American?   271

"Here individuals of all nations are melted into a new race of
men, whose labours and posterity will one day cause great
change in the world."

Alistair Cooke   **The Huddled Masses**   277

"The first thing they heard over the general bedlam were the
clarion voices of inspectors bellowing out numbers in Italian,
German, Polish, Hungarian, Russian, and Yiddish."

Recapture the Flag: 34 Reasons to Love America 287

"The way immigration transforms the nation's eating habits:
Wieners, potatoes, pizza, chow mein, spaghetti, tacos, egg
rolls, curry, mock duck, pad thai."

Anzia Yezierska   **Soap and Water**   291

"Every time I had to come to the dean's office for a private
conference, I prepared for the ordeal of her cold scrutiny, as
a patient prepares for a surgical operation."

Joseph Bruchac   **Ellis Island**   299

"Like millions of others,/I too come to this island,/nine
decades the answerer/of dreams."

PART SEVEN   **Other Worlds**   301

Mark Salzman   **Teacher Mark**   303

" 'Chinese parents love their children, but they also think
that children are like furniture. They own you, and you must
make them comfortable until they decide to let you go.' "

Margaret Atwood   **Canadians: What Do They Want?**   312

"It's hard to explain to Americans what it feels like to be a
Canadian."

George Orwell   **Shooting an Elephant**   318

"In Moulmein, in lower Burma, I was hated by large
numbers of people—the only time in my life that I have
been important enough for this to happen to me."

Ian Buruma   **Conformity and Individuality in Japan** 326

"Talent, being highly individualistic and thus socially
troublesome, is not always highly regarded in Japan."

Laura Bohannan   **Shakespeare in the Bush**   334

"They threatened to tell me no more stories until I told them
one of mine. . . . Realizing that here was my chance to
prove *Hamlet* universally intelligible, I agreed."

Barbara Ehrenreich and Annette Fuentes
Life on the Global Assembly Line   346

"Multinational corporations and Third World governments
alike consider assembly-line work—whether the product is
Barbie dolls or missile parts—to be 'women's work.' "

Jonathan Swift   **A Modest Proposal**   356

". . . a fair, cheap, and easy method of making these children
sound, useful members of the commonwealth . . ."

John David Morley   **Living in a Japanese Home**   365

"The most striking feature of the Japanese house was lack of
privacy; the lack of individual, inviolable space."

Nikki Giovanni   **They Clapped**   372

". . . they finally realized they are strangers all over."

PART EIGHT   **Communicating**   375

Gloria Naylor   **The Meaning of a Word**   377

"I was later to go home and ask the inevitable question that
every black parent must face—'Mommy, what does "nigger"
mean?' "

William Hines   **Hello, Judy. I'm Dr. Smith**   382

". . . it's high time for some consciousness-raising in the
medical profession."

Robin Lakoff   **You Are What You Say**   386

"If we refuse to talk 'like a lady,' we are ridiculed and
criticized as being unfeminine."

Jack G. Shaheen   **The Media's Image of Arabs**   394

"With my children, I have watched animated heroes Heckle
and Jeckle pull the rug from under 'Ali Boo-Boo, the Desert
Rat,' and Laverne and Shirley stop 'Sheik Ha-Mean-Ie' from
conquering 'the U.S. and the world.' "

Myrna Knepler   **Sold at Fine Stores Everywhere,
Naturellement**   398

"Madison Avenue, when constructing ads for high priced
non-necessary items, may use French phrases to suggest to
readers that they are identified as super-sophisticated, subtly
sexy, and privy to the secrets of old world charm and
tradition."

Donna Woolfolk Cross   **Sin, Suffer and Repent**   404

"Under the surface of romantic complications, soap operas
sell a vision of morality and American family life."

Richard Rodriguez   **Public and Private Language**   413

". . . 'Boys and girls, this is Richard Rodriguez.' (I heard her
sound out: *Rich-heard Road-ree-guess.*)"

Ngugi wa Thiong'o   **The Politics of Language**   420

"And then I went to school, a colonial school, and this
harmony was broken. The language of my education was no
longer the language of my culture."

Bernard Malamud   **The German Refugee**   431

"To many of these people, articulate as they were, the great
loss was the loss of language—that they could not say what
was in them to say."

Alan Devenish   **After the Beep**   443

". . . do leave a message/and I or my machine will get back
to you/or your machine."

ACKNOWLEDGMENTS   **445**

AUTHOR/TITLE INDEX   **451**

RHETORICAL CONTENTS

Description (Selections that contain substantial descriptive passages)

Jack Agueros, *Halfway to Dick and Jane: A Puerto Rican Pilgrimage*   25
Mike Rose, *I Just Wanna Be Average*   45
Alfred Kazin, *The Kitchen*   119
Norman Podhoretz, *The Brutal Bargain*   177
Walter White, *I Learn What I Am*   222
Alistair Cooke, *The Huddled Masses*   277
George Orwell, *Shooting an Elephant*   318
John David Morley, *Living in a Japanese Home*   365
Richard Rodriguez, *Public and Private Language*   413

Narration (Personal)

Elizabeth Wong, *The Struggle to Be an All-American Girl*   3
Maya Angelou, *Graduation*   7
Maxine Hong Kingston, *Girlhood Among Ghosts*   19
Jack Agueros, *Halfway to Dick and Jane: A Puerto Rican Pilgrimage*   25
Mike Rose, *I Just Wanna Be Average*   45
John Tarkov, *Fitting In*   71
Toni Morrison, *A Slow Walk of Trees*   76
Sun Park, *Don't Expect Me to Be Perfect*   116
Marcus Mabry, *Living in Two Worlds*   163
Maria L. Muñiz, *Back, but Not Home*   167
Eva Hoffman, *Lost in Translation*   171
Norman Podhoretz, *The Brutal Bargain*   177
Malcolm X, *Hair*   187
Brent Staples, *Night Walker*   217
Walter White, *I Learn What I Am*   222
Jeanne Wakatsuki Houston and James D. Houston, *Arrival at Manzanar*   229
Piri Thomas, *Alien Turf*   240
Bette Bao Lord, *Walking in Lucky Shoes*   257
Mark Salzman, *Teacher Mark*   303
George Orwell, *Shooting an Elephant*   318

Narration (Observation and reporting)

Anton Shammas, *Amérka, Amérka: A Palestinian Abroad in the Land of the Free*   96
Susan Chira, *The Good Mother: Searching for an Ideal*   129

Christopher Columbus, *Journal of Discovery, October
    10th to 12th, 1492*   261
Alistair Cooke, *The Huddled Masses*   277
Laura Bohannan, *Shakespeare in the Bush*   334
Barbara Ehrenreich and Annette Fuentes, *Life on the
    Global Assembly Line*   346

Definition

Jane Howard, *Families*   123
Susan Chira, *The Good Mother: Searching for an Ideal*   129
David Gates, *Who Was Columbus?*   266
Michel Guillaume St. Jean de Crèvecoeur, *What Is an
    American?*   271
Gloria Naylor, *The Meaning of a Word*   377
Robin Lakoff, *You Are What You Say*   386

Classification and Division

Jane Howard, *Families*   123
Recapture the Flag: 34 Reasons to Love America   287
Ian Buruma, *Conformity and Individuality in Japan*   326
Barbara Ehrenreich and Annette Fuentes, *Life on the
    Global Assembly Line*   346
Ngugi wa Thiong'o, *The Politics of Language*   420

Comparison and Contrast

Toni Morrison, *A Slow Walk of Trees*   76
Arthur L. Campa, *Anglo vs. Chicano: Why?*   90
Marcus Mabry, *Living in Two Worlds*   163
Michael Dorris, *For the Indians, No Thanksgiving*   236
Michel Guillaume St. Jean de Crèvecoeur, *What Is an
    American?*   271
Mark Salzman, *Teacher Mark*   303
Margaret Atwood, *Canadians: What Do They Want?*   312
Laura Bohannan, *Shakespeare in the Bush*   334
John David Morley, *Living in a Japanese Home*   365
Nikki Giovanni, *They Clapped*   372
Myrna Knepler, *Sold at Fine Stores Everywhere,
    Naturellement*   398

Cause and Effect

Lindsy Van Gelder, *The Importance of Being Eleven:
    Carol Gilligan Takes on Adolescence*   39
Countee Cullen, *Incident*   68
Arlene Skolnick, *The Paradox of Perfection*   139
Norman Podhoretz, *The Brutal Bargain*   177
Walter White, *I Learn What I Am*   222
George Orwell, *Shooting an Elephant*   318
Jonathan Swift, *A Modest Proposal*   356

William Hines, *Hello, Judy. I'm Dr. Smith*   382
Jack G. Shaheen, *The Media's Image of Arabs*   394
Donna Woolfolk Cross, *Sin, Suffer and Repent*   404
Richard Rodriguez, *Public and Private Language*   413
Ngugi wa Thiong'o, *The Politics of Language*   420

Argument and Persuasion

Maya Angelou, *Graduation*   7
Mike Rose, *I Just Wanna Be Average*   45
Michael Novak, *In Ethnic America*   82
Norman Podhoretz, *The Brutal Bargain*   177
Malcolm X, *Hair*   187
Gerald Early, *Their Malcolm, My Problem*   190
Margaret Atwood, *Canadians: What Do They Want?*   312
George Orwell, *Shooting an Elephant*   318
Barbara Ehrenreich and Annette Fuentes, *Life on the
     Global Assembly Line*   346
Jonathan Swift, *A Modest Proposal*   356
William Hines, *Hello, Judy. I'm Dr. Smith*   382
Robin Lakoff, *You Are What You Say*   386
Jack G. Shaheen, *The Media's Image of Arabs*   394
Donna Woolfolk Cross, *Sin, Suffer and Repent*   404
Richard Rodriguez, *Public and Private Language*   413
Ngugi wa Thiong'o, *The Politics of Language*   420

Irony, Humor, and Satire

Grace Paley, *The Loudest Voice*   60
Sandra Cisneros, *Barbie-Q*   203
Michael Dorris, *For the Indians, No Thanksgiving*   236
Margaret Atwood, *Canadians: What Do They Want?*   312
Jonathan Swift, *A Modest Proposal*   356
Donna Woolfolk Cross, *Sin, Suffer and Repent*   404

Fiction

Grace Paley, *The Loudest Voice*   60
Harry Mark Petrakis, *Barba Nikos*   106
Amy Tan, *Two Kinds*   148
Sandra Cisneros, *Barbie-Q*   203
Piri Thomas, *Alien Turf*   240
Anzia Yezierska, *Soap and Water*   291
John David Morley, *Living in a Japanese Home*   365
Bernard Malamud, *The German Refugee*   431

Poetry

Countee Cullen, *Incident*   68
Wendy Rose, *Three Thousand Dollar Death Song*   112
Theodore Roethke, *My Papa's Waltz*   160
Gwendolyn Brooks, *We Real Cool*   206

Dwight Okita, *In Response to Executive Order 9066:*
All Americans of Japanese Descent Must Report
to Relocation Centers   252
Joseph Bruchac, *Ellis Island*   299
Nikki Giovanni, *They Clapped*   372
Alan Devenish, *After the Beep*   443

PART ONE

Growing Up

$\mathbf{A}$s we grow up, our awareness of the world around us gradually expands. The learning process begins at birth and never stops. We get to know our physical surroundings—a crib, perhaps, then a room, a house. We become aware of a parent and learn that if we cry, that parent will do something for us. We also learn that others want things from us; much of the time these demands are designed to stop us from doing what we want at that moment. Communication, we find, works in both directions.

What we learn depends of course on our environment, although we do not know that in our early lives. Then we believe that our way of talking—our language—is the only one, and that the way things happen is the only way they can be done. For many Americans, the earliest experiences are confined to one culture. Sooner or later we learn, however, that we coexist with people whose experience or upbringing differs from ours. The discovery of that fact may come as a shock, particularly when we find at the same time that our culture is in some way not welcomed or accepted, that there is a barrier between ours and "theirs," a barrier that we cannot readily cross.

Each author in Part One confronts that barrier while growing up. Elizabeth Wong wants to be an "all-American girl" and fights her mother's attempt to have her keep her Chinese background. Maya Angelou, an African-American student in a segregated

1

elementary school in Arkansas in the 1940s, recoils from the condescending attitude of the white speaker at her graduation from the eighth grade. Maxine Hong Kingston, brought up in a Chinese environment, turns silent when she enters public school. Jack Agueros believes he is an all-American boy until he finds that there is a different America across the hill, one where he is not welcome. Lindsy Van Gelder, a sassy tomboy until age 12, discovers to her horror that girls are supposed to act nice and are to be seen but not heard. Mike Rose, with the help of a dedicated teacher, overcomes the limiting boundaries of working-class life and undereducation. Grace Paley's short story tells about school administrators who, with great unconcern, impose a Christmas pageant on children whose culture is non-Christian. Finally, Countee Cullen speaks simply but tellingly of his first confrontation, at age eight, with prejudice.

THE STRUGGLE TO BE AN ALL-AMERICAN GIRL

Elizabeth Wong

Elizabeth Wong's mother insisted that she learn Chinese and be aware of her cultural background. In her essay, which first appeared in the *Los Angeles Times,* Wong vividly portrays her childhood resistance to her mother's wishes and the anger and embarrassment she felt. Chinese school interfered with her being, as she puts it, "an all-American girl." Here, writing as a young adult, she recognizes in herself a sense of loss.

Elizabeth Wong is a playwright and television writer living in Los Angeles. She grew up in that city's Chinatown, and worked as a news reporter for 10 years before quitting in 1988 to write plays. Her first play premiered off Broadway in 1991. She received a B.A. from the University of Southern California in 1980 and an M.F.A. from New York University in 1991. She is still a frequent contributor to the *Los Angeles Times* editorial pages.

It's still there, the Chinese school on Yale Street where my brother and I   1
used to go. Despite the new coat of paint and the high wire fence, the school I knew 10 years ago remains remarkably, stoically the same.

Every day at 5 P.M., instead of playing with our fourth- and   2
fifth-grade friends or sneaking out to the empty lot to hunt ghosts and animal bones, my brother and I had to go to Chinese school. No amount of kicking, screaming, or pleading could dissuade my mother, who was solidly determined to have us learn the language of our heritage.

Forcibly, she walked us the seven long, hilly blocks from our home   3
to school, depositing our defiant tearful faces before the stern principal. My only memory of him is that he swayed on his heels like a palm tree, and he always clasped his impatient twitching hands behind his back. I recognized him as a repressed maniacal child killer, and knew that if we ever saw his hands we'd be in big trouble.

We all sat in little chairs in an empty auditorium. The room smelled   4
like Chinese medicine, an imported faraway mustiness. Like ancient mothballs or dirty closets. I hated that smell. I favored crisp new scents.

3

Like the soft French perfume that my American teacher wore in public school.

There was a stage far to the right, flanked by an American flag and the flag of the Nationalist Republic of China, which was also red, white and blue but not as pretty.

Although the emphasis at the school was mainly language—speaking, reading, writing—the lessons always began with an exercise in politeness. With the entrance of the teacher, the best student would tap a bell and everyone would get up, kowtow, and chant, "Sing san ho," the phonetic for "How are you, teacher?"

Being ten years old, I had better things to learn than ideographs copied painstakingly in lines that ran right to left from the tip of a *moc but,* a real ink pen that had to be held in an awkward way if blotches were to be avoided. After all, I could do the multiplication tables, name the satellites of Mars, and write reports on "Little Women" and "Black Beauty." Nancy Drew, my favorite book heroine, never spoke Chinese.

The language was a source of embarrassment. More times than not, I had tried to disassociate myself from the nagging loud voice that followed me wherever I wandered in the nearby American supermarket outside Chinatown. The voice belonged to my grandmother, a fragile woman in her seventies who could outshout the best of the street vendors. Her humor was raunchy, her Chinese rhythmless, patternless. It was quick, it was loud, it was unbeautiful. It was not like the quiet, lilting romance of French or the gentle refinement of the American South. Chinese sounded pedestrian. Public.

In Chinatown, the comings and goings of hundreds of Chinese on their daily tasks sounded chaotic and frenzied. I did not want to be thought of as mad, as talking gibberish. When I spoke English, people nodded at me, smiled sweetly, said encouraging words. Even the people in my culture would cluck and say that I'd do well in life. "My, doesn't she move her lips fast," they would say, meaning that I'd be able to keep up with the world outside Chinatown.

My brother was even more fanatical than I about speaking English. He was especially hard on my mother, criticizing her, often cruelly, for her pidgin speech—smatterings of Chinese scattered like chop suey in her conversation. "It's not 'What it is,' Mom," he'd say in exasperation. "It's 'What *is* it, what *is* it, what *is* it!'" Sometimes Mom might leave out an occasional "the" or "a," or perhaps a verb of being. He would stop her in mid-sentence: "Say it again, Mom. Say it right." When he tripped over his own tongue, he'd blame it on her: "See, Mom, it's all your fault. You set a bad example."

What infuriated my mother most was when my brother cornered her on her consonants, especially "r." My father had played a cruel joke on Mom by assigning her an American name that her tongue wouldn't allow her to say. No matter how hard she tried, "Ruth" always ended up "Luth" or "Roof."

After two years of writing with a *moc but* and reciting words with   12
multiples of meanings, I finally was granted a cultural divorce. I was permitted to stop Chinese school.

I thought of myself as multicultural. I preferred tacos to egg rolls; I   13
enjoyed Cinco de Mayo more than Chinese New Year.

At last, I was one of you; I wasn't one of them.   14

Sadly, I still am.   15

Exercises

Some Important Words

stoically (paragraph 1), dissuade (2), defiant (3), stern (3), maniacal (3), mustiness (4), kowtow (6), phonetic (6), ideographs (7), disassociate (8), raunchy (8), pedestrian (8), chaotic (9), frenzied (9), gibberish (9), fanatical (10), pidgin (10), smatterings (10), exasperation (10), infuriated (11), multicultural (13), *Cinco de Mayo*—fifth of May: a Mexican national holiday (13).

Some of the Issues

1. Cite some of the characteristics of the Chinese school as Wong describes it; how does it differ from her American school?
2. Why was the Chinese language "a source of embarrassment" to Wong? What are her feelings about speaking English?
3. Consider the last sentence: "Sadly, I still am." Why "sadly"?
*4. Read Maxine Hong Kingston's "Girlhood Among Ghosts." Compare Kingston's attitude toward Chinese school with Wong's.
*5. Read Maria Muñiz's "Back, but Not Home." What similarities do you notice in her experiences and Wong's? What differences?

The Way We Are Told

6. Consider the title. To what extent does Wong succeed in becoming the "all-American Girl" she wanted to be? Explain why the title could be considered ironic.
7. What details does Wong give about her experience in Chinese school to make her feelings explicit? What senses does she appeal to?

---

*Asterisks used in this context denote questions and essay topics that draw on more than one selection.

8. How does the description of the principal in paragraph 3 reflect the fact that Wong sees him through the eyes of a child?
9. In paragraph 14 whom do "you" and "them" refer to?
10. Wong does not state a thesis directly. Nevertheless a thesis statement that sums up the essay could be constructed. What might the thesis be? What do you think the author would gain or lose by stating it directly?

Some Subjects for Writing

11. Describe an experience you disliked. Try, like Wong, to build your case by the way you describe the details.
* 12. Read Maria Muñiz's "Back, but Not Home." Compare Wong's and Muñiz's attitudes toward their respective cultures. How does each woman's experience explain her attitude?

GRADUATION

Maya Angelou

Maya Angelou, born Marguerite Johnson in 1928, spent her child-hood in Stamps, Arkansas. She grew up in a rigidly segregated society. The Civil War (1861–65) had ended slavery but had not eliminated segregation. In fact, several decisions of the Supreme Court reaffirmed its legality. In the case of *Plessy v. Ferguson* (1896) in particular, the Court gave its approval to segregation, declaring it to be constitutional as long as the affected facilities, such as public schools, were "separate but equal." Schools were separate after that in large parts of the country, but not equal, as Angelou's memory of the early 1940s demonstrates. In 1954 the Supreme Court reversed itself in *Brown v. Board of Education,* declaring that segregation was "inherently unequal" and, therefore, unconstitutional.

Angelou—writer, actress, and civil rights activist—is the author of numerous books of prose and poetry, among them *All God's Children Need Traveling Shoes* (1991), *I Shall Not Be Moved* (1990), and *I Know Why the Caged Bird Sings,* the first volume in an autobiographical series that includes *Gather Together in My Name* (1975), *Singin' and Swingin'* and *Merry Like Christmas* (1976), and *The Heart of a Woman* (1981). This selection is taken from *I Know Why the Caged Bird Sings.*

On January 20, 1993, at the invitation of President Clinton, before a crowd of 200,000, Angelou delivered the first original poem written especially for a presidential inauguration, entitled "On the Pulse of Morning."

The children in Stamps trembled visibly with anticipation. Some adults were excited too, but to be certain the whole young population had come down with graduation epidemic. Large classes were graduating from both the grammar school and the high school. Even those who were years removed from their own day of glorious release were anxious to help with preparations as a kind of dry run. The junior students who were moving into the vacating classes' chairs were tradition-bound to show their talents for leadership and management. They strutted through the school and around the campus exerting pressure on the lower

1

grades. Their authority was so new that occasionally if they pressed a little too hard it had to be overlooked. After all, next term was coming, and it never hurt a sixth grader to have a play sister in the eighth grade, or a tenth-year student to be able to call a twelfth grader Bubba. So all was endured in a spirit of shared understanding. But the graduating classes themselves were the nobility. Like travelers with exotic destinations on their minds, the graduates were remarkably forgetful. They came to school without their books, or tablets or even pencils. Volunteers fell over themselves to secure replacements for the missing equipment. When accepted, the willing workers might or might not be thanked, and it was of no importance to the pregraduation rites. Even teachers were respectful of the now quiet and aging seniors, and tended to speak to them, if not as equals, as beings only slightly lower than themselves. After tests were returned and grades given, the student body, which acted like an extended family, knew who did well, who excelled, and what piteous ones had failed.

Unlike the white high school, Lafayette County Training School 2
distinguished itself by having neither lawn, nor hedges, nor tennis court, nor climbing ivy. Its two buildings (main classrooms, the grade school and home economics) were set on a dirt hill with no fence to limit either its boundaries or those of bordering farms. There was a large expanse to the left of the school which was used alternately as a baseball diamond or a basketball court. Rusty hoops on the swaying poles represented the permanent recreational equipment, although bats and balls could be borrowed from the P.E. teacher if the borrower was qualified and if the diamond wasn't occupied.

Over this rocky area relieved by a few shady tall persimmon trees the 3
graduating class walked. The girls often held hands and no longer bothered to speak to the lower students. There was a sadness about them, as if this old world was not their home and they were bound for higher ground. The boys, on the other hand, had become more friendly, more outgoing. A decided change from the closed attitude they projected while studying for finals. Now they seemed not ready to give up the old school, the familiar paths and classrooms. Only a small percentage would be continuing on to college—one of the South's A & M (agricultural and mechanical) schools, which trained Negro youths to be carpenters, farmers, handymen, masons, maids, cooks and baby nurses. Their future rode heavily on their shoulders, and blinded them to the collective joy that had pervaded the lives of the boys and girls in the grammar school graduating class.

Parents who could afford it had ordered new shoes and ready-made 4
clothes for themselves from Sears and Roebuck or Montgomery Ward. They also engaged the best seamstresses to make the floating graduating dresses and to cut down secondhand pants which would be pressed to a military slickness for the important event.

Oh, it was important, all right. Whitefolks would attend the cere- 5
mony, and two or three would speak of God and home, and the
Southern way of life, and Mrs. Parsons, the principal's wife, would play
the graduation march while the lower-grade graduates paraded down the
aisles and took their seats below the platform. The high school seniors
would wait in empty classrooms to make their dramatic entrance.

In the Store I was the person of the moment. The birthday girl. The 6
center. Bailey had graduated the year before, although to do so he had to
forfeit all pleasures to make up for his time lost in Baton Rouge.

My class was wearing butter-yellow piqué dresses, and Momma 7
launched out on mine. She smocked the yoke into tiny crisscrossing
puckers, then shirred the rest of the bodice. Her dark fingers ducked in
and out of the lemony cloth as she embroidered raised daisies around the
hem. Before she considered herself finished she had added a crocheted
cuff on the puff sleeves, and a pointy crocheted collar.

I was going to be lovely. A walking model of all the various styles of 8
fine hand sewing and it didn't worry me that I was only twelve years old
and merely graduating from the eighth grade. Besides, many teachers in
Arkansas Negro schools had only that diploma and were licensed to
impart wisdom.

The days had become longer and more noticeable. The faded beige 9
of former times had been replaced with strong and sure colors. I began to
see my classmates' clothes, their skin tones, and the dust that waved off
pussy willows. Clouds that lazed across the sky were objects of great
concern to me. Their shiftier shapes might have held a message that in
my new happiness and with a little bit of time I'd soon decipher. During
that period I looked at the arch of heaven so religiously my neck kept a
steady ache. I had taken to smiling more often, and my jaws hurt from the
unaccustomed activity. Between the two physical sore spots, I suppose I
could have been uncomfortable, but that was not the case. As a member
of the winning team (the graduating class of 1940) I had outdistanced
unpleasant sensations by miles. I was headed for the freedom of open
fields.

Youth and social approval allied themselves with me and we 10
trammeled memories of slights and insults. The wind of our swift passage
remodeled my features. Lost tears were pounded to mud and then to
dust. Years of withdrawal were brushed aside and left behind, as hanging
ropes of parasitic moss.

My work alone had awarded me a top place and I was going to be 11
one of the first called in the graduating ceremonies. On the classroom
blackboard, as well as on the bulletin board in the auditorium, there
were blue stars and white stars and red stars. No absences, no tardi-
nesses, and my academic work was among the best of the year. I could

say the preamble to the Constitution even faster than Bailey. We timed ourselves often: "WethepeopleoftheUnitedStatesinordertoformamore perfectunion. . ." I had memorized the Presidents of the United States from Washington to Roosevelt in chronological as well as alphabetical order.

My hair pleased me too. Gradually the black mass had lengthened and thickened, so that it kept at last to its braided pattern, and I didn't have to yank my scalp off when I tried to comb it.   12

Louise and I had rehearsed the exercises until we tired out ourselves. Henry Reed was class valedictorian. He was a small, very black boy with hooded eyes, a long, broad nose and an oddly shaped head. I had admired him for years because each term he and I vied for the best grades in our class. Most often he bested me, but instead of being disappointed I was pleased that we shared top places between us. Like many Southern Black children, he lived with his grandmother, who was as strict as Momma and as kind as she knew how to be. He was courteous, respectful and soft-spoken to elders, but on the playground he chose to play the roughest games. I admired him. Anyone, I reckoned, sufficiently afraid or sufficiently dull could be polite. But to be able to operate at a top level with both adults and children was admirable.   13

His valedictory speech was entitled "To Be or Not to Be." The rigid tenth-grade teacher had helped him write it. He'd been working on the dramatic stresses for months.   14

The weeks until graduation were filled with heady activities. A group of small children were to be presented in a play about buttercups and daisies and bunny rabbits. They could be heard throughout the building practicing their hops and their little songs that sounded like silver bells. The older girls (nongraduates, of course) were assigned the task of making refreshments for the night's festivities. A tangy scent of ginger, cinnamon, nutmeg and chocolate wafted around the home economics building as the budding cooks made samples for themselves and their teachers.   15

In every corner of the workshop, axes and saws split fresh timber as the woodshop boys made sets and stage scenery. Only the graduates were left out of the general bustle. We were free to sit in the library at the back of the building or look in quite detachedly, naturally, on the measures being taken for our event.   16

Even the minister preached on graduation the Sunday before. His subject was, "Let your light so shine that men will see your good works and praise your Father, Who is in Heaven." Although the sermon was purported to be addressed to us, he used the occasion to speak to backsliders, gamblers and general ne'er-do-wells. But since he had called our names at the beginning of the service we were mollified.   17

Among Negroes the tradition was to give presents to children going   18
only from one grade to another. How much more important this was
when the person was graduating at the top of the class. Uncle Willie and
Momma had sent away for a Mickey Mouse watch like Bailey's. Louise
gave me four embroidered handkerchiefs. (I gave her three crocheted
doilies.) Mrs. Sneed, the minister's wife, made me an underskirt to wear
for graduation, and nearly every customer gave me a nickel or maybe
even a dime with the instruction "Keep on moving to higher ground," or
some such encouragement.

Amazingly the great day finally dawned and I was out of bed before   19
I knew it. I threw open the back door to see it more clearly, but Momma
said, "Sister, come away from that door and put your robe on."

I hoped the memory of that morning would never leave me.   20
Sunlight was itself still young, and the day had none of the insistence
maturity would bring it in a few hours. In my robe and barefoot in the
backyard, under cover of going to see about my new beans, I gave
myself up to the gentle warmth and thanked God that no matter what
evil I had done in my life He had allowed me to live to see this day.
Somewhere in my fatalism I had expected to die, accidentally, and never
have the chance to walk up the stairs in the auditorium and gracefully
receive my hard-earned diploma. Out of God's merciful bosom I had won
reprieve.

Bailey came out in his robe and gave me a box wrapped in   21
Christmas paper. He said he had saved his money for months to pay for
it. It felt like a box of chocolates, but I knew Bailey wouldn't save money
to buy candy when we had all we could want under our noses.

He was as proud of the gift as I. It was a soft-leather-bound copy of   22
a collection of poems by Edgar Allan Poe, or, as Bailey and I called him,
"Eap." I turned to "Annabel Lee" and we walked up and down the
garden rows, the cool dirt between our toes, reciting the beautifully sad
lines.

Momma made a Sunday breakfast although it was only Friday. After   23
we finished the blessing, I opened my eyes to find the watch on my
plate. It was a dream of a day. Everything went smoothly and to my
credit. I didn't have to be reminded or scolded for anything. Near evening
I was too jittery to attend to chores, so Bailey volunteered to do all before
his bath.

Days before, we had made a sign for the Store, and as we turned   24
out the lights Momma hung the cardboard over the doorknob. It read
clearly: CLOSED. GRADUATION.

My dress fitted perfectly and everyone said that I looked like a   25
sunbeam in it. On the hill, going toward the school, Bailey walked
behind with Uncle Willie, who muttered, "Go on, Ju." We wanted him to
walk ahead with us because it embarrassed him to have to walk so

slowly. Bailey said he'd let the ladies walk together, and the men would bring up the rear. We all laughed, nicely.

Little children dashed by out of the dark like fireflies. Their crepe-paper dresses and butterfly wings were not made for running and we heard more than one rip, dryly, and the regretful "uh uh" that followed.   26

The school blazed without gaiety. The windows seemed cold and unfriendly from the lower hill. A sense of ill-fated timing crept over me, and if Momma hadn't reached for my hand I would have drifted back to Bailey and Uncle Willie, and possibly beyond. She made a few slow jokes about my feet getting cold, and tugged me along to the now-strange building.   27

Around the front steps, assurance came back. There were my fellow "greats," the graduating class. Hair brushed back, legs oiled, new dresses and pressed pleats, fresh pocket handkerchiefs and little handbags, all homesewn. Oh, we were up to snuff, all right. I joined my comrades and didn't even see my family go in to find seats in the crowded auditorium.   28

The school band struck up a march and all classes filed in as had been rehearsed. We stood in front of our seats, as assigned, and on a signal from the choir director, we sat. No sooner had this been accomplished than the band started to play the national anthem. We rose again and sang the song, after which we recited the pledge of allegiance. We remained standing for a brief minute before the choir director and the principal signaled to us, rather desperately I thought, to take our seats. The command was so unusual that our carefully rehearsed and smooth-running machine was thrown off. For a full minute we fumbled for our chairs and bumped into each other awkwardly. Habits change or solidify under pressure, so in our state of nervous tension we had been ready to follow our usual assembly pattern: the American national anthem, then the pledge of allegiance, then the song every Black person I knew called the Negro National Anthem. All done in the same key, with the same passion and most often standing on the same foot.   29

Finding my seat at last, I was overcome with a presentiment of worse things to come. Something unrehearsed, unplanned, was going to happen, and we were going to be made to look bad. I distinctly remember being explicit in the choice of pronoun. It was "we," the graduating class, the unit, that concerned me then.   30

The principal welcomed "parents and friends" and asked the Baptist minister to lead us in prayer. His invocation was brief and punchy, and for a second I thought we were getting back on the high road to right action. When the principal came back to the dais, however, his voice had changed. Sounds always affected me profoundly and the principal's voice was one of my favorites. During assembly it melted and lowed weakly into the audience. It had not been in my plan to listen to him, but my curiosity was piqued and I straightened up to give him my attention.   31

He was talking about Booker T. Washington, our "late great leader," 32
who said we can be as close as the fingers on the hand, etc. . . . . Then he
said a few vague things about friendship and the friendship of kindly
people to those less fortunate than themselves. With that his voice nearly
faded, thin, away. Like a river diminishing to a stream and then to a
trickle. But he cleared his throat and said, "Our speaker tonight, who is
also our friend, came from Texarkana to deliver the commencement
address, but due to the irregularity of the train schedule, he's going to, as
they say, 'speak and run.' " He said that we understood and wanted the
man to know that we were most grateful for the time he was able to give
us and then something about how we were willing always to adjust to
another's program, and without more ado—"I give you Mr. Edward
Donleavy."

Not one but two white men came through the door offstage. The 33
shorter one walked to the speaker's platform, and the tall one moved
over to the center seat and sat down. But that was our principal's seat,
and already occupied. The dislodged gentleman bounced around for a
long breath or two before the Baptist minister gave him his chair, then
with more dignity than the situation deserved, the minister walked off
the stage.

Donleavy looked at the audience once (on reflection, I'm sure that 34
he wanted only to reassure himself that we were really there), adjusted
his glasses and began to read from a sheaf of papers.

He was glad "to be here and to see the work going on just as it was 35
in the other schools."

At the first "Amen" from the audience I willed the offender to 36
immediate death by choking on the word. But Amens and Yes, sir's
began to fall around the room like rain through a ragged umbrella.

He told us of the wonderful changes we children in Stamps had in 37
store. The Central School (naturally, the white school was Central) had
already been granted improvements that would be in use in the fall. A
well-known artist was coming from Little Rock to teach art to them. They
were going to have the newest microscopes and chemistry equipment for
their laboratory. Mr. Donleavy didn't leave us long in the dark over who
made these improvements available to Central High. Nor were we to be
ignored in the general betterment scheme he had in mind.

He said that he had pointed out to people at a very high level that 38
one of the first-line football tacklers at Arkansas Agricultural and Mechanical College had graduated from good old Lafayette County Training
School. Here fewer Amens were heard. Those few that did break through
lay dully in the air with the heaviness of habit.

He went on to praise us. He went on to say how he had bragged 39
that "one of the best basketball players at Fisk sank his first ball right here
at Lafayette County Training School."

The white kids were going to have a chance to become Galileos   40
and Madame Curies and Edisons and Gauguins, and our boys (the girls
weren't even in on it) would try to be Jesse Owenses and Joe Louises.

Owens and the Brown Bomber were great heroes in our world, but   41
what school official in the white-goddom of Little Rock had the right to
decide that those two men must be our only heroes? Who decided that
for Henry Reed to become a scientist he had to work like George
Washington Carver, as a bootblack, to buy a lousy microscope? Bailey
was obviously always going to be too small to be an athlete, so which
concrete angel glued to what county seat had decided that if my brother
wanted to become a lawyer he had to first pay penance for his skin by
picking cotton and hoeing corn and studying correspondence books at
night for twenty years?

The man's dead words fell like bricks around the auditorium and   42
too many settled in my belly. Constrained by hard-learned manners I
couldn't look behind me, but to my left and right the proud graduating
class of 1940 had dropped their heads. Every girl in my row had found
something new to do with her handkerchief. Some folded the tiny
squares into love knots, some into triangles, but most were wadding
them, then pressing them flat on their yellow laps.

On the dais, the ancient tragedy was being replayed. Professor   43
Parsons sat, a sculptor's reject, rigid. His large, heavy body seemed
devoid of will or willingness, and his eyes said he was no longer with us.
The other teachers examined the flag (which was draped stage right) or
their notes, or the windows which opened on our now-famous playing
diamond.

Graduation, the hush-hush magic time of frills and gifts and   44
congratulations and diplomas, was finished for me before my name was
called. The accomplishment was nothing. The meticulous maps, drawn
in three colors of ink, learning and spelling decasyllabic words, memo-
rizing the whole of *The Rape of Lucrece*—it was for nothing. Donleavy
had exposed us.

We were maids and farmers, handymen and washerwomen, and   45
anything higher that we aspired to was farcical and presumptuous.

Then I wished that Gabriel Prosser and Nat Turner had killed all   46
whitefolks in their beds and that Abraham Lincoln had been assassinated
before the signing of the Emancipation Proclamation, and that Harriet
Tubman had been killed by that blow on her head and Christopher
Columbus had drowned in the *Santa María*.

It was awful to be Negro and have no control over my life. It was   47
brutal to be young and already trained to sit quietly and listen to charges
brought against my color with no chance of defense. We should all be
dead. I thought I should like to see us all dead, one on top of the other.
A pyramid of flesh with the whitefolks on the bottom, as the broad base,

then the Indians with their silly tomahawks and teepees and wigwams and treaties, the Negroes with their mops and recipes and cotton sacks and spirituals sticking out of their mouths. The Dutch children should all stumble in their wooden shoes and break their necks. The French should choke to death on the Louisiana Purchase (1803) while silkworms ate all the Chinese with their stupid pigtails. As a species, we were an abomination. All of us.

Donleavy was running for election, and assured our parents that if he won we could count on having the only colored paved playing field in that part of Arkansas. Also—he never looked up to acknowledge the grunts of acceptance—also, we were bound to get some new equipment for the home economics building and the workshop.   48

He finished, and since there was no need to give any more than the most perfunctory thank-you's, he nodded to the men on the stage, and the tall white man who was never introduced joined him at the door. They left with the attitude that now they were off to something really important. (The graduation ceremonies at Lafayette County Training School had been a mere preliminary.)   49

The ugliness they left was palpable. An uninvited guest who wouldn't leave. The choir was summoned and sang a modern arrangement of "Onward, Christian Soldiers," with new words pertaining to graduates seeking their place in the world. But it didn't work. Elouise, the daughter of the Baptist minister, recited "Invictus," and I could have cried at the impertinence of "I am the master of my fate, I am the captain of my soul."   50

My name had lost its ring of familiarity and I had to be nudged to go and receive my diploma. All my preparations had fled. I neither marched up to the stage like a conquering Amazon, nor did I look in the audience for Bailey's nod of approval. Marguerite Johnson, I heard the name again, my honors were read, there were noises in the audience of appreciation, and I took my place on the stage as rehearsed.   51

I thought about colors I hated: ecru, puce, lavender, beige and black.   52

There was shuffling and rustling around me, then Henry Reed was giving his valedictory address, "To Be or Not to Be." Hadn't he heard the whitefolks? We couldn't *be,* so the question was a waste of time. Henry's voice came out clear and strong. I feared to look at him. Hadn't he got the message? There was no "nobler in the mind" for Negroes because the world didn't think we had minds, and they let us know it. "Outrageous fortune"? Now, that was a joke. When the ceremony was over I had to tell Henry Reed some things. That is, if I still cared. Not "rub," Henry, "erase." "Ah, there's the erase." Us.   53

Henry had been a good student in elocution. His voice rose on tides of promise and fell on waves of warnings. The English teacher had   54 helped him to create a sermon winging through Hamlet's soliloquy. To be a man, a doer, a builder, a leader, or to be a tool, an unfunny joke, a crusher of funky toadstools. I marveled that Henry could go through with the speech as if we had a choice.

I had been listening and silently rebutting each sentence with my   55 eyes closed; then there was a hush, which in an audience warns that something unplanned is happening. I looked up and saw Henry Reed, the conservative, the proper, the A student, turn his back to the audience and turn to us (the proud graduating class of 1940) and sing, nearly speaking,

> "Lift ev'ry voice and sing
> Till earth and heaven ring
> Ring with the harmonies of Liberty . . ."*

It was the poem written by James Weldon Johnson. It was the music composed by J. Rosamond Johnson. It was the Negro national anthem. Out of habit we were singing it.

Our mothers and fathers stood in the dark hall and joined the hymn   56 of encouragement. A kindergarten teacher led the small children onto the stage and the buttercups and daisies and bunny rabbits marked time and tried to follow:

> "Stony the road we trod
> Bitter the chastening rod
> Felt in the days when hope, unborn, had died.
> Yet with a steady beat
> Have not our weary feet
> Come to the place for which our fathers sighed?"

Every child I knew had learned that song with his ABC's and along   57 with "Jesus Loves Me This I Know." But I personally had never heard it before. Never heard the words, despite the thousands of times I had sung them. Never thought they had anything to do with me.

On the other hand, the words of Patrick Henry had made such an   58 impression on me that I had been able to stretch myself tall and trembling and say, "I know not what course others may take, but as for me, give me liberty or give me death."

And now I heard, really for the first time: 59

*"Lift Ev'ry Voice and Sing"—words by James Weldon Johnson and music by J. Rosamond Johnson. Copyright by Edward B. Marks Music Corporation. Used by permission.

"We have come over a way that with tears
has been watered,
We have come, treading our path through
the blood of the slaughtered."

While echoes of the song shivered in the air, Henry Reed bowed his   60
head, said "Thank you," and returned to his place in the line. The tears
that slipped down many faces were not wiped away in shame.

We were on top again. As always, again. We survived. The depths   61
had been icy and dark, but now a bright sun spoke to our souls. I was no
longer simply a member of the proud graduating glass of 1940; I was a
proud member of the wonderful, beautiful Negro race.

Exercises

Some Important Words

strutted (paragraph 1), exotic (1), rites (1), extended family (1), pervaded
(3), forfeit (6), piqué (7), decipher (9), parasitic (10), heady (15), fatalism
(20), piqued (31), Booker T. Washington (32), Galileo (40), Madame
Curie (40), Edison (40), Gauguin (40), Jesse Owens (40), Joe Louis (40),
Brown Bomber (41), George Washington Carver (41), *The Rape of
Lucrece* (44), Gabriel Prosser (46), Nat Turner (46), Harriet Tubman (46),
abomination (47), perfunctory (49), palpable (50), "Invictus" (50), ecru
(52), puce (52), elocution (54), soliloquy (54), rebutting (55).

Some of the Issues

1. How does Angelou establish the importance of the graduation? How
   does she build it stage by stage?
2. Why does Angelou distinguish between the high school graduates
   (paragraph 3, end) and the eighth-graders like herself? How do their
   attitudes differ? Why is she happier?
3. How does Angelou describe her rising expectations for "the great
   day" in paragraphs 15 through 23?
4. At what point in the narrative do we first get the idea that things
   may be going wrong with the "dream of a day"? What are later
   indications that something is wrong?
5. In paragraph 29 the children are confronted with a change in the
   usual order of things. Why does Angelou make this seem important?
   Why does the principal "rather desperately" signal for the children
   to sit down?
6. How do the first words Mr. Donleavy says indicate what his attitude is?

7. In paragraphs 50 through 60 Angelou describes her shifting thoughts and emotions. Explain them in your own words and relate them to the conclusion reached in paragraph 61.

The Way We Are Told

8. Paragraph 1 talks about the graduates and their schoolmates. Paragraphs 2 and 3 describe the school. Why does Angelou write in that order? What distinguishes paragraph 1 from 2 and 3 in addition to the content?
9. Why does Angelou introduce Henry Reed so early (paragraphs 12 and 13)?
10. Explain the irony Angelou sees in Henry Reed's "To Be or Not to Be" speech.

Some Subjects for Writing

11. Have you ever experienced an event—a dance, a party, a trip—that you looked forward to and that turned out to be a disaster? Or have you ever dreaded an event, such as an interview or a blind date, that turned out better than you had expected? Tell it, trying to make the reader feel the anticipation and the change through the specific, descriptive details you cite, rather than by direct statements. (You will find that the indirect way—making the reader feel or see the event—is more effective than simply saying, "I was bored" or "I found out it was a great evening after all.")
12. Describe a ceremony you have witnessed or participated in. Do it in two separate essays. In the first, describe the event simply in a neutral way. In the second, tell it from the point of view of a witness or participant.
*13. Read Grace Paley's "The Loudest Voice." Compare Mr. Donleavy's insensitivity to that shown by Shirley's teachers in the story. Cite specific instances to explain similarities and differences.

GIRLHOOD AMONG GHOSTS

Maxine Hong Kingston

Maxine Hong Kingston's parents came to America from China in the 1930s. She was born in Stockton, California, in 1940 and was graduated from the University of California at Berkeley.

The following selection comes from *The Woman Warrior: Memories of a Girlhood Among Ghosts* (1976), for which Kingston received the National Book Critics Circle Award. The ghosts she refers to are of several kinds: the spirits and demons that Chinese peasants believed in, the ghosts of the dead, and, more significantly, the whole of non-Chinese America, peopled with strange creatures who seem very powerful but not quite human, and whose behavior is often inexplicable.

Kingston continued her autobiography with *China Men* (1981). Since then she has also written *Hawaii One Summer* (1981) and a novel, *Tripmaster Monkey* (1988).

Long ago in China, knot-makers tied string into buttons and frogs, and 1
rope into bell pulls. There was one knot so complicated that it blinded the knot-maker. Finally an emperor outlawed this cruel knot, and the nobles could not order it anymore. If I had lived in China, I would have been an outlaw knot-maker.

Maybe that's why my mother cut my tongue. She pushed my 2
tongue up and sliced the frenum. Or maybe she snipped it with a pair of nail scissors. I don't remember her doing it, only her telling me about it, but all during childhood I felt sorry for the baby whose mother waited with scissors or knife in hand for it to cry—and then, when its mouth was wide open like a baby bird's, cut. The Chinese say "a ready tongue is an evil."

I used to curl up my tongue in front of the mirror and tauten my 3
frenum into a white line, itself as thin as a razor blade. I saw no scars in my mouth. I thought perhaps I had had two frena, and she had cut one. I made other children open their mouths so I could compare theirs to mine. I saw perfect pink membranes stretching into precise edges that looked easy enough to cut. Sometimes I felt very proud that my mother

committed such a powerful act upon me. At other times I was terrified—
the first thing my mother did when she saw me was to cut my tongue.

"Why did you do that to me, Mother?"   4

"I told you."   5

"Tell me again."   6

"I cut it so that you would not be tongue-tied. Your tongue would   7
be able to move in any language. You'll be able to speak languages that
are completely different from one another. You'll be able to pronounce
anything. Your frenum looked too tight to do those things, so I cut it."

"But isn't 'a ready tongue an evil'?"   8

"Things are different in this ghost country."   9

"Did it hurt me? Did I cry and bleed?"   10

"I don't remember. Probably."   11

She didn't cut the other children's. When I asked cousins and other   12
Chinese children whether their mothers had cut their tongues loose, they
said. "What?"

"Why didn't you cut my brothers' and sisters' tongues?"   13

"They didn't need it."   14

"Why not? Were theirs longer than mine?"   15

"Why don't you quit blabbering and get to work?"   16

If my mother was not lying she should have cut more, scraped   17
away the rest of the frenum skin, because I have a terrible time talking.
Or she should not have cut at all, tampering with my speech. When I
went to kindergarten and had to speak English for the first time, I became
silent. A dumbness—a shame—still cracks my voice in two, even when I
want to say "hello" casually, or ask an easy question in front of the
check-out counter, or ask directions of a bus driver. I stand frozen, or I
hold up the line with the complete, grammatical sentence that comes
squeaking out at impossible length. "What did you say?" says the cab
driver, or "Speak up," so I have to perform again, only weaker the second
time. A telephone call makes my throat bleed and takes up that day's
courage. It spoils my day with self-disgust when I hear my broken voice
come skittering out into the open. It makes people wince to hear it. I'm
getting better, though. Recently I asked the postman for special-issue
stamps; I've waited since childhood for postmen to give me some of their
own accord. I am making progress, a little every day.

My silence was thickest—total—during the three years that I   18
covered my school paintings with black paint. I painted layers of black
over houses and flowers and suns, and when I drew on the blackboard,
I put a layer of chalk on top. I was making a stage curtain, and it was the
moment before the curtain parted or rose. The teachers called my parents
to school, and I saw they had been saving my pictures, curling and
cracking, all alike and black. The teachers pointed to the pictures and
looked serious, talked seriously too, but my parents did not understand

English. ("The parents and teachers of criminals were executed," said my father.) My parents took the pictures home. I spread them out (so black and full of possibilities) and pretended the curtains were swinging open, flying up, one after another, sunlight underneath, mighty operas.

During the first silent year I spoke to no one at school, did not ask   19
before going to the lavatory, and flunked kindergarten. My sister also said nothing for three years, silent in the playground and silent at lunch. There were other quiet Chinese girls not of our family, but most of them got over it sooner than we did. I enjoyed the silence. At first it did not occur to me I was supposed to talk or to pass kindergarten. I talked at home and to one or two of the Chinese kids in class. I made motions and even made some jokes. I drank out of a toy saucer when the water spilled out of the cup, and everybody laughed, pointing at me, so I did it some more. I didn't know that Americans don't drink out of saucers.

I liked the Negro students (Black Ghosts) best because they   20
laughed the loudest and talked to me as if I were a daring talker too. One of the Negro girls had her mother coil braids over her ears Shanghai-style like mine; we were Shanghai twins except that she was covered with black like my paintings. Two Negro kids enrolled in Chinese school, and the teachers gave them Chinese names. Some Negro kids walked me to school and home, protecting me from the Japanese kids, who hit me and chased me and stuck gum in my ears. The Japanese kids were noisy and tough. They appeared one day in kindergarten, released from concentration camp, which was a tic-tac-toe mark, like barbed wire, on the map.

It was when I found out I had to talk that school became a misery,   21
that the silence became a misery. I did not speak and felt bad each time that I did not speak. I read aloud in first grade, though, and heard the barest whisper with little squeaks come out of my throat. "Louder," said the teacher, who scared the voice away again. The other Chinese girls did not talk either, so I knew the silence had to do with being a Chinese girl.

Reading out loud was easier than speaking because we did not   22
have to make up what to say, but I stopped often, and the teacher would think I'd gone quiet again. I could not understand "I." The Chinese "I" has seven strokes, intricacies. How could the American "I," assuredly wearing a hat like the Chinese, have only three strokes, the middle so straight? Was it out of politeness that this writer left off strokes the way a Chinese has to write her own name small and crooked? No, it was not politeness; "I" is a capital and "you" is lowercase. I stared at the middle line and waited so long for its black center to resolve into tight strokes and dots that I forgot to pronounce it. The other troublesome word was "here," no strong consonant to hang on to, and so flat, when "here" is two mountainous ideographs. The teacher, who had already told me every day how to read "I" and "here" put me in the low corner under the stairs again, where the noisy boys usually sat.

When my second grade class did a play, the whole class went to the   23
auditorium except the Chinese girls. The teacher, lovely and Hawaiian,
should have understood about us, but instead left us behind in the
classroom. Our voices were too soft or nonexistent, and our parents
never signed the permission slips anyway. They never signed anything
unnecessary. We opened the door a crack and peeked out, but closed it
again quickly. One of us (not me) won every spelling bee, though.

I remember telling the Hawaiian teacher, "We Chinese can't sing   24
'land where our fathers died.' " She argued with me about politics, while
I meant because of curses. But how can I have that memory when I
couldn't talk? My mother says that we, like the ghosts, have no memories.

After American school, we picked up our cigar boxes, in which   25
we had arranged books, brushes, and an inkbox neatly, and went to
Chinese school, from 5:00 to 7:30 P.M. There we chanted together,
voices rising and falling, loud and soft, some boys shouting, everybody
reading together, reciting together and not alone with one voice. When
we had a memorization test, the teacher let each of us come to his desk
and say the lesson to him privately, while the rest of the class practiced
copying or tracing. Most of the teachers were men. The boys who were
so well behaved in the American school played tricks on them and
talked back to them. The girls were not mute. They screamed and
yelled during recess, when there were no rules; they had fistfights.
Nobody was afraid of children hurting themselves or of children hurting
school property. The glass doors to the red and green balconies with
the gold joy symbols were left wide open so that we could run out and
climb the fire escapes. We played capture-the-flag in the auditorium,
where Sun Yat-sen and Chiang Kai-shek's pictures hung at the back of
the stage, the Chinese flag on their left and the American flag on their
right. We climbed the teak ceremonial chairs and made flying leaps off
the stage. One flag headquarters was behind the glass door and the
other on stage right. Our feet drummed on the hollow stage. During
recess the teachers locked themselves up in their office with the
shelves of books, copybooks, inks from China. They drank tea and
warmed their hands at a stove. There was no play supervision. At
recess we had the school to ourselves, and also we could roam as far
as we could go—downtown, Chinatown stores, home—as long as we
returned before the bell rang.

At exactly 7:30 the teacher again picked up the brass bell that sat on   26
his desk and swung it over our heads, while we charged down the stairs,
our cheering magnified in the stairwell. Nobody had to line up.

Not all of the children who were silent at American school found   27
voice at Chinese school. One new teacher said each of us had to get up
and recite in front of the class, who was to listen. My sister and I had
memorized the lesson perfectly. We said it to each other at home, one

chanting, one listening. The teacher called on my sister to recite first. It was the first time a teacher had called on the second-born to go first. My sister was scared. She glanced at me and looked away; I looked down at my desk. I hoped that she could do it because if she could, then I would have to. She opened her mouth and a voice came out that wasn't a whisper, but it wasn't a proper voice either. I hoped that she would not cry, fear breaking up her voice like twigs underfoot. She sounded as if she were trying to sing though weeping and strangling. She did not pause or stop to end the embarrassment. She kept going until she said the last word, and then she sat down. When it was my turn, the same voice came out, a crippled animal running on broken legs. You could hear splinters in my voice, bones rubbing jagged against one another. I was loud, though. I was glad I didn't whisper. There was one little girl who whispered.

Exercises

Some Important Words

frenum (paragraph 2), tauten (3), tampering (17), skittering (17), wince (17), intricacies (22), ideographs (22), mute (25), Sun Yat-sen (25), Chiang Kai-shek (25).

Some of the Issues

1. After reading the selection explain why Kingston says in the first paragraph, "In China, I would have been an outlaw knot-maker." Why does she call herself an outlaw? And, considering the legend she tells, why would she have been a knot-maker?
2. "Maybe that's why my mother cut my tongue." That startling sentence introduces a remembered conversation with her mother. Is it possible that the tongue-cutting never took place? What evidence do you find either way?
3. Kingston is silent in some situations but not in others. When is she silent and when not?
4. How did the American and the Chinese schools differ in the way they were run? In the way they affected the children?

The Way We Are Told

5. Kingston uses several symbols: the knot, the tongue, the Chinese word for *I.* Explain their meaning and use.
6. What is the effect of the first sentence of paragraph 2?

7. Kingston departs from strict chronological order in telling her story. What is the effect?

Some Subjects for Writing

8. Kingston describes times when she was embarrassed or "tongue-tied." Describe a time when you were afraid to speak. Include descriptions of your feelings before, during, and after the incident.
9. Kingston suggests that in Chinese-American culture girls are brought up very differently from boys. In your own experience of the culture in which you were raised does gender make an important difference in upbringing? Give examples in your answer.
*10. Read Richard Rodriguez's "Public and Private Language." Both he and Kingston describe the experience of attending school for the first time with children different from themselves. Compare and contrast their reactions.

HALFWAY TO DICK AND JANE: A PUERTO RICAN PILGRIMAGE

Jack Agueros

Dick and Jane are no longer with us, but generations of American children learned to read with them. In Agueros's childhood they were the central characters in the most popular first-grade reader: two children with their dog Spot, their aproned mother keeping house, and their pipe-smoking father going out to earn the money that would keep the family firmly anchored to the middle class. They were a kindly, friendly family living the American Dream in an immaculate house with a white picket fence. Agueros speaks not only for himself but for many others when he says that he never got more than halfway toward that dreamland. In fact, it receded further as he was growing up.

Jack Agueros was born in New York City in 1934 of parents who had recently migrated from the island of Puerto Rico. He grew up in Spanish Harlem, was graduated from Brooklyn College, and has served in the administration of New York City. He is the author of *Correspondence Between the Stonehaulers* (1991). The following essay from 1971 was his first published work.

Puerto Rico, conquered by Spain in the early sixteenth century, became part of the United States as a result of the Spanish-American War (1898). Since 1917, Puerto Ricans have been U.S. citizens. They elect their governor and legislature but cannot vote for president. A resident commissioner (without vote) represents them in the U.S. Congress. Many Puerto Ricans have come to the mainland either to settle or to work for a time.

I was born in Harlem in 1934. We lived on 111th Street off Fifth Avenue.   1
It was a block of mainly three-story buildings—with brick fronts, or brownstone, or limestone imitations of brownstone. Our apartment was a three-room first-floor walk-up. It faced north and had three windows on the street, none in back. There was a master bedroom, a living room,

a kitchen-dining room, a foyer with a short hall, and a bathroom. In the kitchen there was an air shaft to evacuate cooking odors and grease—we converted it to a chimney for Santa Claus.

The kitchen was dominated by a large Victorian china closet, and 2 the built-in wall shelves were lined with oilcloth, trimmed with ruffle, both decorated by brilliant and miniature fruits. Prominent on a wall of the kitchen was a large reproduction of a still life, a harvest table full of produce, framed and under glass. From it, I learned to identify apples, pumpkins, bananas, pears, grapes, and melons, and "peaches without worms." A joke between my mother and me. (A peach we had bought in the city market, under the New Haven's elevated tracks, bore, like the trains above, passengers.)

On one shelf of the kitchen, over the stove, there was a lineup of 3 ceramic canisters that carried words like "nutmeg," "ginger," and "basil." I did not know what those words meant and I don't know if my mother did either. "Spices," she would say, and that was that. They were of a yellow color that was not unlike the yellow of the stove. The kitchen was itself painted yellow, I think, very pale. But I am sure of one thing, it was not "Mickey Moused." "Mickey Mousing" was a technique used by house painters to decorate the areas of the walls that were contained by wood molding. Outside the molding they might paint a solid green. Inside the wood mold, the same solid green. Then with a twisted-up rag dipped in a lighter green they would trace random patterns.

We never used wallpaper or rugs. Our floors were covered with 4 linoleum in every room. My father painted the apartment every year before Christmas, and in addition, he did all the maintenance, doing his own plastering and plumbing. No sooner would we move into an apartment than my father would repair holes or cracks, and if there were bulges in the plaster, he would break them open and redo the area— sometimes a whole wall. He would immediately modify the bathrooms to add a shower with separate valves, and usually as a routine matter, he cleaned out all the elbow traps, and changed all the washers on faucets. This was true of the other families in the buildings where I lived. Not a December came without a painting of the apartment.

We had Louis XIV furniture in the living room, reflected in the 5 curved glass door and curved glass sides of the china closet. On the walls of the living room hung two prints that I loved. I would spend hours playing games with my mother based on the pictures, making up stories, etc. One day at Brooklyn College, a slide projector slammed, and I awoke after having dozed off during a dull lecture to see Van Gogh's "The Gleaners" on the screen. I almost cried. Another time I came across the other print in a book. A scene of Venice by Canaletto.

The important pieces of the living room, for me, were a Detrola 6 radio with magic-eye tuning and the nightingale, Keero. The nightingale and the radio went back before my recollection. The bird could not stop singing, and people listened on the sidewalk below and came upstairs offering to buy Keero.

The Detrola, shaped like a Gothic arch with inlaid woodwork, was   7
a great source of entertainment for the family. I memorized all the hit songs sung by Libertad Lamarque and Carlos Gardel. Sundays I listened to the Canary Hour presented by Hartz Mountain Seed Company. Puppy, a white Spitz, was my constant companion. Puppy slept at the foot of my bed from the first day he came to our house till the day he died, when I was eleven or twelve and he was seven or eight.

I am an only child. My parents and I always talked about my   8
becoming a doctor. The law and politics were not highly regarded in my house. Lawyers, my mother would explain, had to defend people whether they were guilty or not, while politicians, my father would say, were all crooks. A doctor helped everybody, rich and poor, white and black. If I became a doctor, I could study hay fever and find a cure for it, my godmother would say. Also, I could take care of my parents when they were old. I liked the idea of helping, and for nineteen years my sole ambition was to study medicine.

My house had books, not many, but my parents encouraged me to   9
read. As I became a good reader they bought books for me and never refused me money for their purchase. My father once built a bookcase for me. It was an important moment, for I had always believed that my father was not too happy about my being a bookworm. The atmosphere at home was always warm. We seemed to be a popular family. We entertained frequently, with two standing parties a year—at Christmas and for my birthday. Parties were always large. My father would dismantle the beds and move all the furniture so that the full two rooms could be used for dancing. My mother would cook up a storm, particularly at Christmas. *Pasteles, lechon asado, arroz con gandules,* and a lot of *coquito* to drink (meat-stuffed plantain, roast pork, rice with pigeon peas, and coconut nog). My father always brought in a band. They played without compensation and were guests at the party. They ate and drank and danced while a victrola covered the intermissions. One year my father brought home a whole pig and hung it in the foyer doorway. He and my mother prepared it by rubbing it down with oil, oregano, and garlic. After preparation, the pig was taken down and carried over to a local bakery where it was cooked and returned home. Parties always went on till daybreak, and in addition to the band, there were always volunteers to sing and declaim poetry.

My mother kept an immaculate household. Bedspreads (chenille   10
seemed to be very in) and lace curtains, washed at home like everything else, were hung up on huge racks with rows of tight nails. The racks were assembled in the living room, and the moisture from the wet

bedspreads would fill the apartment. In a sense, that seems to be the lasting image of that period of my life. The house was clean. The neighbors were clean. The streets, with few cars, were clean. The buildings were clean and uncluttered with people on the stoops. The park was clean. The visitors to my house were clean, and the relationships that my family had with other Puerto Rican families, and the Italian families that my father had met through baseball and my mother through the garment center, were clean. Second Avenue was clean and most of the apartment windows had awnings. There was always music, there seemed to be no rain, and snow did not become slush. School was fun, we wrote essays about how grand America was, we put up hunchbacked cats at Halloween, we believed Santa Claus visited everyone. I believed everyone was Catholic. I grew up with dogs, nightingales, my godmother's guitar, rocking chair, cat, guppies, my father's occasional roosters, kept in a cage on the fire escape. Laundry delivered and collected by horse and wagon, fruits and vegetables sold the same way, windowsill refrigeration in winter, iceman and box in summer. The police my friends, likewise the teachers.

In short, the first seven or so years of my life were not too great a   11
variation on Dick and Jane, the school book figures who, if my memory serves me correctly, were blond Anglo-Saxons, not immigrants, not migrants like the Puerto Ricans, and not the children of either immigrants or migrants.

My family moved in 1941 to Lexington Avenue into a larger   12
apartment where I could have my own room. It was a light, sunny, railroad flat on the top floor of a well-kept building. I transferred to a new school, and whereas before my classmates had been mostly black, the new school had few blacks. The classes were made up of Italians, Irish, Jews, and a sprinkling of Puerto Ricans. My block was populated by Jews, Italians, and Puerto Ricans.

And then a whole series of different events began. I went to junior   13
high school. We played in the backyards, where we tore down fences to build fires to cook stolen potatoes. We tore up whole hedges, because the green tender limbs would not burn when they were peeled, and thus made perfect skewers for our stolen "mickies." We played tag in the abandoned buildings, tearing the plaster off the walls, tearing the wire lath off the wooden slats, tearing the wooden slats themselves, good for fires, for kites, for sword fighting. We ran up and down the fire escapes playing tag and over and across many rooftops. The war ended and the heavy Puerto Rican migration began. The Irish and the Jews disappeared from the neighborhood. The Italians tried to consolidate east of Third Avenue.

What caused the clean and open world to end? Many things. Into   14
an ancient neighborhood came pouring four to five times more people than it had been designed to hold. Men who came running at the

promise of jobs were jobless as the war ended. They were confused. They could not see the economic forces that ruled their lives as they drank beer on the corners, reassuring themselves of good times to come while they were hell-bent toward alcoholism. The sudden surge in numbers caused new resentments, and prejudice was intensified. Some were forced to live in cellars, and were then characterized as cave dwellers. Kids came who were confused by the new surroundings; their Puerto Ricanness forced us against a mirror asking, "If they are Puerto Ricans, what are we?" and thus they confused us. In our confusion we were sometimes pathetically reaching out, sometimes pathologically striking out. Gangs. Drugs. Wine. Smoking. Girls. Dances and slow-drag music. Mambo. Spics, Spooks, and Wops. Territories, brother gangs, and war councils establishing rules for right of way on blocks and avenues and for seating in the local theater. Pegged pants and zip guns. Slang.

Dick and Jane were dead, man. Education collapsed. Every class- 15 room had ten kids who spoke no English. Black, Italian, Puerto Rican relations in the classroom were good, but we all knew we couldn't visit one another's neighborhoods. Sometimes we could not move too freely within our own blocks. On 109th, from the lamp post west, the Latin Aces, and from the lamp post east, the Senecas, the "club" I belonged to. The kids who spoke no English became known as Marine Tigers, picked up from a popular Spanish song. (The *Marine Tiger* and the *Marine Shark* were two ships that sailed from San Juan to New York and brought over many, many migrants from the island.)

The neighborhood had its boundaries. Third Avenue and east, 16 Italian. Fifth Avenue and west, black. South, there was a hill on 103rd Street known locally as Cooney's Hill. When you got to the top of the hill, something strange happened: America began, because from the hill south was where the "Americans" lived. Dick and Jane were not dead; they were alive and well in a better neighborhood.

When, as a group of Puerto Rican kids, we decided to go swimming 17 to Jefferson Park Pool, we knew we risked a fight and a beating from the Italians. And when we went to La Milagrosa Church in Harlem, we knew we risked a fight and a beating from the blacks. But when we went over Cooney's Hill, we risked dirty looks, disapproving looks, and questions from the police like, "What are you doing in this neighborhood?" and "Why don't you kids go back where you belong?"

Where we belonged! Man, I had written compositions about 18 America. Didn't I belong on the Central Park tennis courts, even if I didn't know how to play? Couldn't I watch Dick play? Weren't these policemen working for me too?

Junior high school was a waste. I can say with 90 per cent accuracy 19 that I learned nothing. The woodshop was used to manufacture stocks for "home-mades" after Macy's stopped selling zipguns. We went from classroom to classroom answering "here," and trying to be "good." The math class was generally permitted to go to the gym after roll call. English was still a good class. Partly because of a damn good, tough teacher named Miss Beck, and partly because of the grade-number system (7-1 the smartest seventh grade and 7-12, the dumbest). Books were left in school, there was little or no homework, and the whole thing seemed to be a holding operation until high school. Somehow or other, I passed the entrance exam to Brooklyn Technical High School. But I couldn't cut the mustard, either academically or with the "American" kids. After one semester, I came back to PS 83, waited a semester, and went on to Benjamin Franklin High School.

I still wanted to study medicine and excelled in biology. English was   20 always an interesting subject, and I still enjoyed writing compositions and reading. In the neighborhood it was becoming a problem being categorized as a bookworm and as one who used "Sunday words," or "big words." I dug school, but I wanted to be one of the boys more. I think the boys respected my intelligence, despite their ribbing. Besides which, I belonged to a club with a number of members who were interested in going to college, and so I wasn't so far out.

My introduction to marijuana was in junior high school in 1948. A   21 kid named Dixie from 124th street brought a pack of joints to school and taught about twelve guys to smoke. He told us we could buy joints at a quarter each or five for a dollar. Bombers, or thicker cigarettes, were thirty-five cents each or three for a dollar. There were a lot of experimenters, but not too many buyers. Actually, among the boys there was a strong taboo on drugs, and the Spanish word *"motto"* was a term of disparagement. Many clubs would kick out members who were known to use drugs. Heroin was easily available, and in those days came packaged in capsules or "caps" which sold for fifty cents each. Method of use was inhalation through the nose, or "sniffing," or "snorting."

I still remember vividly the first kid I ever saw who was mainlining.   22 Prior to this encounter, I had known of "skin-popping," or subcutaneous injection, but not of mainlining. Most of the sniffers were afraid of skin-popping because they knew of the danger of addiction. They seemed to think that you could not become addicted by sniffing.

I went over to 108th Street and Madison where we played softball   23 on an empty lot. This kid came over who was maybe sixteen or seventeen and asked us if we wanted to buy Horse. He started telling us about shooting up and showed me his arms. He had tracks, big black marks on the inside of his arm from the inner joint of the elbow down to his wrist and then over onto the back of his hand. I was stunned. Then he said, "That's nothing, man. I ain't hooked, and I ain't no junky. I can stop anytime I want to." I believe that he believed what he was saying.

Invariably the kids talking about their drug experiences would say over and over, "I ain't hooked. I can stop anytime."

But they didn't stop; and the drug traffic grew greater and more   24 open. Kids were smoking on the corners and on the stoops. Deals were made on the street, and you knew fifteen places within a block radius where you could buy anything you wanted. Cocaine never seemed to catch on although it was readily available. In the beginning, the kids seemed to be able to get money for stuff easily. As the number of shooters grew and the prices wei t up, the kids got more desperate and apartment robbing became a real problem.

More of the boys began to leave school. We didn't use the term   25 drop out; rather, a guy would say one day, after forty-three truancies, "I'm quitting school." And so he would. It was an irony, for what was really happening was that after many years of being rejected, ignored, and shuffled around by the school, the kid wanted to quit. Only you can't quit something you were never a part of, nor can you drop out if you were never in.

Some kids lied about their age and joined the army. Most just hung   26 around. Not drifting to drugs or crime or to work either. They used to talk about going back at night and getting the diploma. I believe that they did not believe they could get their diplomas. They knew that the schools had abandoned them a long time ago—that to get the diploma meant starting all over again and that was impossible. Besides, day or night, it was the same school, the same staff, the same shit. But what do you say when you are powerless to get what you want, and what do you say when the other side has all the cards and writes all the rules? You say, "Tennis is for fags," and "School is for fags."

My mother leads me by the hand and carries a plain brown   27 shopping bag. We enter an immense airplane hangar. Structural steel crisscrosses on the ceiling and walls; large round and square rivets look like buttons or bubbles of air trapped in the girders. There are long metallic counters with people bustling behind them. It smells of C.N. disinfectant. Many people stand on many lines up to these counters; there are many conversations going on simultaneously. The huge space plays tricks with voices and a very eerie combination of sounds results. A white cabbage is rolled down a counter at us. We retaliate by throwing down stamps.

For years I thought that sequence happened in a dream. The rolling   28 cabbage rolled in my head, and little unrelated incidents seemed to bring it to the surface of my mind. I could not understand why I remembered a once-dreamt dream so vividly. I was sixteen when I picked up and read Freud's *The Interpretation of Dreams*. One part I understood immediately and well, sex and symbolism. In no time, I had hung my shingle;

Streetcorner Analyst. My friends would tell me their dreams and with the most outrageous sexual explanations we laughed whole evenings away. But the rolling cabbage could not be stopped and neither quack analysis nor serious thought could explain it away. One day I asked my mother if she knew anything about it.

"That was home relief, 1937 or 1938. You were no more than four   29
years old then. Your father had been working at a restaurant and I had a job downtown. I used to take you every morning to Dona Eduvije who cared for you all day. She loved you very much, and she was very clean and neat, but I used to cry on my way to work, wishing I could stay home with my son and bring him up like a proper mother would. But I guess I was fated to be a workhorse. When I was pregnant, I would get on the crowded subway and go to work. I would get on a crowded elevator up. Then down. Then back on the subway. Every day I was afraid that the crowd would hurt me, that I would lose my baby. But I had to work. I worked for the WPA right into my ninth month."

My mother was telling it "like it was," and I sat stupefied, for I could   30
not believe that what she said applied to the time I thought of as open and clean. I had been existing in my life like a small plant in a bell jar, my parents defining my awareness. There were things all around me I could not see.

"When you were born we had been living as boarders. It was hard   31
to find an apartment, even in Harlem. You saw signs that said 'No Renting to Colored or Spanish.' That meant Puerto Ricans. We used to say, 'This is supposed to be such a great country?' But with a new baby we were determined not to be boarders and we took an apartment on 111th Street. Soon after we moved, I lost my job because my factory closed down. Your father was making seven or eight dollars a week in a terrible job in a carpet factory. They used to clean rugs, and your father's hands were always in strong chemicals. You know how funny some of his fingernails are? It was from that factory. He came home one night and he was looking at his fingers, and he started saying that he didn't come to this country to lose his hands. He wanted to hold a bat and play ball and he wanted to work—but he didn't want to lose his hands. So he quit the job and went to a restaurant for less pay. With me out of work, a new apartment and therefore higher rent, we couldn't manage. Your father was furious when I mentioned home relief. He said he would rather starve than go on relief. But I went and filled out the papers and answered all the questions and swallowed my pride when they treated me like an intruder. I used to say to them, 'Find me a job—get my husband a better job—we don't want home relief.' But we had to take it. And all that mess with the stamps in exchange for food. And they used to have weekly 'specials' sort of—but a lot of things were useless—because they were American food. I don't remember if we went once a week or

once every two weeks. You were so small I don't know how you remember that place and the long lines. It didn't last long because your father had everybody trying to find him a better job and finally somebody did. Pretty soon I went into the WPA and thank God, we never had to deal with those people again. I don't know how you remember that place, but I wish you didn't. I wish I could forget that home relief thing myself. It was the worst time for your father and me. He still hates it.

(He still hates it and so do many people. The expression, "I'd rather 32 starve than go on welfare" is common in the Puerto Rican community. This characteristic pride is well chronicled throughout Spanish literature. For example, one episode of *Lazarillo de Tormes,* the sixteenth-century picaresque novel, tells of a squire who struts around all day with his shiny sword and pressed cape. At night the squire takes food from the boy, Lazarillo—who has begged or stolen it—explaining that it is not proper for a squire to beg or steal, or even to work! Without Lazarillo to feed him, the squire would probably starve.)

"You don't know how hard it was being married to your father 33 then. He was young and very strong and very active and he wanted to work. Welfare deeply disturbed him, and I was afraid that he would actually get very violent if an investigator came to the house. They had a terrible way with people, like throwing that cabbage, that was the way they gave you everything, the way we used to throw the kitchen slop to the pigs in Puerto Rico. Some giving! Your father was, is, *muy macho,* and I used to worry if anybody says anything or gives him that why-do-you-people-come-here-to-ruin-things look he'll be in jail for thirty years. He almost got arrested once when you were just a baby. We went to a hospital clinic—I don't remember now if it was Sydenham or Harlem Hospital—you had a swelling around your throat—and the doctor told me, 'Put on cold compresses.' I said I did that and it didn't help. The doctor said, 'Then put hot compresses.' Your father blew up. In his broken English, he asked the doctor to do that to his mother, and then invited him to transfer over to the stable on 104th Street. 'You do better with horses—maybe they don't care what kind of compresses they get.'

"One morning your father tells me, 'I got a new job. I start today 34 driving a truck delivering soft drinks.' That night I ask him about the job—he says, 'I quit—bunch of Mafia—I went to the first four places on my list and each storeowner said, "I didn't order any soda." So I got the idea real fast. The Mafia was going to leave soda in each place and then make the guys buy from them only. As soon as I figured it out, I took the truck back, left it parked where I got it, and didn't even say good-bye.' The restaurant took him back. They liked him. The chef used to give him eggs and meats; it was very important to us. Your father never could keep still (still can't), so he was loved wherever he worked. I feel sorry for people on welfare—forget about the cabbage—I never should have taken you there."

My father and I are walking through East Harlem, south down Lexington from 112th toward 110th, in 1952. Saturday in late spring, I am eighteen years old, sun brilliant on the streets, people running back and forth on household errands. My father is telling me a story about how back in nineteen thirty something, we were very poor and Con Ed light meters were in every apartment. "The Puerto Ricans, maybe everybody else, would hook up a shunt wire around the meter, specially in the evenings when the use was heavy—that way you didn't pay for all the electric you used. We called it *'pillo'* (thief)."   35

We arrive at 110th Street and all the cart vendors are there peddling plantains, avocados, yams, various subtropical roots. I make a casual remark about how foolish it all seemed, and my father catches that I am looking down on them. "Are they stealing?" he asks. "Are they selling people colored water? Aren't they working honestly? Are they any different from a bank president? Aren't they hung like you and me? They are *machos,* and to be respected. Don't let college go to your head. You think a Ph.D. is automatically better than a peddler? Remember where you come from—poor people. I mopped floors for people and I wasn't ashamed, but I never let them look down on me. Don't you look down on anybody."   36

We walk for a way in silence, I am mortified, but he is not angry. "One day I decide to play a joke on your mother. I come home a little early and knock. When she says 'Who?' I say 'Edison man.' Well, there is this long silence and then a scream. I open the door and run in. Your mother's on a chair, in tears, her right arm black from pinky to elbow. She ran to take the *pillo* out, but in her nervousness she got a very slight shock, the black from the spark. She never has forgiven me. After that, I always thought through my jokes."   37

We walk some more and he says, "I'll tell you another story. This one on me. I was twenty-five years old and was married to your mother. I took her down to Puerto Rico to meet Papa and Mama. We were sitting in the living room, and I remember it like it happened this morning. The room had rattan furniture very popular in that time. Papa had climbed in rank back to captain and had a new house. The living room had double doors which opened onto a large *balcón*. At the other end of the room you could see the dining table with a beautiful white handmade needlework cloth. We were sitting and talking and I took out a cigarette. I was smoking Chesterfields then. No sooner had I lit up than Papa got up, came over, and smacked me in the face. 'You haven't received my permission to smoke,' he said. Can you imagine how I felt?" So my father dealt with his love for me through lateral actions: building bookcases, and through tales of how he got his wounds, he anointed mine.   38

What is a migration? What does it happen to? Why are the Eskimos   39
still dark after living in that snow all these centuries? Why don't they have
a word for snow? What things are around me with such high saturation that
I have not named them? What is a migration? If you rob my purse, are you
really a fool? Can a poor boy really be president? In America? Of anything?
If he is not white? Should one man's achievement fulfill one million
people? Will you let us come near your new machine: after all, there is no
more ditch digging? What is a migration? What does it happen to?

The most closely watched migrants of this world are birds. Birds   40
migrate because they get bored singing in the same place to the same
people. And they see that the environment gets hostile. Men move for
the same reasons. When a Puerto Rican comes to America, he comes
looking for a job. He takes the cold as one of a negative series of givens.
The mad hustle, the filthy city, filthy air, filthy housing, sardine transportation, are in the series. He knows life will be tough and dangerous. But
he thinks he can make a buck. And in his mind, there is only one tableau:
himself retired, owner of his home in Puerto Rico, chickens cackling in
the back yard.

It startles me still, though it has been five years since my parents   41
went back to the island. I never believed them. My father, driving around
New York for the Housing Authority, knowing more streets in more
boroughs than I do, and my mother, curious in her later years about
museums and theaters, and reading my books as fast as I would put them
down, then giving me cryptic reviews. Salinger is really silly *(Catcher in
the Rye),* but entertaining. That evil man deserved to die *(Moby Dick).*
He's too much (Dostoevski in *Crime and Punishment).* I read this when
I was a little girl in school *(Hamlet* and *Macbeth).* It's too sad for me *(Cry,
the Beloved Country).*

My father, intrigued by the thought of passing the foreman's exam,   42
sitting down with a couple of arithmetic books, and teaching himself at
age fifty-five to do work problems and mixture problems and fractions
and decimals, and going into the civil service exam and scoring a
seventy-four and waiting up one night for me to show me three poems
he had written. These two cosmopolites, gladiators without skills or
language, battling hostile environments and prejudiced people and
systems, had graduated from Harlem to the Bronx, had risen into
America's dream-cherished lower middle class, and then put it down for
Puerto Rico after thirty plus years.

What is a migration, when is it not just a long visit?   43

I was born in Harlem, and I live downtown. And I am a migrant, for   44
if a migration is anything, it is a state of mind. I have known those
Eskimos who lived in America twenty and thirty years and never voted,
never attended a community meeting, never filed a complaint against a
landlord, never informed the police when they were robbed or swindled,

or when their daughters were molested. Never appeared at the State or City Commission on Human Rights, never reported a business fraud, never, in other words, saw the snow.

And I am very much a migrant because I am still not quite at home   45
in America. Always there are hills; on the other side—people inclined to throwing cabbages. I cannot "earn and return"—there is no position for me in my father's tableau.

However, I approach the future with optimism. Fewer Puerto Ricans   46
like Eskimos, a larger number of leaders like myself, trained in the university, tempered in the ghetto, and with a vision of America moving from its unexecuted policy to a society open and clean, accessible to anyone.

Dick and Jane? They, too, were tripped by the society, and in our   47
several ways, we are all still migrating.

Exercises

Some Important Words

Harlem (paragraph 1), evacuate (1), Victorian (2), Louis XIV furniture (5), Van Gogh (5), Canaletto (5), compensation (9), foyer (9), immaculate (10), Anglo-Saxon (11), railroad flat (12), pathologically (14), disparagement (21), subcutaneous (22), immense (27), stupefied (30), mortified (37), lateral (38), anointed (38), migration (39), saturation (39), tableau (40), cryptic (41), cosmopolites (42), gladiators (42).

Some of the Issues

1. The first seven paragraphs describe Agueros's first house: its layout, its furnishings, and decorations. What impression does Agueros's description give you? Cite details that contribute to this impression.
2. In paragraph 4 Agueros lists the activities of his father in the home. In paragraph 10 he does the same for his mother's work. How do their roles differ? Are these differences similar to those in homes you know?
3. What is the key word in paragraph 10? How does it contribute to the impression the author gives of his childhood?
4. In paragraph 11 Agueros sums up his feelings about his childhood. How do the preceding paragraphs, and paragraph 10 in particular, justify that conclusion?
5. Compare the early experiences of Agueros, as he remembers them, with his experiences in junior high. "What caused the clean and open world to end?"

6. Explain what Agueros means when he says, "Their Puerto Ricanness forced us against a mirror, asking, 'If they are Puerto Rican, what are we?' "

7. Paragraphs 13 through 26 describe the author's progression through junior high and high school. What changes does he record? What are the way stations?

8. During the Great Depression of the 1930s Agueros's family went on relief. Much later he finds out about that time from his mother when he learns that the story of the cabbage (27) was not a dream. Compare that adult experience with his recollection of childhood in paragraph 10. Which is the real dream world?

9. In paragraphs 35 through 38 Agueros describes a talk with his father. What do we learn from their conversation?

10. In the last part of the essay Agueros repeatedly asks, "What is a migration?" What does he mean by that question? In what ways has he remained a migrant? What is he trying to tell the reader about migration?

*11. Which family is more distant, in your opinion, from "mainstream" America: Agueros's or Kingston's as described in "Girlhood Among Ghosts"? Explain.

The Way We Are Told

12. Find the various references to Dick and Jane in the text. How does the author use them to express his theme? What does the essay's title mean?

13. How does paragraph 13 serve as a transition?

14. Note the last few lines of paragraph 14 and the opening sentence of paragraph 15. What is their effect? How has the language changed since paragraph 10?

15. Why does Agueros change to the present tense for paragraph 27? (He reverts to the past tense in paragraph 28.)

16. Agueros tells of the talk with his father (paragraphs 35 through 38) in the present tense as well. Are his reasons for doing so the same as in the cabbage story? Look at paragraphs 39 through 46 before you answer.

Some Subjects for Writing

17. Compare two schools you have attended and explain the differences between them. To what do you attribute these differences: your classmates, your teachers, the administration, different locations, or changes in you?

18. Agueros describes several objects that were important to him as a child. Describe an object that was important to you and explain its meaning. How would it affect you now?
19. "I am a migrant, for if migration is anything, it is a state of mind." (44) Describe yourself as a migrant; consider in what ways you have "moved," not necessarily physically, but mentally or emotionally.

THE IMPORTANCE OF BEING ELEVEN: CAROL GILLIGAN TAKES ON ADOLESCENCE

Lindsy Van Gelder

In this 1990 *Ms.* article, Van Gelder reviews the results of a study on adolescent girls undertaken by the Project on the Psychology of Women and the Development of Girls at Harvard University and published in *Making Connections: The Relational Worlds of Adolescent Girls at Emma Willard School* (1989). Their findings indicate that as girls get older, they seem to undergo a crisis in response to adolescence and to the demands placed on girls in mainstream American culture. As a consequence, girls learn to "think in ways that differ from what they really think." A second book published by Carol Gilligan, Lyn Mikel Brown, and others from the Harvard Project, *Meeting at the Crossroads; Women's Psychology and Girls' Development* (1992), contains interviews and reports of ongoing research about girls growing into adulthood.

Van Gelder is chief writer for *Allure,* a contributing editor to *Ms.* magazine, and coauthor with Pamela Robin Brandt of *Are You Two . . . Together? A Gay and Lesbian Travel Guide to Europe* (1991). She was born in 1944 and has two daughters.

The summer before sixth grade, I grew six inches. So, probably, did my [1] breasts. In June, my nickname was "Ace," and my favorite possession was a pair of boys' black hightoppers with a decal of the Lone Ranger on the ankle; by September, I had given up sports (this being the pre-aerobics 1950s), changed my name to "Lyn," learned to sleep in iron maiden hair rollers, and begun getting crushes on boys instead of on their haberdashery. The adults in my life were visibly relieved at my "decision," and I remember being happy that I apparently seemed to be the one in control. On the inside it felt more like putting a gun to my own head just before the enemy army burst through the ramparts. Around the same time as my fall from tomboy grace, but seemingly unrelated to it, I also stopped doing something else I loved: writing poetry. There was no reason to leave it behind; the poetry was the one part of my smart-ass fifth-grade self that teachers and parents wholeheartedly approved of. Nonetheless, it simply disappeared.

According to the ongoing research of Harvard University's Project   2
on the Psychology of Women and the Development of Girls, I was hardly the only girl in our culture who, in one way or another, choked off her own voice at adolescence. The project—whose best known member is Carol Gilligan, author of *In a Different Voice*—has uncovered strong evidence that girls at puberty get the message that the culture doesn't value their experience; it literally doesn't want to listen to what they have to say. They "adjust" by stifling themselves. Indeed, in self-defense most of them stop even consciously knowing the things that the choked-off voice would want to say.

At 10 or 11, girls have clear-eyed views of the world and their own   3
right to be heard, says Gilligan. "At this age, they're often called 'bossy'—a word that virtually disappears later on. They're not afraid of conflict. They care deeply about relationships, but they understand that there's often jealously and anger in relationships as well as joy and comfort." Above all, they aren't worried about being "nice."

Consider the girl who is asked to complete the sentence "What gets   4
me into trouble is" and adds: "Chewing gum and not tucking my shirt in (but it's usually worth it)." Or the girl who's mad at her friend for ignoring her when a third friend is around and who plans to "get even" by doing the same thing—at which point her friend will empathize with how *she* felt, and they can be friends again. Or the girl who gets annoyed when she thinks her family isn't paying enough attention to what she has to say at the dinner table—and whips out a whistle and blows it. In the stunned silence that follows, she cheerfully notes in a normal voice: "That's much nicer."

But by seventh grade, the girls have started to use the phrase "I   5
don't know" as a sort of conversational mantra ("I thought it was, like—I don't know—a little unfair") or later, even to preface their opinions with remarks like "This may sound mediocre, but . . ." Instead of living comfortably inside their own skin, they measure themselves against an idealized, perfect girl. And they start to frame dilemmas in relationships not in terms of conflicts between two people but in terms of how "nice" and "good" and self-sacrificing they can be. One legacy of all this shoehorning into an impossible ideal is that girls' relationships (precisely the thing they really *were* "good" at) may become inauthentic—since one's "real" self needs constantly to be tamed, denigrated, glossed over, or buried. It's an endless loop—or it will be if we don't find our way back to what we all knew, effortlessly, in fifth grade.

As recently as a decade ago, according to Gilligan, there wasn't   6
enough adolescent girl-specific research to fill even a chapter in a

psychology textbook. "The study of adolescence had been the study of males," Gilligan notes. "You'd have titles like 'The Psychological World of the Teenager: A Study of 175 Boys.' These studies were passing government review boards and peer review boards, and they were being published in journals, and they weren't studying girls. I think it's one of the most interesting pieces of intellectual history of this century that nobody saw this, neither women nor men."

Then in 1980 Robert Parker moved from a New England boys' prep school to become headmaster of Emma Willard, a girls' private high school near Albany, New York. Parker did notice that the trajectory into adulthood for his new female students seemed to be very different from that of boys. He invited Gilligan (whose *In a Different Voice* had focused on variations in the way men and women approach moral choices) to study his students. The book based on that research (*Making Connections: The Relational Worlds of Adolescent Girls at Emma Willard School*, edited by Gilligan, Nona P. Lyons, and Trudy J. Hanmer) has just been published by Harvard University Press.

"What could you possibly learn," one of the Emma Willard girls asked the researchers early on, "by studying *us?*" The girl may have been asking the question out of a typical conviction that girls don't really count, but the researchers themselves didn't have an agenda. The most basic question at the time was simply: "What will we hear about adolescence if we start listening to girls?" As the project grew, the group listened to girls beyond the Emma Willard sample: black, Irish, and Hispanic girls at after-school clubs in three inner-city Boston neighborhoods, as well as girls in public, private, coed, and all-girls school settings.

In hindsight, the breakthrough probably came when project member Lyn Mikel Brown began studying girls at a private school in the Midwest. Because it was an elementary as well as a secondary school, Brown had the opportunity to mount a five-year longitudinal comparative study of girls in four different age groups: second, fifth, seventh, and tenth grades. Brown saw changes among the age groups, and over time, saw individual girls change. As Gilligan notes, "It was as if we had been filling in a mosaic piece by piece. With Lyn's pieces, a real picture emerged: and the picture was of an 11-year-old."

That the 11-year-old's sea change might be a pivotal life event was also radical news. "As psychologists we're used to thinking of early childhood as the most crucial time," Gilligan explains. The project's research certainly suggests, however, that psychologists should look at adolescence when they look at girls. Gilligan also finds cultural clues pointing in the same direction: "Look at all the coming-of-age stories written by men, from *David Copperfield* to *Tom Jones* to *Portrait of the Artist*. They almost always begin in infancy or childhood. Then look at what women write. Jane Eyre was ten at the beginning of the novel. Claudia in Toni Morrison's *The Bluest Eye* is nine. Or look at Margaret Atwood's *Cat's Eye* or Jamaica Kincaid's *Annie John* or Carson McCullers' *Member of the Wedding*. It's much more likely that *our* stories start at nine or ten." The new work is likely to invite controversy precisely because the team members at this stage analyze only girls' responses. Ironically, Gilligan's *In a Different Voice,* which did compare men and women, was attacked for providing ammunition to those who would use differences between men and women as a basis for discrimination.

I deliberately began this article with my own personal experience   11
because, ultimately, research on girls doubles back to our own ten-year-old selves. I learned to write, and you learned to read, and the Harvard researchers learned to collect and interpret data precisely in the language of the culture that didn't hear what we had to say. The Journalism Voice I learned was one that insisted on pretending that the writer was "objective" and not part of the story. The Researcher Voice assumes no personal connection between interviewer and subject (in this case a girl who may in fact be looking for clues about life from a former girl—or vice versa).

Traditional research also assumes that interviews proceed in a linear   12
way and can be codified according to long-standing traditions of social science. Project members felt in their guts that this approach wasn't fine-tuned to the way girls really talk about themselves—but what was the alternative? For several years, literally, the group wrestled with this basic dilemma of language. Ultimately, they came up with a method of interpreting interviews that proceeds from a metaphor not of language at all, but of music. Each interview is gone over four times, like a song played in four different keys, with researchers listening for different elements: the "plot" of whatever story is being told, the teller's sense of self, her concern for justice, and her sensitivity to caring. Researchers also listen for what *isn't* said.

"We now see what's said as polyphonic, and we listen for the   13
counterpoint and the orchestration of voices," Gilligan explains. The metaphor seemed even more apt when project member Annie Rogers researched the etymology of the word "counterpoint" and found that it came from *contre-point*—or quilt-making.

Another image that project members are using a lot these days is   14
that of "resistance." Not all girls stop knowing what they knew in fifth grade; some girls simply take that knowledge "underground" without losing it. "It's a brilliant but risky strategy," says Gilligan, "because when you're thirteen years old, it really *is* hard to confront the authority of the culture. So you keep your mouth shut, and you take a deep dive. Friendships become treacherous, because who do you trust? Will they turn out to be double agents?"

Current project work includes research into the role of friendships   15
in adolescence and workshops on how to build resistance in girls.
(Writing helps, since it keeps girls in touch with their own voice, as do
activities that emphasize group efforts rather than competition.) The
group is also studying girls whom society has labeled "at risk." Much
preliminary research indicates that it may be precisely those "trouble-
making" girls who are among the strongest resisters—and who may even
drop out of school as a way to protect their sense of self.

Adds Gilligan: "It's often the ones who seem to be doing *well* who   16
may, from our perspective, be the ones who are in trouble."

Exercises

Some Important Words

haberdashery (paragraph 1), puberty (2), mantra (5), inauthentic (5),
denigrated (5), trajectory (7), longitudinal (9), pivotal (10), codified (12),
polyphonic (13).

Some of the Issues

1. What analogy does Van Gelder use to describe her internal response
   to the "decision" she made in the sixth grade (paragraph 1)? What
   does this image say about her feelings?
2. What can you infer about Van Gelder's parents' attitude toward her
   behavior at that time?
3. According to the research findings, why do girls change their
   personalities at adolescence (paragraph 2)?
4. How would you characterize the behavior of the girls cited in
   paragraph 4?
5. What are the noticeable features of the speech of seventh-grade girls
   quoted in paragraph 5? How do you interpret these patterns of
   speech?
6. Why do you suppose research on adolescence before 1980 focused
   only on male behavior?
7. Who are the subjects in the Lyn Mikel Brown research (paragraph 9)?
8. Describe the procedure used to interpret the girls' responses to the
   interviewers. How does it differ from traditional research methods in
   the social sciences?
9. What strong claims about at-risk girls does the preliminary research
   purport?
10. Explain the significance of Gilligan's comment in the last lines of the
    article.

The Way We Are Told

11. What strategies does Van Gelder use in the first paragraph to capture the reader's attention?
12. What further motivation does she give (paragraph 11) for beginning in this way?
13. In paragraph 10, what other kinds of evidence does Gilligan examine to support the claim that age eleven is a critical psychological period for girls?
14. In paragraph 11, Van Gelder characterizes the "language" of our culture, i.e., the "Journalism Voice" and the "Researcher Voice." How is her "voice" different?

Some Subjects for Writing

15. Journal writing, poetry writing, and free writing are ways to stay in touch with our own voices. For one week, write for at least 10 minutes a day to see what you can discover about yourself. You might wish to begin by reflecting on some of the questions asked in the Harvard University Project:
    a. How would you describe yourself to yourself?
    b. A woman should always . . .
    c. What gets me into trouble is . . .
16. In your opinion, is the development of boys radically different from that of girls? Use your own family history or that of friends and relatives to support your idea.

I JUST WANNA BE AVERAGE

Mike Rose

Mike Rose was born in Chicago in 1938 and, when he was seven, moved with his parents to the South Side of Los Angeles. His parents, who had immigrated from Italy and arrived at Ellis Island in the 1910s and 1920s, never escaped poverty; however, they managed to save enough money to send Rose to a parochial school. He was an average student but, after junior high, was misplaced in the vocational education track in high school, where he "drifted to the level of a really mediocre and unprepared student." His experience in "Voc. Ed." illustrates how students placed in the lower tracks live down to the expectations of their classrooms. Fortunately, Rose's biology teacher noticed his ability, looked at his academic record, and discovered that his grades had been switched with those of another student named Rose. Subsequently, he was reassigned to the college track. In his senior year, he encountered a nontraditional teacher who opened up the world of poetry, ideas, language, and life and who helped Rose to get a scholarship to Loyola University in Los Angeles.

Rose became a teacher and worked with others on the margins of society: inner-city kids, Vietnam veterans, and underprepared adults. He is now the associate director of the writing program at UCLA, where he continues to teach underprepared students to enter and succeed in the academic world.

In the following excerpts from his book *Lives on the Boundary* (1989), he relates how poverty contributes to deep, lasting feelings of self-doubt, and how one caring person can make a fundamental difference in the lives of others.

The house was on a piece of land that rose about four feet up from heavily trafficked Vermont Avenue. The yard sloped down to the street, and three steps and a short walkway led up the middle of the grass to our front door. There was a similar house immediately to the south of us. Next to it was Carmen's Barber Shop. Carmen was a short, quiet Italian who, rumor had it, had committed his first wife to the crazy house to get her money. In the afternoons, Carmen could be found in the lot behind his shop playing solitary catch, flinging a tennis ball high into the air and running under it. One day the police arrested Carmen on charges of child molesting. He was released but became furtive and suspicious. I never saw him in the lot again. Next to Carmen's was a junk store where, one summer, I made a little money polishing brass and rewiring old lamps. Then came a dilapidated real estate office, a Mexican restaurant, an empty lot, and an appliance store owned by the father of Keith Grateful, the streetwise, chubby boy who would become my best friend.

Right to the north of us was a record shop, a barber shop presided over by old Mr. Graff, Walt's Malts, a shoe repair shop with a big Cat's Paw decal in the window, a third barber shop, and a brake shop. It's as I write this that I realize for the first time that three gray men could have had a go at your hair before you left our street.

Behind our house was an unpaved alley that passed, just to the north, a power plant the length of a city block. Massive coils atop the building hissed and cracked through the day, but the doors never opened. I used to think it was abandoned—feeding itself on its own wild arcs—until one sweltering afternoon a man was electrocuted on the roof. The air was thick and still as two firemen—the only men present—brought down a charred and limp body without saying a word.

The north and south traffic on Vermont was separated by tracks for the old yellow trolley cars, long since defunct. Across the street was a huge garage, a tiny hot dog stand run by a myopic and reclusive man named Freddie, and my dreamland, the Vermont Bowl. Distant and distorted behind thick lenses, Freddie's eyes never met yours; he would look down when he took your order and give you your change with a mumble. Freddie slept on a cot in the back of his grill and died there one night, leaving tens of thousands of dollars stuffed in the mattress.

My father would buy me a chili dog at Freddie's, and then we would walk over to the bowling alley where Dad would sit at the lunch counter and drink coffee while I had a great time with pinball machines, electric shooting galleries, and an ill-kept dispenser of cheese corn. There was a small, dark bar abutting the lanes, and it called to me. I would devise reasons to walk through it: " 'Scuse me, is the bathroom in here?" or "Anyone see my dad?" though I can never remember my father having a drink. It was dark and people were drinking and I figured all sorts of mysterious things were being whispered. Next to the Vermont Bowl was a large vacant lot overgrown with foxtails and dotted with car parts, bottles, and rotting cardboard. One day Keith heard that the police had found a human head in the brush. After that we explored the lot periodically, coming home with stickers all the way up to our waists. But we didn't find a thing. Not even a kneecap.

When I wasn't with Keith or in school, I would spend most of my day with my father or with the men who were renting the one-room

apartments behind our house. Dad and I whiled away the hours in the
bowling alley, watching TV, or planting a vegetable garden that never
seemed to take. When he was still mobile, he would walk the four blocks
down to St. Regina's Grammar School to take me home to my favorite
lunch of boiled wieners and chocolate milk. There I'd sit, dunking my hot
dog in a jar of mayonnaise and drinking my milk while Sheriff John tuned
up the calliope music on his "Lunch Brigade." Though he never
complained to me, I could sense that my father's health was failing, and
I began devising child's ways to make him better. We had a box of rolled
cotton in the bathroom, and I would go in and peel off a long strip and
tape it around my jaw. Then I'd rummage through the closet, find a
sweater of my father's, put on one of his hats—and sneak around to the
back door. I'd knock loudly and wait. It would take him a while to get
there. Finally, he'd open the door, look down, and quietly say, "Yes,
Michael?" I was disappointed. Every time. Somehow I thought I could
fool him. And, I guess, if he had been fooled, I would have succeeded in
redefining things: I would have been the old one, he much younger,
more agile, with strength in his legs.

The men who lived in the back were either retired or didn't work   7
that much, so one of them was usually around. They proved to be, over
the years, an unusual set of companions for a young boy. Ed Gionotti
was the youngest of the lot, a handsome man whose wife had run off and
who spoke softly and never smiled. Bud Hall and Lee McGuire were two
out-of-work plumbers who lived in adjacent units and who weekly drank
themselves silly, proclaiming in front of God and everyone their undying
friendship or their unequivocal hatred. Old Cheech was a lame Italian
who used to hobble along grabbing his testicles and rolling his eyes
while he talked about the women he claimed to have on a string. There
was Lester, the toothless cabbie, who several times made overtures to me
and who, when he moved, left behind a drawer full of syringes and burnt
spoons. Mr. Smith was a rambunctious retiree who lost his nose to an
untended skin cancer. And there was Mr. Berryman, a sweet and gentle
man who eventually left for a retirement hotel only to be burned alive in
an electrical fire.

Except for Keith, there were no children on my block and only one   8
or two on the immediate side streets. Most of the people I saw day to day
were over fifty. People in their twenties and thirties working in the shoe
shop or the garages didn't say a lot; their work and much of what they
were working for drained their spirits. There were gang members who
sauntered up from Hoover Avenue, three blocks to the east, and
occasionally I would get shoved around, but they had little interest in me
either as member or victim. I was a skinny, bespectacled kid and had
neither the coloring nor the style of dress or carriage that marked me as
a rival. On the whole, the days were quiet, lazy, lonely. The heat

shimmering over the asphalt had no snap to it; time drifted by. I would lie on the couch at night and listen to the music from the record store or from Walt's Malts. It was new and quick paced, exciting, a little dangerous (the church had condemned Buddy Knox's "Party Doll"), and I heard in it a deep rhythmic need to be made whole with love, or marked as special, or released in some rebellious way. Even the songs about lost love—and there were plenty of them—lifted me right out of my socks with their melodious longing:

> Came the dawn,
> and my heart and her love and the night
> were gone.
> But I know I'll never forget
> her kiss in the moonlight Oooo . . .
> such a kiss Oooo Oooo such a night . . .

In the midst of the heat and slow time the music brought the promise of its origins, a promise of deliverance, a promise that, if only for a moment, life could be stirring and dreamy.

But the anger and frustration of South Vermont could prove too strong for music's illusion; then it was violence that provided deliverance of a different order. One night I watched as a guy sprinted from Walt's to toss something on our lawn. The police were right behind, and a cop tackled him, smashing his face into the sidewalk. I ducked out to find the packet: a dozen glassine bags of heroin. Another night, one August midnight, an argument outside the record store ended with a man being shot to death. And the occasional gang forays brought with them some fated kid who would fumble his moves and catch a knife.   9

It's popular these days to claim you grew up on the streets. Men tell   10
violent tales and romanticize the lessons violence brings. But, though it was occasionally violent, it wasn't the violence in South L.A. that marked me, for sometimes you can shake that ugliness off. What finally affected me was subtler, but more pervasive: I cannot recall a young person who was crazy in love or lost in work or one old person who was passionate about a cause or an idea. I'm not talking about an absence of energy— the street toughs and, for that fact, old Cheech had energy. And I'm not talking about an absence of decency, for my father was a thoughtful man. The people I grew up with were retired from jobs that rub away the heart or were working hard at jobs to keep their lives from caving in or were anchorless and in between jobs and spouses or were diving headlong into a barren tomorrow: junkies, alcoholics, and mean kids walking along Vermont looking to throw a punch. I developed a picture of human existence that rendered it short and brutish or sad and aimless or long and quiet with rewards like afternoon naps, the evening newspaper,

walks around the block, occasional letters from children in other states. When, years later, I was introduced to humanistic psychologists like Abraham Maslow and Carl Rogers, with their visions of self-actualization, or even Freud with his sober dictum about love and work, it all sounded like a glorious fairy tale, a magical account of a world full of possibility, full of hope and empowerment. Sindbad and Cinderella couldn't have been more fanciful.

Some people who manage to write their way out of the working class 11 describe the classroom as an oasis of possibility. It became their intellectual playground, their competitive arena. Given the richness of my memories of this time, it's funny how scant are my recollections of school. I remember the red brick building of St. Regina's itself, and the topography of the playground: the swings and basketball courts and peeling benches. There are images of a few students: Erwin Petschaur, a muscular German boy with a strong accent; Dave Sanchez, who was good in math; and Sheila Wilkes, everyone's curly-haired heartthrob. And there are two nuns: Sister Monica, the third-grade teacher with beautiful hands for whom I carried a candle and who, to my dismay, had wedded herself to Christ; and Sister Beatrice, a woman truly crazed, who would sweep into class, eyes wide, to tell us about the Apocalypse.

All the hours in class tend to blend into one long, vague stretch of 12 time. What I remember best, strangely enough, are the two things I couldn't understand and over the years grew to hate: grammar lessons and mathematics. I would sit there watching a teacher draw her long horizontal line and her short, oblique lines and break up sentences and put adjectives here and adverbs there and just not get it, couldn't see the reason for it, turned off to it. I would hide by slumping down in my seat and page through my reader, carried along by the flow of sentences in a story. She would test us, and I would dread that, for I always got Cs and Ds. Mathematics was a bit different. For whatever reasons, I didn't learn early math very well, so when it came time for more complicated operations, I couldn't keep up and started day-dreaming to avoid my inadequacy. This was a strategy I would rely on as I grew older. I fell further and further behind. A memory: The teacher is faceless and seems very far away. The voice is faint and is discussing an equation written on the board. It is raining, and I am watching the streams of water form patterns on the windows.

I realize now how consistently I defended myself against the 13 lessons I couldn't understand and the people and events of South L.A. that were too strange to view head-on. I got very good at watching a blackboard with minimum awareness. And I drifted more and more into a variety of protective fantasies. I was lucky in that although my parents didn't read or write very much and had no more than a few books around the house, they never debunked my pursuits. And when they could, they bought me what I needed to spin my web.

One early Christmas they got me a small chemistry set. My father   14
brought home an old card table from the secondhand store, and on that table I spread out my test tubes, my beaker, my Erlenmeyer flask, and my gas-generating apparatus. The set came equipped with chemicals, minerals, and various treated papers—all in little square bottles. You could send away to someplace in Maryland for more, and I did, saving pennies and nickels to get the substances that were too exotic for my set, the Junior Chemcraft: Congo red paper, azurite, glycerine, chrome alum, cochineal—this from female insects!—tartaric acid, chameleon paper, logwood. I would sit before my laboratory and play for hours. My father rested on the purple couch in front of me watching wrestling or *Gunsmoke* while I measured powders or heated crystals or blew into solutions that my breath would turn red or pink. I was taken by the blends of names and by the colors that swirled through the beaker. My equations were visual and phonetic. I would hold a flask up to the hall light, imagining the veils of a million atoms dancing. Sulfur and alcohol hung in the air. I wanted to shake down the house.

One day my mother came home from Coffee Dan's with an awful   15
story. The teenage brother of one of her waitress friends was in the hospital. He had been fooling around with explosives in his garage "where his mother couldn't see him," and something happened, and "he blew away part of his throat. For God's sake, be careful," my mother said. "Remember poor Ada's brother." Wow! I thought. How neat! Why couldn't my experiments be that dangerous? I really lost heart when I realized that you could probably eat the chemicals spread across my table.

I knew what I had to do. I saved my money for a week and then   16
walked with firm resolve past Walt's Malts, past the brake shop, across Ninetieth Street, and into Palazolla's market. I bought a little bottle of Alka-Seltzer and ran home. I chipped up the wafers and mixed them into a jar of white crystals. When my mother came home, dog tired, and sat down on the edge of the couch to tell me and Dad about her day, I gravely poured my concoction into a beaker of water, cried something about the unexpected, and ran out from behind my table. The beaker foamed ominously. My father swore in Italian. The second time I tried it, I got something milder—in English. And by my third near-miss with death, my parents were calling my behavior cute. Cute! Who wanted cute? I wanted to toy with the disaster that befell Ada Pendleton's brother. I wanted all those wonderful colors to collide in ways that could blow your voice box right off.

But I was limited by the real. The best I could do was create a toxic   17
antacid. I loved my chemistry set—its glassware and its intriguing

labels—but it wouldn't allow me to do the things I wanted to do. St. Regina's had an all-purpose room, one wall of which was lined with old books—and one of those shelves held a row of plastic-covered space novels. The sheen of their covers was gone, and their futuristic portraits were dotted with erasures and grease spots like a meteor shower of the everyday. I remember the rockets best. Long cylinders outfitted at the base with three slick fins, tapering at the other end to a perfect conical point, ready to pierce out of the stratosphere and into my imagination: X-fifteens and Mach 1, the dark side of the moon, the Red Planet, Jupiter's Great Red Spot, Saturn's rings—and beyond the solar system to swirling wisps of galaxies, to stardust.

Students will float to the mark you set. I and the others in the vocational   18
classes were bobbing in pretty shallow water. Vocational education has aimed at increasing the economic opportunities of students who do not do well in our schools. Some serious programs succeed in doing that, and through exceptional teachers—like Mr. Gross in *Horace's Compromise*—students learn to develop hypotheses and troubleshoot, reason through a problem, and communicate effectively—the true job skills. The vocational track, however, is most often a place for those who are just not making it, a dumping ground for the disaffected. There were a few teachers who worked hard at education; young Brother Slattery, for example, combined a stern voice with weekly quizzes to try to pass along to us a skeletal outline of world history. But mostly the teachers had no idea of how to engage the imaginations of us kids who were scuttling along at the bottom of the pond.

And the teachers would have needed some inventiveness, for none   19
of us was groomed for the classroom. It wasn't just that I didn't know things—didn't know how to simplify algebraic fractions, couldn't identify different kinds of clauses, bungled Spanish translations—but that I had developed various faulty and inadequate ways of doing algebra and making sense of Spanish. Worse yet, the years of defensive tuning out in elementary school had given me a way to escape quickly while seeming at least half alert. During my time in Voc. Ed., I developed further into a mediocre student and a somnambulant problem solver, and that affected the subjects I did have the wherewithal to handle: I detested Shakespeare; I got bored with history. My attention flitted here and there. I fooled around in class and read my books indifferently—the intellectual equivalent of playing with your food. I did what I had to do to get by, and I did it with half a mind.

But I did learn things about people and eventually came into my   20
own socially. I liked the guys in Voc. Ed. Growing up where I did, I understood and admired physical prowess, and there was an abundance of muscle here. There was Dave Snyder, a sprinter and halfback of true

quality. Dave's ability and quick wit gave him a natural appeal, and he was welcome in any clique, though he always kept a little independent. He enjoyed acting the fool and could care less about studies, but he possessed a certain maturity and never caused the faculty much trouble. It was a testament to his independence that he included me among his friends—I eventually went out for track, but I was no jock. Owing to the Latin alphabet and a dearth of *R*s and *S*s, Snyder sat behind Rose, and we started exchanging one-liners and became friends.

There was Ted Richard, a much-touted Little League pitcher. He was 21 chunky and had a baby face and came to Our Lady of Mercy as a seasoned street fighter. Ted was quick to laugh and he had a loud, jolly laugh, but when he got angry he'd smile a little smile, the kind that simply raises the corner of the mouth a quarter of an inch. For those who knew, it was an eerie signal. Those who didn't found themselves in big trouble, for Ted was very quick. He loved to carry on what we would come to call philosophical discussions: What is courage? Does God exist? He also loved words, enjoyed picking up big ones like *salubrious* and *equivocal* and using them in our conversation—laughing at himself as the word hit a chuckhole rolling off his tongue. Ted didn't do all that well in school—baseball and parties and testing the courage he'd speculated about took up his time. His textbooks were *Argosy* and *Field and Stream,* whatever newspapers he'd find on the bus stop—from the *Daily Worker* to pornography—conversations with uncles or hobos or businessmen he'd meet in a coffee shop, *The Old Man and the Sea.* With hindsight, I can see that Ted was developing into one of those rough-hewn intellectuals whose sources are a mix of the learned and the apocryphal, whose discussions are both assured and sad.

And then there was Ken Harvey. Ken was good-looking in a puffy 22 way and had a full and oily ducktail and was a car enthusiast . . . a hodad. One day in religion class, he said the sentence that turned out to be one of the most memorable of the hundreds of thousands I heard in those Voc. Ed. years. We were talking about the parable of the talents, about achievement, working hard, doing the best you can do, blah-blah-blah, when the teacher called on the restive Ken Harvey for an opinion. Ken thought about it, but just for a second, and said (with studied, minimal affect), "I just wanna be average." That woke me up. Average?! Who wants to be average? Then the athletes chimed in with the clichés that make you want to laryngectomize them, and the exchange became a platitudinous melee. At the time, I thought Ken's assertion was stupid, and I wrote him off. But his sentence has stayed with me all these years, and I think I am finally coming to understand it.

Ken Harvey was gasping for air. School can be a tremendously 23 disorienting place. No matter how bad the school, you're going to encounter notions that don't fit with the assumptions and beliefs that you grew up with—maybe you'll hear these dissonant notions from teachers, maybe from the other students, and maybe you'll read them. You'll also be thrown in with all kinds of kids from all kinds of backgrounds, and that can be unsettling—this is especially true in places of rich ethnic and linguistic mix, like the L.A. basin. You'll see a handful of students far excel you in courses that sound exotic and that are only in the curriculum of the elite: French, physics, trigonometry. And all this is happening while you're trying to shape an identity, your body is changing, and your emotions are running wild. If you're a working-class kid in the vocational track, the options you'll have to deal with this will be constrained in certain ways: You're defined by your school as "slow"; you're placed in a curriculum that isn't designed to liberate you but to occupy you, or, if you're lucky, train you, though the training is for work the society does not esteem; other students are picking up the cues from your school and your curriculum and interacting with you in particular ways. If you're a kid like Ted Richard, you turn your back on all this and let your mind roam where it may. But youngsters like Ted are rare. What Ken and so many others do is protect themselves from such suffocating madness by taking on with a vengeance the identity implied in the vocational track. Reject the confusion and frustration by openly defining yourself as the Common Joe. Champion the average. Rely on your own good sense. Fuck this bullshit. Bullshit, of course, is everything you— and the others—fear is beyond you: books, essays, tests, academic scrambling, complexity, scientific reasoning, philosophical inquiry.

The tragedy is that you have to twist the knife in your own gray   24
matter to make this defense work. You'll have to shut down, have to reject intellectual stimuli or diffuse them with sarcasm, have to cultivate stupidity, have to convert boredom from a malady into a way of confronting the world. Keep your vocabulary simple, act stoned when you're not or act more stoned than you are, flaunt ignorance, materialize your dreams. It is a powerful and effective defense—it neutralizes the insult and the frustration of being a vocational kid and, when perfected, it drives teachers up the wall, a delightful secondary effect. But like all strong magic, it exacts a price.

Jack MacFarland couldn't have come into my life at a better time. My   25
father was dead, and I had logged up too many years of scholastic indifference. Mr. MacFarland had a master's degree from Columbia and decided, at twenty-six, to find a little school and teach his heart out. He never took any credentialing courses, couldn't bear to, he said, so he had to find employment in a private system. He ended up at Our Lady of Mercy teaching five sections of senior English. He was a beatnik who was born too late. His teeth were stained, he tucked his sorry tie in between the third and fourth buttons of his shirt, and his pants were chronically

wrinkled. At first, we couldn't believe this guy, thought he slept in his car. But within no time, he had us so startled with work that we didn't much worry about where he slept or if he slept at all. We wrote three or four essays a month. We read a book every two to three weeks, starting with the *Iliad* and ending up with Hemingway. He gave us a quiz on the reading every other day. He brought a prep school curriculum to Mercy High.

MacFarland's lectures were crafted, and as he delivered them he   26
would pace the room jiggling a piece of chalk in his cupped hand, using it to scribble on the board the names of all the writers and philosophers and plays and novels he was weaving into his discussion. He asked questions often, raised everything from Zeno's paradox to the repeated last line of Frost's "Stopping by Woods on a Snowy Evening." He slowly and carefully built up our knowledge of Western intellectual history— with facts, with connections, with speculations. We learned about Greek philosophy, about Dante, the Elizabethan world view, the Age of Reason, existentialism. He analyzed poems with us, had us reading sections from John Ciardi's *How Does a Poem Mean?*, making a potentially difficult book accessible with his own explanations. We gave oral reports on poems Ciardi didn't cover. We imitated the styles of Conrad, Hemingway, and *Time* magazine. We wrote and talked, wrote and talked. The man immersed us in language.

Even MacFarland's barbs were literary. If Jim Fitzsimmons, hung   27
over and irritable, tried to smart-ass him, he'd rejoin with a flourish that would spark the indomitable Skip Madison—who'd lost his front teeth in a hapless tackle—to flick his tongue through the gap and opine, "good chop," drawing out the single "o" in stinging indictment. Jack MacFarland, this tobacco-stained intellectual, brandished linguistic weapons of a kind I hadn't encountered before. Here was this *egghead,* for God's sake, keeping some pretty difficult people in line. And from what I heard, Mike Dweetz and Steve Fusco and all the notorious Voc. Ed. crowd settled down as well when MacFarland took the podium. Though a lot of guys groused in the schoolyard, it just seemed that giving trouble to this particular teacher was a silly thing to do. Tomfoolery, not to mention assault, had no place in the world he was trying to create for us, and instinctively everyone knew that. If nothing else, we all recognized MacFarland's considerable intelligence and respected the hours he put into his work. It came to this: The troublemaker would look foolish rather than daring. Even Jim Fitzsimmons was reading *On the Road* and turning his incipient alcoholism to literary ends.

There were some lives that were already beyond Jack MacFarland's   28
ministrations, but mine was not. I started reading again as I hadn't since elementary school. I would go into our gloomy little bedroom or sit at the dinner table while, on the television, Danny McShane was paralyzing Mr.

Moto with the atomic drop, and work slowly back through *Heart of Darkness*, trying to catch the words in Conrad's sentences. I certainly was not MacFarland's best student; most of the other guys in College Prep, even my fellow slackers, had better backgrounds than I did. But I worked very hard, for MacFarland had hooked me. He tapped my old interest in reading and creating stories. He gave me a way to feel special by using my mind. And he provided a role model that wasn't shaped on physical prowess alone, and something inside me that I wasn't quite aware of responded to that. Jack MacFarland established a literacy club, to borrow a phrase of Frank Smith's, and invited me—invited all of us—to join.

29   There's been a good deal of research and speculation suggesting that the acknowledgment of school performance with extrinsic rewards—smiling faces, stars, numbers, grades—diminishes the intrinsic satisfaction children experience by engaging in reading or writing or problem solving. While it's certainly true that we've created an educational system that encourages our best and brightest to become cynical grade collectors and, in general, have developed an obsession with evaluation and assessment, I must tell you that venal though it may have been, I loved getting good grades from MacFarland. I now know how subjective grades can be, but then they came tucked in the back of essays like bits of scientific data, some sort of spectroscopic readout that said, objectively and publicly, that I had made something of value. I suppose I'd been mediocre for too long and enjoyed a public redefinition. And I suppose the workings of my mind, such as they were, had been private for too long. My linguistic play moved into the world; like the intergalactic stories I told years before on Frank's berry-splattered truck bed, these papers with their circled, red B-pluses and A-minuses linked my mind to something outside it. I carried them around like a club emblem.

30   One day in the December of my senior year, Mr. MacFarland asked me where I was going to go to college. I hadn't thought much about it. Many of the students I teach today spent their last year in high school with a physics text in one hand and the Stanford catalog in the other, but I wasn't even aware of what "entrance requirements" were. My folks would say that they wanted me to go to college and be a doctor, but I don't know how seriously I ever took that; it seemed a sweet thing to say, a bit of supportive family chatter, like telling a gangly daughter she's graceful. The reality of higher education wasn't in my scheme of things: No one in the family had gone to college; only two of my uncles had completed high school. I figured I'd get a night job and go to the local junior college because I knew that Snyder and Company were going there to play ball. But I hadn't even prepared for that. When I finally said, "I don't know," MacFarland looked down at me—I was seated in his office—and said, "Listen, you can write."

My grades stank. I had A's in biology and a handful of B's in a few   31
English and social science classes. All the rest were C's—or worse.
MacFarland said I would do well in his class and laid down the law about
doing well in the others. Still, the record for my first three years wouldn't
have been acceptable to any four-year school. To nobody's surprise, I
was turned down flat by USC and UCLA. But Jack MacFarland was on the
case. He had received his bachelor's degree from Loyola University, so he
made calls to old professors and talked to somebody in admissions and
wrote me a strong letter. Loyola finally accepted me as a probationary
student. I would be on trial for the first year, and if I did okay, I would be
granted regular status. MacFarland also intervened to get me a loan, for I
could never have afforded a private college without it. Four more years of
religion classes and four more years of boys at one school, girls at
another. But at least I was going to college. Amazing.

In my last semester of high school, I elected a special English   32
course fashioned by Mr. MacFarland, and it was through this elective that
there arose at Mercy a fledgling literati. Art Mitz, the editor of the school
newspaper and a very smart guy, was the kingpin. He was joined by me
and by Mark Dever, a quiet boy who wrote beautifully and who would
die before he was forty. MacFarland occasionally invited us to his
apartment, and those visits became the high point of our apprenticeship:
We'd clamp on our training wheels and drive to his salon.

He lived in a cramped and cluttered place near the airport, tucked   33
away in the kind of building that architectural critic Reyner Banham calls
a *dingbat*. Books were all over: stacked, piled, tossed, and crated,
underlined and dog eared, well worn and new. Cigarette ashes crusted
with coffee in saucers or spilled over the sides of motel ashtrays. The
little bedroom had, along two of its walls, bricks and boards loaded with
notes, magazines, and oversized books. The kitchen joined the living
room, and there was a stack of German newspapers under the sink. I had
never seen anything like it: a great flophouse of language furnished by
City Lights and Café le Metro. I read every title. I flipped through
paperbacks and scanned jackets and memorized names: Gogol, *Finne-
gan's Wake,* Djuna Barnes, Jackson Pollock, *A Coney Island of the Mind,*
F. O. Matthiessen's *American Renaissance,* all sorts of Freud, *Troubled
Sleep,* Man Ray, *The Education of Henry Adams,* Richard Wright, *Film as
Art,* William Butler Yeats, Marguerite Duras, *Redburn, A Season in Hell,
Kapital.* On the cover of Alain-Fournier's *The Wanderer* was an Edward
Gorey drawing of a young man on a road winding into dark trees. By the
hotplate sat a strange Kafka novel called *Amerika,* in which an adoles-
cent hero crosses the Atlantic to find the Nature Theater of Oklahoma. Art
and Mark would be talking about a movie or the school newspaper, and
I would be consuming my English teacher's library. It was heady stuff. I
felt like a Pop Warner athlete on steroids.

Art, Mark, and I would buy stogies and triangulate from MacFar-   34
land's apartment to the Cinema, which now shows X-rated films but was
then L.A.'s premiere art theater, and then to the musty Cherokee
Bookstore in Hollywood to hobnob with beatnik homosexuals—
smoking, drinking bourbon and coffee, and trying out awkward phrases
we'd gleaned from our mentor's bookshelves. I was happy and precocious and a little scared as well, for Hollywood Boulevard was thick with
a kind of decadence that was foreign to the South Side. After the
Cherokee, we would head back to the security of MacFarland's apartment, slaphappy with hipness.

Let me be the first to admit that there was a good deal of adolescent   35
passion in this embrace of the avant-garde: self-absorption, sexually
charged pedantry, an elevation of the odd and abandoned. Still it was a
time during which I absorbed an awful lot of information: long lists of
titles, images from expressionist paintings, new wave shibboleths, snippets of philosophy, and names that read like Steve Fusco's misspellings—
Goethe, Nietzsche, Kierkegaard. Now this is hardly the stuff of deep
understanding. But it was an introduction, a phrase book, a Baedeker to
a vocabulary of ideas, and it felt good at the time to know all these
words. With hindsight I realize how layered and important that knowledge was.

It enabled me to do things in the world. I could browse bohemian   36
bookstores in far-off, mysterious Hollywood; I could go to the Cinema
and see events through the lenses of European directors; and, most of all,
I could share an evening, talk that talk, with Jack MacFarland, the man I
most admired at the time. Knowledge was becoming a bonding agent.
Within a year or two, the persona of the disaffected hipster would prove
too cynical, too alienated to last. But for a time it was new and exciting:
It provided a critical perspective on society, and it allowed me to act as
though I were living beyond the limiting boundaries of South Vermont.

Exercises

Some Important Words

defunct (paragraph 4), myopic (4), calliope (6), unequivocal (7), rambunctious (7), bespectacled (8), forays (9), rendered (10), humanistic
(10), self-actualization (10), Freud (10), dictum (10), Apocalypse (11),
debunked (13), stratosphere (17), scuttling (18), bungled (19), somnambulant (19), wherewithal (19), sprinter (20), clique (20), touted (21),
seasoned (21), salubrious (21), equivocal (21), chuckhole (21), hindsight
(21), apocryphal (21), ducktail (22), hodad (22), parable (22), restive
(22), laryngectomize (22), platitudinous (22), melee (22), disorienting

(23), dissonant (23), constrained (23), stimuli (24), diffuse (24), malady (24), flaunt (24), *Iliad* (25), Hemingway (25), Frost (26), Dante (26), Elizabethan (26), existentialism (26), Conrad (26), barbs (27), rejoin (27), flourish (27), indomitable (27), hapless (27), opine (27), brandished (27), groused (27), *On the Road* (27), incipient (27), ministrations (28), *Heart of Darkness* (28), slackers (28), extrinsic (29), intrinsic (29), venal (29), spectroscopic (29), fledgling (32), literati (32), heady (33), stogies (34), triangulate (34), hobnob (34), gleaned (34), precocious (34), avant-garde (35), expressionist (35), shibboleths (35), Baedeker (35), persona (36), disaffected (36).

Some of the Issues

1. Give a physical description of the neighborhood where Rose grew up.
2. How would you characterize the men who lived in the area (paragraph 7)?
3. Considering the view of life on Vermont Avenue, can you infer why Rose doesn't mention any women?
4. How do you think he felt about growing up in his neighborhood? What lines from the text support your idea?
5. The author says that his childhood days were quiet, lazy, and lonely. What kinds of neighborhood activities did attract his attention?
6. What defense mechanism did Rose develop to cope with school and the hopelessness of the neighborhood (paragraph 12)?
7. Rose spent hours with his chemistry set, yet he was disappointed that it didn't allow him "to do the things I wanted to do." Based on what you know about his life, what "things" do you suppose he had in mind?
8. According to Rose, what are the job skills that vocational education programs should teach (paragraphs 18 and 19)?
9. In paragraphs 22–24, how does Rose interpret Ken Harvey's sentence, "I just wanna be average"?
10. What kind of a person is Jack MacFarland? If you were a film director, which actor would you cast to play him?
11. What do you think was the key to MacFarland's success as a teacher?
12. The knowledge that Rose gained during his senior year enabled him "to do things in the world" and "to act as though I were living beyond the limiting boundaries of South Vermont." How does all this relate to his childhood dreams? Find lines from earlier portions of the text that support your idea.
*13. Read "The Brutal Bargain" by Norman Podhoretz. Compare his journey out of his lower-class neighborhood to Rose's experience.

The Way We Are Told

14. Reread Rose's description of his neighborhood (paragraphs 1-8). Which images best capture the feeling of place for you?
15. How would you characterize Rose's use of language in paragraph 18, "students will float to the mark you set. I and the others in the vocational classes were bobbing in pretty shallow water." Can you find similar phrases in paragraphs 18-24 that continue the comparison?

Some Subjects for Writing

16. Rose describes several of his classmates in Voc. Ed. who attempted to cope with the "disorienting" atmosphere of their high school (paragraphs 20-24). Did you or any of your high school classmates develop special ways of coping with the system or with the teachers? Recount this experience.
17. In paragraphs 18-24, Rose sharply criticizes traditional vocational education programs. What kinds of programs do you think are appropriate for students who do not plan to go to college or who want to enter the job market immediately after high school?
18. Rose says that a mystique surrounds those who grow up in urban environments: "It's popular these days to claim you grew up on the streets" (paragraph 10). Do you agree? What cultural factors might influence this attitude?

THE LOUDEST VOICE

Grace Paley

Grace Paley grew up in the Bronx, New York, where she was born in 1922. Her first published collection of short stories, *The Little Disturbances of Man,* which appeared in 1959, contained the story included here. Since then she has published *Enormous Changes at the Last Minute* (1974), *Later the Same Day* (1985), *Leaning Forward* (1985), and *Long Walks and Intimate Talks* (1991).

Three of the stories in *Enormous Changes at the Last Minute* have been made into a movie by the same name. Most of Paley's stories are set in New York and treat the lives of a great range of people of different backgrounds, Jews, African-Americans, Italians, Puerto Ricans, and Irish. She is noted particularly for her ability to catch the flavor of urban American speech.

In her short story "The Loudest Voice" Grace Paley tells how an unthinking school administration dealt with the children under its authority. There are almost no Christian children in Shirley Abramowitz's grade school, but the teachers find it natural to foist a Christmas pageant on them. The results are hilarious as well as thought provoking.

There is a certain place where dumb-waiters boom, doors slam, dishes 1 crash; every window is a mother's mouth bidding the street shut up, go skate somewhere else, come home. My voice is the loudest.

There, my own mother is still as full of breathing as me and the 2 grocer stands up to speak to her. "Mrs. Abramowitz," he says, "people should not be afraid of their children."

"Ah, Mr. Bialik," my mother replies, "if you say to her or her father 3 'Ssh,' they say, 'In the grave it will be quiet.' "

"From Coney Island to the cemetery," says my papa. "It's the same 4 subway; it's the same fare."

I am right next to the pickle barrel. My pinky is making tiny 5 whirlpools in the brine. I stop a moment to announce: "Campbell's Tomato Soup. Campbell's Vegetable Beef Soup. Campbell's S-c-otch Broth . . ."

"Be quiet," the grocer says, "the labels are coming off."   6

"Please, Shirley, be a little quiet," my mother begs me.   7

In that place the whole street groans: Be quiet! Be quiet! but steals   8
from the happy chorus of my inside self not a tittle or a jot.

There, too, but just around the corner, is a red brick building that   9
has been old for many years. Every morning the children stand before it
in double lines which must be straight. They are not insulted. They are
waiting anyway.

I am usually among them. I am, in fact, the first, since I begin with "A."   10

One cold morning the monitor tapped me on the shoulder. "Go to   11
Room 409, Shirley Abramowitz," he said. I did as I was told. I went in a
hurry up a down staircase to Room 409, which contained sixth-graders. I
had to wait at the desk without wiggling until Mr. Hilton, their teacher,
had time to speak.

After five minutes he said, "Shirley?"   12

"What?" I whispered.   13

He said, "My! My! Shirley Abramowitz! They told me you had a   14
particularly loud, clear voice and read with lots of expression. Could that
be true?"

"Oh yes," I whispered.   15

"In that case, don't be silly; I might very well be your teacher   16
someday. Speak up, speak up."

"Yes," I shouted.   17

"More like it," he said. "Now, Shirley, can you put a ribbon in your   18
hair or a bobby pin? It's too messy."

"Yes!" I bawled.   19

"Now, now, calm down." He turned to the class. "Children, not a   20
sound. Open at page 39. Read till 52. When you finish, start again." He
looked me over once more. "Now, Shirley, you know, I suppose, that
Christmas is coming. We are preparing a beautiful play. Most of the parts
have been given out. But I still need a child with a strong voice, lots of
stamina. Do you know what stamina is? You do? Smart kid. You know, I
heard you read 'The Lord is my shepherd' in Assembly yesterday. I was
very impressed. Wonderful delivery. Mrs. Jordan, your teacher, speaks
highly of you. Now listen to me, Shirley Abramowitz, if you want to take
the part and be in the play, repeat after me, 'I swear to work harder than
I ever did before.' "

I looked to heaven and said at once, "Oh, I swear." I kissed my   21
pinky and looked at God.

"That is an actor's life, my dear," he explained. "Like a soldier's,   22
never tardy or disobedient to his general, the director. Everything," he
said, "absolutely everything will depend on you."

That afternoon, all over the building, children scraped and   23
scrubbed the turkeys and the sheaves of corn off the schoolroom

windows. Goodbye Thanksgiving. The next morning a monitor brought red paper and green paper from the office. We made new shapes and hung them on the walls and glued them to the doors.

The teachers became happier and happier. Their heads were   24
ringing like the bells of childhood. My best friend Evie was prone to evil, but she did not get a single demerit for whispering. We learned "Holy Night" without an error. "How wonderful!" said Miss Glacé, the student teacher. "To think that some of you don't even speak the language!" We learned "Deck the Halls" and "Hark! The Herald Angels." . . . They weren't ashamed and we weren't embarrassed.

Oh, but when my mother heard about it all, she said to my father: 25
"Misha, you don't know what's going on there. Cramer is the head of the Tickets Committee."

"Who?" asked my father. "Cramer! Oh yes, an active woman."   26

"Active? Active has to have a reason. Listen," she said sadly, "I'm   27
surprised to see my neighbors making tra-la-la for Christmas."

My father couldn't think of what to say to that. Then he decided: 28
"You're in America! Clara, you wanted to come here. In Palestine the Arabs would be eating you alive. Europe you had pogroms. Argentina is full of Indians. Here you got Christmas. . . . Some joke, ha?"

"Very funny, Misha. What is becoming of you? If we came to a new   29
country a long time ago to run away from tyrants, and instead we fall into a creeping pogrom, that our children learn a lot of lies, so what's the joke? Ach, Misha, your idealism is going away."

"So is your sense of humor."   30

"That I never had, but idealism you had a lot of."   31

"I'm the same Misha Abramovitch, I didn't change an iota. Ask   32
anyone."

"Only ask me," says my mama, may she rest in peace. "I got the   33
answer."

Meanwhile the neighbors had to think of what to say too.   34

Marty's father said: "You know, he has a very important part, my boy."   35

"Mine also," said Mr. Sauerfeld.   36

"Not my boy!" said Mrs. Klieg. "I said to him no. The answer is no.   37
When I say no! I mean no!"

The rabbi's wife said, "It's disgusting!" But no one listened to her.   38
Under the narrow sky of God's great wisdom she wore a strawberry-blond wig.

Every day was noisy and full of experience. I was Right-hand Man.   39
Mr. Hilton said: "How could I get along without you, Shirley?"

He said: "Your mother and father ought to get down on their knees   40
every night and thank God for giving them a child like you."

He also said: "You're absolutely a pleasure to work with, my dear,   41
dear child."

Sometimes he said: "For God's sakes, what did I do with the script? 42
Shirley! Shirley! Find it."

Then I answered quietly: "Here it is, Mr. Hilton." 43

Once in a while, when he was very tired, he would cry out: 44
"Shirley, I'm just tired of screaming at those kids. Will you tell Ira Pushkov
not to come in till Lester points to that star the second time?"

Then I roared: "Ira Pushkov, what's the matter with you? Dope! Mr. 45
Hilton told you five times already, don't come in till Lester points to that
star the second time."

"Ach, Clara," my father asked, "what does she do there till six 46
o'clock she can't even put the plates on the table?"

"Christmas," said my mother coldly. 47

"Ho! Ho!" my father said. "Christmas. What's the harm? After all, 48
history teaches everyone. We learn from reading this is a holiday from
pagan times also, candles, lights, even Chanukah. So we learn it's not
altogether Christian. So if they think it's a private holiday, they're only
ignorant, not patriotic. What belongs to history, belongs to all men. You
want to go back to the Middle Ages? Is it better to shave your head with
a secondhand razor? Does it hurt Shirley to learn to speak up? It does not.
So maybe someday she won't live between the kitchen and the shop.
She's not a fool."

I thank you, Papa, for your kindness. It is true about me to this day. 49
I am foolish but I am not a fool.

That night my father kissed me and said with great interest in my 50
career, "Shirley, tomorrow's your big day. Congrats."

"Save it," my mother said. Then she shut all the windows in order 51
to prevent tonsillitis.

In the morning it snowed. On the street corner a tree had been 52
decorated for us by a kind city administration. In order to miss its chilly
shadow our neighbors walked three blocks east to buy a loaf of bread.
The butcher pulled down black window shades to keep the colored
lights from shining on his chickens. Oh, not me. On the way to school,
with both my hands I tossed it a kiss of tolerance. Poor thing, it was a
stranger in Egypt.

I walked straight into the auditorium past the staring children. "Go 53
ahead, Shirley!" said the monitors. Four boys, big for their age, had
already started work as propmen and stagehands.

Mr. Hilton was very nervous. He was not even happy. Whatever he 54
started to say ended in a sideward look of sadness. He sat slumped in the
middle of the first row and asked me to help Miss Glacé. I did this,
although she thought my voice too resonant and said, "Show-off!"

Parents began to arrive long before we were ready. They wanted to 55
make a good impression. From among the yards of drapes I peeked out
at the audience. I saw my embarrassed mother.

Ira, Lester, and Meyer were pasted to their beards by Miss Glacé.   56
She almost forgot to thread the star on its wire, but I reminded her. I
coughed a few times to clear my throat. Miss Glacé looked around and
saw that everyone was in costume and on line waiting to play his part.
She whispered, "All right . . ." Then:

Jackie Sauerfeld, the prettiest boy in first grade, parted the curtains   57
with his skinny elbow and in a high voice sang out:

"Parents dear
We are here
To make a Christmas play in time.
It we give
In narrative
And illustrate with pantomime."

He disappeared.   58

My voice burst immediately from the wings to the great shock of   59
Ira, Lester, and Meyer, who were waiting for it but were surprised all the
same.

"I remember, I remember, the house where I was born . . ."   60

Miss Glacé yanked the curtain open and there it was, the   61
house—an old hayloft, where Celia Kornbluh lay in the straw with Cindy
Lou, her favorite doll. Ira, Lester, and Meyer moved slowly from the
wings toward her, sometimes pointing to a moving star and sometimes
ahead to Cindy Lou.

It was a long story and it was a sad story. I carefully pronounced all   62
the words about my lonesome childhood, while little Eddie Braunstein
wandered upstage and down with his shepherd's stick, looking for
sheep. I brought up lonesomeness again, and not being understood at all
except by some women everybody hated. Eddie was too small for that
and Marty Groff took his place, wearing his father's prayer shawl. I
announced twelve friends, and half the boys in the fourth grade
gathered round Marty, who stood on an orange crate while my voice
harangued. Sorrowful and loud, I declaimed about love and God and
Man, but because of the terrible deceit of Abie Stock we came suddenly
to a famous moment. Marty, whose remembering tongue I was, waited at
the foot of the cross. He stared desperately at the audience. I groaned,
"My God, my God, why hast thou forsaken me?" The soldiers who were
sheiks grabbed poor Marty to pin him up to die, but he wrenched free,
turned again to the audience, and spread his arms aloft to show despair
and the end. I murmured at the top of my voice, "The rest is silence, but
as everyone in this room, in this city—in this world—now knows, I shall
have life eternal."

That night Mrs. Kornbluh visited our kitchen for a glass of tea.   63

"How's the virgin?" asked my father with a look of concern.   64

"For a man with a daughter, you got a fresh mouth, Abramovitch."   65

"Here," said my father kindly, "have some lemon, it'll sweeten your   66
disposition."

They debated a little in Yiddish, then fell in a puddle of Russian and   67
Polish. What I understood next was my father, who said, "Still and all, it
was certainly a beautiful affair, you have to admit, introducing us to the
beliefs of a different culture."

"Well, yes," said Mrs. Kornbluh. "The only thing . . . you know   68
Charlie Turner—that cute boy in Celia's class—a couple others? They got
very small parts or no part at all. In very bad taste, it seemed to me. After
all, it's their religion."

"Ach," explained my mother, "what could Mr. Hilton do? They got   69
very small voices; after all, why should they holler? The English language
they know from the beginning by heart. They're blond like angels. You
think it's so important they should get in the play? Christmas . . . the
whole piece of goods . . . they own it."

I listened and listened until I couldn't listen any more. Too sleepy, I   70
climbed out of bed and kneeled. I made a little church of my hands and
said, "Hear, O Israel . . ." Then I called out in Yiddish, "Please, good
night, good night. Ssh." My father said, "Ssh yourself," and slammed the
kitchen door.

I was happy. I fell asleep at once. I had prayed for everybody: my   71
talking family, cousins far away, passersby, and all the lonesome Christians. I expected to be heard. My voice was certainly the loudest.

Exercises

Some Important Words

dumb-waiter (paragraph 1), Coney Island—amusement park in New
York City (4), a tittle or a jot (8), monitor (11), stamina (20), demerit (24),
Palestine (28), pogroms (28), iota (32), pagan (48), Chanukah (48),
tonsillitis (51), tolerance (52), resonant (54), pantomime (57), hayloft
(61), harangued (62), declaimed (62), disposition (66), Yiddish (67).

Some of the Issues

1. In paragraphs 1 through 8 Paley tells about "a certain place." How
   does she describe it? Do we know what it looked like? What it
   sounded like? How do we know that it is a place in Shirley's
   memory?
2. In paragraph 9 we move to another place, just around the corner.
   How are we told about that place?

3. Shirley has the loudest voice in the school, but at some points she whispers or talks softly. When and why?
4. Mr. Hilton has a number of ways of getting Shirley and the other children to do what he wants them to do. What technique does he use? How sincere do you think he is? How much do he and the other teachers seem to understand or care about the children in the school?
5. Shirley's mother and father disagree with one another at several points in the story. Find the points where they disagree. What position does the father take consistently? The mother?
6. In paragraph 24 Miss Glacé, the student teacher, makes a comment. Does she believe it is a compliment? Is it really? Does her remark, and others made by teachers in the school, give any indication of their attitudes toward the children and their families?
7. Read the last sentences of paragraph 24; who is referred to as "we"? As "they"?
8. Paragraphs 34 through 38 tell how the neighbors react to the upcoming school play. What is their reaction? Why does no one pay attention to the rabbi's wife?
9. Read paragraph 52. Explain the people's reaction to "the tree." Why is it a stranger in Egypt?
10. Paragraphs 57 through 62 tell abut the actual performance of the Christmas play. What is the story being told in the play? What parts are each of the children playing? How well do the children seem to understand the story and their parts?
11. Examine the last paragraph. Whom does Shirley pray for and why? In what way can Shirley be said to have triumphed?

The Way We Are Told

12. Grace Paley is known for her good ear for dialog. She is said to create dialog that sounds natural and conveys a sense of her characters' personalities. A large part of this story is told through dialog. Examine it, and show how it conveys the sense of each character who speaks and how it carries the story along.
13. Did you find the story funny? If so, why? Does the humorous tone help or hinder its serious purpose?

Some Subjects for Writing

14. We know Shirley, and indeed all of the characters in the story, through their voices. Unlike many authors, Paley gives few visual descriptions. We are not told the color of Shirley's hair, or how tall she is, or even exactly how old she is. We may, however, be able to form images in our minds about what she and others are like, from

our knowledge of what they say and how they say it. Imagine that "The Loudest Voice" is to be filmed. You are the casting director. Tell how you would visualize Paley's characters: Shirley, her parents, and the various teachers.

15. In this story Paley describes people and places by means of sound, not appearance. Write a paragraph giving a vivid description of a place you know well, using primarily sounds to describe it, and avoiding visual details as much as possible.

16. Have you ever, as a child or as an adult, participated in a cultural or religious ceremony that was unfamiliar to you, in which you perhaps felt out of place? Describe it in an essay.

* 17. Like Paley, Maya Angelou in "Graduation" describes a school ceremony in which officials are insensitive to the lives of the children and their parents. How do the two situations differ? In what way are they the same? Explain in an essay.

* 18. In Paley's story and in Maxine Hong Kingston's "Girlhood Among Ghosts" the image of voice plays a major role. In an essay compare and contrast the two central characters' experience in losing and finding a voice.

INCIDENT

Countee Cullen

Countee Cullen (1903–46) gained recognition for his poetry while still in high school and published his first volume of poetry at the age of 22. He attended New York University and Harvard and continued to publish poetry and fiction. "Incident" first appeared in *Color* (1925).

Once riding in old Baltimore
  Heart-filled head-filled with glee,
I saw a Baltimorean
  Keep looking straight at me.

Now I was eight and very small,
  And he was no whit bigger,
And so I smiled, but he poked out
  His tongue, and called me, "Nigger."

I saw the whole of Baltimore
  From May until December;
Of all the things that happened there
  That's all that I remember.

PART TWO

Heritage

All of us inherit something: in some cases, it is money, property or some object—a family heirloom such as a grandmother's wedding dress or a father's set of tools. But beyond that, all of us inherit something else, something much less concrete and tangible, something we may not even be fully aware of. It may be a way of doing a daily task, or the way we solve a particular problem or decide a moral issue for ourselves. It may be a special way of keeping a holiday or a tradition to have a picnic on a certain date. It may be something important or central to our thinking, or something minor that we have long accepted quite casually.

For many Americans who are descended from immigrants, refugees, former slaves, and native peoples, the notion of heritage often includes more than one culture. Often, such cross-cultural heritage gives rise to mixed feelings, especially in the children of immigrants. A sense of pride in the distant land a father or mother came from may be mingled with a sense of embarrassment when that parent tries—and does not quite succeed at—being part of the son's or daughter's new life-style. In the first selection, "Fitting In," John Tarkov, son of a Russian father, reveals such mingled sentiments. In the story "Barba Nikos" by Harry Mark Petrakis the narrator illustrates the conflict that often arises between first- and second-generation immigrants when the ways of the Old Country—and their parents' accented English—become a source of embarrassment. Toni Morrison, granddaughter of a slave, describes in "A Slow Walk of Trees" how her parents and grandparents strove to overcome a set of obstacles, very different from those facing immigrants like John Tarkov's father or the old Greek grocer in "Barba Nikos."

Michael Novak's essay "In Ethnic America" is a defense of the people from eastern and southern Europe, millions of whom immigrated to the United States in the early twentieth century. Mostly of peasant origin, they have a strong heritage of hard work—and silence, including a silent acceptance of the disregard for them, as Novak asserts, by mainstream America. In the selection "Anglo vs. Chicano: Why?" Arthur L. Campa attributes the strain between the English-speaking and Spanish-speaking people in the southeastern states to several elements in their different heritages.

One general trait that is part of the American heritage is a belief in the importance of individual rights. In "Amérka, Amérka" Anton Shammas illustrates how immigrants can live in this country and keep their native traditions if they so choose. "This country is big," he says, "it has room not only for the newcomers, but for their portable homelands."

Part Two concludes with a poem, "The Three Thousand Dollar Death Song" by Wendy Rose, which protests the tendency to treat Native American heritage as something dead and fossilized, rather than a living, contributing force to "our heritage."

FITTING IN

John Tarkov

John Tarkov is a writer and editor who lives in Queens, New York. "This newspaper" (paragraph 12) refers to the *New York Times*, in whose *Sunday Magazine* the following selection was published on July 7, 1985. In this autobiographical essay, Tarkov speaks about the question of identity from the point of view of a second-generation American. He loves his Russian immigrant father and yet is exasperated by him—as much by his attempts to be American as by his foreignness.

Russian Americans of John Tarkov's father's generation often encountered an added difficulty in integrating themselves into mainstream America. Deeply attached to their homeland, they were out of sympathy with the communist government under Josef Stalin—a government, moreover, disliked and often feared by a majority of Americans.

Not quite two miles and 30 years from the church where these thoughts 1 came to me, is a small, graveled parking lot cut out of the New Jersey pines, behind a restaurant and a dance hall. On road signs, the town is called Cassville. But to the several generations of Russian-Americans whose center of gravity tipped to the Old World, it was known as Roova Farms. I think the acronym stands for Russian Orthodox Outing and Vacation Association. In the summers, the place might as well have been on the Black Sea.

One day during one of those summers, my old man showed up 2 from a job, just off a cargo ship. He made his living that way, in the merchant marine. With him, he had a brittle new baseball glove and a baseball as yet unmarked by human error. We went out to that parking lot and started tossing the ball back and forth; me even at the age of 8 at ease with the motions of this American game, him grabbing at the ball with his bare hands then sending it back with an unpolished stiff-armed heave. It was a very hot day. I remember that clearly. What I can't remember is who put the first scuff mark on the ball. Either I missed it, or he tossed it out of my reach.

I chased it down, I'm sure with American-kid peevishness. I wonder if I said anything. Probably I mouthed off about it. **3**

Last winter, the phone call comes on a Saturday morning. The old man's heart had stopped. They had started it beating again. When I get to the hospital, he's not conscious. They let me in to see him briefly. Then comes an afternoon of drinking coffee and leaning on walls. Around 4 o'clock, two doctors come out of coronary care. One of them puts his hand on my arm and tells me. A nurse takes me behind the closed door. **4**

Two fragments of thought surface. One is primitive and it resonates from somewhere deep: *This all began in Russia long ago.* The other is sentimental: *He died near the sea.* **5**

I joined the tips of the first three fingers of my right hand and touch them to his forehead, then his stomach, then one side of his chest, then the other. It's what I believe. I pause just briefly, then give him a couple of quick cuffs on the side of his face, the way men do when they want to express affection but something stops them from embracing. The nurse takes me downstairs to sign some forms. **6**

He never did quite get the hang of this country. He never went to the movies. Didn't watch television on his own. Didn't listen to the radio. Ate a lot of kielbasa. Read a lot. Read the paper almost cover to cover every day. He read English well, but when he talked about what he'd read, he'd mispronounce some words and put a heavy accent on them all. The paper was the window through which he examined a landscape and a people that were nearly as impenetrable to him as they were known and manageable to me. For a touch of home, he'd pick up *Soviet Life.* "I'm not a Communist," he used to tell me. "I'm a Russian." Then he'd catch me up about some new hydroelectric project on the Dnieper. **7**

And so he vaguely embarrassed me. Who knows how many times, over the years, this story has repeated itself: the immigrant father and the uneasy son. This Melting Pot of ours absorbs the second generation over a flame so high that the first is left encrusted on the rim. In college, I read the literature—Lenski on the three-generation hypothesis, stuff like that—but I read it to make my grades, not particularly to understand that I was living it. **8**

When he finally retired from the ocean, he took his first real apartment, on the Lower East Side, and we saw each other more regularly. We'd sit there on Saturday or Sunday afternoons, drinking beer and eating Chinese food. He bought a television set for our diversion, and, depending on the season, the voices of Keith Jackson and Ara Parseghian or Ralph Kiner and Lindsey Nelson would overlap with, and sometimes submerge, our own. **9**

After the game, he'd get us a couple more beers, and we would become emissaries: from land and sea, America and ports of destination. We were never strangers—never that—but we dealt, for the most part, in **10** small talk. It was a son trying—or maybe trying to try—to share what little he knew with his father, and flinching privately at his father's foreignness. And it was a father outspokenly proud of his son, beyond basis in reason, yet at times openly frustrated that the kid had grown up unlike himself.

Every father has a vision of what he'd like his son to be. Every son 11 has a vision in kind of his father. Eventually, one of them goes, and the one remaining has little choice but to extinguish the ideal and confront the man of flesh and blood who was. Time and again it happens: The vision shed, the son, once vaguely embarrassed by the father, begins to wear the old man's name and story with pride.

Though he read it daily, the old man hated this newspaper. 12 Sometimes I think he bought it just to make himself angry. He felt the sports editor was trying to suppress the growth of soccer in America. So naturally, I would egg him on. I'd say things like: "Yeah, you're right. It's a conspiracy. The sports editor plus 200 million other Americans." Then we'd start yelling.

But when it came time to put the obituary announcements in the 13 press, after I phoned one in to the Russian-language paper, I started to dial The Times. And I remembered. And I put the phone down. And started laughing. "O.K.," I said. "O.K. They won't get any of our business."

So he went out Russian, like he came in. Up on the hill, the 14 church is topped by weathered gold onion domes—sort of like back in the Old Country, but in fact just down the road from his attempt to sneak us both into America through a side door in New Jersey, by tossing a baseball back and forth on a hot, still, bake-in-the-bleachers kind of summer day.

I believe he threw the thing over my head, actually. It *was* a 15 throwing error, the more I think about it. No way I could have caught it. But it was only a baseball, and he was my father, so it's no big deal. I bounced a few off his shins that day myself. Next time, the baseball doesn't touch the ground.

Exercises

Some Important Words

acronym (paragraph 1), Black Sea (1), merchant marine (2), brittle (2), heave (2), peevishness (3), resonates (5), sentimental (5), kielbasa (7), impenetrable (7), hydroelectric (7), Melting Pot (8), encrusted (8), hypothesis (8), diversion (9), submerge (9), emissaries (10), flinching (10), extinguish (11), conspiracy (12), obituary (13), onion domes (14).

Some of the Issues

1. Tarkov begins his reminiscence with a description of a summer day. Describe the location and the event.
2. Paragraphs 4 through 6 abruptly change the time and location. What are Tarkov's thoughts and actions on that day?
3. Tarkov says of his father: "He never did quite get the hang of this country." What examples does he give?
4. What does the father say after reading *Soviet Life,* and what does he mean by it?
5. Explain the sentence in paragraph 8: "This Melting Pot of ours absorbs the second generation over a flame so high that the first is left encrusted on the rim."
6. Tarkov cites several incidents when his father's behavior embarrassed him. What are they? In your opinion, is Tarkov embarrassed because his father was an immigrant, or does Tarkov feel what many children feel about their parents from time to time?
7. In several instances the roles of father and son seem to be reversed: the son is more knowledgeable than the father and at one point speaks in the father's voice. Cite come examples of this reversal of roles.
8. In paragraph 8 Tarkov mentions reading a book as a student, without realizing that it might have personal relevance to him. Why did he not understand it at that time?
9. What does paragraph 10 tell you about the relationship between father and son? Why are they "emissaries from land and sea"?
10. In paragraph 12 Tarkov describes an argument with his father. What is its significance?
11. Why did Tarkov refuse to put an obituary in the *New York Times?*
12. Examine the final paragraph. Why is it important to Tarkov to determine who was responsible for an error in a baseball game long ago?

The Way We Are Told

13. The essay begins with the description of a place—Roova Farms—and an activity—baseball. Why would Tarkov choose to describe this particular place and activity?
14. Tarkov looks at the relationship between himself and his father at several different points in their lives. How would the character of the essay be changed if he had put his account in chronological order?
15. Tarkov uses colloquial language or slang several times, such as "my old man" (paragraphs 2 and 4) and "mouthed off" (paragraph 3). Find some additional examples. Are such expressions appropriate in an otherwise serious essay?

16. Paragraph 7 contains several intentional sentence fragments. Identify them. What effect do they have?
17. Cite other examples of the use of informal and formal language. Is the combination effective for Tarkov's purposes?

Some Subjects for Writing

18. In his essay Tarkov explains the ways in which he is both a part of and separate from his heritage. Write an essay in which you describe some specific aspect of your own heritage. Examine the ways in which you have departed from it, or have accepted it.
19. Tarkov writes about a relationship with one person that changes, yet in some ways stays the same over a long period of time. In an essay, describe your own relationship with someone whom you have known over a long time, perhaps your own parents, perhaps another relative or a friend of long standing. Give "snapshots" of at least three different periods in the relationship and explain how it has changed over time.
*20. Read Harry Mark Petrakis's "Barba Nikos." Tarkov and the character created by Petrakis both are children of immigrants to America, and both reflect on what their heritage meant to them in their youth, and later on. In your essay first describe and then compare their experiences and attitudes.

A SLOW WALK OF TREES

Toni Morrison

Toni Morrison was born in 1931 in Lorrain, a small town near Cleveland, Ohio. She received a B.A. degree from Howard University and an M.A. from Cornell. Since 1964 she has lived in New York, where she is an editor for Random House. In that capacity she has worked on the autobiographies of Angela Davis, an activist in the civil rights movement, and Muhammad Ali, among other books. Morrison is the author of six novels: *The Bluest Eye* (1969), *Sula* (1973), *Song of Solomon* (1977), *Tar Baby* (1981); the 1987 Pulitzer Prize winner, *Beloved;* and *Jazz* (1992). Her fiction captures small-town African-American life and is characterized by vivid narration and dialog of the Black experience.

The article included here was first published in the *New York Times Magazine* on July 4, 1976, the date of the American bicentennial. Morrison describes as well as contrasts the attitudes of her grandparents and parents toward the discrimination that was a central factor in their lives. In each of the two generations, she explains, the male had an essentially pessimistic outlook that nothing could be done; the female, on the other hand, set out to cope with whatever particular adversity was likely to befall her family. At the same time, Morrison sees a generational difference between the views of her grandparents and her parents that indicates some progress: an increased belief in the possibility of assuming control of their lives.

His name was John Solomon Willis, and when at age 5 he heard from the old folks that "the Emancipation Proclamation was coming," he crawled under the bed. It was his earliest recollection of what was to be his habitual response to the promise of white people: horror and an instinctive yearning for safety. He was my grandfather, a musician who managed to hold on to his violin but not his land. He lost all 88 acres of his Indian mother's inheritance to legal predators who built their fortunes on the likes of him. He was an unreconstructed black pessimist who, in spite of or because of emancipation, was convinced for 85 years that there was no hope whatever for black people in this country. His rancor

76

was legitimate, for he, John Solomon, was not only an artist but a first-rate carpenter and farmer, reduced to sending home to his family money he had made playing the violin because he was not able to find work. And this during the years when almost half the black male population were skilled craftsmen who lost their jobs to white ex-convicts and immigrant farmers.

His wife, however, was of a quite different frame of mind and believed that all things could be improved by faith in Jesus and an effort of the will. So it was she, Ardelia Willis, who sneaked her seven children out of the back window into the darkness, rather than permit the patron of their sharecropper's existence to become their executioner as well, and headed north in 1912, when 99.2 percent of all black people in the U.S. were native-born and only 60 percent of white Americans were. And it was Ardelia who told her husband that they could not stay in the Kentucky town they ended up in because the teacher didn't know long division.

They have been dead now for 30 years and more and I still don't know which of them came closer to the truth about the possibilities of life for black people in this country. One of their grandchildren is a tenured professor at Princeton. Another, who suffered from what the Peruvian poet called "anger that breaks a man into children," was picked up just as he entered his teens and emotionally lobotomized by the reformatories and mental institutions specifically designed to serve him. Neither John Solomon nor Ardelia lived long enough to despair over one or swell with pride over the other. But if they were alive today each would have selected and collected enough evidence to support the accuracy of the other's original point of view. And it would be difficult to convince either one that the other was right.

Some of the monstrous events that took place in John Solomon's America have been duplicated in alarming detail in my own America. There was the public murder of a President in a theater in 1865 and the public murder of another President on television in 1963. The Civil War of 1861 had its encore as the civil rights movement of 1960. The torture and mutilation of a black West Point Cadet (Cadet Johnson Whittaker) in 1880 had its rerun with the 1970's murders of students at Jackson State College, Texas Southern and Southern University in Baton Rouge. And in 1976 we watch for what must be the thousandth time a pitched battle between the children of slaves and the children of immigrants—only this time, it is not the New York draft riots of 1863, but the busing turmoil in Paul Revere's home town, Boston.

Hopeless, he'd said. Hopeless. For he was certain that white people of every political, religious, geographical and economic background would band together against black people everywhere when they felt the threat of our progress. And a hundred years after he sought safety from the white man's "promise," somebody put a bullet in Martin Luther King's brain. And not long before that some excellent samples of the master race demonstrated their courage and virility by dynamiting some little black girls to death. If he were here now, my grandfather, he would shake his head, close his eyes and pull out his violin—too polite to say, "I told you so." And his wife would pay attention to the music but not to the sadness in her husband's eyes, for she would see what she expected to see—not the occasional historical repetition, but, *like the slow walk of certain species of trees from the flatlands up into the mountains,* she would see the signs of irrevocable and permanent change. She, who pulled her girls out of an inadequate school in the Cumberland Mountains, knew all along that the gentlemen from Alabama who had killed the little girls would be rounded up. And it wouldn't surprise her in the least to know that the number of black college graduates jumped 12 percent in the last three years: 47 percent in 20 years. That there are 140 black mayors in this country; 14 black judges in the District Circuit, 4 in the Courts of Appeals and one on the Supreme Court. That there are 17 blacks in Congress, one in the Senate; 276 in state legislatures—223 in state houses, 53 in state senates. That there are 112 elected black police chiefs and sheriffs, 1 Pulitzer Prize winner; 1 winner of the Prix de Rome; a dozen or so winners of the Guggenheim; 4 deans of predominantly white colleges. . . . Oh, her list would go on and on. But so would John Solomon's sweet sad music.

While my grandparents held opposite views on whether the fortunes of black people were improving, my own parents struck similarly opposed postures, but from another slant. They differed about whether the moral fiber of white people would ever improve. Quite a different argument. The old folks argued about how and if black people could improve themselves, who could be counted on to help us, who would hinder us and so on. My parents took issue over the question of whether it was possible for white people to improve. They assumed that black people were the humans of the globe, but had serious doubts about the quality and existence of white humanity. Thus my father, distrusting every word and every gesture of every white man on earth, assumed that the white man who crept up the stairs one afternoon had come to molest his daughters and threw him down the stairs and then our tricycle after him. (I think my father was wrong, but considering what I have seen since, it may have been very healthy for me to have witnessed that as my first black-white encounter.) My mother, however, *believed* in them—their possibilities. So when the meal we got on relief was bug-ridden, she wrote a long letter to Franklin Delano Roosevelt. And when white bill collectors came to our door, it was she who received them civilly and explained in a sweet voice that we were people of honor and that the debt would be taken care of. Her message to Roosevelt got through—our meal improved. Her message to the bill collectors did not always get through and there was occasional violence when my father (self-exiled to the bedroom for fear he could not hold his temper) would hear that her reasonableness had failed. My mother was always wounded by these scenes, for she thought the bill collector knew that she loved good credit more than life and that being in arrears on a payment horrified her probably more than it did him. So she thought he was rude because he was white. For years she walked to utility companies and department stores to pay bills in person and even now she does not seem convinced that checks are legal tender. My father loved excellence, worked hard (he held three jobs at once for 17 years) and was so outraged by the suggestion of personal slackness that he could explain it to himself only in terms of racism. He was a fastidious worker who was frightened of one thing: unemployment. I can remember now the dooms-day-cum-graveyard sound of "laid off" and how the minute school was out he asked us, "Where you workin'?" Both my parents believed that all succor and aid came from themselves and their neighborhood, since "they"—white people in charge and those not in charge but in obstruc-tionist positions—were in some way fundamentally, genetically corrupt.

So I grew up in a basically racist household with more than a child's [7] share of contempt for white people. And for each white friend I acquired who made a small crack in that contempt, there was another who repaired it. For each one who related to me as a person, there was one who in my presence at least, became actively "white." And like most black people of my generation, I suffer from racial vertigo that can be cured only by taking what one needs from one's ancestors. John Solomon's cynicism and his deployment of his art as both weapon and solace, Ardelia's faith in the magic that can be wrought by sheer effort of the will; my mother's open-mindedness in each new encounter and her habit of trying reasonableness first; my father's temper, his impatience and his efforts to keep "them" (throw them) out of his life. And it is out of these learned and selected attitudes that I look at the quality of life for my people in this country now. These widely disparate and sometimes conflicting views, I suspect, were held not only by me, but by most black people. Some I know are clearer in their positions, have not sullied their anger with optimism or dirtied their hope with despair. But most of us are plagued by a sense of being worn shell-thin by constant repression and hostility as well as the impression of being buoyed by visible testimony of tremendous strides. There *is* repetition of the grotesque in our history. And there *is* the miraculous walk of trees. The question is whether our walk is progress or merely movement. O.J. Simpson leaning on a Hertz car *is* better than the Gold Dust Twins on the back of a soap box. But is "Good Times" better than Stepin Fetchit? Has the first order of business been taken care of? Does the law of the land work for us?

Exercises

Some Important Words

Emancipation Proclamation (paragraph 1), predators (1), unreconstructed (1), rancor (1), sharecropper (2), tenured (3), lobotomized
(3), turmoil (4), Paul Revere (4), Martin Luther King (5), master race (5),
virility (5), irrevocable (5), moral fiber (6), Franklin Delano Roosevelt
(6), civilly (6), self-exiled (6), in arrears (6), legal tender (6), fastidious (6),
doomsday (6), succor (6), obstructionist (6), genetically (6), vertigo
(7), cynicism (7), deployment (7), solace (7), disparate (7), sullied (7),
buoyed (7), grotesque (7).

Some of the Issues

1. Toni Morrison describes her grandfather as a pessimist and says that
   "his rancor was legitimate." Why does she call it legitimate? Toward
   whom was it directed?
2. What was the difference in basic outlook between Morrison's
   grandfather and grandmother? What did the grandmother believe?
   How does the author show that she lived up to her beliefs?
3. Why does Morrison cite the lives of their two grandchildren in
   paragraph 3? How do these lives relate to their grandparents' beliefs?
   In what way does Morrison think these lives would have affected her
   grandparents' beliefs?
4. Reread paragraph 4. What bearing does what Morrison tells here
   have on the grandparents' views?
5. After rereading paragraph 5, explain the title of the essay. Whose
   beliefs does Morrison reflect in this paragraph?
6. Explain the distinction Morrison makes between the views of her
   grandparents and her parents. What if the difference between the
   views of her father and mother?
7. Morrison says: "So I grew up in a basically racist household." How
   does Morrison trace her views back to the influence of her parents
   and grandparents?

The Way We Are Told

8. Morrison uses a mix of personal anecdotes and more general
   observations, including statistics, to support her thesis. How are
   these used to support the idea of black progress of the lack of it?
9. As Morrison tells it, one each of her parents and grandparents was an
   optimist, the other a pessimist. Try to determine Morrison's own
   stand. Whose side is she on?

Some Subjects for Writing

10. How would you characterize your own family's outlook on life? Is it more on the optimistic or pessimistic side? How have your family's attitudes influenced you?
11. With which of her grandparents or parents does Morrison identify most? Support your argument with specific references drawn from the essay.

IN ETHNIC AMERICA

Michael Novak

Michael Novak, an American of Slovak descent, was born in Johnstown, Pennsylvania, in 1933 and has been a resident scholar at the American Enterprise Institute, a conservative think tank, since 1978. He holds honorary degrees from several universities. A prolific author, Novak's books include *The American Vision* (1978), *The Spirit of Democratic Capitalism* (1982), *Moral Clarity in the Nuclear Age* (1983), *Freedom and Justice* (1984), *Character and Crime* (1986), *The Consensus on Family and Welfare* (1987), and *This Hemisphere of Liberty: A Philosophy of the Americas* (1992).

The selection included here is an excerpt from one of his earlier books, *The Rise of the Unmeltable Ethnics* (1972). It is a spirited defense of the cultural roles of southern and eastern European immigrants to America. These immigrants, often referred to collectively as "ethnics," arrived in large numbers in the late nineteenth and early twentieth centuries. Mostly of peasant origin, they have been, Novak asserts, discriminated against in many ways. Yet, Novak claims, whereas other minorities who suffer from discrimination have aroused the sympathy and concern of many mainstream Americans, ethnics have been treated with neglect and often with scorn.

To learn more about the conditions under which immigrants like Novak's ancestors came to the United States, read Alistair Cooke's "The Huddled Masses."

Growing up in America has been an assault upon my sense of worthiness. It has also been a kind of liberation and delight. 1

There must be countless women in America who have known for years that something is peculiarly unfair, yet who only recently have found it possible, because of Women's Liberation, to give tongue to their pain. In recent months I have experienced a similar inner thaw, a gradual relaxation, a willingness to think about feelings heretofore shepherded out of sight. 2

I am born of PIGS—those Poles, Italians, Greeks, and Slavs, those non-English-speaking immigrants numbered so heavily among the work- 3 ingmen of this nation. Not particularly liberal or radical; born into a history not white Anglo-Saxon and not Jewish; born outside what, in America, is considered the intellectual mainstream—and thus privy to neither power nor status nor intellectual voice.

Those Poles of Buffalo and Milwaukee—so notoriously taciturn, sullen, nearly speechless. Who has ever understood them? It is not that Poles do not feel emotion—what is their history if not dark passion, romanticism, betrayal, courage, blood? But where in America is there anywhere a language for voicing what a Christian Pole in this nation feels? He has no Polish culture left him, no Polish tongue. Yet Polish feelings do not go easily into the idiom of happy America, the America of the Anglo-Saxons and yes, in the arts, the Jews. (The Jews have long been a culture of the word, accustomed to exile, skilled in scholarship and in reflection. The Christian Poles are largely of peasant origin, free men for hardly more than a hundred years.) Of what shall the young man of Lackawanna think on his way to work in the mills, departing his relatively dreary home and street? What roots does he have? What language of the heart is available to him?

The PIGS are not silent willingly. The silence burns like hidden coals in the chest.

All four of my grandparents, unknown to one another, arrived in America from the same country in Slovakia. My grandfather had a small farm in Pennsylvania; his wife died in a wagon accident. Meanwhile, Johanna, fifteen, arrived on Ellis Island, dizzy from witnessing births and deaths and illnesses aboard the crowded ship. She had a sign around her neck lettered PASSAIC. There an aunt told her of a man who had lost his wife in Pennsylvania. She went. They were married. She inherited his three children.

Each year for five years Grandma had a child of her own. She was among the lucky; only one died. When she was twenty-two and the mother of seven (my father was the last), her husband died. "Grandma Novak," as I came to know her many years later, resumed the work she had begun in Slovakia at the town home of a man known to my father only as "the Professor"; she housecleaned and she laundered.

I heard this story only weeks ago. Strange that I had not asked insistently before. Odd that I should have such shallow knowledge of my roots. Amazing to me that I do not know what my family suffered, endured, learned, and hoped these last six or seven generations. It is as if there were no project in which we all have been involved, as if history in some way began with my father and with me.

The estrangement I have come to feel derives not only from lack of family history. Early in life, I was made to feel a slight uneasiness when I said my name. When I was very young, the "American" kids still made something out of names unlike their own, and their earnest, ambitious mothers thought long thoughts when I introduced myself.

Under challenge in grammar school concerning my nationality, I   10
had been instructed by my father to announce proudly: "American."
When my family moved from the Slovak ghetto of Johnstown to the
WASP suburb on the hill, my mother impressed upon us how well we
must be dressed, and show good manners, and behave—people think of
us as "different" and we mustn't give them any cause. "Whatever you do,
marry a Slovak girl," was other advice to a similar end: "They cook. They
clean. They take good care of you. For your own good." I was taught to
be proud of being Slovak, but to recognize that others wouldn't know
what it meant, or care.

Nowhere in my schooling do I recall any attempt to put me in touch   11
with my own history. The strategy was clearly to make an American of
me. English literature, American literature, and even the history books, as
I recall them, were peopled mainly by Anglo-Saxons from Boston (where
most historians seemed to live). Not even my native Pennsylvania, let
alone my Slovak forebears, counted for very many paragraphs. (We did
have something called "Pennsylvania History" somewhere; I seem to
remember its puffs for industry. It could have been written by a Mellon.)
I don't remember feeling envy or regret: a feeling, perhaps, of unimpor-
tance, of remoteness, of not having heft enough to count.

The fact that I was born a Catholic also complicated life. What is a   12
Catholic but what everybody else is in reaction against? Protestants
reformed "the whore of Babylon." Others were "enlightened" from it,
and Jews had reason to help Catholicism and the social structure it was
rooted in fall apart. The history books and the whole of education
hummed in upon that point (for during crucial years I attended a public
school): to be modern is decidedly not to be medieval; to be reasonable
is not to be dogmatic; to be free is clearly not to live under ecclesiastical
authority; to be scientific is not to attend ancient rituals, cherish irrational
symbols, indulge in mythic practices. It is hard to grow up Catholic in
America without becoming defensive, perhaps a little paranoid, feeling
forced to divide the world between "us" and "them."

We had a special language all our own, our own pronunciation for   13
words we shared in common with others (Augústine, contémplative),
sights and sounds and smells in which few others participated (incense at
Benediction of the Most Blessed Sacrament, Forty Hours, wakes, and
altar bells at the silent consecration of the Host); and we had our own
politics and slant on world affairs. Since earliest childhood, I have known
about a "power elite" that runs America: the boys from the Ivy League in
the State Department as opposed to the Catholic boys in Hoover's FBI
who (as Daniel Moynihan once put it), keep watch on them. And on a
whole host of issues, my people have been, though largely Democratic,

conservative: on censorship, on communism, on abortion, on religious schools, etc. "Harvard" and "Yale" long meant "them" to us.

We did not feel this country belonged to us. We felt fierce pride in   14 it, more loyalty than anyone could know. But we felt blocked at every turn. There were not many intellectuals among us, not even very many professional men. Laborers mostly. Small businessmen, agents for corporations perhaps. Content with a little, yes, modest in expectation, and content. But somehow feeling cheated. For a thousand years the Slovaks survived Hungarian hegemony and our strategy here remained the same: endurance and steady work. Slowly, one day, we would overcome.

A special word is required about a complicated symbol: sex. To this   15 day my mother finds it hard to spell the word intact, preferring to write "s--." Not that much was made of sex in our environment. And that's the point: silence. Demonstrative affection, emotive dances, an exuberance Anglo-Saxons seldom seem to share; but on the realities of sex, discretion. Reverence, perhaps; seriousness, surely. On intimacies, it was as though our tongues had been stolen, as though in peasant life for a thousand years—as in the novels of Tolstoi, Sholokhov, and even Kosinski—the context had been otherwise. Passion, certainly; romance, yes; family and children, certainly; but sex rather a minor if explosive part of life.

Imagine, then, the conflict in the generation of my brothers, sister,   16 and myself. Suddenly, what for a thousand years was minor becomes an all-absorbing investigation. Some view it as a drama of "liberation" when the ruling classes (subscribers to the *New Yorker*, I suppose) move progressively, generation by generation since Sigmund Freud, toward concentration upon genital stimulation, and latterly toward consciousness-raising sessions in Clit. Lib. But it is rather a different drama when we stumble suddenly upon mores staggering any expectation our grandparents ever cherished.

Yet more significant in the ethnic experience in America is the   17 intellectual world one meets: the definition of values, ideas, and purposes emanating from universities, books, magazines, radio, and television. One hears one's own voice echoed back neither by spokesmen of "middle America" (so complacent, smug, nativist, and Protestant), nor by the "intellectuals." Almost unavoidably, perhaps, education in America leads the student who entrusts his soul to it in a direction which, lacking a better word, we might call liberal: respect for individual conscience, a sense of social responsibility, trust in the free exchange of ideas and procedures of dissent, a certain confidence in the ability of men to "reason together" and adjudicate their differences, a frank recognition of the vitality of the unconscious, a willingness to protect workers and the poor against the vast economic power of industrial corporations, and the like.

On the other hand, the liberal imagination has appeared to be   18
astonishingly universalist and relentlessly missionary. Perhaps the metaphor "enlightenment" offers a key. One is *initiated into light*. Liberal
education tends to separate children from their parents, from their roots,
from their history, in the cause of a universal and superior religion.

In particular, I have regretted and keenly felt the absence of that   19
sympathy for PIGS which simple human feeling might have prodded
intelligence to muster, that same sympathy which the educated find so
easy to conjure up for black culture, Chicano culture, Indian culture, and
other cultures of the poor. In such cases one finds the universalist
pretensions of liberal culture suspended; some groups, at least, are
entitled to be both different and respected. Why do the educated classes
find it so difficult to want to understand the man who drives a beer truck,
or the fellow with a helmet working on a site across the street with
plumbers and electricians, while their sensitivities race easily to Mississippi or even Bedford-Stuyvesant?

There are deep secrets here, no doubt, unvoiced fantasies and   20
scarcely admitted historical resentments. Few persons in describing
"middle Americans," "the silent majority," or Scammon and Wattenberg's
" typical American voter" distinguish clearly enough between the nativist
American and the ethnic American. The first is likely to be Protestant, the
second Catholic. Both may be, in various ways, conservative, loyalist,
and unenlightened. Each has his own agonies, fears, betrayed expectations. Neither is ready, quite, to become an ally of the other. Neither has
the same history behind him here. Neither has the same hopes. Neither
lives out the same psychic voyage, shares the same symbols, has the
same sense of reality. The rhetoric and metaphors proper to each differ
from those of the other.

There is overlap, of course. But country music is not a polka; a   21
successful politician in a Chicago ward needs a very different "common
touch" from the one needed by the county clerk in Normal. The urban
experience of immigration lacks that mellifluous, optimistic, biblical
vision of the good America which springs naturally to the lips of
politicians from the Bible Belt. The nativist tends to believe with
Richard Nixon that he "knows America, and the American heart is
good." The ethnic tends to believe that every American who preceded
him has an angle, and that he, by God, will some day find one, too.
(Often, ethnics complain that by working hard, obeying the law,
trusting their political leaders, and relying upon the American dream,
they now have only their own naiveté to blame for rising no higher
than they have.)

Unfortunately, it seems, the ethnics erred in attempting to Ameri-   22
canize themselves before clearing the project with the educated classes.
They learned to wave the flag and to send their sons to war. They

learned to support their President—an easy task, after all, for those accustomed to obeying authority. And where would they have been if Franklin Roosevelt had not sided with them against established interests? They knew a little about communism—the radicals among them in one way, and by far the larger number of conservatives in another. To this day not a few exchange letters with cousins and uncles who did not leave for America when they might have, whose lot is demonstrably harder than their own and less than free.

Finally, the ethnics do not like, or trust, or even understand the 23 intellectuals. It is not easy to feel uncomplicated affection for those who call you "pig," "fascist," "racist." One had not yet grown accustomed to not hearing "hunkie," "Polack," "spic," "mick," "dago," and the rest.

At no little sacrifice, one had apologized for foods that smelled 24 too strong for Anglo-Saxon noses; moderated the wide swings of Slavic and Italian emotion; learned decorum; given oneself to education, American style; tried to learn tolerance and assimilation. Each generation criticized the earlier for its authoritarian and European and old-fashioned ways. "Up-to-date" was a moral lever. And now when the process nears completion, when a generation appears that speaks without accent and goes to college, still you are considered "pigs," "fascists," and "racists." Racists? Our ancestors owned no slaves. Most of us ceased being serfs only in the last two hundred years—the Russians in 1861. . . .

Whereas the Anglo-Saxon model appears to be a system of atomic 25 individuals and high mobility, our model has tended to stress communities of our own, attachment to family and relatives, stability, and roots. Ethnics tend to have a fierce sense of attachment to their homes, having been homeowners for less than three generations: a home is almost fulfillment enough for one man's life. Some groups save arduously in a passion to *own;* others rent. We have most ambivalent feelings about suburban assimilation and mobility. The melting pot is a kind of homogenized soup, and its mores only partly appeal to ethnics: to some, yes, and to others, no.

It must be said that ethnics think they are better people than the 26 blacks. Smarter, tougher, harder working, stronger in their families. But maybe many are not sure. Maybe many are uneasy. Emotions here are delicate; one can understand the immensely more difficult circumstances under which the blacks have suffered; and one is not unaware of peculiar forms of fear, envy, and suspicion across color lines. How much of this we learned in America by being made conscious of our olive skin, brawny backs, accents, names, and cultural quirks is not plain to us. Racism is not our invention; we did not bring it with us; we had prejudices enough and would gladly have been spared new ones. Especially regarding people who suffer more than we.

Exercises

Some Important Words

assault (paragraph 1), privy (3), taciturn (4), WASP (10), Mellon (11), ecclesiastical (12), ritual (12), mythic (12), Augústine (13), contémplative (13), hegemony (14), Tolstoi (15), Sholokhov (15), Kosinski (15), nativist (17), adjudicate (17), unconscious (17), Bedford-Stuyvesant (19), mellifluous (21), authoritarian (24).

Some of the Issues

1. Explain the meaning of the first paragraph after you have read the third. What aspects of his own background does Novak single out? How do they relate to his opening statement?
2. Novak refers to his background in paragraph 3 and returns to his family history in paragraphs 6 through 8. What is his reason for inserting paragraphs 4 and 5 in between?
3. How does Novak's family history reflect the silence of the ethnics to which he refers?
4. In paragraph 14 Novak says, "We did not feel this country belonged to us." What has he said in the preceding part of the essay to substantiate that assertion?
5. Explain the anger Novak reflects in discussing sex (paragraphs 15 and 16).
6. Show the points Novak makes to contrast the ethnic and liberal outlook on life in America.
7. What reasons does Novak give for the liberal, intellectual sympathy for African-Americans, Chicanos, or Native Americans, but not for ethnics?

The Way We Are Told

8. Why does Novak make the analogy between Women's Liberation and his own "inner thaw" (paragraph 2)?
9. In paragraphs 4 and 5 Novak uses emotional terms to characterize ethnics. Find some of them, and then contrast them to the language of paragraphs 6 and 7. Can you explain the reasons for the difference between the two sets of paragraphs?
10. In paragraph 10 Novak refers to his people as "different." Different from whom? How does he show that difference? What do his comments imply about Americans?
11. On a few occasions Novak uses sarcasm, or satirizes the people he considers anti-ethnic, the "them" at the end of paragraph 12. Find some examples of satiric statements.
12. Look at the last sentence of paragraph 14. Do you hear any echoes?

Some Subjects for Writing

13. In paragraph 1 Novak refers to growing up in America as "an assault upon my sense of worthiness" as well as "a kind of liberation and delight." In an essay explain how Novak's experience could be both of these.

14. In an essay determine Novak's intended audience. Is it PIGS, for example? Liberals? Argue from the contents of the essay and the way it is written.

ANGLO VS. CHICANO: WHY?

Arthur L. Campa

Arthur L. Campa (1905–78) was born to American missionary parents in Mexico. He attended the University of New Mexico and Columbia, and was professor and chairman of the Department of Modern Languages at the University of Denver. He also served as cultural attaché at several United States embassies. The following selection appeared in the *Western Review*.

In his essay Campa discusses the differences between the two main cultures that meet in the southwestern United States: he contrasts the Anglo culture derived from English sources and the Chicano, whose cultural sources are Hispanic. He uses history, geography, and language to show how and why these two cultures living side by side find it hard to overcome the differences between them.

The cultural differences between Hispanic and Anglo-American people 1 have been dwelt upon by so many writers that we should all be well informed about the values of both. But audiences are usually of the same persuasion as the speakers, and those who consult published works are for the most part specialists looking for affirmation of what they believe. So, let us consider the same subject, exploring briefly some of the basic cultural differences that cause conflict in the Southwest, where Hispanic and Anglo-American cultures meet.

Cultural differences are implicit in the conceptual content of the 2 languages of these two civilizations, and their value systems stem from a long series of historical circumstances. Therefore, it may be well to consider some of the English and Spanish cultural configurations before these Europeans set foot on American soil. English culture was basically insular, geographically and ideologically; was more integrated on the whole, except for some strong theological differences; and was particularly zealous of its racial purity. Spanish culture was peninsular, a geographical circumstance that made it a catchall of Mediterranean,

90

central European and north African peoples. The composite nature of the population produced a marked regionalism that prevented close integration, except for religion, and led to a strong sense of individualism. These differences were reflected in the colonizing enterprise of the two cultures. The English isolated themselves from the Indians physically and culturally; the Spanish, who had strong notions about *pureza de sangre* [purity of blood] among the nobility, were not collectively averse to adding one more strain to their racial cocktail. Cortés led the way by siring the first *mestizo* in North America, and the rest of the conquistadores followed suit. The ultimate products of these two orientations meet today in the Southwest.

3   Anglo-American culture was absolutist at the onset; that is, all the dominant values were considered identical for all, regardless of time and place. Such values as justice, charity, honesty were considered the superior social order for all men and were later embodied in the American Constitution. The Spaniard brought with him a relativistic viewpoint and saw fewer moral implications in man's actions. Values were looked upon as the result of social and economic conditions.

4   The motives that brought Spaniards and Englishmen to America also differed. The former came on an enterprise of discovery, searching for a new route to India initially, and later for new lands to conquer, the fountain of youth, minerals, the Seven Cities of Cíbola and, in the case of the missionaries, new souls to win for the Kingdom of Heaven. The English came to escape religious persecution, and once having found a haven, they settled down to cultivate the soil and establish their homes. Since the Spaniards were not seeking a refuge or running away from anything, they continued their explorations and circled the globe 25 years after the discovery of the New World.

5   This peripatetic tendency of the Spaniard may be accounted for in part by the fact that he was the product of an equestrian culture. Men on foot do not venture far into the unknown. It was almost a century after the landing on Plymouth Rock that Governor Alexander Spotswood of Virginia crossed the Blue Ridge Mountains, and it was not until the nineteenth century that the Anglo-Americans began to move west of the Mississippi.

6   The Spaniard's equestrian role meant that he was not close to the soil, as was the Anglo-American pioneer, who tilled the land and built the greatest agricultural industry in history. The Spaniard cultivated the land only when he had Indians available to do it for him. The uses to which the horse was put also varied. The Spanish horse was essentially a mount, while the more robust English horse was used in cultivating the soil. It is therefore not surprising that the viewpoints of these two cultures should differ when we consider that the pioneer is looking at the world at the level of his eyes while the *caballero* [horseman] is looking beyond and down at the rest of the world.

One of the most commonly quoted, and often misinterpreted, 7
characteristics of Hispanic peoples is the deeply ingrained individualism
in all walks of life. Hispanic individualism is a revolt against the incursion
of collectivity, strongly asserted when it is felt that the ego is being fenced
in. This attitude leads to a deficiency in those social qualities based on
collective standards, an attitude that Hispanos do not consider negative
because it manifests a measure of resistance to standardization in order to
achieve a measure of individual freedom. Naturally, such an attitude has
no *reglas fijas* [fixed rules].

Anglo-Americans who achieve a measure of success and security 8
through institutional guidance not only do not mind a few fixed rules but
demand them. The lack of a concerted plan of action, whether in
business or in politics, appears unreasonable to Anglo-Americans. They
have a sense of individualism, but they achieve it through action and
self-determination. Spanish individualism is based on feeling, on something that is the result not of rules and collective standards but of a
person's momentary, emotional reaction. And it is subject to change
when the mood changes. In contrast to Spanish emotional individualism,
the Anglo-American strives for objectivity when choosing a course of
action or making a decision.

The Southwestern Hispanos voiced strong objections to the lack of 9
courtesy of the Anglo-Americans when they first met them in the early
days of the Santa Fe trade. The same accusation is leveled at the
Americanos today in many quarters of the Hispanic world. Some of this
results from their different conceptions of polite behavior. Here too one
can say that the Spanish have no *reglas fijas* because for them courtesy is
simply an expression of the way one person feels toward another. To
some they extend the hand, to some they bow and for the more *íntimos*
there is the well-known *abrazo*. The concepts of "good or bad" or "right
and wrong" in polite behavior are moral considerations of an absolutist
culture.

Another cultural contrast appears in the way both cultures share 10
part of their material substance with others. The pragmatic Anglo-
American contributes regularly to such institutions as the Red Cross, the
United Fund and a myriad of associations. He also establishes foundations and quite often leaves millions to such institutions. The Hispano
prefers to give his contribution directly to the recipient so he can see the
person he is helping.

A century of association has inevitably acculturated both Hispanos 11
and Anglo-Americans to some extent, but there still persist a number of
culture traits that neither group has relinquished altogether. Nothing is
more disquieting to an Anglo-American who believes that time is money
than the time perspective of Hispanos. They usually refer to this attitude
as the "*mañana* psychology." Actually, it is more of a "today psychology,"

because Hispanos cultivate the present to the exclusion of the future; because the latter has not arrived yet, it is not a reality. They are reluctant to relinquish the present, so they hold on to it until it becomes the past. To an Hispano, nine is nine until it is ten, so when he arrives at nine-thirty, he jubilantly exclaims: "*¡Justo!*" [right on time]. This may be why the clock is slowed down to a walk in Spanish while in English it runs. In the United States, our future-oriented civilization plans our lives so far in advance that the present loses its meaning. January magazine issues are out in December; 1973 cars have been out since October; cemetery plots and even funeral arrangements are bought on the installment plan. To a person engrossed in living today the very idea of planning his funeral sounds like the tolling of the bells.

It is a natural corollary that a person who is present oriented should be compensated by being good at improvising. An Anglo-American is told in advance to prepare for an "impromptu speech," but an Hispano usually can improvise a speech because "*Nosotros lo improvisamos todo*" [we improvise everything]. 12

Another source of cultural conflict arises from the difference between *being* and *doing*. Even when trying to be individualistic, the Anglo-American achieves it by what he does. Today's young generation decided to be themselves, to get away from standardization, so they let their hair grow, wore ragged clothes and even went barefoot in order to be different from the Establishment. As a result they all ended up doing the same things and created another stereotype. The freedom enjoyed by the individuality of *being* makes it unnecessary for Hispanos to strive to be different. 13

In 1963 a team of psychologists from the University of Guadalajara in Mexico and the University of Michigan compared 74 upper-middle-class students from each university. Individualism and personalism were found to be central values for the Mexican students. This was explained by saying that a Mexican's value as a person lies in his *being* rather than, as is the case of the Anglo-Americans, in concrete accomplishments. Efficiency and accomplishments are derived characteristics that do not affect worthiness in the Mexican, whereas in the American it is equated with success, a value of highest priority in the American culture. Hispanic people disassociate themselves from material things or from actions that may impugn a person's sense of being, but the Anglo-American shows great concern for material things and assumes responsibility for his actions. This is expressed in the language of each culture. In Spanish one says, "*Se me cayó la taza*" [the cup fell away from me] instead of "I dropped the cup." 14

In English, one speaks of money, cash and all related transactions with frankness because material things of this high order do not trouble Anglo-Americans. In Spanish such materialistic concepts are circumvented by referring to cash as *efectivo* [effective] and when buying or 15 selling as something *al contado* [counted out], and when without it by saying *No tengo fondos* [I have no funds]. This disassociation from material things is what produces *sobriedad* [sobriety] in the Spaniard according to Miguel de Unamuno, but in the Southwest the disassociation from materialism leads to *dejadez* [lassitude] and *desprendimiento* [disinterestedness]. A man may lose his life defending his honor but is unconcerned about the lack of material things. *Desprendimiento* causes a man to spend his last cent on a friend, which when added to lack of concern for the future may mean that tomorrow he will eat beans as a result of today's binge.

The implicit differences in words that appear to be identical in   16
meaning are astonishing. Versatile is a compliment in English and an insult in Spanish. An Hispano student who is told to apologize cannot do it, because the word doesn't exist in Spanish. *Apología* means words in praise of a person. The Anglo-American either apologizes, which is a form of retraction abhorrent in Spanish, or compromises, another concept foreign to Hispanic culture. *Compromiso* means a date, not a compromise. In colonial Mexico City, two hidalgos once entered a narrow street from opposite sides, and when they could not go around, they sat in their coaches for three days until the viceroy ordered them to back out. All this because they could not work out a compromise.

It was that way then and to some extent now. Many of today's   17
conflicts in the Southwest have their roots in polarized cultural differences, which need not be irreconcilable when approached with mutual respect and understanding.

Exercises

Some Important Words

implicit (paragraph 2), conceptual (2), configuration (2), zealous (2), *mestizo*—mixed blood (2), conquistadores (2), absolutist (3), relativistic (3), peripatetic (5), equestrian (5), incursion (7), collectivity (7), *abrazo*—embrace, greeting (9), circumvented (15), versatile (16), *hidalgo*—gentleman, nobleman (16).

Some of the Issues

1. Find the sentence that most precisely states the thesis of the essay.
2. It is relatively easy to find the thesis statements for the various paragraphs. Find them for paragraphs 3, 7, and 10. What is the arrangement of supporting evidence in each case?

3. Campa makes a number of assertions throughout the essay. Examine the evidence he presents for each. Which ones do you find to be strongly supported? Which are less well sustained?
4. According to Campa, individuality is a virtue in both Anglo and Hispanic cultures. How do the notions of individuality differ in the two cultures?

The Way We Are Told

5. Make an outline of the essay, showing its organizational pattern.
6. Each paragraph (or small group of paragraphs) deals with a particular contrast between Anglos and Chicanos. In your view, would the essay be more or less effective if the author had used a different pattern, that is, if he had developed the Anglo and Hispanic characteristics in two major, separate sections? Support your opinion.
7. How objective do you find Campa's article? Does the author favor one side? If you think he does, what evidence can you cite for your view?

Some Subjects for Writing

8. Write an essay comparing and contrasting two related subjects you know well: high school and college; an old home and your present one; two jobs.

AMÉRKA, AMÉRKA:
A PALESTINIAN ABROAD
IN THE LAND OF THE FREE

Anton Shammas

Anton Shammas is a Palestinian born in Israel in 1950. He attended
Hebrew University and came to the United States in 1987 as a
Rockefeller Fellow at the University of Michigan. He is the author of
the novel *Arabesques* (1989) and has published numerous essays.
Shammas teaches in the Department of Near Eastern Studies at the
University of Michigan.

     Palestine is a historic region on the eastern coast of the
Mediterranean. The 10,000-square-mile region is sacred land to three
major religions—Judaism, Christianity, and Islam—and throughout
history, ownership of this land has been often and bitterly contested.
In the twentieth century, Arab and Jewish nationalists made conflicting claims to the region, a brutal and costly dispute that Palestinian
and Israeli leaders agreed to end in September 1993. In this essay
published in *Harper's* magazine (1991), Shammas speaks of Arab
immigrants who, although physically separated from their home in
the Middle East, carry with them the spiritual and cultural heritage of
their "lost Palestine."

Some years ago, in San Francisco, I heard the following tale from a   1
young, American-educated Palestinian engineer. We had found a rustic,
trendy place and managed to find a quiet table. Over lukewarm beers,
rather than small cups of lukewarm cardamomed coffee, we talked about
his family, which had wandered adrift in the Arab world for some time
before finding its moorings on the West Coast, and in particular of a
relative of his living to the south of San Francisco whom we were
planning to visit the following day. We never did make that visit—that is
a story, too—but the story about this man has fluttered inside my head
ever since.

    We will call him Abu-Khalil. Imagine him as a fortysomething   2
Palestinian (he is now past sixty) whose West Bank homeland was, once

again in his lifetime, caving in on him in June 1967 after what the Arabs call the Defeat of Hazieran 5 and the Israelis and Americans call the Six-Day War. Where was he to spend the occupation years of his life? Where could he get as far away from the Israeli "benign" presence as his captive mind could go? The choices were essentially two: He could cross the Allenby Bridge to His Majesty's Jordan, or he could take an unhijack-able flight west, from Ben-Gurion Airport. He chose the latter, a plane that would carry him to the faraway U.S.A.—to those members of his large family (Arabs always seem to have *large* families) who had discovered the New World centuries after Columbus. (They had discov-ered the New World, as they would tell him later, in a sort of belated westbound revenge for the eastbound expulsion of their great ancestors from Andalusia/Spain the same year that Columbus's Spanish ships arrived on the shores of his imaginary India.)

To continue our tale: Abu-Khalil lands in San Francisco one warm   3
September afternoon, clad in a heavy black coat that does not astonish his waiting relatives a bit, since they are familiar with the man's eccentricities. But what about the security guys at Ben-Gurion Airport? Didn't the out-of-season coat merit suspicion and a frisking? Apparently not. Abu-Khalil is, as far as I can tell, the only Palestinian to have seeped out through the thick security screenings at Ben-Gurion Airport—née Lydda—unsearched. How else to account for the fact that he had managed to carry on board with him a veritable Little Palestine—flora, fauna, and all?

His bags were heavy with small plants and seeds that went   4
undetected by Israeli security. (It should be said, of course, that flora poised to explode is not what they look for in a Palestinian's luggage at Ben-Gurion Airport.) As for U.S. Customs Form 6059B, which inbound foreigners are graciously asked to fill out before they land—it prohibits passengers from importing "fruits, vegetables, plants, plant products, soil, meats, meat products, birds, snails, and other live animals and animal products"—our passenger, to the best of the storyteller's authorial knowledge (and mine), could not read English, and no American officer, lawful or otherwise, bothered to verify his declarations—albeit not made—through questioning, much less through physical search, these being two procedures that Palestinians are much accustomed to in their comings and goings in the Middle East.

So that's how Abu-Khalil managed to bring to California some   5
representative plants of Palestine, many still rooted in their original, fecund soil. It seems, however, that he took pride mainly—think of it as a feather in his kaffiyeh—in his having managed to smuggle out of the West Bank, through Israel, and into the United States seven representa-tive birds of his homeland. The duri, the hassoun, the sununu, the shahrur, the bulbul, the summan, and the hudhud, small-talk companion to King Solomon himself—they all surrounded him now in California,

re-chirping Palestine away in his ears from inside their unlocked American cages. "They will not leave their open cages," Abu-Khalil would say, or so the story went, "till I leave mine."

Abu-Khalil's was a cage of his own making; he has not left it to this   6
very day. But I was mainly interested in the birds, in their mute, wondrous migration. In the years that followed, I asked the storyteller, did they forget their mother chirp? Did they eventually adopt the mellow sounds of California? And how, I asked, did he manage to smuggle in these birds in the first place? "Well," said my friend, "he had a coat of many pockets, you see."

I found the story hard to believe at the time; but one has to trust the   7
storyteller, even a Palestinian. After all, where else could the birds of Palestine go "after the last sky," in the words of the poet Mahmoud Darwish, but to the Land of the Free.

My storyteller and I belong to a different generation from Abu-Khalil's.   8
We, and others like us, are too young to think of smuggling roots and soil, though not young enough to forget all about the birds we left behind. We travel light, empty-pocketed, with the vanity of those who think home is a portable idea, something that dwells mainly in the mind or within a text. Celebrating the modern powers of imagination and of fiction, we have lost faith in our old idols—memory, storytelling. We are not even sure anymore whether there ever was a home out there, a territory, a homeland. We owe allegiance to no memory; and we have adopted as our anthem Derek Walcott's perhaps too-often-quoted line: "I had no nation now but the imagination." Our language, Arabic, was de-territorialized by another, and only later did we realize that Arabic does not even have a word for "territory." The act of de-territorialization, then, took place outside our language, so we could not talk, much less write, about our plight in our mother tongue. Now we need the language of the Other for that, the language that can categorize the new reality and sort it out for us in upper and lower cases; the language that can re-territorialize us, as imaginary as that might be, giving us some allegedly solid ground. It is English for my San Francisco storyteller-friend, French for others, Hebrew for me: the unlocked cages of our own choices. In short, we are Palestine's post–Abu-Khalilians, if you like.

Many Middle Eastern Abu-Khalils have immigrated to the U.S.A. over the   9
years, driven out of their respective homelands by wars, greedy foreigners, and pangs of poverty. At the turn of the century, when the Ottomans—who had been ruling the Middle East since 1517—were practicing some refined forms of their famine policy, Arabs left their homes and families and sailed to the Americas. Brazil and Argentina had their charm; Michigan, too. Today, Michigan is home to the largest

Arab-American community in North America. If you were to take a stroll through the streets of Dearborn, a south-by-southwest suburb of Detroit, the signs and names might remind you of some ancient legend.

Bereft of names and deeds, these Arabs came to Michigan to make [10] names for themselves as a twentieth-century self-mocking variation on the old Mesopotamian tradition of the *shuma shakanu,* the preservation of one's name and deeds. That also was the original aim of those who followed Nimrod the Hunter in his biblical endeavor to reach heaven and said, "Let us make us a name for ourselves" (Gen. 11:4). An American heaven of sorts and, in this case, an American name; no concealed Nimrods.

Hoping for a happier ending than the biblical one, they have come [11] from places whose names Mark Twain, the great American nomenclator, traveling with "the innocents abroad" some 123 years ago, found impossible to pronounce. "One of the great drawbacks to this country," he wrote in September 1867, from Palestine, "is its distressing names that nobody can get the hang of. . . .You may make a stagger of pronouncing these names, but they will bring any Christian to grief that tries to spell them. I have an idea that if I can only simplify the nomenclature of this country, it will be of the greatest service to Americans who may travel here in the future."

This may account for the notorious Hollywood tradition, many [12] years after tongue-in-cheek Twain, of assuming that all men Middle Eastern—if fortunate enough to actually have names of their own in the films—should be called Abdul. (In fact, Abdul is but the first half of a common Middle Eastern compound.) So all these anonymous Abduls are here now, trying, so far away from home, to complete their names, in a new world that has been practicing the renaming of things now for five centuries and counting.

* * * * *

From Fassuta, my small village in the Galilee, émigrés went mainly to [13] Brazil and Argentina. My grandfather and his brothers and brother-in-law left for Argentina in 1896, only to return home, empty-handed, a year later. Then, on the eve of the First World War, my grandfather tried his luck again, this time on his own, heading once more to Argentina (at least that's what he told my grandmother the night before he took off), where he vanished for about ten years, leaving behind three daughters and three sons, all of them hungry. His youngest son, my uncle Jiryes, followed in his footsteps in 1928, leaving his wife and child behind, never to come back.

One of my childhood heroes, an old villager whom we, the [14] children of Fassuta, always blamed for having invented school, had actually been to Salt Lake City. I don't have the foggiest idea what he did there for three years before the Depression; his deeds remain a sealed and, I suspect, quite salty book, but he certainly did not betray the Catholic faith, no sir. I still remember him in the late 1950s, breathing down my neck during Mass at the village's church. He used to wear impeccable white American shirts under his Arab *abaya,* even some thirty years after he had returned to the village. But that was the only American fingerprint on him; the rest was Middle Eastern.

The most famous American immigrant from my village, though, was   15
M., my aunt Najeebeh's brother-in-law, Najeebeh being my father's sister. I hate to be finicky about the exact relationship, but that is simply the was it is in Arabic: There are different words to refer to the father's and the mother's side of the family. At any rate, M. left the village in the early 1920s and came back to visit his brothers some forty years later, with his non-Arabic-speaking sons. As a matter of fact, he was the only one of a long, winding line of immigrants who had really made it, or "had it fixed," as the Galileans would say. He came to own a chain of fast-food restaurants, quite famous in the Midwest. Before I myself left the Mideast for these parts, I went to see his nephews—my cousins—in the village and promised them, under oath, that I would certainly look M. up one day and introduce myself, or at least pop into one of his restaurants and, naturally, ask for a free meal. I have not yet done the former and am still keeping the latter for a rainy Michigan day. However, whenever I come across his chain's emblem, a plump plastic boy holding a plate high above his plumply combed head, I remember my late aunt Najeebeh and think how disconcerted she would be had she known what kind of a mnemonic-device-in-the-form-of-a-cultural-shock she had become for her nephew, in faraway Amérka, as it is called in my part of the world.

Upon first arriving in Amérka, one of my first cultural shocks was the   16
otherwise trivial American fact that shirts had not only a neck size but also a sleeve size. Fassuta's Salt Lake City visitor and I, we both come from a culture where, insofar as shirts are concerned, one's arm length doesn't matter much. People in the Middle East are still immersed in figuring out the length of their postcolonial borders, personal and otherwise, and all indications show that a long time will elapse before they start paying attention to the lonely business of their sleeve size.

Which may or may not have something to do with the fact that in   17
a culture with an oral background of storytelling, where choices continue, even in postcolonial times, to be made for you (be they by God, fate, nature, or the ruler), you don't enjoy the luxuries of the novel's world, where characters make their own choices and have to live, subsequently, with the consequences, sleeve size and all. The storyteller's world revolves around memory; the novelist's, around imagination. And what people in places like the Middle East are struggling to do, I

think, is to shrug off the bondage of their memory and decolonize their imagination. So, in this regard, for a Middle Easterner to have a sleeve size would be a sign of such a decolonization.

My first stroll ever on American soil took place in a park along the Iowa River, in Iowa City. I was thirty years old, and there were so many things I had not seen before. On that day I saw my first squirrel. There are many jittery, frail creatures in the Middle East, but, to the best of my zoological knowledge, there are no squirrels. However, people do talk of the *sinjabi,* the squirrelish color. I remember thinking, during my walk, that if there were no squirrels in the Middle East, how come the Arabs use the word *sinjabi?* [18]

Not long after the day I took my walk, I found out, as I had expected, that there were *sinjabs* in Iran and that the word *sinjabi* was derived from the Persian, a language that had given Arabic, long before the Koran, so many beautiful words. Some 1,300 years later, at the very time of my stay in Iowa, the Ayatollah Khomeini was busy squirreling away some ideas about a new order, about the Mesopotamian tradition of the *shuma shakanu.* A half-world away, Salman Rushdie was, apparently, squirreling away some counter-ideas of his own. It was not hard to imagine, later, who would play the Crackers, and who—or on whose— Nuts. [19]

My Galilean friend J., not to be confused with the biblical author, came to America some sixteen years ago. We'd met at the Hebrew University in Jerusalem, in the early Seventies. He was my instructor in the Introduction to Arabic Literature course, and I'm still indebted to him for teaching me the first steps of academic research and, most importantly, for being so decent a friend as to have unabashedly explained to me how I would never have the proper discipline. [20]

At that time he was mulling over the idea that he should perhaps come to this country to work on a Ph.D. in modern Arabic literature. Once he had made up his mind, he started frantically looking for a wife with whom to share the burden of American self-exile. I asked him once whether it wouldn't be wiser to find himself an already naturalized American lady, to which he replied: "I'm looking for a woman that when I put my weary head against her arm, I want to hear her blood murmuring in Arabic." He did eventually find one, and they both immigrated to Amérka and have been happily listening to each other's blood ever since. [21]

J. was looking for the blood tongue, for the primordial language, wherein the names of things, long before the confusion of tongues, were so deeply lodged in the things they designated that no human eye could decipher the sign. Had he been a Cabalist, he would have believed that what God introduced into the world was written words, not murmurings [22] of blood. But J. came from the oral Middle East to the literate West, and he knew upon arriving in Amérka that he would be expected to trade in his mother tongue and keep the secret language circulating only in his veins.

I saw the already "naturalized" J. again, in Jerusalem, some ten   23
years after he'd left. At the end of a very long night of catching up, he picked up a Hebrew literary magazine from my desk and browsed through it. Something caught his eye; he paused for a moment. "What is *this* doing here?" "This" turned out to be an ad for a famous Israeli brand of women's underwear. I wasn't sure what he meant. It was a full-page ad, an exact replica of the famous photograph of Marilyn Monroe standing on a grate in the street, her dress blowing above her waist. "You know what the reference is to, right?" I asked. No, he did not. And I thought, How could a bright guy like J. live for so long in the U.S.A., be an *American citizen,* and not be familiar with what I thought were the basics of American iconography?

I had been settled for a year in Ann Arbor when I went to visit J. and   24
his wife in Ohio. Having just returned from a short visit to our Galilee home, I brought J., who has a green thumb, what he had asked me to: some local lubia peas for his thriving backyard garden. We were reminiscing late at night, with Fayruz, the famous Lebanese singer, on the stereo in the background and some Middle Eastern munchies on the coffee table, when I suddenly remembered that night in Jerusalem years before and the ad with the Marilyn knockoff. It would be nice if you did recognize the American icon, I thought to myself, but it is nice too that you can live in this country for decades without being forced to go native. You can always pick up your own fold of the huge map and chart yourself into it.

Now it is my fourth year in Ann Arbor. I moved in early in September of   25
1987, and for three months my relationship with the squirrels outside my window was quite good. "Quite good," as my English professor at the Hebrew University in Jerusalem used to say, means "yes, good, but there's no need to be so excited about it." So I was developing an unexciting relationship with these creatures, especially with one of them, whom I told myself I was able to tell from the others, although they all did look alike, if I may say so without prejudice. Anyway, I would open the door early in the morning to pick up the *New York Times* from the doorstep, and he would be goofing around its blue, transparent wrap (that's how the paper is home-delivered in Michigan), unalarmed by my invasion of *his* kingdom.

But one morning, as I reached down for the paper, he froze, all of   26
a sudden, in the middle of one of his silly gesticulations, gaping at me in utter terror, and then fled away as if I were about to—well, throw a stone

at him. Maybe it was a morning in December 1987, and he had peeked at the *Times*. Maybe I will never cease to look east for my images and metaphors.

For J., for my friend in San Francisco, for me, the Old World will   27
never cease to hold us hostage in this way. Sometimes I think that no matter how deep I have traveled *into* the American life, I still carry my own miniature Abu-Khalils in my pockets and a miniature Middle East in my mind. There is little space for Amérka in the most private of my maps.

And speaking of maps, how many adult Americans know where the   28
"heartbroken piece of territory" Mark Twain was talking about actually is?

Still, would it matter if they did?   29

I don't think it would. After all, modern colonialism (sometimes   30
euphemistically referred to as "our American interests"), unlike its old-fashioned, European counterpart, is not geographically oriented. Geographical literacy is defunct; its demise was caused by the invention of the remote control. And if you happen to live in this vast country, your sense of geography is necessarily numbed by what Aldous Huxley would have called one's "local validity." Paradoxically, the vastness of the land provides Americans with a continental alibi. A look at the map of the U.S.A. from, say, a Palestinian point of view would psychologically suffice to make a clear-cut distinction between the American people and their government's policy. Unlike England, for instance, where every Brit seems to be living in London and has something or another to do with the business of running the rather rusty machinery of a worn-out colonialism, there is an utter distinction when it comes to the United States between the Americans on Capitol Hill and the *real* Americans who, on a good day, want absolutely nothing to do with Washington's follies.

Maybe that's why Abu-Khalil can feel at home in California,   31
surrounded by the artifacts of his lost Palestine. This country is *big;* it has enough room not only for the newcomers but also for their portable homelands. Among other achievements, Amérka has made homesickness obsolete.

Exercises

Some Important Words

West Bank (paragraph 2), the Six-Day War (2), benign (2), clad (3), née (3), albeit (4), fecund (5), kaffiyeh (5), deterritorialized (8), plight (8), reterritorialize (8), allegedly (8), bereft (10), nomenclator (11), Galilee (13), mnemonic device (15), Ayatollah Khomeini (19), Salman Rushdie (19), unabashedly (20), primordial (22), Cabalist (22), naturalized (23), iconography (23), gesticulations (26), colonialism (30), euphemistically (30), defunct (30), demise (30), obsolete (31).

Some of the Issues

1. What is the significance of Abu-Khalil's smuggling seven birds out of Palestine to the United States? What do these birds represent?
2. How is Shammas's concept of home different from Abu-Khalil's? What historical events have shaped younger Arabs' views?
3. Explain what Shammas means by "unlocked cages of our own choices" in paragraph 8.
4. How does Shammas distinguish the storyteller from the novelist in paragraphs 8 and 17?
5. In paragraph 17, Shammas asserts that many Middle Easterners are struggling to cast off "the bondage of their memory and decolonize their imagination." What are the political implications of this statement?
6. Shammas's friend J. married an Arab woman before coming to America. Why is it important for him to keep "the secret language circulating only in his veins?" (paragraph 22)?
7. In paragraph 23, what is the source of his friend J.'s confusion over the underwear ad in the Hebrew literary magazine? How does his friend's ignorance strike Shammas?
8. How do you understand the last line, "Amérka has made homesickness obsolete?"

The Way We Are Told

9. How does the squirrel metaphor in paragraphs 18 and 19 and 25-27 relate to the Middle Eastern experience?
10. Shammas uses part of Mark Twain's description of Palestine as that "most hopeless, dreary, heartbroken piece of territory out of Arizona" to underscore the fact that many Americans are geographically illiterate. He cites this American characteristic as a possible advantage. Why?
11. Find several examples of the author's humorous or sarcastic tone.
12. In paragraph 23, why is the word *naturalized* in quotation marks?

Some Subjects for Writing

*13. ". . . Home is a portable idea, something that dwells mainly in the mind or within a text" (paragraph 8). In an essay, consider what home means to you and develop a personal definition of "home." Illustrate your idea with your experience and if appropriate, the experiences of various authors in the text, among them, Maria L.

Muñiz in "Back, but Not Home," Marcus Mabry in "Living in Two Worlds," and John David Morley in "Living in a Japanese Home."

*14. Read Michel Guillaume St. Jean de Crèvecoeur's essay "What Is an American?" in which he describes the fusion of people of different nationalities into a new "race of men"—Americans. Contrast Shammas's description of America as a place where one can accommodate a "portable homeland." Do you concur with Shammas that in the Land of the Free it is fitting that one can live for decades without "being forced to go native?"

BARBA NIKOS

Harry Mark Petrakis

Harry Mark Petrakis was born in St. Louis in 1923 but has spent most of his life in and around Chicago. A novelist and short story writer, his books include *Pericles on 31st Street* (1965), *A Dream of Kings* (1966), and *Stelmark: A Family Recollection* (1970), from which the following selection is an excerpt.

In more recent years he has written *Reflections on a Writer's Life and Work* (1983) and published his *Collected Stories* (1983). Petrakis, himself of Greek descent, often sets the scene of his writing among Greek Americans and immigrants.

The story Petrakis tells describes the strains that can come between first- and second-generation immigrants, when the ways of the Old Country—and their parents' accented English—become a source of embarrassment. Young people, trying to conform with their peers, may find this situation particularly trying.

Located in the eastern Mediterranean, Greece has some 10 million inhabitants. It gained its independence in the nineteenth century after centuries of rule by the Turkish empire. It is a relatively poor country, many of whose people have sought their fortunes elsewhere, often in the United States, which has a large population of Greek descent.

Ancient Greece, the Greece Barba Nikos talks about so proudly, has often been called "the cradle of Western civilization." Among its many small city states, Athens stands out as the first representative democracy. Of the earliest philosophers, poets, historians, and scientists whose works have been preserved, most are Athenians. Achilles, whom Barba Nikos mentions, is a mythical warrior who plays a central role in Homer's *Iliad,* the epic poem about the war between the Greek city states and Troy. Alexander the Great, King of Macedonia, conquered the Middle East as far as India some 2,300 years ago. Marathon was not a race but a city in Greece where, in 490 B.C., the Athenians won a major battle against the invading Persians. According to legend, a Greek soldier ran from Marathon to Athens to carry the news of victory—before collapsing dead from the strain. He ran the same distance as the thousands who now run in marathons all over the world, except he ran it in full armor.

There was one storekeeper I remember above all others in my youth. It
was shortly before I became ill, spending a good portion of my time with
a motley group of varied ethnic ancestry. We contended with one
another to deride the customs of the old country. On our Saturday forays
into neighborhoods beyond our own, to prove we were really Americans,
we ate hot dogs and drank Cokes. If a boy didn't have ten cents for this
repast he went hungry, for he dared not bring a sandwich from home
made of the spiced meats our families ate.

One of our untamed games was to seek out the owner of a pushcart
or a store, unmistakably an immigrant, and bedevil him with a chorus of
insults and jeers. To prove allegiance to the gang it was necessary to
reserve our fiercest malevolence for a storekeeper or peddler belonging
to our own ethnic background.

For that reason I led a raid on the small, shabby grocery of old
Barba Nikos, a short, sinewy Greek who walked with a slight limp and
sported a flaring, handlebar mustache.

We stood outside his store and dared him to come out. When he
emerged to do battle, we plucked a few plums and peaches from the
baskets on the sidewalk and retreated across the street to eat them while
he watched. He waved a fist and hurled epithets at us in ornamental
Greek.

Aware that my mettle was being tested, I raised my arm and threw
my half-eaten plum at the old man. My aim was accurate and the plum
struck him on the cheek. He shuddered and put his hand to the stain. He
stared at me across the street, and although I could not see his eyes, I felt
them sear my flesh. He turned and walked silently back into the store.
The boys slapped my shoulders in admiration, but it was a hollow victory
that rested like a stone in the pit of my stomach.

At twilight when we disbanded, I passed the grocery alone on my
way home. There was a small light burning in the store and the shadow
of the old man's body outlined against the glass. Goaded by remorse, I
walked to the door and entered.

The old man moved from behind the narrow wooden counter and
stared at me. I wanted to turn and flee, but by then it was too late. As he
motioned for me to come closer, I braced myself for a curse or a blow.

"You were the one," he said, finally, in a harsh voice.

I nodded mutely.

"Why did you come back?"

I stood there unable to answer.

"What's your name?"

"Haralambos," I said, speaking to him in Greek.

He looked at me in shock. "You are Greek!" he cried. "A Greek boy
attacking a Greek grocer!" He stood appalled at the immensity of my
crime. "All right," he said coldly. "You are here because you wish to make

amends." His great mustache bristled in concentration. "Four plums, two peaches," he said. "That makes a total of 78 cents. Call it 75. Do you have 75 cents, boy?"

I shook my head.   15

"Then you will work it off," he said. "Fifteen cents an hour into 75   16
cents makes"—he paused—"five hours of work. Can you come here Saturday morning?"

"Yes," I said.   17

"Yes, Barba Nikos," he said sternly. "Show respect."   18

"Yes, Barba Nikos," I said.   19

"Saturday morning at eight o'clock," he said. "Now go home and   20
say thanks in your prayers that I did not loosen your impudent head with a solid smack on the ear." I needed no further urging and fled.

Saturday morning, still apprehensive, I returned to the store. I   21
began by sweeping, raising clouds of dust in dark and hidden corners. I washed the windows, whipping the squeegee swiftly up and down the glass in a fever of fear that some member of the gang would see me. When I finished I hurried back inside.

For the balance of the morning I stacked cans, washed the counter,   22
and dusted bottles of yellow wine. A few customers entered, and Barba Nikos served them. A little after twelve o'clock he locked the door so he could eat lunch. He cut himself a few slices of sausage, tore a large chunk from a loaf of crisp-crusted bread, and filled a small cup with a dozen black shiny olives floating in brine. He offered me the cup. I could not help myself and grimaced.

"You are a stupid boy," the old man said. "You are not really Greek,   23
are you?"

"Yes, I am."   24

"You might be," he admitted grudgingly. "But you do not act Greek.   25
Wrinkling your nose at these fine olives. Look around this store for a minute. What do you see?"

"Fruits and vegetables," I said. "Cheese and olives and things like   26
that."

He stared at me with a massive scorn. "That's what I mean," he said.   27
"You are a bonehead. You don't understand that a whole nation and a people are in this store."

I looked uneasily toward the storeroom in the rear, almost expect-   28
ing someone to emerge.

"What about olives?" he cut the air with a sweep of his arm. "There   29
are olives of many shapes and colors. Pointed black ones from Kalamata, oval ones from Amphissa, pickled green olives and sharp tangy yellow ones. Achilles carried black olives to Troy and after a day of savage battle leading his Myrmidons, he'd rest and eat cheese and ripe black olives such as these right here. You have heard of Achilles, boy, haven't you?"

"Yes," I said.   30

"Yes, Barba Nikos."   31

"Yes, Barba Nikos," I said.   32

He motioned at the row of jars filled with varied spices. "There is   33
origanon there and basilikon and daphne and sesame and miantanos, all
the marvelous flavorings that we have used in our food for thousands of
years. The men of Marathon carried small packets of these spices into
battle, and the scents reminded them of their homes, their families, and
their children."

He rose and tugged his napkin free from around his throat.   34
"Cheese, you said. Cheese! Come closer, boy, and I educate your abysmal
ignorance." He motioned toward a wooden container on the counter.
"That glistening white delight is feta, made from goat's milk, packed in
wooden buckets to retain the flavor. Alexander the Great demanded it on
his table with his casks of wine when he planned his campaigns."

He walked limping from the counter to the window where the piles   35
of tomatoes, celery, and green peppers clustered. "I suppose all you see
here are some random vegetables?" He did not wait for me to answer.
"You are dumb again. These are some of the ingredients that go to make
up a Greek salad. Do you know what a Greek salad really is? A meal in
itself, an experience, an emotional involvement. It is created deftly and
with grace. First, you place large lettuce leaves in a big, deep bowl." He
spread his fingers and moved them slowly, carefully, as if he were
arranging the leaves. "The remainder of the lettuce is shredded and piled
in a small mound," he said. "Then comes celery, cucumbers, tomatoes
sliced lengthwise, green peppers, origanon, green olives, feta, avocado
and anchovies. At the end you dress it with lemon, vinegar, and pure
olive oil, glinting golden in the light."

He finished with a heartfelt sigh and for a moment closed his eyes.   36
Then he opened one eye to mark me with a baleful intensity. "The story
goes that Zeus himself created the recipe and assembled and mixed the
ingredients on Mount Olympus one night when he had invited some of
the other gods to dinner."

He turned his back on me and walked slowly again across the store,   37
dragging one foot slightly behind him. I looked uneasily at the clock,
which showed that it was a few minutes past one. He turned quickly and
startled me. "And everything else in here," he said loudly. "White beans,
lentils, garlic, crisp bread, kokoretsi, meat balls, mussels and clams." He
paused and drew a deep, long breath. "And the wine," he went on, "wine
from Samos, Santorini, and Crete, retsina and mavrodaphne, a taste
almost as old as water . . . and then the fragrant melons, the pastries,
yellow diples and golden loukoumades, the honey custard galato-
bouriko. Everything a part of our history, as much a part as the exquisite
sculpture in marble, the bearded warriors, Pan and the oracles at Delphi,

and the nymphs dancing in the shadowed groves under Homer's glittering moon." He paused, out of breath again, and coughed harshly. "Do you understand now, boy?"

He watched my face for some response and then grunted. We stood silent for a moment until he cocked his head and stared at the clock. "It is time for you to leave," he motioned brusquely toward the door. "We are square now. Keep it that way." 38

I decided the old man was crazy and reached behind the counter for my jacket and cap and started for the door. He called me back. From a box he drew out several soft, yellow figs that he placed in a piece of paper. "A bonus because you worked well," he said. "Take them. When you taste them, maybe you will understand what I have been talking about." 39

I took the figs and he unlocked the door and I hurried from the store. I looked back once and saw him standing in the doorway, watching me, the swirling tendrils of food curling like mist about his head. 40

I ate the figs late that night. I forgot about them until I was in bed, and then I rose and took the package from my jacket. I nibbled at one, then ate them all. They broke apart between my teeth with a tangy nectar, a thick sweetness running like honey across my tongue and into the pockets of my cheeks. In the morning when I woke, I could still taste and inhale their fragrance. 41

I never again entered Barba Nikos's store. My spell of illness, which began some months later, lasted two years. When I returned to the streets I had forgotten the old man and the grocery. Shortly afterwards my family moved from the neighborhood. 42

Some twelve years later, after the war, I drove through the old neighborhood and passed the grocery. I stopped the car and for a moment stood before the store. The windows were stained with dust and grime, the interior bare and desolate, a store in a decrepit group of stores marked for razing so new structures could be built. 43

I have been in many Greek groceries since then and have often bought the feta and Kalamata olives. I have eaten countless Greek salads and have indeed found them a meal for the gods. On the holidays in our house, my wife and sons and I sit down to a dinner of steaming, buttered pilaf like my mother used to make and lemon-egg avgolemono and roast lamb richly seasoned with cloves of garlic. I drink the red and yellow wines, and for dessert I have come to relish the delicate pastries coated with honey and powdered sugar. Old Barba Nikos would have been pleased. 44

But I have never been able to recapture the halcyon flavor of those figs he gave me on that day so long ago, although I have bought figs many times. I have found them pleasant to my tongue, but there is something missing. And to this day I am not sure whether it was the figs or the vision and passion of the old grocer that coated the fruit so sweetly I can still recall their savor and fragrance after almost thirty years. 45

Exercises

Some Important Words

motley (paragraph 1), deride (1), foray (1), repast (1), bedevil (2), allegiance (2), appalled (14), immensity (14), Achilles (29), Troy (29), Myrmidons (29), Marathon (33), Alexander the Great (34), Zeus (36), Mount Olympus (36), Pan (37), Delphi (37), Homer (37), halcyon (45).

Some of the Issues

1. Why do the gang members attack immigrants of their own ethnic group?
2. What is the first sign that the narrator will change his mind about his deed?
3. What is the boy's first reaction to the olives? How does it set the scene for later reactions?
4. What does Barba Nikos mean when he says, "a whole nation and a people are in this store"?

The Way We Are Told

5. In the first four paragraphs the author uses a number of rather unusual words and phrases for simple events: *motley, repast, untamed, bedevil, malevolence, to do battle.* What effect is achieved by this choice?
6. Contrast the tone of the narrative frame at the beginning and end of the selection with the telling of the story through dialog in the middle. What is the effect?
7. Examine the various references to Barba Nikos throughout the selection. What impression do we have of him in the beginning? How does it change?
8. List the various references linking food and drink to mythology. What is their purpose?
9. In what way do the last two paragraphs sum up the theme of the essay?

Some Subjects for Writing

10. Describe a time when you did something against your better judgment, perhaps under pressure from friends. What exactly was the pressure that led you to it, and how did you feel afterwards?
*11. Read Michael Novak's "In Ethnic America." Novak asserts that ethnics—Greeks among them—have subtly been made to feel inferior in America. In an essay examine why and how Novak's view accounts for the attitude Petrakis's narrator initially displays.

THREE THOUSAND DOLLAR DEATH SONG

Wendy Rose

Wendy Rose, of Hopi-Miwok ancestry, was born in Oakland, California, in 1948. She received B.A. and M.A. degrees from the University of California at Berkeley. A visual artist, poet, anthropologist, and frequent contributor of articles to anthologies, books, and journals, she has published numerous volumes of poetry, often concerned with Native American themes.

In the following poem from *Lost Copper* (1980), Rose protests museum collections and displays of Native American mummies and skeletal parts. For many Native Americans, the exhibiting of their ancestors' remains is a continued source of pain and humiliation. In recent years, Native American activists and other groups have demanded that the museums return the bones for reburial; in 1990 a federal law took effect requiring the return of such items to the tribe or association.

"Nineteen American Indian Skeletons from Nevada . . . valued at $3000 . . ."

—Museum invoice, 1975

Is it in cold hard cash? the kind
that dusts the insides of mens' pockets
lying silver-polished surface along the cloth.
Or in bills? papering the wallets of they
who thread the night with dark words. Or
checks? paper promises weighing the same
as words spoken once on the other side
of the grown grass and dammed rivers
of history. However it goes, it goes.
Through my body it goes
assessing each nerve, running its edges
along my arteries, planning ahead
for whose hands will rip me

into pieces of dusty red paper,
whose hands will smooth or smatter me
into traces of rubble. Invoiced now,
it's official how our bones are valued
that stretch out pointing to sunrise
or are flexed into one last foetal bend,
that are removed and tossed about,
catalogued, numbered with black ink
on newly-white foreheads.
As we were formed to the white soldier's voice,
so we explode under white students' hands.
Death is a long trail of days
in our fleshless prison.

From this distant point we watch our bones
auctioned with our careful beadwork,
our quilled medicine bundles, even the bridles
of our shot-down horses.   You: who have
priced us, you who have removed us: at what cost?
What price the pits where our bones share
a single bit of memory, how one century
turns our dead into specimens, our history
into dust, our survivors into clowns.
Our memory might be catching, you know;
picture the mortars, the arrowheads, the labrets[1]
shaking off their labels like bears
suddenly awake to find the seasons have ended
while they slept. Watch them touch each other,
measure reality, march out the museum door!
Watch as they lift their faces
and smell about for us; watch our bones rise
to meet them and mount the horses once again!
The cost, then, will be paid
for our sweetgrass-smelling having-been
in clam shell beads and steatite,
dentalia[2] and woodpecker scalp, turquoise
and copper, blood and oil, coal
and uranium, children, a universe
of stolen things.

---

[1]*Labrets* are ornaments of wood or bone worn in a hole pierced through the lip.
[2]*Dentalia* refers to any marine mollusk resembling a tooth.

PART THREE

Families

The American family we used to consider the norm in the postwar generation of the 1940s and 1950s is now the minority. The traditional family in which children grow up in the same household with two biological parents who are married to each other is being replaced by an array of differently formed families. The selections in Part Three examine the lives of children in traditional families, the changing definition of family structures, and the notion of the "perfect" family, mother, or child.

In "Don't Expect Me to Be Perfect" by Sun Park, a 16-year-old Korean-American reacts to her parents' strong expectations that she excel in schoolwork. In the following selection, Alfred Kazin recounts the story of his eastern European immigrant family, held together by the ceaseless work and worry of his mother.

Jane Howard, in "Families," gives 10 characteristics she believes all "good" families must have. In her 1992 *New York Times* article, "The Good Mother," Susan Chira chronicles one change in the definition of the family: the lives of one-parent families headed by the mother. Arlene Skolnick's essay "The Paradox of Perfection" helps us to consider the family in the light of its historical development. As Skolnick reveals, the "traditional" family has actually not been the norm for society except in fairly recent times, and then only in some cultures.

In "Two Kinds" by Amy Tan, a Chinese mother defines the "good" daughter much to her American-born daughter's dismay. Part Three concludes with a poem by Theodore Roethke, a brief glimpse of a child's memory of his father.

115

DON'T EXPECT ME
TO BE PERFECT

Sun Park

This essay first appeared in a 1990 special edition of *Newsweek* for teenagers. Sun Park writes about some of the problems she and others face in trying to meet parental expectations.

I am a 16-year-old Korean-American. My family has been in the United States for six years now. I'll be a junior next fall.

When I first came to the States, it took two years before I could speak English fluently. By the time I started middle school, I realized that most of my fellow students had never met many kids like me before. They had this idea, probably from TV and movies, that all Asians are nerds and all Asians are smart. It's true that some are. I know many smart people. But what about those Asians who aren't so smart? Having a reputation for brains is nice, I guess, but it can also be a pain. For instance, sometimes when my classmates do not know something, they come to me for the answer. Often I can help them. But when I can't, they get these weird expressions on their faces. If I were a genius, I would not mind being treated like one. But since I am not, I do.

The problem isn't just limited to the classroom. My mother and father expect an awful lot from me, too. Like so many Korean parents, and many ambitious American parents, they're very competitive and can't help comparing me with other kids. Mine always say to me, "So and so is smart, works so hard and is so good to his or her parents. Why can't you be more like him or her?" Because I am the oldest kid in my family, they expect me to set a good example for my younger sisters and relatives. They'd rather I concentrate on schoolwork than dating. They want me to be No. 1.

Most of the time I want to do well, too. I'm glad I take all honors classes. But now that I am at those levels, I have to be on my toes to keep doing well. The better I do, the more pressure I seem to place on myself. Because my parents want me to be perfect—or close to perfect—I find myself turning into a perfectionist. When I do a project and make one little error, I can't stand it. Sometimes I stay up as late as 2 A.M. doing homework.

116

I don't think I would be like this if my parents weren't motivating   5
me. But I don't think they know what pressure can do to a teenager. It's
not that they put me down or anything. They have plenty of faith in me.
But to tell the truth, sometimes I really like to be lazy, and it would be
nice just to take it easy and not worry so much about my grades all the
time. Maybe my parents know this. Maybe that's why they encourage me
to be better. Well, it still drives me crazy when they compare me with
others. I wonder if those smart kids have parents like mine.

Sure, I'm proud of who I am, and I love my parents very much. But   6
then there are times I just feel like taking a break and going far away from
parents and teachers. Of course that's impossible, but it's always nice to
dream about it.

Exercises

Some Important Words

fluently (paragraph 2), perfectionist (4), motivating (5).

Some of the Issues

1. What image of Asians do most of Park's classmates have? How does
   this image affect her relationships with other students?
2. How does she react to her parents' wishes that she achieve high marks?
3. What are some of the manifestations of her "perfectionism"? Do you
   think there is anything wrong with this behavior?

The Way We Are Told

4. How would you describe the tone of this essay? How does her
   audience affect the tone? Find specific phrases and words from the
   text to illustrate your answer.
5. What is the author's purpose in writing this essay? What lines best
   express it?
6. What is the author's attitude toward her parents? How do you know?

Some Subjects for Writing

7. Do you know any perfectionists? Describe their behavior and characteristics. What is your own attitude toward perfectionism?
8. Sun Park wonders if other "smart kids have parents like mine." Have
   you ever felt this way? From your own school experiences, have you
   noticed any connection between academic achievement and parental involvement?

9. Park dreams of "going far away from parents and teachers" as a solution to her problem. Have you ever had these feelings? Can you think of better options?

*10. Read "The Media's Image of Arabs," in which Jack G. Shaheen enumerates the negative images of Arabs in the American media. Park believes that Asians are also depicted as stereotypes, yet with images that many would view as positive—intelligent and hard-working. Is one stereotype less damaging than another?

THE KITCHEN

Alfred Kazin

Alfred Kazin, born in New York in 1915, has taught at several universities, most recently at the City University of New York. He has held several distinguished fellowships and is a member of the American Academy of Arts and Sciences. His books include *On Native Grounds* (1942), *The Inmost Leaf* (1955), *Starting Out in the Thirties* (1965), *New York Jew* (1978), and *An American Procession* (1984).

In this selection from *A Walker in the City* (1957) Kazin describes the setting in which he grew up. It was not unusual for its time and place: a tenement district in a large American city, peopled with immigrants from eastern Europe, working hard, struggling for a life for themselves and more importantly for their children.

The large-scale immigration that brought as many as one million new inhabitants annually from Europe to America lasted from the 1880s to the First World War. The majority of the immigrants in those years came from eastern, southern, and central Europe. They included large numbers of Jewish families like Kazin's, escaping not only the stifling poverty of their regions but also the outright persecution, the pogroms, to which they were subjected in Czarist Russia.

In Brownsville tenements the kitchen is always the largest room and the center of the household. As a child I felt we lived in a kitchen to which four other rooms were annexed. My mother, a "home" dressmaker, had her workshop in the kitchen. She told me once that she had begun dressmaking in Poland at thirteen; as far back as I can remember, she was always making dresses for the local women. She had an innate sense of design, a quick eye for all the subtleties in the latest fashions, even when she despised them, and great boldness. For three or four dollars she would study the fashion magazines with a customer, go with the customer to the remnants store on Belmont Avenue to pick out the material, argue the owner down—all remnants stores, for some reason, were supposed to be shady, as if the owners dealt in stolen goods—and then for days would patiently fit and baste and sew and fit again. Our apartment was always full of women in their housedresses sitting around the kitchen table waiting for a fitting. My little bedroom next to the kitchen was the fitting room. The sewing machine, an old nut-brown Singer with golden scrolls painted along the black arm and engraved along the two tiers of little drawers massed with needles and thread on each side of the treadle, stood next to the window and the great coal-black stove which up to my last year in college was our main source of heat. By December the two outer bedrooms were closed off, and used to chill bottles of milk and cream, cold borscht and jellied calves' feet.

The kitchen held our lives together. My mother worked in it all day long, we ate in it almost all meals except the Passover *seder,* I did my homework and first writing at the kitchen table, and in winter I often had a bed made up for me on three kitchen chairs near the stove. On the wall just over the table hung a long horizontal mirror that sloped to a ship's prow at each end and was lined in cherry wood. It took up the whole wall, and drew every object in the kitchen to itself. The walls were a fiercely stippled whitewash, so often rewhitened by my father in slack seasons that the paint looked as if it had been squeezed and cracked into the walls. A large electric bulb hung down the center of the kitchen at the end of a chain that had been hooked into the ceiling; the old gas ring and key still jutted out of the wall like antlers. In the corner next to the toilet was the sink at which we washed, and the square tub in which my mother did our clothes. Above it, tacked to the shelf on which were pleasantly ranged square, blue bordered white sugar and spice jars, hung calendars from the Public National Bank on Pitkin Avenue and the Minsker Progressive Branch of the Workman's Circle; receipts for the payment of insurance premiums, and household bills on a spindle; two little boxes engraved with Hebrew letters. One of these was for the poor, the other to buy back the Land of Israel. Each spring a bearded little man would suddenly appear in our kitchen, salute us with a hurried Hebrew blessing, empty the boxes (sometimes with a sidelong look of disdain if they were not full), hurriedly bless us again for remembering our less fortunate Jewish brothers and sisters, and so take his departure until the next spring, after vainly trying to persuade my mother to take still another box. We did occasionally remember to drop coins in the boxes, but this was usually only on the dreaded morning of "mid-terms" and final examinations, because my mother thought it would bring me luck. She was extremely superstitious, but embarrassed about it, and always laughed at herself whenever, on the morning of an examination, she counseled me to leave the house on my right foot. "I know it's silly," her smile seemed to say, "but what harm can it do? It may calm God down."

The kitchen gave a special character to our lives; my mother's character. All my memories of that kitchen are dominated by the nearness of my mother sitting all day long at her sewing machine, by the clacking of the treadle against the linoleum floor, by the patient twist of her right shoulder as she automatically pushed at the wheel with one hand or lifted the foot to free the needle where it had got stuck in a thick piece of material. The kitchen was her life. Year by year, as I began to take in her fantastic capacity for labor and her anxious zeal, I realized it was ourselves she kept stitched together. I can never remember a time when she was not working. She worked because the law of her life was work, work and anxiety; she worked because she would have found life meaningless without work. She read almost no English; she could read the Yiddish paper, but never felt she had time to. We were always talking of a time when I would teach her how to read, but somehow there was never time. When I awoke in the morning she was already at her machine, or in the great morning crowd of housewives at the grocery getting fresh rolls for breakfast. When I returned from school she was at her machine, or conferring over *McCall's* with some neighborhood woman who had come in pointing hopefully to an illustration—"Mrs. Kazin! Mrs. Kazin! Make me a dress like it shows here in the picture!" When my father came home from work she had somehow mysteriously interrupted herself to make supper for us, and the dishes cleared and washed, was back at her machine. When I went to bed at night, often she was still there, pounding away at the treadle, hunched over the wheel, her hands steering a piece of gauze under the needle with a finesse that always contrasted sharply with her swollen hands and broken nails. Her left hand had been pierced through when as a girl she had worked in the infamous Triangle Shirtwaist Factory on the East Side. A needle had gone straight through the palm, severing a large vein. They had sewn it up for her so clumsily that a tuft of flesh always lay folded over the palm.

The kitchen was the great machine that set our lives running; it 4 whirred down a little only on Saturdays and holy days. From my mother's kitchen I gained my first picture of life as a white, overheated, starkly lit workshop redolent with Jewish cooking, crowded with women in housedresses, strewn with fashion magazines, patterns, dress material, spools of thread—and at whose center, so lashed to her machine that bolts of energy seemed to dance out of her hands and feet as she worked, my mother stamped the treadle hard against the floor, hard, hard, and silently, grimly at war, beat out the first rhythm of the world for me.

Exercises

Some Important Words

tenement (paragraph 1), innate (1), Passover *seder* (2), stippled (2), Triangle Shirtwaist Factory (3).

Some of the Issues

1. Kazin writes about the kitchen in his childhood home. Is he writing from the point of view of a child or an adult? What indications do you have of one or the other?
2. In speaking of his mother, Kazin says, "The law of her life was work, work and anxiety." In an age in which many people's goal is self-fulfillment this does not seem to be a happy life. Can you find any evidence as to whether Mrs. Kazin was happy or unhappy? What pleasures did she have?
3. What is the meaning of the first sentence in paragraph 4? Why does Kazin call the kitchen "the great machine"?

The Way We Are Told

4. The same two words are repeated in the first sentence of each paragraph. What purpose does that repetition serve?
5. Compare the first two paragraphs. How do they differ from each other in content and in the way they are written?
6. Kazin talks about the kitchen of his childhood home but does not describe it until the second paragraph. What would be the effect if he had started with that description?
7. Reread the second paragraph. What details does Kazin give? How are they arranged—in which kind of order? Could an artist draw a picture on the basis of Kazin's description? Could an architect draw a plan from it?
8. Kazin describes several items in detail—the sewing machine, aspects of the kitchen itself, and his mother's work. Find some adjectives that stand out because they are unusual or that add precision or feeling to his descriptions.

Some Subjects for Writing

9. Write a paragraph about a place of significance for you, using Kazin's second paragraph as your model. Try to show its significance by the way you describe it.
10. Consider the role of work in the life of Kazin's mother. If you know someone whose life seems completely tied up with some specific activity, describe that person through his or her activity.
11. More and more women are joining the work force in America in the 1990s. Many of them are married and have children. Write an essay in which you discuss the causes for this major social change and argue either for or against it.
*12. Read Arlene Skolnick's "The Paradox of Perfection." Examine the extent to which Kazin's family represents the kind of family Skolnick describes, particularly in paragraphs 23–27.

FAMILIES

Jane Howard

Jane Howard, born in Springfield, Illinois, in 1935, is a reporter, editor, and writer. Among her books are *Please Touch: A Guided Tour of the Human Potential Movement* (1970), the autobiographical *A Different Woman* (1973), and *Families* (1978). Her latest book is *Margaret Mead: A Life* (1984). She has taught at several universities.

Howard explains 10 characteristics good families should have. Her definition of a family includes not only the one you are born into but also those we may develop through close friendships.

Each of us is born into one family not of our choosing. If we're going to go around devising new ones, we might as well have the luxury of picking their members ourselves. Clever picking might result in new families whose benefits would surpass or at least equal those of the old. The new ones by definition cannot spawn us—as soon as they do that, they stop being new—but there is plenty they can do. I have seen them work wonders. As a member in reasonable standing of six or seven tribes in addition to the one I was born to, I have been trying to figure which earmarks are common to both kinds of families.

(1) Good families have a chief, or a heroine, or a founder— someone around whom others cluster, whose achievements as the Yiddish word has it, let them *kvell,* and whose example spurs them on to like feats. Some blood dynasties produce such figures regularly; others languish for as many as five generations between demigods, wondering with each new pregnancy whether this, at last, might be the messianic baby who will redeem us. Look, is there not something gubernatorial about her footstep, or musical about the way he bangs with his spoon on his cup? All clans, of all kinds, need such a figure now and then. Sometimes clans based on water rather than blood harbor several such personages at one time. The Bloomsbury Group in London six decades ago was not much hampered by its lack of a temporal history.

(2) Good families have a switchboard operator—someone like my mother who cannot help but keep track of what all the others are up to, who plays Houston Mission Control to everyone else's Apollo. This role, like the foregoing one, is assumed rather than assigned. Someone always

123

volunteers for it. That person often also has the instincts of an archivist, and feels driven to keep scrapbooks and photograph albums up to date, so that the clan can see proof of its own continuity.

(3) Good families are much to all their members, but everything to   4
none. Good families are fortresses with many windows and doors to the outer world. The blood clans I feel most drawn to were founded by parents who are nearly as devoted to whatever it is they do outside as they are to each other and their children. Their curiosity and passion are contagious. Everybody, where they live, is busy. Paint is spattered on eyeglasses. Mud lurks under fingernails. Person-to-person calls come in the middle of the night from Tokyo and Brussels. Catchers' mitts, ballet slippers, overdue library books and other signs of extrafamilial concerns are everywhere.

(4) Good families are hospitable. Knowing that hosts need guests as   5
much as guests need hosts, they are generous with honorary member-ships for friends, whom they urge to come early and often and to stay late. Such clans exude a vivid sense of surrounding rings of relatives, neighbors, teachers, students and godparents, any of whom at any time might break or slide into the inner circle. Inside that circle a wholesome, tacit emotional feudalism develops: you give me protection, I'll give you fealty. Such treaties begin with, but soon go far beyond, the jolly exchange of pie at Thanksgiving for cake on birthdays. It means you can ask me to supervise your children for the fortnight you will be in the hospital, and that however inconvenient this might be for me, I shall manage to. It means I can phone you on what for me is a dreary, wretched Sunday afternoon and for you is the eve of a deadline, knowing you will tell me to come right over, if only to watch you type. It means we need not dissemble. ("To yield to seeming," as Buber wrote, "is man's essential cowardice, to resist it is his essential courage . . . one must at times pay dearly for life lived from the being, but it is never too dear.")

(5) Good families deal squarely with direness. Pity the tribe that   6
doesn't have, and cherish, at least one flamboyant eccentric. Pity too the one that supposes it can avoid for long the woes to which all flesh is heir. Lunacy, bankruptcy, suicide and other unthinkable fates sooner or later afflict the noblest of clans with an undertow of gloom. Family life is a set of givens, someone once told me, and it takes courage to see certain givens as blessings rather than as curses. Contradictions and inconsisten-cies are givens, too. So is the war against what the Oregon patriarch Kenneth Babbs calls malarkey. "There's always malarkey lurking, bub-bles in the cesspool, fetid bubbles that pop and smell. But I don't put up with malarkey, between my stepkids and my natural ones or anywhere else in the family."

(6) Good families prize their rituals. Nothing welds a family more   7
than these. Rituals are vital especially for clans without histories, because

they evoke a past, imply a future, and hint at continuity. No line in the Seder service at Passover reassures more than the last: "Next year in Jerusalem!" A clan becomes more of a clan each time it gathers to observe a fixed ritual (Christmas, birthdays, Thanksgiving, and so on), grieve at a funeral (anyone may come to most funerals; those who do declare their tribalness), and devises a new rite of its own. Equinox breakfasts and all-white dinners can be at least as welding as Memorial Day parades. Several of us in the old *Life* magazine years used to meet for lunch every Pearl Harbor Day, preferably to eat some politically neutral fare like smorgasbord, to "forgive" our only ancestrally Japanese colleague Irene Kubota Neves. For that and other reasons we became, and remain, a sort of family.

"Rituals," a California friend of mine said, "aren't just externals and   8
holidays. They are the performances of our lives. They are a kind of shorthand. They can't be decreed. My mother used to try to decree them. She's make such a goddamn fuss over what we talked about at dinner, aiming at Topics of Common Interest, topics that celebrated our cohesion as a family. These performances were always hollow, because the phenomenology of the moment got sacrificed for the *idea* of the moment. Real rituals are discovered in retrospect. They emerge around constitutive moments, moments that only happen once, around whose memory meanings cluster. You don't choose those moments. They choose themselves." A lucky clan includes a born mythologizer, like my blood sister, who has the gift of apprehending such a moment when she sees it, and who cannot help but invent new rituals everywhere she goes.

(7) Good families are affectionate. This is of course a matter of   9
style. I know clans whose members greet each other with gingerly handshakes or, in what pass for kisses, with hurried brushes of side jawbones, as if the object were to touch not the lips but the ears. I don't see how such people manage. "The tribe that does not hug," as someone who has been part of many *ad hoc* families recently wrote to me, "is no tribe at all. More and more I realize that everybody, regardless of age, needs to be hugged and comforted in a brotherly or sisterly way now and then. Preferably now."

(8) Good families have a sense of place, which these days is not   10
achieved easily. As Susanne Langer wrote in 1957, "Most people have no home that is a symbol of their childhood, not even a definite memory of one place to serve that purpose . . . all the old symbols are gone." Once I asked a roomful of supper guests who, if anyone, felt any strong pull to any certain spot on the face of the earth. Everyone was silent, except for a visitor from Bavaria. The rest of us seemed to know all too well what Walker Percy means in *The Moviegoer* when he tells of the "genie-soul of the place which every place has or else is not a place [and which]

wherever you go, you must meet and master or else be met and mastered." All that meeting and mastering saps plenty of strength. It also underscores our need for tribal bases of the sort which soaring real estate taxes and splintering families have made all but obsolete.

So what are we to do, those of us whose habit and pleasure and doom is our tendency, as a Georgia lady put it, to "fly off at every other whipstitch?" Think in terms of movable feasts, for a start. Live here, wherever here may be, as if we were going to belong here for the rest of our lives. Learn to hallow whatever ground we happen to stand on or land on. Like medieval knights who took their tapestries along on Crusades, like modern Afghanis with their yurts, we must pack such totems and icons as we can to make short-term quarters feel like home. Pillows, small rugs, watercolors can dispel much of the chilling anonymity of a sublet apartment or motel room. When we can, we should live in rooms with stoves or fireplaces or anyway candlelight. The ancient saying still is true: Extinguished hearth, extinguished family. Round tables help, too, and as a friend of mine once put it, so do "too many comfortable chairs, with surfaces to put feet on, arranged so as to encourage a maximum of eye contact." Such rooms inspire good talk, of which good clans can never have enough.

(9) Good families, not just the blood kind, find some way to connect with posterity. "To forge a link in the humble chain of being, encircling heirs to ancestors," as Michael Novak has written, "is to walk within a circle of magic as primitive as humans knew in caves." He is talking of course about babies, feeling them leap in wombs, giving them suck. Parenthood, however, is a state which some miss by chance and others by design, and a vocation to which not all are called. Some of us, like the novelist Richard P. Brickner, "look on as others name their children who in turn name their own lives, devising their own flags from their parents' cloth." What are we who lack children to do? Build houses? Plant trees? Write books or symphonies or laws? Perhaps, but even if we do these things, there still should be children on the sidelines, if not at the center, of our lives. It is a sadly impoverished tribe that does not allow access to, and make much of, some children. Not too much, of course: it has truly been said that never in history have so many educated people devoted so much attention to so few children. Attention, in excess, can turn to fawning, which isn't much better than neglect. Still, if we don't regularly see and talk to and laugh with people who can expect to outlive us by twenty years or so, we had better get busy and find some.

(10) Good families also honor their elders. The wider the age range, the stronger the tribe. Jean-Paul Sartre and Margaret Mead, to name two spectacularly confident former children, have both remarked on the central importance of grandparents in their own early lives.

Grandparents now are in much more abundant supply than they were a generation or two ago when old age was more rare. If actual grandparents are not at hand, no family should have too hard a time finding substitute ones to whom to give unfeigned homage. The Soviet Union's enchantment with day care centers, I have heard, stems at least in part from the state's eagerness to keep children away from their presumably subversive grandparents. Let that be a lesson to clans based on interest as well as to those based on genes.

Exercises

Some Important Words

messianic (paragraph 2), Bloomsbury Group (2), temporal (2), exude (5), feudalism (5), fortnight (5), direness (6), flamboyant (6), inconsistencies (6), Passover (7), Equinox (7), smorgasbord (7), decreed (8), constitutive (8), whipstitch (11), Crusades (11), anonymity (11), posterity (12), fawning (12), Jean-Paul Sartre (13), Margaret Mead (13).

Some of the Issues

1. In paragraph 1, and elsewhere in her book *Families,* Howard suggests that people should build their own families, "devising new ones" with friends, supplementing (or replacing?) natural families. What do you think of her idea?
2. In offering her 10 "earmarks . . . common to both kinds of families" does she distinguish at any time between "natural" and "new" families? If so, in what way?
3. Look at each of the 10 points, and consider if each one is convincing. If you agree, try to add evidence from your own experience. If you disagree, try to develop counterarguments.
*4. Read Alfred Kazin's "The Kitchen." Which of the 10 points fit that family and why?

The Way We Are Told

5. Each of the 10 points begins in exactly the same way. What is the effect of this repetition?
6. Describe how each of the points is constructed. How is the content arranged? How consistent is the arrangement?
7. Howard frequently uses what one can call "the part for the whole"; examples are the last two sentences of point 3; or, in point 4, "you can ask me to supervise your children for the fortnight you will be in the hospital." Find other examples. What is their effect?

Some Subjects for Writing

8. Select a topic similar to Howard's, for example, "The good citizen," or "An educated person," or "An effective teacher." Then treat it as Howard might, developing the points one by one that together constitute a series of definitions of the subject.
9. Are gangs families? Argue for or against that proposition.
10. Howard's definitions are implicitly based on mainstream American culture. On the basis of your experience or reading, would you say that her definitions hold for families in another culture?

THE GOOD MOTHER: SEARCHING FOR AN IDEAL

Susan Chira

This article first appeared in the *New York Times* on October 4, 1992, as the first in a series on the changing roles of mothers. Preview the reporter's main ideas by skimming the title, headings, and subheadings of the text. Then examine the evidence that Chira marshals to support her claim that the definition of motherhood has changed. Use the data from the Census Bureau and American Demographics on the accompanying charts and map to track the changes in the traditional family unit.

The American mother—that self-sacrificing, self-effacing, cookie-baking   1
icon—has been shoved into the center of a political morality play, one where stick-figure mothers battle in a debate that does not begin to suggest the complexity, diversity and confusion of being a mother in 1992.

Instead of Marilyn Quayle and Hillary Clinton, those emblems of   2
stay-at-home and working mothers, talk to Toni Rumsey, who cried when her first child was born and realized she would have to keep her factory job at Gerber Baby Foods here in Fremont or face living in a trailer.

Or Stacy Murdock, who watches every penny on her farm in   3
Murray, Ky., because her family's income dropped by more than half when she quit teaching, unable to bear leaving her children.

Or Nancy Cassidy, a garment worker in Easton, Pa., who loves to   4
work and believes her children are the better for it.

These mothers are haunted by the ghost of the mythical 1950's   5
television mother—one that most women today cannot be, even if they want to. Caught between a fictional ideal, changing expectations of women's roles and the reality that many mothers now work because they must, women around the country are groping for a new definition of the good mother.

129

Reshaping Motherhood

The old images linger, but they fit fewer people's lives. Motherhood in America has undergone a breathtaking transformation in little more than 30 years, propelled by shrinking wages of husbands and changing social attitudes.   6

In 1960, 20 percent of mothers with children under 6 years old were in the labor force; by last year the figure had swelled to 58 percent, with most of them working full time. Twenty-nine percent of all American families are now headed by one parent.   7

Some more affluent women choose to work for self-fulfillment, and some who started out that way found that they could not afford to leave their jobs as the economy soured. Whether or not a conservative backlash movement is trying to shame women into staying at home, more and more mothers see work as a financial and personal necessity.   8

Small wonder, then, that Republican strategists quickly folded their family values banner when they found the reality of motherhood in this election year at odds with campaign slogans. With politicians in both parties now courting middle America, many of these same working-class women have been forced to take jobs outside the home, often monotonous and regimented ones at low wages that may not allow them to buy help with child care and housecleaning.   9

As interviews with more than 30 mothers around the country show, politicians have waded into one of the most wrenching issues of American life.   10

"I never feel like I'm a full mom," said Mrs. Rumsey, a 34-year-old mother of two who checks Gerber's baby food for shards of glass and signs of spoilage from 7 A.M. to 3 P.M. "I make the cookies, the homemade costumes for Halloween. I volunteer for everything to make up to them for not being here. When I do all that, I make myself so tired that they lose a happy cheerful mom, and then I'm cheating them again. It's hard when you were raised with Donna Reed and the Beav's mom."   11

In another factory in Easton, Pa., Mrs. Cassidy inspects sportswear, and her life as a working mother, for flaws. "I think you can work and be a good mother," said the 42-year-old mother of two. "We're doing it. When people compliment you that they're nice children, then I think you've been a terrific mother."   12

The Old Ideal: Mythic Verities and Apple Pie

Some women have found that they could not be good mothers in the old sense because working has become so important to their identities.   13

These women say they know in their hearts that being at home all day does not automatically make a good mother.

"You can be there without being there," said Cheryl Moorefield, a labor nurse in Winston-Salem, N.C., who has two children.   14

Yet ask most women their image of a good mother, and the old verities come tumbling forth. "A mother doesn't have a right to be tired or sick," said Deborah Gray, a 38-year-old mother of six whose shift can run 12 hours a day during the busy summer season at Heinz's pickling plant in Holland, Mich. "A mother must be available no matter what. A mother is a person that can perform miracles."   15

In Murray, Ky., which boasts the National Scouting Museum, tobacco and soybean farms, a state university branch and what seems like a church on every corner, Stacy Murdock comes close to this cherished ideal. Mrs. Murdock, who gave up her teaching job, is up at 6 A.M., starts breakfast and then wakes her three children a half-hour later. The whole family eats breakfast at 7 A.M., and then her husband drives the two older children to school. Her husband, one of a vanishing breed of small farmers who can work close to home, tends his 600 acres of corn, beans, wheat and cattle while his wife plays with her 14-month-old daughter, cleans, cooks and pays bills. At noon he returns for a hot meal with his family.   16

By 2:30 P.M., Mrs. Murdock is on her way to school to pick up her older daughters. Some afternoons she takes them to dancing school, which she pays for by keeping the school's books. On Wednesdays the children's grandmother drops by to baby-sit so that Mrs. Murdock can volunteer at the older children's school.   17

"The most important thing you're going to get in your life is your children," Mrs. Murdock said, explaining why the family has given up eating out, planning for a bigger house and having many other extras. "I just can't imagine giving that responsibility to someone else."   18

It is precisely because convictions about what kind of mother is best run so strong and deep that family values became such an explosive issue. Despite all the talk about fathers' becoming more involved with children, it is mothers who remain at the center of this debate, and mothers who shoulder the praise or blame. Most women interviewed said they were worried about the future of the family, but many said the debate, at least as conducted by politicians, seemed irrelevant or insulting.   19

"Family values is a cheap way out," Mrs. Rumsey said. "We all believe in family morals and values. I'm not going to put down what you're doing and don't put me down for what I'm trying to do."   20

For some, the debate intensified their own guilt. "My heart pounds a little bit," said Kris Northrop, the mother of a 4-month-old girl, who has just returned to her job running a candy-wrapping machine at the Life   21

Savers plant in Holland, Mich. "I think, Is this right? Should I try to not be a working mother, even though my image is of an independent mother?"

And for others the verdict is clear: working and mothering small   22
children cannot mix. "I had these children and I wanted to raise them," said Celisa Cunningham, a Baptist minister's wife who returned to work designing and supervising asphalt mixes once her children started school. "I've given 10 years to my children and I'm going to give 30 to my career, and I'm going to see more from those 10 years in the long run than from the 30. I think many mothers cop out and make a life-style choice."

The New Reality: Harried Jugglers on a Tightrope

But for many working-class women, Mrs. Murdock's life, and the com-   23
fortable certainties invoked by the champions of family values, are as remote as the television characters that helped shape their idea of the good mother.

Instead of family breakfasts and school volunteer work, Jan Flint   24
works nights and her husband works days in a Welch's juice and jam plant in Lawton, Mich., so that one of them can always be home with the children.

"That's what God meant for me—to stay at home, cook and sew,   25
and I can't do that," said Mrs. Flint, who had to return to work seven years ago when money got tight. "I used to have a clean house all the time. I always enjoyed being involved in my older two's education. Last night was open house and my children wanted me to go. I bribed them—'I'll let you bring friends over if I don't go.' That's what's happening to the American family. Nobody's there, and children don't have full-time guidance."

Measuring themselves against such an exacting, idealized standard,   26
where good mothering equals how much time is spent with the children rather than how secure or happy the children are, many working women feel they fall short. For the most part, these women struggle without help from society or their employers, who seldom give them long maternity leaves or flexible hours.

And because motherhood itself has been transformed in less than a   27
generation, these mothers have no guides. "What is happening now is that parents are relying on child care who themselves were often raised

by their mothers," said Deborah Phillips, a psychologist and expert in child development at the University of Virginia. "So there is incredible anxiety and uncertainty, especially in a society that holds firmly to the belief that mother care is superior."

Sheila Lencki, a mother of four who works as a school secretary in Murray, Ky., says she fears she is failing to meet the standard her own mother set.   28

"My own mother stayed at home, and that's what I wanted to do," she said. "I respect my mother so much. I think that everything she does is right."   29

Even more troubling, many women fear they have somehow relinquished their children. "When I put them in day care, I did feel a pull; I'm not the one raising my children," said Mrs. Moorefield, who raised her two children alone for seven years until her remarriage several years ago. "Who's teaching them values?"   30

That anxiety deepens if mothers suspect their child care is not very good, a suspicion that experts in the field say is often correct. Working-class women usually cannot afford to buy one-on-one attention for their children; most of the women interviewed either left their children with relatives or took them to the home of another mother who was looking after several children for pay.   31

The quality of such care, in both the physical settings and the attention the children receive, varies considerably. The best care is also often the most expensive, and many women said government could help them most by giving them some financial help with child care.   32

Many women said they felt lucky to have found help from their families or loving baby sitters. But some said they were making compromises that disturbed them, either leaving children as young as 9 at home alone until they returned from work or having to switch baby sitters frequently.   33

Although she loves her work, Mrs. Moorefield is torn because she believes her recent change to a 12-hour shift may be hurting her children, who are not doing well in school. She is considering sharing a job, but she must first wait to see whether her husband, who works in an airline stockroom, goes on strike.   34

Generally, though, most women say, with an air of surprise, that they believe their children are actually turning out all right, even if working interferes with their ideal of a good mother.   35

"For me, looking at my kids tells me I'm doing O.K.," Mrs. Rumsey said. "My kids are excellent students. They are outgoing. They have minds of their own. No matter how much I've never wanted to work, there's never been any drastic indication from my kids that I shouldn't."   36

Blazing a New Path: Leaving the Land of Make-believe

With little chance of living out their ideal of the good mother, many   37
mothers are searching for a new way to think about motherhood.

Elesha Lindsay works days checking references at Forsyth Memorial   38
Hospital in Winston-Salem, N.C., and two nights a week studying for a
higher-paying job as a medical stenographer while her husband juggles
four jobs as a cook. She leaves her 16-month-old daughter at the
hospital's day-care center, where she believes her daughter is happy and
well-cared for. Yet she cried all week when she first had to return to
work, when her daughter was 9 weeks old. She and a friend filled in for
each other so she could add three weeks onto the hospital's normal
six-week maternity leave.

Although she would rather work part time when her daughter is   39
small, Mrs. Lindsay sees herself as a good mother, and work as a
welcome part of her life.

"Being a good mother depends on what type of person you are and   40
what you instill," she said. "My mother wasn't there the majority of the
time, but I was watching her, knowing the type of person she was. We
knew what our mother expected from us. That child is spending more
time with that day-care giver than you, but I still feel like I'm a better
person for her, out working, financially helping the family."

Mrs. Cassidy, the garment worker, also believes that too many   41
mothers become obsessed with motherhood's gestures rather than its
substance. "It doesn't matter if you bake cookies for them, and don't take
them to Cub Scouts every time," she said. "You're not going to be there
for their first step. But I never heard mine say, 'You were never there
when I needed you.' "

Still, many mothers worry that they may be deluding themselves.   42
"It looks fine to me," Mrs. Lencki said, "but maybe I'm not looking."

While there is debate about the effects of extensive nonmaternal   43
care early in life, experts agree that with conscientious, loving parents
and high-quality care the vast majority of children do just fine, by any
measurement of intellectual and emotional development. Some studies
suggest that mothers' attitudes are crucial; if they are happy, whether
staying at home or working, that will have an enormous impact on their
relationship with their children.

Employer flexibility clearly makes a difference, said Arlie Hochs-   44
child, a sociologist and author of "The Second Shift: Working Parents and
the Revolution at Home" (Viking, 1989), who is now studying the
workplace and its effects on family life. "We have to acknowledge that
the majority of American women will work for the majority of their lives

through their childbearing years and we have to adapt the workplace," she said. "Don't pretend they're men who have wives at home to do this."

One reason Mrs. Cassidy feels little guilt is that she was able to take   45
off work to watch her children in school plays, or tend them when they were sick. But other companies, particularly factories where workers' absences may slow assembly lines, are not so lenient. Several women said their employers required 24-hour notice for sick days—an impossibility with children—or docked their pay if they wanted to go to an event at their children's schools.

But even if they did not choose to work, some mothers have found   46
that working has brought unexpected benefits: a new sense of identity, a role in a broader community, pride in their independence, a temporary escape from children that may allow them to be better mothers in the time they share.

And while women may yearn for the safe world of mythic families,   47
they have seen enough of the sobering reality of divorce and widowhood to cherish the financial independence that working confers. "My mother stayed home, and when my father divorced her she had nothing to fall back on," said Donna King, a hospital laboratory supervisor who is a mother of four.

In fact, most of the women interviewed said they would prefer   48
working to staying at home—but most wanted to work part time.

These days, some more affluent and educated women say they   49
would feel embarrassed to tell their friends that they did not work. Yet many working-class mothers who have found that they are happy working treat it like a guilty secret. Mrs. Lencki dropped her voice almost to a whisper when she talked about enjoying her job, despite her guilt that her youngest son had not had her full-time presence.

Pride, embarrassment and defiance competed as Mrs. Moorefield   50
talked about work. "For me, the ideal mother is one who is able to choose," Mrs. Moorefield said. "Even if we could financially afford that I could not work, I still think I would need at least some other contact, part time. You want to be there for your children, and on the other hand you want to be able to provide for them well. This sounds like I'm anti-family values. . . .'"

Exercises

Some Important Words

self-effacing (paragraph 1), icon (1), affluent (8), backlash (8), shards (11), Donna Reed (11), the Beav (11), verities (15), convictions (19), exacting (26), deluding (42).

According to the Census Bureau, half of all marriages end in divorce. Births to single mothers now make up one-quarter of total births. One in four Americans over age 18 have never married. These factors have whittled away at the number of households that fit the Republican ideal.

The charts track the decline of the traditional family unit and the map shows places around the United States where such families are a large presence.

Family Arrangements:
Percentage of all U.S. households in 1991. "Children" refer to a family's own child or children under age 18.

Shrinking Minority:
Married couples with a child or children under age 18, as a percentage of all households.

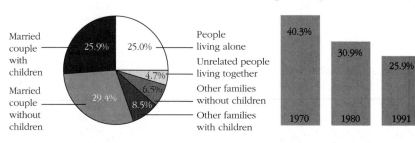

Some of the Issues

1. Why are Marilyn Quayle and Hillary Clinton referred to as "stick-figure" mothers in the opening paragraphs?
2. What makes Toni Rumsey (paragraph 2), Stacy Murdock (paragraph 3), or Nancy Cassidy (paragraph 4) different from Quayle and Clinton?
3. Although social attitudes are changing, why do some mothers still feel guilty about working outside the home?
4. Describe the life of Stacy Murdock, the women who fits the traditional image of motherhood (paragraph 16). Do you know people who lead similar lives?
5. According to Deborah Phillips, an expert in child development, many working mothers feel anxious and uncertain about child care. Summarize the reasons for their anxiety given in paragraphs 26–34.
6. In paragraphs 46 and 47, most of the women interviewed said that they wanted to work at least part time. What are some of the unexpected benefits of working that these women have discovered?
7. Refer to the charts and the map on pages 136 and 137 and answer the questions that follow:
   a. Locate your county on the map. Is your area one of those where 33 percent or more of the households consist of the "traditional" family unit? What might account for the household figure of your area?

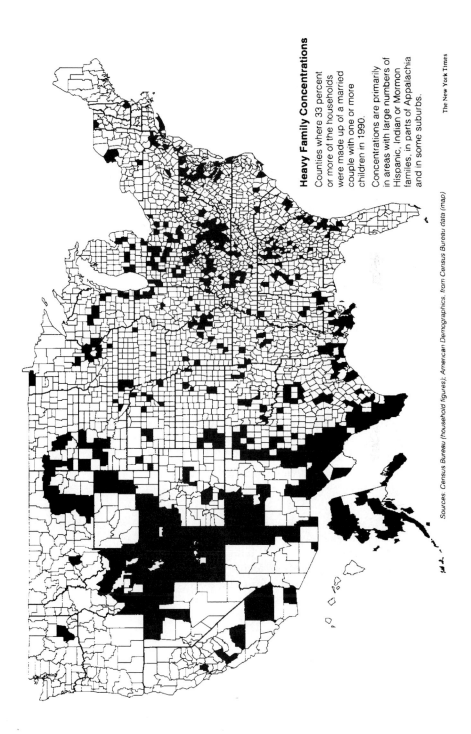

Heavy Family Concentrations

Counties where 33 percent
or more of the households
were made up of a married
couple with one or more
children in 1990.

Concentrations are primarily
in areas with large numbers of
Hispanic, Indian or Mormon
families, in parts of Appalachia
and in some suburbs.

The New York Times

Sources: Census Bureau (household figures); American Demographics, from Census Bureau data (map)

b. What percentage of the U.S. population lives in a household like yours?
c. Do the percentages given in the bar graph corroborate the information on the traditional family unit in the text?

The Way We Are Told

8. Cite several instances in which Chira supports a general assertion with specific examples drawn from mothers from around the country.
9. In addition to the women interviewed, what other expert sources does Chira cite to support her hypothesis?
10. What is meant by the subheading "Leaving the Land of Make-believe" in the last section of this essay?
11. What social changes does the author advocate?

Some Subjects for Writing

12. During the 1992 Republican Convention, Marilyn Quayle, the wife of the vice president, urged women not to stray from their "essential natures," and to return to "family values." In your opinion, have women's essential natures changed? Use the information given by the women interviewed in this article and your own experience to define what a "good" mother and "good" family values mean in the 1990s.

*13. In "The Paradox of Perfection" Arlene Skolnick speaks of a "new realism," or pluralism in the way we regard the American family. Examine whether this approach can also be applied to the way in which our society views motherhood.

THE PARADOX OF PERFECTION

Arlene Skolnick

Arlene Skolnick is a research psychologist at the Institute of Human Development, University of California at Berkeley. Born in 1933, she received her undergraduate education at Queens College and her Ph.D. in psychology from Yale in 1962. She is the author of *The Intimate Environment* (1973), *The Psychology of Human Development* (1986), and *Embattled Paradise: The American Family in an Age of Uncertainty* (1991).

The article reprinted here first appeared in the *Wilson Quarterly*. In examining the development of the family from colonial times to the present, Skolnick finds that in recent times we have come to look upon the ideal as if it were the norm, making every state less than perfection seem like failure.

In examining the myth of perfection, Skolnick makes reference to *Brigadoon* (paragraph 8), a Broadway musical and Hollywood film. Brigadoon was an imaginary town that came to life every one hundred years, never changing from its idealized state. Dr. Benjamin Spock's (paragraph 31) advice to new parents, especially his best-selling book *Baby and Child Care,* has shaped family life for a generation. Alexis de Tocqueville (1805–59), mentioned in paragraph 24, was a French aristocrat who traveled throughout America. Deeply impressed with what he saw as a new society, he published his observations and reflections in *Democracy in America.*

The American Family, as even readers of *Popular Mechanics* must know 1 by now, is in what Sean O'Casey would have called "a terrible state of chassis." Yet, there are certain ironies about the much-publicized crisis that give one pause.

True, the statistics seem alarming. The U.S. divorce rate, though it 2 has reached something of a plateau in recent years, remains the highest in American history. The number of births out-of-wedlock among all races and ethnic groups continues to climb. The plight of many elderly Americans subsisting on low fixed incomes is well known.

What puzzles me is an ambiguity, not in the facts, but in what we   3
are asked to make of them. A series of opinion polls conducted in 1978
by Yankelovich, Skelley, and White, for example, found that 38 percent of
those surveyed had recently witnessed one or more "destructive activities" (e.g., a divorce, a separation, a custody battle) within their own
families or those of their parents or siblings. At the same time, 92 percent
of the respondents said the family was highly important to them as a
"personal value."

Can the family be at once a cherished "value" and a troubled   4
institution? I am inclined to think, in fact, that they go hand in hand. A
recent "Talk of the Town" report in *The New Yorker* illustrates what I
mean:

> A few months ago word was heard from Billy Gray, who used to play
> brother Bud in "Father Knows Best," the 1950s television show about the
> nice Anderson family who lived in the white frame house on a side street
> in some mythical Springfield—the house at which the father arrived each
> night swinging open the front door and singing out "Margaret, I'm home!"
> Gray said he felt "ashamed" that he had ever had anything to do with the
> show. It was all "totally false," he said, and had caused many Americans to
> feel inadequate, because they thought that was the way life was supposed
> to be and that their own lives failed to measure up.

As Susan Sontag has noted in *On Photography*, mass-produced   5
images have "extraordinary powers to determine our demands upon
reality." The family is especially vulnerable to confusion between truth
and illusion. What, after all, is "normal"? All of us have a backstairs view
of our own families, but we know The Family, in the aggregate, only
vicariously.

Like politics or athletics, the family has become a media event.   6
Television offers nightly portrayals of lump-in-the-throat family "normalcy" ("The Waltons," "Little House on the Prairie") and, nowadays,
even humorous "deviance" ("One Day at a Time," "The Odd Couple").
Family advisers sally forth in syndicated newspaper columns to uphold
standards, mend relationships, suggest counseling, and otherwise lead
their readers back to the True Path. For commercial purposes, advertisers
spend millions of dollars to create stirring vignettes of glamorous-but-
ordinary families, the kind of family most 11-year-olds wish they had.

All Americans do not, of course, live in such a family, but most share   7
an intuitive sense of what the "ideal" family should be—reflected in the
precepts of religion, the conventions of etiquette, and the assumptions of
law. And, characteristically, Americans tend to project the ideal back into
the past, the time when virtues of all sorts are thought to have flourished.

We do not come off well by comparison with that golden age, nor   8
could we, for it is as elusive and mythical as Brigadoon. If Billy Gray

shames too easily, he has a valid point: While Americans view the family as the proper context for their own lives—9 out of 10 people live in one—they have no realistic context in which to view the family. Family history, until recently, was as neglected in academe as it still is in the press. The familiar, depressing charts of "leading family indicators"— marriage, divorce, illegitimacy—in newspapers and newsmagazines rarely survey the trends before World War II. The discussion, in short, lacks ballast.

Let us go back to before the American Revolution.   9

Perhaps what distinguishes the modern family most from its colonial   10
counterpart is its newfound privacy. Throughout the 17th and 18th centuries, well over 90 percent of the American population lived in small rural communities. Unusual behavior rarely went unnoticed, and neighbors often intervened directly in a family's affairs, to help or to chastise.

The most dramatic example was the rural "charivari," prevalent in   11
both Europe and the United States until the early 19th century. The purpose of these noisy gatherings was to censure community members for familial transgressions—unusual sexual behavior, marriages between persons of grossly discrepant ages, or "household disorder," to name but a few. As historian Edward Shorter describes it in *The Making of the Modern Family:*

> Sometimes the demonstration would consist of masked individuals circling somebody's house at night, screaming, beating on pans, and blowing cow horns . . . on other occasions, the offender would be seized and marched through the streets, seated perhaps backwards on a donkey or forced to wear a placard describing his sins.

The state itself had no qualms about intruding into a family's affairs   12
by statute, if necessary. Consider 17th-century New England's "stubborn child" laws that, though never actually enforced, sanctioned the death penalty for chronic disobedience to one's parents.

If the boundaries between home and society seem blurred during   13
the colonial era, it is because they were. People were neither very emotional nor very self-conscious about family life, and, as historian John Demos points out, family and community were "joined in a relation of profound reciprocity." In his *Of Domesticall Duties,* William Gouge, a 17th-century Puritan preacher, called the family "a little community." The home, like the larger community, was as much an economic as a social unit; all members of the family worked, be it on the farm, or in a shop, or in the home.

There was not much to idealize. Love was not considered the basis   14
for marriage but one possible result of it. According to historian Carl

Degler, it was easier to obtain a divorce in colonial New England than anywhere else in the Western world, and the divorce rate climbed steadily throughout the 18th century, though it remained low by contemporary standards. Romantic images to the contrary, it was rare for more than two generations (parents and children) to share a household, for the simple reason that very few people lived beyond the age of 60. It is ironic that our nostalgia for the extended family—including grandparents and grandchildren—comes at a time when, thanks to improvements in health care, its existence is less threatened than ever before.

Infant mortality was high in colonial days, though not as high as we 15 are accustomed to believe, since food was plentiful and epidemics, owing to generally low population density, were few. In the mid-1700s, the average age of marriage was about 24 for men, 21 for women—not much different from what it is now. Households, on average, were larger, but not startlingly so: A typical household in 1790 included about 5.6 members, versus about 3.5 today. Illegitimacy was widespread. Premarital pregnancies reached a high in 18th-century America (10 percent of all first births) that was not equalled until the 1950s.

In simple demographic terms, then, the differences between the 16 American family in colonial times and today are not all that stark; the similarities are sometimes striking.

The chief contrast is psychological. While Western societies have 17 always idealized the family to some degree, the *most vivid* literary portrayals of family life before the 19th century were negative or, at best, ambivalent. In what might be called the "high tragic" tradition—including Sophocles, Shakespeare, and the Bible, as well as fairy tales and novels—the family was portrayed as a high-voltage emotional setting, laden with dark passions, sibling rivalries, and violence. There was also the "low comic" tradition—the world of hen-pecked husbands and tyrannical mothers-in-law.

It is unlikely that our 18th-century ancestors ever left the book of 18 Genesis or *Tom Jones* with the feeling that their own family lives were seriously flawed.

By the time of the Civil War, however, American attitudes toward 19 the family had changed profoundly. The early decades of the 19th century marked the beginnings of America's gradual transformation into an urban, industrial society. In 1820, less than 8 percent of the U.S. population lived in cities; by 1860, the urban concentration approached 20 percent, and by 1900 that proportion had doubled.

Structurally, the American family did not immediately undergo a 20 comparable transformation. Despite the large families of many immigrants and farmers, the size of the *average* family declined—slowly but steadily—as it had been doing since the 17th century. Infant mortality remained about the same, and may even have increased somewhat, owing to poor sanitation in crowded cities. Legal divorces were easier to obtain than they had been in colonial times. Indeed, the rise in the divorce rate was a matter of some concern during the 19th century, though death, not divorce, was the prime cause of one-parent families, as it was up to 1965.

Functionally, however, America's industrial revolution had a lasting 21 effect on the family. No longer was the household typically a group of interdependent workers. Now, men went to offices and factories and became breadwinners; wives stayed home to mind the hearth; children went off to the new public schools. The home was set apart from the dog-eat-dog arena of economic life; it came to be viewed as a utopian retreat or, in historian Christopher Lasch's phrase, a "haven in a heartless world." Marriage was now valued primarily for its emotional attractions. Above all, the family became something to worry about.

The earliest and most saccharine "sentimental model" of the family 22 appeared in the new mass media that proliferated during the second quarter of the 19th century. Novels, tracts, newspaper articles, and ladies' magazines—there were variations for each class of society—elaborated a "Cult of True Womanhood" in which piety, submissiveness, and domesticity dominated the pantheon of desirable feminine qualities. This quotation from *The Ladies Book* (1830) is typical:

> See, she sits, she walks, she speaks, she looks—unutterable things! Inspiration springs up in her very paths—it follows her footsteps. A halo of glory encircles her, and illuminates her whole orbit. With her, man not only feels safe, but actually renovated.

In the late 1800s, science came into the picture. The "professional- 23 ization" of the housewife took two different forms. One involved motherhood and childrearing, according to the latest scientific understanding of children's special physical and emotional needs. (It is no accident that the publishing of children's books became a major industry during this period.) The other was the domestic science movement— "home economics," basically—which focused on the woman as full-time homemaker, applying "scientific" and "industrial" rationality to shopping, making meals, and housework.

The new ideal of the family prompted a cultural split that has 24 endured, one that Tocqueville had glimpsed (and rather liked) in 1835. Society was divided more sharply into man's sphere and woman's sphere. Toughness, competition, and practicality were the masculine values that ruled the outside world. The softer values—affection, tranquility, piety—were worshiped in the home and the church. In contrast to the colonial view, the ideology of the "modern" family implied a critique of everything beyond the front door.

What is striking as one looks at the writings of the 19th-century   25
"experts"—the physicians, clergymen, phrenologists, and "scribbling
ladies"—is how little their essential message differs from that of the
sociologists, psychiatrists, pediatricians, and women's magazine writers
of the 20th century, particularly since World War II.

Instead of men's and women's spheres, of course, sociologists   26
speak of "instrumental" and "expressive" roles. The notion of the family
as a retreat from the harsh realities of the outside world crops up as
"functional differentiation." And, like the 19th-century utopians who
believed society could be regenerated through the perfection of family
life, 20th-century social scientists have looked at the failed family as the
source of most American social problems.

None of those who promoted the sentimental model of the family—   27
neither the popular writers nor the academics—considered the paradox of
perfectionism: the ironic possibility that it would lead to trouble. Yet it has.
The image of the perfect, happy family makes ordinary families seem like
failures. Small problems loom as big problems if the "normal" family is
thought to be one where there are no real problems at all.

One sees this phenomenon at work on the generation of Americans   28
born and reared during the late 19th century, the first generation reared
on the mother's milk of sentimental imagery. Between 1900 and 1920,
the U.S. divorce rate doubled, from four to eight divorces annually per
1,000 married couples. The jump—comparable to the 100 percent
increase in the divorce rate between 1960 and 1980—is not attributable
to changes in divorce laws, which were not greatly liberalized. Rather, it
would appear that, as historian Thomas O'Neill believes, Americans were
simply more willing to dissolve marriages that did not conform to their
ideal of domestic bliss—and perhaps try again.

If anything, family standards became even more demanding as the   29
20th century progressed. The new fields of psychology and sociology
opened up whole new definitions of familial perfection. "Feelings"—fun,
love, warmth, good orgasm—acquired heightened popular significance
as the invisible glue of successful families.

Psychologist Martha Wolfenstein, in an analysis of several decades   30
of government-sponsored infant care manuals, has documented the
emergence of a "fun morality." In former days, being a good parent
meant carrying out certain tasks with punctilio; if your child was clean
and reasonably obedient, you had no cause to probe his psyche. Now,
we are told, parents must commune with their own feelings and those of
their children—an edict which has seeped into the ethos of education as
well. The distinction is rather like that between religions of deed and
religions of faith. It is one thing to make your child brush his teeth; it is
quite another to transform the whole process into a joyous "learning
experience."

The task of 20th-century parents has been further complicated by 31
the advice offered them. The experts disagree with each other and often
contradict themselves. The kindly Dr. Benjamin Spock, for example, is
full of contradictions. In a detailed analysis of *Baby and Child Care,*
historian Michael Zuckerman observes that Spock tells mothers to relax
("trust yourself") yet warns them that they have an "ominous power" to
destroy their children's innocence and make them discontented "for
years" or even "forever."

Since the mid-1960s, there has been a youth rebellion of sorts, a 32
new "sexual revolution," a revival of feminism, and the emergence of the
two-worker family. The huge postwar Baby-Boom generation is pairing
off, accounting in part for the upsurge in the divorce rate (half of all
divorces occur within seven years of a first marriage). Media images of
the family have become more "realistic," reflecting new patterns of family
life that are emerging (and old patterns that are re-emerging).

Among social scientists, "realism" is becoming something of an 33
ideal in itself. For some of them, realism translates as pluralism: All forms
of the family, by virtue of the fact that they happen to exist, are equally
acceptable—from communes and cohabitation to one-parent households, homosexual marriages, and, come to think of it, the nuclear family.
What was once labeled "deviant" is now merely "variant." In some
college texts, "the family" has been replaced by "family systems." Yet, this
new approach does not seem to have squelched perfectionist standards.
Indeed, a palpable strain of perfectionism runs through the pop literature
on "alternative" family lifestyles.

For the majority of scholars, realism means a more down-to-earth 34
view of the American household. Rather than seeing the family as a
haven of peace and tranquility, they have begun to recognize that even
"normal" families are less than ideal, that intimate relations of any sort
inevitably involve antagonism as well as love. Conflict and change are
inherent in social life. If the family is now in a state of flux, such is the
nature of resilient institutions; if it is beset by problems, so is life. The
family will survive.

Exercises

Some Important Words

paradox (title), plateau (paragraph 2), plight (2), subsisting (2), ambiguity
(3), custody (3), mythical (4), vulnerable (5), vicariously (5), deviance
(6), syndicated (6), vignettes (6), intuitive (7), elusive (8), academe (8),
ballast (8), chastise (10), prevalent (11), qualms (12), chronic (13),
nostalgia (14), demographic (16), ambivalent (17), Sophocles (17), sibling

(17), henpecked (17), utopian (21), haven (21), saccharine (22), proliferated (22), tracts (22), submissiveness (22), phrenologists (25), regenerated (26), ironic (27), phenomenon (28), imagery (28), punctilio (29), psyche (30), ethos (30), nostrums (32), pluralism (33), palpable (33), resilient (34).

Some of the Issues

1. Skolnick begins her analysis by saying that just about everyone knows that the family is in crisis. How does she support that assertion in the first three paragraphs?

2. Why is the family, according to Skolnick, "particularly vulnerable to the confusion between truth and illusion"? How have the media increased that confusion?

3. In paragraph 8 Skolnick says: "While Americans view the family as the proper context for their own lives . . . they have no realistic context in which to view the family." What does she mean? How do Billy Gray's attitude (paragraph 4) and the examples drawn from the media (paragraphs 5 – 7) support her statement?

4. What reasons does Skolnick give for her decision to go back to before the American Revolution in tracing the history of the American family (paragraph 8)? What is the chief distinction she sees between the modern family and the family of 200 years ago? On the other hand, in what respects is the difference not very great?

5. What was the gradual effect on the family of the change from a predominantly rural society to an industrial, urban one (paragraphs 19 – 21)?

6. What were the causes for the increasing division of family roles into a man's sphere and a woman's sphere, according to Skolnick? How do the two spheres differ?

7. In paragraph 27, Skolnick turns to the "paradox" she has referred to in her title. What is it? What is the irony in seeking perfectionism for the family?

8. What are the more demanding standards that modern social science has imposed on the family according to Skolnick (paragraphs 29 – 31)?

9. In the last two paragraphs (33 and 34) Skolnick speaks of a new realism. What does she mean?

* 10. Compare and contrast the "realism" Skolnick talks about in the last two paragraphs to Jane Howard's view of what constitutes a good family in her essay "Families."

The Way We Are Told

11. In paragraph 1 Skolnick first states the commonly held view that the family is in a sorry state. In what way does the second sentence foreshadow the argument she will make?

12. Consider paragraph 8; how does Skolnick make a transition from her analysis of the contemporary family to the topic she introduces with her one-line paragraph 9?

13. Skolnick puts words or sentences in quotation marks, but these "quotes" are of two kinds. One is the regular kind, as for example those in paragraph 3. The other is used for some specific effect, such as "normalcy" (paragraph 6) or "ideal" (paragraph 7). Find further examples of the second kind and explain their effect.

Some Subjects for Writing

14. In her final paragraph Skolnick gives the reader a rather optimistic view of the future of the family. Examine if her arguments based on history justify that conclusion, and why (or why not).

15. Skolnick claims that in 1980, when this essay was written, TV programs presenting family situations were becoming more realistic. Examine a current show that deals with family life. How realistic is the picture of family life, in terms of the situations, attitudes, and relationships presented?

TWO KINDS

Amy Tan

Amy Tan was born in Oakland, California, in 1952, two and one-half years after her parents immigrated to the United States. Tan's semiautobiographical first novel, *The Joy Luck Club* (1989), from which this excerpt is taken, is the story of the lives of four Chinese women in pre–1949 China and the lives of their American daughters in California.

It is a Chinese custom for daughters to honor and listen obediently to their mothers. This tradition is challenged by the generation of daughters who were raised in the American culture and language. Jing-mei disdains her mother's constant criticism and insists on making her own way. Only at the end of the novel, when after her mother's death she is reunited with her sisters in China, can she say, "Now I see what part of me is Chinese. It is so obvious. It is my family. It is in our blood. After all these years, it can finally be let go."

Tan published a second novel, *The Kitchen God's Wife,* in 1991.

My mother believed you could be anything you wanted to be in America. 1
You could open a restaurant. You could work for the government and get good retirement. You could buy a house with almost no money down. You could become rich. You could become instantly famous.

"Of course you can be prodigy, too," my mother told me when I 2
was nine. "You can be best anything. What does Auntie Lindo know? Her daughter, she is only best tricky."

America was where all my mother's hopes lay. She had come here 3
in 1949 after losing everything in China: her mother and father, her family home, her first husband, and two daughters, twin baby girls. But she never looked back with regret. There were so many ways for things to get better.

We didn't immediately pick the right kind of prodigy. At first my mother 4
thought I could be a Chinese Shirley Temple. We'd watch Shirley's old movies on TV as though they were training films. My mother would poke my arm and say, *"Ni kan"*—You watch. And I would see Shirley tapping

her feet, or singing a sailor song, or pursing her lips into a very round O while saying, "Oh my goodness."

"*Ni kan,*" said my mother as Shirley's eyes flooded with tears. "You already know how. Don't need talent for crying!"

Soon after my mother got this idea about Shirley Temple, she took me to a beauty training school in the Mission district and put me in the hands of a student who could barely hold the scissors without shaking. Instead of getting big fat curls, I emerged with an uneven mass of crinkly black fuzz. My mother dragged me off to the bathroom and tried to wet down my hair.

"You look like Negro Chinese," she lamented, as if I had done this on purpose.

The instructor of the beauty training school had to lop off these soggy clumps to make my hair even again. "Peter Pan is very popular these days," the instructor assured my mother. I now had hair the length of a boy's with straight-across bangs that hung at a slant two inches above my eyebrows. I liked the haircut and it made me actually look forward to my future fame.

In fact, in the beginning, I was just as excited as my mother, maybe even more so. I pictured this prodigy part of me as many different images, trying each one on for size. I was a dainty ballerina girl standing by the curtains, waiting to hear the right music that would send me floating on my tiptoes. I was like the Christ child lifted out of the straw manger, crying with holy indignity. I was Cinderella stepping from her pumpkin carriage with sparkly cartoon music filling the air.

In all of my imaginings, I was filled with a sense that I would soon become *perfect*. My mother and father would adore me. I would be beyond reproach. I would never feel the need to sulk for anything.

But sometimes the prodigy in me became impatient. "If you don't hurry up and get me out of here, I'm disappearing for good," it warned. "And then you'll always be nothing."

Every night after dinner, my mother and I would sit at the Formica kitchen table. She would present new tests, taking her examples from stories of amazing children she had read in *Ripley's Believe It or Not,* or *Good Housekeeping, Reader's Digest,* and a dozen other magazines she kept in a pile in our bathroom. My mother got these magazines from people whose houses she cleaned. And since she cleaned many houses each week, we had a great assortment. She would look through them all, searching for stories about remarkable children.

The first night she brought out a story about a three-year-old boy who knew the capitals of all the states and even most of the European countries. A teacher was quoted as saying the little boy could also pronounce the names of the foreign cities correctly.

"What's the capital of Finland?" my mother asked me, looking at the   14
magazine story.

All I knew was the capital of California, because Sacramento was   15
the name of the street we lived on in Chinatown. "Nairobi!" I guessed,
saying the most foreign word I could think of. She checked to see if that
was possibly one way to pronounce "Helsinki" before showing me the
answer.

The tests got harder—multiplying numbers in my head, finding the   16
queen of hearts in a deck of cards, trying to stand on my head without
using my hands, predicting the daily temperatures in Los Angeles, New
York, and London.

One night I had to look at a page from the Bible for three minutes   17
and then report everything I could remember. "Now Jehoshaphat had
riches and honor in abundance and . . . that's all I remember, Ma," I said.

And after seeing my mother's disappointed face once again,   18
something inside of me began to die. I hated the tests, the raised hopes
and failed expectations. Before going to bed that night, I looked in the
mirror above the bathroom sink and when I saw only my face staring
back—and that it would always be this ordinary face—I began to cry.
Such a sad, ugly girl! I made high-pitched noises like a crazed animal,
trying to scratch out the face in the mirror.

And then I saw what seemed to be the prodigy side of me—   19
because I had never seen that face before. I looked at my reflection,
blinking so I could see more clearly. The girl staring back at me was
angry, powerful. This girl and I were the same. I had new thoughts,
willful thoughts, or rather thoughts filled with lots of won'ts. I won't let
her change me, I promised myself. I won't be what I'm not.

So now on nights when my mother presented her tests, I performed   20
listlessly, my head propped on one arm. I pretended to be bored. And I
was. I got so bored I started counting the bellows of the foghorns out on
the bay while my mother drilled me in other areas. The sound was
comforting and reminded me of the cow jumping over the moon. And
the next day, I played a game with myself, seeing if my mother would
give up on me before eight bellows. After a while I usually counted only
one, maybe two bellows at most. At last she was beginning to give up
hope.

Two or three months had gone by without any mention of my being a   21
prodigy again. And then one day my mother was watching *The Ed
Sullivan Show* on TV. The TV was old and the sound kept shorting out.
Every time my mother got halfway up from the sofa to adjust the set, the
sound would go back on and Ed would be talking. As soon as she sat
down, Ed would go silent again. She got up, the TV broke into loud
piano music. She sat down. Silence. Up and down, back and forth, quiet

and loud. It was like a stiff embraceless dance between her and the TV set. Finally she stood by the set with her hand on the sound dial.

She seemed entranced by the music, a little frenzied piano piece   22
with this mesmerizing quality, sort of quick passages and then teasing lilting ones before it returned to the quick playful parts.

"*Ni kan,*" my mother said, calling me over with hurried hand   23
gestures, "Look here."

I could see why my mother was fascinated by the music. It was   24
being pounded out by a little Chinese girl, about nine years old, with a Peter Pan haircut. The girl had the sauciness of a Shirley Temple. She was proudly modest like a proper Chinese child. And she also did this fancy sweep of a curtsy, so that the fluffy skirt of her white dress cascaded slowly to the floor like the petals of a large carnation.

In spite of these warning signs, I wasn't worried. Our family had no   25
piano and we couldn't afford to buy one, let alone reams of sheet music and piano lessons. So I could be generous in my comments when my mother bad-mouthed the little girl on TV.

"Play note right, but doesn't sound good! No singing sound,"   26
complained my mother.

"What are you picking on her for?" I said carelessly. "She's pretty   27
good. Maybe she's not the best, but she's trying hard." I knew almost immediately I would be sorry I said that.

"Just like you," she said. "Not the best. Because you not trying." She   28
gave a little huff as she let go of the sound dial and sat down on the sofa.

The little Chinese girl sat down also to play an encore of "Anitra's   29
Dance" by Grieg. I remember the song, because later on I had to learn how to play it.

Three days after watching *The Ed Sullivan Show*, my mother told me   30
what my schedule would be for piano lessons and piano practice. She had talked to Mr. Chong, who lived on the first floor of our apartment building. Mr. Chong was a retired piano teacher and my mother had traded housecleaning services for weekly lessons and a piano for me to practice on every day, two hours a day, from four until six.

When my mother told me this, I felt as though I had been sent to hell.   31
I whined and then kicked my foot a little when I couldn't stand it anymore.

"Why don't you like me the way I am? I'm *not* a genius! I can't play   32
the piano. And even if I could, I wouldn't go on TV if you paid me a million dollars!" I cried.

My mother slapped me. "Who ask you be genius?" she shouted.   33
"Only ask you be your best. For you sake. You think I want you be genius? Hnnh! What for! Who ask you!"

"So ungrateful," I heard her mutter in Chinese. "If she had so much   34
talent as she has temper, she would be famous now."

Mr. Chong, whom I secretly nicknamed Old Chong, was very   35
strange, always tapping his fingers to the silent music of an invisible
orchestra. He looked ancient in my eyes. He had lost most of the hair on
top of his head and he wore thick glasses and had eyes that always
looked tired and sleepy. But he must have been younger than I thought,
since he lived with his mother and was not yet married.

I met Old Lady Chong once and that was enough. She had this   36
peculiar smell like a baby that had done something in its pants. And her
fingers felt like a dead person's, like an old peach I once found in the
back of the refrigerator; the skin just slid off the meat when I picked it up.

I soon found out why Old Chong had retired from teaching piano.   37
He was deaf. "Like Beethoven!" he shouted to me. "We're both listening
only in our head!" And he would start to conduct his frantic silent sonatas.

Our lessons went like this. He would open the book and point to   38
different things, explaining their purpose: "Key! Treble! Bass! No sharps
or flats! So this is C major! Listen now and play after me!"

And then he would play the C scale a few times, a simple chord,   39
and then, as if inspired by an old, unreachable itch, he gradually added
more notes and running trills and a pounding bass until the music was
really something quite grand.

I would play after him, the simple scale, the simple chord, and then   40
I just played some nonsense that sounded like a cat running up and
down on top of garbage cans. Old Chong smiled and applauded and
then said, "Very good! But now you must learn to keep time!"

So that's how I discovered that Old Chong's eyes were too slow to   41
keep up with the wrong notes I was playing. He went through the
motions in half-time. To help me keep rhythm, he stood behind me,
pushing down on my right shoulder for every beat. He balanced pennies
on top of my wrists so I would keep them still as I slowly played scales
and arpeggios. He had me curve my hand around an apple and keep that
shape when playing chords. He marched stiffly to show me how to make
each finger dance up and down, staccato like an obedient little soldier.

He taught me all these things, and that was how I also learned I   42
could be lazy and get away with mistakes, lots of mistakes. If I hit the
wrong notes because I hadn't practiced enough, I never corrected myself.
I just kept playing in rhythm. And Old Chong kept conducting his own
private reverie.

So maybe I never really gave myself a fair chance. I did pick up the   43
basics pretty quickly, and I might have become a good pianist at that
young age. But I was so determined not to try, not to be anybody
different that I learned to play only the most ear-splitting preludes, the
most discordant hymns.

Over the next year, I practiced like this, dutifully in my own way.   44
And then one day I heard my mother and her friend Lindo Jong both

talking in a loud bragging tone of voice so others could hear. It was after church, and I was leaning against the brick wall wearing a dress with stiff white petticoats. Auntie Lindo's daughter, Waverly, who was about my age, was standing farther down the wall about five feet away. We had grown up together and shared all the closeness of two sisters squabbling over crayons and dolls. In other words, for the most part, we hated each other. I thought she was snotty. Waverly Jong had gained a certain amount of fame as "Chinatown's Littlest Chinese Chess Champion."

"She bring home too many trophy," lamented Auntie Lindo that Sunday. "All day she play chess. All day I have no time do nothing but dust off her winnings." She threw a scolding look at Waverly, who pretended not to see her.   45

"You lucky you don't have this problem," said Auntie Lindo with a sigh to my mother.   46

And my mother squared her shoulders and bragged: "Our problem worser than yours. If we ask Jing-mei wash dish, she hear nothing but music. It's like you can't stop this natural talent."   47

And right then, I was determined to put a stop to her foolish pride.   48

A few weeks later, Old Chong and my mother conspired to have me play in a talent show which would be held in the church hall. By then, my parents had saved up enough to buy me a secondhand piano, a black Wurlitzer spinet with a scarred bench. It was the showpiece of our living room.   49

For the talent show, I was to play a piece called "Pleading Child" from Schumann's *Scenes from Childhood*. It was a simple, moody piece that sounded more difficult than it was. I was supposed to memorize the whole thing, playing the repeat parts twice to make the piece sound longer. But I dawdled over it, playing a few bars and then cheating, looking up to see what notes followed. I never really listened to what I was playing. I day-dreamed about being somewhere else, about being someone else.   50

The part I liked to practice best was the fancy curtsy: right foot out, touch the rose on the carpet with a pointed foot, sweep to the side, left leg bends, look up and smile.   51

My parents invited all the couples from the Joy Luck Club to witness my debut. Auntie Lindo and Uncle Tin were there. Waverly and her two older brothers had also come. The first two rows were filled with children both younger and older than I was. The littlest ones got to go first. They recited simple nursery rhymes, squawked out tunes on miniature violins, twirled Hula Hoops, pranced in pink ballet tutus, and when they bowed or curtsied, the audience would sigh in unison, "Awww," and then clap enthusiastically.   52

When my turn came, I was very confident. I remember my childish excitement. It was as if I knew, without a doubt, that the prodigy side of   53 me really did exist. I had no fear whatsoever, no nervousness. I remember thinking to myself, This is it! This is it! I looked out over the audience, at my mother's blank face, my father's yawn, Auntie Lindo's stiff-lipped smile, Waverly's sulky expression. I had on a white dress layered with sheets of lace, and a pink bow in my Peter Pan haircut. As I sat down I envisioned people jumping to their feet and Ed Sullivan rushing up to introduce me to everyone on TV.

And I started to play. It was so beautiful. I was so caught up in how 54 lovely I looked that at first I didn't worry how I would sound. So it was a surprise to me when I hit the first wrong note and I realized something didn't sound quite right. And then I hit another and another followed that. A chill started at the top of my head and began to trickle down. Yet I couldn't stop playing, as though my hands were bewitched. I kept thinking my fingers would adjust themselves back, like a train switching to the right track. I played this strange jumble through two repeats, the sour notes staying with me all the way to the end.

When I stood up, I discovered my legs were shaking. Maybe I had 55 just been nervous and the audience, like Old Chong, had seen me go through the right motions and had not heard anything wrong at all. I swept my right foot out, went down on my knee, looked up and smiled. The room was quiet, except for Old Chong, who was beaming and shouting, "Bravo! Bravo! Well done!" But then I saw my mother's face, her stricken face. The audience clapped weakly, and as I walked back to my chair, with my whole face quivering as I tried not to cry, I heard a little boy whisper loudly to his mother, "That was awful," and the mother whispered back, "Well, she certainly tried."

And now I realized how many people were in the audience, the 56 whole world it seemed. I was aware of eyes burning into my back. I felt the shame of my mother and father as they sat stiffly throughout the rest of the show.

We could have escaped during intermission. Pride and some 57 strange sense of honor must have anchored my parents to their chairs. And so we watched it all: the eighteen-year-old boy with a fake mustache who did a magic show and juggled flaming hoops while riding a unicycle. The breasted girl with white makeup who sang from *Madama Butterfly* and got honorable mention. And the eleven-year-old boy who won first prize playing a tricky violin song that sounded like a busy bee.

After the show, the Hsus, the Jongs, and the St. Clairs from the Joy 58 Luck Club came up to my mother and father.

"Lots of talented kids," Auntie Lindo said vaguely, smiling broadly. 59

"That was somethin' else," said my father, and I wondered if he was 60 referring to me in a humorous way, or whether he even remembered what I had done.

Waverly looked at me and shrugged her shoulders. "You aren't a   61
genius like me," she said matter-of-factly. And if I hadn't felt so bad, I
would have pulled her braids and punched her stomach.

But my mother's expression was what devastated me: a quiet, blank   62
look that said she had lost everything. I felt the same way, and it seemed
as if everybody were now coming up, like gawkers at the scene of an
accident, to see what parts were actually missing. When we got on the bus
to go home, my father was humming the busy-bee tune and my mother was
silent. I kept thinking she wanted to wait until we got home before shouting
at me. But when my father unlocked the door to our apartment, my mother
walked in and then went to the back, into the bedroom. No accusations. No
blame. And in a way, I felt disappointed. I had been waiting for her to start
shouting, so I could shout back and cry and blame her for all my misery.

I assumed my talent-show fiasco meant I never had to play the piano   63
again. But two days later, after school, my mother came out of the
kitchen and saw me watching TV.

"Four clock," she reminded me as if it were any other day. I was   64
stunned, as though she were asking me to go through the talent-show
torture again. I wedged myself more tightly in front of the TV.

"Turn off TV," she called from the kitchen five minutes later.   65

I didn't budge. And then I decided. I didn't have to do what my   66
mother said anymore. I wasn't her slave. This wasn't China. I had listened
to her before and look what happened. She was the stupid one.

She came out from the kitchen and stood in the arched entryway of   67
the living room. "Four clock," she said once again, louder.

"I'm not going to play anymore," I said nonchalantly. "Why should   68
I? I'm not a genius."

She walked over and stood in front of the TV. I saw her chest was   69
heaving up and down in an angry way.

"No!" I said, and I now felt stronger, as if my true self had finally   70
emerged. So this was what had been inside me all along.

"No! I won't!" I screamed.   71

She yanked me by the arm, pulled me off the floor, snapped off the   72
TV. She was frighteningly strong, half pulling, half carrying me toward
the piano as I kicked the throw rugs under my feet. She lifted me up and
onto the hard bench. I was sobbing by now, looking at her bitterly. Her
chest was heaving even more and her mouth was open, smiling crazily as
if she were pleased I was crying.

"You want me to be someone that I'm not!" I sobbed. "I'll never be   73
the kind of daughter you want me to be!"

"Only two kinds of daughters," she shouted in Chinese. "Those   74
who are obedient and those who follow their own mind! Only one kind
of daughter can live in this house. Obedient daughter!"

"Then I wish I wasn't your daughter. I wish you weren't my   75
mother," I shouted. As I said these things I got scared. It felt like worms
and toads and slimy things crawling out of my chest, but it also felt good,
as if this awful side of me had surfaced, at last.

"Too late change this," said my mother shrilly.   76

And I could sense her anger rising to its breaking point. I wanted to   77
see it spill over. And that's when I remembered the babies she had lost in
China, the ones we never talked about. "Then I wish I'd never been
born!" I shouted. "I wish I were dead! Like them."

It was as if I had said the magic words. Alakazam!—and her face   78
went blank, her mouth closed, her arms went slack, and she backed out
of the room, stunned, as if she were blowing away like a small brown
leaf, thin, brittle, lifeless.

It was not the only disappointment my mother felt in me. In the years   79
that followed, I failed her so many times, each time asserting my own
will, my right to fall short of expectations. I didn't get straight As. I didn't
become class president. I didn't get into Stanford. I dropped out of
college.

For unlike my mother, I did not believe I could be anything I   80
wanted to be. I could only be me.

And for all those years, we never talked about the disaster at the   81
recital or my terrible accusations afterward at the piano bench. All that
remained unchecked, like a betrayal that was now unspeakable. So I
never found a way to ask her why she had hoped for something so large
that failure was inevitable.

And even worse, I never asked her what frightened me the most: 82
Why had she given up hope?

For after our struggle at the piano, she never mentioned my playing   83
again. The lessons stopped. The lid to the piano was closed, shutting out
the dust, my misery, and her dreams.

So she surprised me. A few years ago, she offered to give me the   84
piano, for my thirtieth birthday. I had not played in all those years. I saw
the offer as a sign of forgiveness, a tremendous burden removed.

"Are you sure?" I asked shyly. "I mean, won't you and Dad miss it?"   85

"No, this your piano," she said firmly. "Always your piano. You only   86
one can play."

"Well, I probably can't play anymore," I said. "It's been years."   87

"You pick up fast," said my mother, as if she knew this was certain.   88
"You have natural talent. You could been genius if you want to."

"No I couldn't."   89

"You just not trying," said my mother. And she was neither angry   90
nor sad. She said it as if to announce a fact that could never be disproved.
"Take it," she said.

But I didn't at first. It was enough that she had offered it to me. And after that, every time I saw it in my parents' living room, standing in front of the bay windows, it made me feel proud, as if it were a shiny trophy I had won back.   91

Last week I sent a tuner over to my parents' apartment and had the piano reconditioned, for purely sentimental reasons. My mother had died a few months before and I had been getting things in order for my father, a little bit at a time. I put the jewelry in special silk pouches. The sweaters she had knitted in yellow, pink, bright orange—all the colors I hated—I put those in moth-proof boxes. I found some old Chinese silk dresses, the kind with little slits up the sides. I rubbed the old silk against my skin, then wrapped them in tissue and decided to take them home with me.   92

After I had the piano tuned, I opened the lid and touched the keys. It sounded even richer than I remembered. Really, it was a very good piano. Inside the bench were the same exercise notes with handwritten scales, the same secondhand music books with their covers held together with yellow tape.   93

I opened up the Schumann book to the dark little piece I had played at the recital. It was on the left-hand side of the page, "Pleading Child." It looked more difficult than I remembered. I played a few bars, surprised at how easily the notes came back to me.   94

And for the first time, or so it seemed, I noticed the piece on the right-hand side. It was called "Perfectly Contented." I tried to play this one as well. It had a lighter melody but the same flowing rhythm and turned out to be quite easy. "Pleading Child" was shorter but slower; "Perfectly Contented" was longer, but faster. And after I played them both a few times, I realized they were two halves of the same song.   95

Exercises

Some Important Words

prodigy (paragraph 2), reproach (10), sulk (10), listlessly (20), foghorns (20), arpeggios (41), staccato (41), reverie (42), preludes (43), discordant (43), dawdled (50), fiasco (63), nonchalantly (68), shrilly (76).

Some of the Issues

1. Amy Tan opens the story with the mother's philosophy of life in America. How are her views similar to those of other immigrants? In what way are they unusual?

2. In paragraph 4, Jing-mei says "We didn't immediately pick the right kind of prodigy. At first my mother thought I could be a Chinese Shirley Temple." Why wasn't Shirley Temple the "right kind"?

3. In paragraph 9, Jing-mei is excited by the prospect of becoming a prodigy. What do the images she envisions reveal about her self-concept?

4. In paragraph 19, how does seeing her reflection in the mirror change her idea of a prodigy?

5. In paragraph 33, her mother insists that she is not asking her daughter to be a genius—only to do her best—for her own sake. Do you believe that this is true?

6. How would you characterize the dynamics of the relationship between her mother and her friend Auntie Lindo?

7. Right before her piano recital in paragraph 53, Jing-mei talks about her confidence and lack of fear or nervousness. How can this self-confidence be explained, given her piano-playing ability? What role might others have played in fostering this attitude?

8. How do the responses of the audience, Auntie Lindo, and Waverly affect Jing-mei and her mother? What can you infer from her father's comment in paragraph 60?

9. In paragraph 62, why does she want her mother to scold her for her performance at the talent show?

10. In paragraphs 81 and 82, Jing-mei wonders why her mother "hoped for something so large that failure was inevitable," and yet she is frightened that her mother has given up hope. How do you understand this apparent contradiction?

The Way We Are Told

11. What effect does Tan achieve by representing her mother's nonfluent English speech?

12. Tan's sense of humor characterizes her style as a storyteller. Select some examples of humor from the narrative and discuss their effectiveness.

13. Paragraphs 72–78 recount the dramatic scene wherein her mother demands that Jing-mei be the kind of daughter who is obedient. Jing-mei explodes with anger, describing it as feeling "like worms and toads and slimy things crawling out of my chest." What do these images suggest to you about her anger?

14. How do the details of the colored hand-knit sweaters and the Chinese silk dresses contribute to your understanding of Jing-mei's relationship with her mother?

15. In the last paragraphs after the death of her mother, Jing-mei discovers her old music books inside the piano bench. How do the titles of the two musical pieces relate to the whole story?

Some Subjects for Writing

16. Do you think that children of immigrant parents are under more parental pressure to achieve than children of American-born parents? Why or why not?

* 17. Read "Don't Expect Me to Be Perfect." Have you ever been in a situation, like Jing-mei or Sun Park, where you were expected to live up to or even surpass the performance of others? Did this expectation motivate you, or discourage you from trying?

* 18. Read "Fitting In" by John Tarkov. What parallels can you draw between his experience with his father and Jing-mei's relationship with her mother?

MY PAPA'S WALTZ

Theodore Roethke

Theodore Roethke (1908–63), a widely published and much honored American poet, received a Pulitzer Prize in 1953 and a Bollingen Prize in 1958, among other awards. Two of his collections of poems, *Words for the Wind* (1958) and *The Far Field* (1964), received National Book Awards. His *Collected Poems* appeared in 1966. He taught at several universities, last as Poet in Residence at the University of Washington.

This brief poem is like a snapshot—a recollection of a moment that sums up the relationship of father and son.

The whiskey on your breath
Could make a small boy dizzy;
But I hung on like death:
Such waltzing was not easy.

We romped until the pans
Slid from the kitchen shelf;
My mother's countenance
Could not unfrown itself.

The hand that held my wrist
Was battered on one knuckle;
At every step you missed
My right ear scraped a buckle.

You beat time on my head
With a palm caked hard by dirt,
Then waltzed me off to bed
Still clinging to your shirt.

PART FOUR

Identities

Each of us carries a number of identities. We are identified as sons or daughters, as parents, as students, as members of clubs or teams, professions or unions, religious denominations, or social classes. In some cases our particular identities will not only associate us with specific groups of people, but also type us. In American society, as multiethnic and multiracial as it is, this attribution of identity is particularly complex and often carries with it, rightly or wrongly, certain notions about the members of a group.

To compound this complexity, Americans are also a very mobile people. They move physically from one part of the country to another, as well as socially. Young men or women who leave home to go to college may be moving not only a hundred or a thousand miles, but also away from high school friends, associations, and ideas about life. These changes may reshape their identities, the concepts that they and others have of them.

Two of the selections in this section are concerned with education as a cause of such changes in identity. Marcus Mabry, as a college junior, writes about the gap between his earlier and his present life. Returning home to his lower-class neighborhood in New Jersey from the prestigious Stanford University in California, he finds himself with two identities that are hard to reconcile. But the shift from one to the other may have already occurred: at home for spring break, he gets the one good bedroom in the

161

house. He is already "different." A generation older than Mabry, Norman Podhoretz looks back on his high school years, when he fought the relentless efforts of a teacher to transform him from a "slum child" into a member of the educated middle class. Now a member of that class, he realizes that his gains also meant some losses.

A sense of divided identity often results from the shock and disruption of exile and the concomitant need to assimilate into a new culture. Maria L. Muñiz struggled with her Cuban emigré parents to build a new life in America; 16 years later, she yearns to visit friends and relatives left behind in Cuba to preserve and renew "la Cubana" within herself. Likewise, Eva Hoffman feels the pain of nostalgia as she remembers the friends she left in Poland and the sense of strangeness and discomfort with her dual identity.

Pride in African-American identity is fostered in the writings of Malcolm X. He describes how, as a young boy in 1914, he sought to assimilate into white America by straightening his hair, realizing much later in his life the extent to which he had been degrading himself by that attempt. Gerald Early, writing in 1992, argues that African-Americans have given America its particular identity—as a country dedicated to diversity—and cautions against Afrocentric doctrines that preach the necessity of being African at the complete expense of being American. And Gwendolyn Brooks's poem at the end of this section characterizes, in a very few lines, the identities of some who build a wall around themselves—or have others build one around them.

Cultural expectations shape gender identity as well. In a short story, Sandra Cisneros portrays the enormous popularity of Barbie and Ken dolls as both models and reflections of gender roles in America.

LIVING IN TWO WORLDS

Marcus Mabry

Marcus Mabry was a junior at Stanford University when he wrote this
essay for the April 1988 issue of *Newsweek on Campus,* a supplement
to the popular newsmagazine distributed on college campuses. As
he himself tells it, he comes from a poor family in New Jersey whose
lives seem far removed from the life at Stanford, one of the most
affluent universities in the United States. It is this wide gap between
home—African-American, poor—and college—white, mainstream,
and affluent—that Mabry discusses. His double identity attests to
both the mobility in American society and the tensions that it may
create.

A round, green cardboard sign hangs from a string proclaiming, "We built   1
a proud new feeling," the slogan of a local supermarket. It is a souvenir
from one of my brother's last jobs. In addition to being a bagger, he's
worked at a fast-food restaurant, a gas station, a garage and a textile
factory. Now, in the icy clutches of the Northeastern winter, he is
unemployed. He will soon be a father. He is 19 years old.

In mid-December I was at Stanford, among the palm trees and   2
weighty chores of academe. And all I wanted to do was get out. I joined
the rest of the undergrads in a chorus of excitement, singing the praises
of Christmas break. No classes, no midterms, no finals . . . and no
freshmen! (I'm a resident assistant.) Awesome! I was looking forward to
escaping. I never gave a thought to what I was escaping to.

Once I got home to New Jersey, reality returned. My dreaded   3
freshmen had been replaced by unemployed relatives; badgering professors had been replaced by hard-working single mothers, and cold
classrooms by dilapidated bedrooms and kitchens. The room in which
the "proud new feeling" sign hung contained the belongings of myself,
my mom and my brother. But for these two weeks it was mine. They
slept downstairs on couches.

Most students who travel between the universes of poverty and   4
affluence during breaks experience similar conditions, as well as the
guilt, the helplessness and, sometimes, the embarrassment associated
with them. Our friends are willing to listen, but most of them are unable

to imagine the pain of the impoverished lives that we see every six months. Each time I return home I feel further away from the realities of poverty in America and more ashamed that they are allowed to persist. What frightens me most is not that the American socioeconomic system permits poverty to continue, but that by participating in that system I share some of the blame.

Last year I lived in an on-campus apartment, with a (relatively) 5 modern bathroom, kitchen and two bedrooms. Using summer earnings, I added some expensive prints, a potted palm and some other plants, making the place look like the more-than-humble abode of a New York City Yuppie. I gave dinner parties, even a *soirée française.*

For my roommate, a doctor's son, this kind of life was nothing 6 extraordinary. But my mom was struggling to provide a life for herself and my brother. In addition to working 24-hour-a-day cases as a practical nurse, she was trying to ensure that my brother would graduate from high school and have a decent life. She knew that she had to compete for his attention with drugs and other potentially dangerous things that can look attractive to a young man when he sees no better future.

Living in my grandmother's house this Christmas break restored all 7 the forgotten, and the never acknowledged, guilt. I had gone to boarding school on a full scholarship since the ninth grade, so being away from poverty was not new. But my own growing affluence has increased my distance. My friends say that I should not feel guilty: what could I do substantially for my family at this age, they ask. Even though I know that education is the right thing to do, I can't help but feel, sometimes, that I have it too good. There is no reason that I deserve security and warmth, while my brother has to cope with potential unemployment and preju-dice. I, too, encounter prejudice, but it is softened by my status as a student in an affluent and intellectual community.

More than my sense of guilt, my sense of helplessness increases 8 each time I return home. As my success leads me further away for longer periods of time, poverty becomes harder to conceptualize and feels that much more oppressive when I visit with it. The first night of break, I lay in our bedroom, on a couch that let out into a bed that took up the whole room, except for a space heater. It was a little hard to sleep because the springs from the couch stuck through at inconvenient spots. But it would have been impossible to sleep anyway because of the groans coming from my grandmother's room next door. Only in her early 60s, she suffers from many chronic diseases and couldn't help but moan, then pray aloud, then moan, then pray aloud.

This wrenching of my heart was interrupted by the 3 A.M. entry of a 9 relative who had been allowed to stay at the house despite rowdy behavior and threats toward the family in the past. As he came into the house, he slammed the door, and his heavy steps shook the second floor as he stomped into my grandmother's room to take his place, at the foot of her bed. There he slept, without blankets on a bare mattress. This was the first night. Later in the vacation, a Christmas turkey and a Christmas ham were stolen from my aunt's refrigerator on Christmas Eve. We think the thief was a relative. My mom and I decided not to exchange gifts that year because it just didn't seem festive.

A few days after New Year's I returned to California. The Northeast   10
was soon hit by a blizzard. They were there, and I was here. That was the way it had to be, for now. I haven't forgotten; the ache of knowing their suffering is always there. It has to be kept deep down, or I can't find the logic in studying and partying while people, my people, are being killed by poverty. Ironically, success drives me away from those I most want to help by getting an education.

Somewhere in the midst of all that misery, my family has built,   11
within me, "a proud feeling." As I travel between the two worlds it becomes harder to remember just how proud I should be—not just because of where I have come from and where I am going, but because of where they are. The fact that they survive in the world in which they live is something to be very proud of, indeed. It inspires within me a sense of tenacity and accomplishment that I hope every college graduate will someday possess.

Exercises

Some Important Words

academe (paragraph 2), badgering (3), dilapidated (3), affluence (3), socioeconomic (4), abode (5), Yuppie (5), *soirée française*—elegant party in the French style (5), conceptualize (8), wrenching (9), ironically (10), tenacity (11).

Some of the Issues

1. Describe the two worlds Mabry lives in.
2. Mabry looks forward to "escaping" from school (paragraph 2), not an unusual sentiment at the end of a semester. What is he escaping to? Considering the rest of what he tells the reader, what is the real direction of escape?
3. "Once I got home to New Jersey, reality returned" (paragraph 3). Why does Mabry refer to life in New Jersey as "reality"? Is life at Stanford not real?
4. In paragraph 8 Mabry says "More than my sense of guilt, my sense of helplessness increases each time I return home." What events does he describe that contribute to this feeling?

5. Why does Mabry say in paragraph 11 that his family built "a proud feeling" within him?

The Way We Are Told

6. Consider the order of the first two paragraphs. Why does Mabry start with his brother rather than himself? Is the reader likely to be more familiar with the brother's world or Mabry's?
7. In the opening and concluding paragraphs and again in paragraph 3, Mabry refers to the supermarket sign about a "proud new feeling." How does the reference change each time he uses it? How does the repetition of the phrase help him to unify the essay? Try to define the kind of pride he is talking about.
8. Account for Mabry's use of expressions like "weighty chores of academe," "awesome!" "more-than-humble abode," "*soirée française.*" From which of Mabry's two worlds do these phrases come? What does he gain by including them?

Some Subjects for Writing

9. Many people have had the experience of living in two different worlds—perhaps not the same two as Mabry's. If you have had such an experience—in family life, as a result of a job, a vacation, or some other cause—discuss your worlds and your relation to them.
* 10. Read Norman Podhoretz's "The Brutal Bargain." Both he and Mabry originate in an environment of poverty, but they look on it, and their relation to it, in different ways. Compare their attitudes.

BACK, BUT NOT HOME

Maria L. Muñiz

Maria L. Muñiz was born in Cuba in 1958. A few months later, on January 1, 1959, after years of fighting, Fidel Castro led his followers into Havana, Cuba's capital, forcing the dictator Batista to flee the country. Many of Batista's followers left at that time. Later, others disillusioned with the new government joined them.

Muñiz arrived in the United States with her parents when she was five years old, leaving behind, as she explains in this essay, many members of her extended family—grandparents, aunts and uncles, and cousins. As she grew older she felt more keenly a wider sense of cultural loss, which led her to the views expressed in this essay.

In 1978 Muñiz was graduated from New York University and began to work for Catalyst, an organization devoted to expanding career possibilities for women in business and the professions. She has written or edited a number of books on careers for women and published articles in magazines such as *Family Circle* and *Seventeen*.

The essay included here was written when the author was only 20 and first appeared in the *New York Times* on July 13, 1979.

With all the talk about resuming diplomatic relations with Cuba, and with 1 the increasing number of Cuban exiles returning to visit friends and relatives, I am constantly being asked, "Would you ever go back?" In turn, I have asked myself, "Is there any reason for me to go?" I have had to think long and hard before finding my answer. Yes.

I came to the United States with my parents when I was almost five 2 years old. We left behind grandparents, aunts, uncles and several cousins. I grew up in a very middle-class neighborhood in Brooklyn. With one exception, all my friends were Americans. Outside of my family, I do not know many Cubans. I often feel awkward visiting relatives in Miami because it is such a different world. The way of life in Cuban Miami seems very strange to me and I am accused of being too "Americanized." Yet, although I am now an American citizen, whenever anyone has asked me my nationality, I have always and unhesitatingly replied, "Cuban."

Outside American, inside Cuban.   3

I recently had a conversation with a man who generally sympa-   4
thizes with the Castro regime. We talked of Cuban politics and although
the discussion was very casual, I felt an old anger welling inside. After 16
years of living an "American" life, I am still unable to view the revolution
with detachment or objectivity. I cannot interpret its results in social,
political or economic terms. Too many memories stand in my way.

And as I listened to this man talk of the Cuban situation, I began to   5
remember how as a little girl I would wake up crying because I had
dreamed of my aunts and grandmothers and I missed them. I remembered my mother's trembling voice and the sad look on her face
whenever she spoke to her mother over the phone. I thought of the
many letters and photographs that somehow were always lost in transit.
And as the conversation continued, I began to remember how difficult it
often was to grow up Latina in an American world.

It meant going to kindergarten knowing little English. I'd been in   6
this country only a few months and although I understood a good deal of
what was said to me, I could not express myself very well. On the first
day of school I remember one little girl's saying to the teacher: "But how
can we play with her? She's so stupid she can't even talk!" I felt so
helpless because inside I was crying, "Don't you know I can understand
everything you're saying?" But I did not have words for my thoughts and
my inability to communicate terrified me.

As I grew a little older, Latina meant being automatically relegated   7
to the slowest reading classes in school. By now my English was fluent,
but the teachers would always assume I was somewhat illiterate or slow.
I recall one teacher's amazement at discovering I could read and write
just as well as her American pupils. Her incredulity astounded me. As a
child, I began to realize that Latina would always mean proving I was as
good as the others. As I grew older, it became a matter of pride to prove
I was better than the others.

As an adult I have come to terms with these memories and they   8
don't hurt as much. I don't look or sound very Cuban. I don't speak with
an accent and my English is far better than my Spanish. I am beginning
my career and look forward to the many possibilities ahead of me.

But a persistent little voice is constantly saying, "There's something   9
missing. It's not enough." And this is why when I am now asked, "Do you
want to go back?" I say "yes" with conviction.

I do not say to Cubans, "It is time to lay aside the hurt and forgive   10
and forget." It is impossible to forget an event that has altered and scarred
all our lives so profoundly. But I find I am beginning to care less and less
about politics. And I am beginning to remember and care more about the
child (and how many others like her) who left her grandma behind. I have
to return to Cuba one day because I want to know that little girl better.

When I try to review my life during the past 16 years, I almost feel   11
as if I've walked into a theater right in the middle of a movie. And I'm
afraid I won't fully understand or enjoy the rest of the movie unless I can
see and understand the beginning. And for me, the beginning is Cuba. I
don't want to go "home" again; the life and home we all left behind are
long gone. My home is here and I am happy. But I need to talk to my
family still in Cuba.

Like all immigrants, my family and I have had to build a new life   12
from almost nothing. It was often difficult, but I believe the struggle
made us strong. Most of my memories are good ones.

But I want to preserve and renew my cultural heritage. I want to   13
keep "la Cubana" within me alive. I want to return because the journey
back will also mean a journey within. Only then will I see the missing
piece.

Exercises

Some Important Words

exile (paragraph 1), Latina (5), relegated (7), illiterate (7), incredulity (7).

Some of the Issues

1. In paragraph 1 Muñiz says "yes" when she asks herself if there is any
   reason to go back to Cuba. What does she say in paragraphs 2 - 5 that
   helps us to understand her response?
2. What were the difficulties Muñiz encountered in school (paragraphs
   6 and 7)? What bearing do these experiences have on her wish to
   visit Cuba?
3. In paragraph 8, Muñiz, at 20, states that she has "come to terms"
   with her memories. How does she describe herself?
4. What does the "persistent little voice" (paragraph 9) tell Muñiz?
   What is missing? Why is it not enough?
5. What does Muñiz mean by saying in the final paragraph that "the
   journey back will also mean a journey within"?
*6. Read Elizabeth Wong's "The Struggle to Be an All-American Girl";
   then consider Muñiz's characterization of herself as "Outside
   American, inside Cuban." Would a similar statement ("Outside
   American, inside Chinese") apply to Wong? Why or why not?
*7. Read Jack Agueros's "Halfway to Dick and Jane." Both he and Muñiz
   see themselves as half in one culture, half out of it. Compare and
   contrast their experiences.

The Way We Are Told

8. Muñiz uses a common introductory technique: a question whose answer will be the focus of her essay. What are the advantages of this technique?
9. In paragraphs 1, 4, and 10 Muñiz interrupts her personal story with references to more general political issues. What does she gain by doing so?
10. Paragraph 3 consists of one striking statement. How does it sum up what Muñiz has said in the preceding paragraphs? How does it anticipate what she will say later?

Some Subjects for Writing

11. Muñiz was underestimated by teachers and later proved her ability. Recall a time when you or someone else doubted your ability. Describe the circumstances and the outcome.
12. Have you had the experience of returning to a place you knew as a young child? If so, describe that experience telling what you saw and what you felt.
13. Do you believe it is possible or advisable for a person exposed to two cultures to maintain the customs and language of both? You may want to examine other essays that refer to the bicultural experience, such as those by Kingston, Agueros, Wong, and Rodriguez. You may also want to interview someone who has had that experience.

LOST IN TRANSLATION

Eva Hoffman

Eva (Ewa) Hoffman was born in 1945. In 1959 her family emigrated from postwar Poland to Canada. As an adult she has taught literature and written on a variety of cultural subjects. She is the author of a memoir, *Lost in Translation, A Life in a New Language* (1989), and a book about eastern Europe, *Exit into History* (1994). In this excerpt from *Lost in Translation,* she describes the anguish of an adolescent with a bicultural identity in the suburbs of Vancouver.

The car is full of my new friends, or at least the crowd that has more or less accepted me as one of their own, the odd "greener" tag-along. They're as lively as a group of puppies, jostling each other with sharp elbows, crawling over each other to change seats, and expressing their well-being and amiability by trying to outshout each other. It's Saturday night, or rather Saturday Night, and party spirits are obligatory. We're on our way to the local White Spot, an early Canadian version of McDonald's, where we'll engage in the barbarous—as far as I'm concerned—rite of the "drive-in." This activity of sitting in your car in a large parking lot, and having sloppy, big hamburgers brought to you on a tray, accompanied by greasy french fries bounding out of their cardboard containers, mustard, spilly catsup, and sickly smelling relish, seems to fill these peers of mine with warm, monkeyish, groupy comfort. It fills me with a finicky distaste. I feel my lips tighten into an unaccustomed thinness—which, in turn, fills me with a small dislike for myself.

"Come on, foreign student, cheer up," one of the boys sporting a flowery Hawaiian shirt and a crew cut tells me, poking me in the ribs good-naturedly. "What's the matter, don't you like it here?" So as the car caroms off, I try to get in the mood. I try to giggle coyly as the girls exchange insinuating glances—though usually my titter comes a telling second too late. I try to join in the general hilarity, as somebody tells the latest elephant joke. Then—it's always a mistake to try too hard—I decide to show my goodwill by telling a joke myself. Finding some interruption in which to insert my uncertain voice, I launch into a translation of some slightly off-color anecdote I'd heard my father tell in Polish, no doubt hoping to get points for being risqué as well as a good

171

sport. But as I hear my choked-up voice straining to assert itself, as I hear myself missing every beat and rhythm that would say "funny" and "punch line," I feel a hot flush of embarrassment. I come to a lame ending. There's a silence. "I suppose that's supposed to be funny," somebody says. I recede into the car seat.

Ah, the humiliation, the misery of failing to amuse! The incident is   3
as rankling to my amour propre as being told I'm graceless or ugly. Telling a joke is like doing a linguistic pirouette. If you fall flat, it means not only that you don't have the wherewithal to do it well but also that you have misjudged your own skill, that you are fool enough to undertake something you can't finish—and that lack of self-control or self-knowledge is a lack of grace.

But these days, it takes all my will to impose any control on the   4
words that emerge from me. I have to form entire sentences before uttering them; otherwise, I too easily get lost in the middle. My speech, I sense, sounds monotonous, deliberate, heavy—an aural mask that doesn't become me or express me at all. This willed self-control is the opposite of real mastery, which comes from a trust in your own verbal powers and allows for a free streaming of speech, for those bursts of spontaneity, the quickness of response that can rise into pleasure and overflow in humor. Laughter is the lightning rod of play, the eroticism of conversation; for now, I've lost the ability to make the sparks fly.

I've never been prim before, but that's how I am seen by my new   5
peers. I don't try to tell jokes too often, I don't know the slang, I have no cool repartee. I love language too much to maul its beats, and my pride is too quick to risk the incomprehension that greets such forays. I become a very serious young person, missing the registers of wit and irony in my speech, though my mind sees ironies everywhere.

If primness is a small recoil of distaste at things that give others   6
simple and hearty pleasure, then prim is what I'm really becoming. Although I'm not brave enough or hermit enough to stay home by myself every night, I'm a pretend teenager among the real stuff. There's too much in this car I don't like; I don't like the blue eye shadow on Cindy's eyelids, or the grease on Chuck's hair, or the way the car zooms off with a screech and then slows down as everyone plays we're-afraid-of-the-policeman. I don't like the way they laugh. I don't care for their "ugly" jokes, or their five-hundred-pound canary jokes, or their pickle jokes, or their elephant jokes either. And most of all, I hate having to pretend.

Perhaps the extra knot that strangles my voice is rage. I am enraged   7
at the false persona I'm being stuffed into, as into some clumsy and overblown astronaut suit. I'm enraged at my adolescent friends because they can't see through the guise, can't recognize the light-footed dancer I really am. They only see this elephantine creature who too often sounds as if she's making pronouncements.

It will take years before I pick and choose, from the Babel of American language, the style of wit that fits. It will take years of practice before its nuances and patterns snap smartly into the synapses of my brain so they can generate verbal electricity. It will take years of observing the discreet sufferings of the corporate classes before I understand the equally discreet charm of *New Yorker* cartoons. 8

For now, when I come across a *New Yorker* issue, I stare at the drawings of well-heeled people expressing some dissatisfaction with their condition as yet another demonstration of the weirdness all around me. "What's funny about that?" my mother asks in puzzlement. "I don't know," I answer, and we both shrug and shake our heads. And, as the car veers through Vancouver's neatly shrubberied and sparsely populated streets, I know that, among my other faculties, I've lost my sense of humor. I am not about to convert my adolescent friends to anti-Russian jokes. I swallow my injury, and giggle falsely at the five-hundred-pound canary. 9

Happy as larks, we lurch toward the White Spot. 10

If you had stayed there, your hair would have been straight, and you would have worn a barrette on one side. 11

But maybe by now you would have grown it into a ponytail? Like the ones you saw on those sexy faces in the magazine you used to read? 12

I don't know. You would have been fifteen by now. Different from thirteen. 13

You would be going to the movies with Zbyszek, and maybe to a café after, where you would meet a group of friends and talk late into the night. 14

But maybe you would be having problems with Mother and Father. They wouldn't like your staying out late. 15

That would have been fun. Normal. Oh God, to be a young person trying to get away from her parents. 16

But you can't do that. You have to take care of them. Besides, with whom would you go out here? One of these churlish boys who play spin the bottle? You've become more serious than you used to be. 17

What jokes are your friends in Cracow exchanging? I can't imagine. What's Basia doing? Maybe she's beginning to act. Doing exactly what she wanted. She must be having fun. 18

But you might have become more serious even there. 19

Possible. 20

But you would have been different, very different. 21

No question. 22

And you prefer her, the Cracow Ewa. 23

Yes, I prefer her. But I can't be her. I'm losing track of her. In a few years, I'll have no idea what her hairdo would have been like. 24

But she's more real, anyway.   25
Yes, she's the real one.   26

For my birthday, Penny gives me a diary, complete with a little lock and   27
key to keep what I write from the eyes of all intruders. It is that little
lock—the visible symbol of the privacy in which the diary is meant to
exist—that creates my dilemma. If I am indeed to write something
entirely for myself, in what language do I write? Several times, I open the
diary and close it again. I can't decide. Writing in Polish at this point
would be a little like resorting to Latin or ancient Greek—an eccentric
thing to do in a diary, in which you're supposed to set down your most
immediate experiences and unpremeditated thoughts in the most unme-
diated language. Polish is becoming a dead language, the language of the
untranslatable past. But writing for nobody's eyes in English? That's like
doing a school exercise, or performing in front of yourself, a slightly
perverse act of self-voyeurism.

Because I have to choose something, I finally choose English. If I'm   28
to write about the present, I have to write in the language of the present,
even if it's not the language of the self. As a result, the diary becomes
surely one of the more impersonal exercises of that sort produced by an
adolescent girl. These are no sentimental effusions of rejected love,
eruptions of familial anger, or consoling broodings about death. English
is not the language of such emotions. Instead, I set down my reflections
on the ugliness of wrestling; on the elegance of Mozart, and on how
Dostoyevsky puts me in mind of El Greco. I write down Thoughts. I
Write.

There is a certain pathos to this naïve snobbery, for the diary is an   29
earnest attempt to create a part of my persona that I imagine I would
have grown into in Polish. In the solitude of this most private act, I write,
in my public language, in order to update what might have been my
other self. The diary is about me and not about me at all. But on one
level, it allows me to make the first jump. I learn English through writing,
and, in turn, writing gives me a written self. Refracted through the double
distance of English and writing, this self—my English self—becomes
oddly objective; more than anything, it perceives. It exists more easily in
the abstract sphere of thoughts and observations than in the world. For
a while, this impersonal self, this cultural negative capability, becomes
the truest thing about me. When I write, I have a real existence that is
proper to the activity of writing—an existence that takes place midway
between me and the sphere of artifice, art, pure language. This language
is beginning to invent another me. However, I discover something odd.
It seems that when I write (or, for that matter, think) in English, I am
unable to use the word "I." I do not go as far as the schizophrenic

"she"—but I am driven, as by a compulsion, to the double, the Siamese-twin "you."

Exercises

Some Important Words

jostling (paragraph 1), amiability (1), obligatory (1), barbarous (1), rite (1), finicky (1), caroms (2), coyly (2), insinuating (2), titter (2), anecdote (2), risqué (2), lame (2), rankling (3), amour propre (3), pirouette (3), aural (4), prim (5), repartee (5), recoil (6), persona (7), guise (7), pronouncements (7), synapses (8), discreet (8), *New Yorker* (8), well-heeled (9), faculties (9), churlish (17), Cracow (18), eccentric (27), self-voyeurism (27), effusions (28), broodings (28), pathos (29), refracted (29), artifice (29).

Some of the Issues

1. With what details does the author describe the "barbarous" Saturday Night at the White Spot? (paragraphs 1 and 2)?
*2. Compare Hoffman's voice in the joke-telling (paragraph 2) with Maxine Hong Kingston's voice in the school recitation in "Girlhood Among Ghosts" (paragraph 27). What stands out in each author's memory of voice?
3. What is her definition of *prim* in paragraph 6? What do you think is the underlying reason for her primness?
4. In paragraph 8, what does Hoffman say is the key to understanding the humor in *New Yorker* cartoons? What can you infer about the author's appreciation of the cartoons today?
5. In what way does the little lock on her diary create a dilemma (paragraph 27)?
6. Describe Hoffman's "English self" (paragraph 29).
7. How does that persona contrast with her "real self" (paragraphs 25 and 26)?
8. What does Hoffman mean when she says she created herself through writing?

The Way We Are Told

9. What analogy does the author use in paragraph 3 to describe telling a joke? Explain the comparison.
10. In paragraphs 11–26, there is a sudden shift in diction and in audience. What effect does this shift achieve?

11. What evidence in the text illustrates her compulsion to use "the Siamese-twin 'you' " (paragraph 29)?

Some Subjects for Writing

12. In this excerpt, Hoffman is nostalgic for her teenage friends in Cracow. Have you ever experienced a longing to go back to an earlier time or place? Describe a sound, a place, a smell, or a memory of a person that evokes nostalgic feelings for you.
13. Recount an experience from your adolescence and show what it revealed about your developing sense of self.

THE BRUTAL BARGAIN

Norman Podhoretz

As the editor-in-chief of *Commentary,* Norman Podhoretz today is a member of the New York literary establishment. He received a B.A. degree from Columbia University in 1950 at the age of twenty, and a further B.A. from Cambridge University in England two years later. He has written a number of books, including *Breaking Ranks* (1979), *The Present Danger* (1980), *Why We Were in Viet Nam* (1982), *The Bloody Crossroads* (1986), and *Making It* (1964), from which the following selection is taken.

Like Alfred Kazin (see "The Kitchen"), Podhoretz is a child of Jewish immigrants from eastern Europe. He grew up in Brooklyn where, as he tells it, he wanted as a teenager to conform to the ways of his peers, children of poor immigrant origin whose sights were definitely not set on an intellectual career. Podhoretz describes his early, fierce resistance to one of his high school teachers who was determined to turn the "dirty slum child" into a Harvard swan. He wins some of his battles with her, but in the end he loses the war. Looking back he sees the "brutal bargain" he struck. Getting his new identity was a wrenching process of gain and loss.

One of the longest journeys in the world is the journey from Brooklyn to   1
Manhattan—or at least from certain neighborhoods in Brooklyn to certain parts of Manhattan. I have made that journey, but it is not from the experience of having made it that I know how very great the distance is, for I started on the road many years before I realized what I was doing, and by the time I did realize it I was for all practical purposes already there. At so imperceptible a pace did I travel, and with so little awareness, that I never felt footsore or out of breath or weary at the thought of how far I still had to go. Yet whenever anyone who has remained back there where I started— remained not physically but socially and culturally, for the neighborhood is now a Negro ghetto and the Jews who have "remained" in it mostly reside in the less affluent areas of Long Island—whenever anyone like that happens into the world in which I now live with such perfect ease, I can see that in his eyes I have become a fully acculturated citizen of a country as foreign to him as China and infinitely more frightening.

That country is sometimes called the upper middle class; and   2
indeed I am a member of that class, less by virtue of my income than by
virtue of the way my speech is accented, the way I dress, the way I
furnish my home, the way I entertain and am entertained, the way I
educate my children—the way, quite simply, I look and I live. It appalls
me to think what an immense transformation I had to work on myself in
order to become what I have become: if I had known what I was doing
I would surely not have been able to do it, I would surely not have
wanted to. No wonder the choice had to be blind; there was a kind of
treason in it: treason toward my family, treason toward my friends. In
choosing the road I chose, I was pronouncing a judgment upon them,
and the fact that they themselves concurred in the judgment makes the
whole thing sadder but no less cruel.

When I say that the choice was blind, I mean that I was never   3
aware—obviously not as a small child, certainly not as an adolescent, and
not even as a young man already writing for publication and working on
the staff of an important intellectual magazine in New York—how
inextricably my "noblest" ambitions were tied to the vulgar desire to rise
above the class into which I was born; nor did I understand to what an
astonishing extent these ambitions were shaped and defined by the
standards and values and tastes of the class into which I did not know I
wanted to move. It is not that I was or am a social climber as that term is
commonly used. High society interests me, if at all, only as a curiosity; I
do not wish to be a member of it; and in any case, it is not, as I have
learned from a small experience of contact with the very rich and
fashionable, my "scene." Yet precisely because social climbing is not one
of my vices (unless what might be called celebrity climbing, which very
definitely *is* one of my vices, can be considered the contemporary variant
of social climbing), I think there may be more than a merely personal
significance in the fact that class has played so large a part both in my life
and in my career.

But whether or not the significance is there, I feel certain that my   4
longtime blindness to the part class was playing in my life was not
altogether idiosyncratic. "Privilege," Robert L. Heilbroner has shrewdly
observed in *The Limits of American Capitalism,* "is not an attribute we
are accustomed to stress when we consider the construction of *our* social
order." For a variety of reasons, says Heilbroner, "privilege under
capitalism is much less 'visible,' especially to the favored groups, than
privilege under other systems" like feudalism. This "invisibility" extends
in America to class as well.

No one, of course, is so naïve as to believe that America is a   5
classless society or that the force of egalitarianism, powerful as it has
been in some respects, has ever been powerful enough to wipe out class
distinctions altogether. There was a moment during the 1950's, to be

sure, when social thought hovered on the brink of saying that the country had to all intents and purposes become a wholly middle-class society. But the emergence of the civil-rights movements in the 1960's and the concomitant discovery of the poor—to whom, in helping to discover them, Michael Harrington interestingly enough applied, in *The Other America,* the very word ("invisible") that Heilbroner later used with reference to the rich—has put at least a temporary end to that kind of talk. And yet if class has become visible again, it is only in its grossest outlines—mainly, that is, in terms of income levels—and to the degree that manners and style of life are perceived as relevant at all, it is generally in the crudest of terms. There is something in us, it would seem, which resists the idea of class. Even our novelists, working in a genre for which class has traditionally been a supreme reality, are largely indifferent to it—which is to say, blind to its importance as a factor in the life of the individual.

In my own case, the blindness to class always expressed itself in an 6 outright and very often belligerent refusal to believe that it had anything to do with me at all. I no longer remember when or in what form I first discovered that there was such a thing as class, but whenever it was and whatever form the discovery took, it could only have coincided with the recognition that criteria existed by which I and everyone I knew were stamped as inferior: we were in the *lower* class. This was not a proposition I was willing to accept, and my way of not accepting it was to dismiss the whole idea of class as a prissy triviality.

Given the fact that I had literary ambitions even as a small boy, it 7 was inevitable that the issue of class would sooner or later arise for me with a sharpness it would never acquire for most of my friends. But given the fact also that I was on the whole very happy to be growing up where I was, that I was fiercely patriotic about Brownsville (the spawning-ground of so many famous athletes and gangsters), and that I felt genuinely patronizing toward other neighborhoods, especially the "better" ones like Crown Heights and East Flatbush which seemed by comparison colorless and unexciting—given the fact, in other words, that I was not, for all that I wrote poetry and read books, an "alienated" boy dreaming of my escape—my confrontation with the issue of class would probably have come later rather than sooner if not for an English teacher in high school who decided that I was a gem in the rough and who took it upon herself to polish me to as high a sheen as she could manage and I would permit.

I resisted—far less effectively, I can see now, than I then thought, 8 though even then I knew that she was wearing me down far more than I would ever give her the satisfaction of admitting. Famous throughout the school for her altogether outspoken snobbery, which stopped short by only a hair, and sometimes did not stop short at all, of an old-fashioned kind of patrician anti-Semitism, Mrs. K. was also famous for being an extremely good teacher; indeed, I am sure that she saw no distinction between the hopeless task of teaching the proper use of English to the young Jewish barbarians whom fate had so unkindly deposited into her charge and the equally hopeless task of teaching them the proper "manners." (There were as many young Negro barbarians in her charge as Jewish ones, but I doubt that she could ever bring herself to pay very much attention to them. As she never hesitated to make clear, it was punishment enough for a woman of her background—her family was old-Brooklyn and, she would have us understand, extremely distinguished—to have fallen among the sons of East European immigrant Jews.)

For three years, from the age of thirteen to the age of sixteen, I was   9 her special pet, though that word is scarcely adequate to suggest the intensity of the relationship which developed between us. It was a relationship right out of *The Corn Is Green,* which may, for all I know, have served as her model; at any rate, her objective was much the same as the Welsh teacher's in that play: she was determined that I should win a scholarship to Harvard. But whereas (an irony much to the point here) the problem the teacher had in *The Corn Is Green* with her coal-miner pupil in the traditional class society of Edwardian England was strictly academic, Mrs. K.'s problem with me in the putatively egalitarian society of New Deal America was strictly social. My grades were very high and would obviously remain so, but what would they avail me if I continued to go about looking and sounding like a "filthy little slum child" (the epithet she would invariably hurl at me whenever we had an argument about "manners")?

Childless herself, she worked on me like a dementedly ambitious   10 mother with a somewhat recalcitrant son; married to a solemn and elderly man (she was then in her early forties or thereabouts), she treated me like a callous, ungrateful adolescent lover on whom she had humiliatingly bestowed her favors. She flirted with me and flattered me, she scolded me and insulted me. Slum child, filthy little slum child, so beautiful a mind and so vulgar a personality, so exquisite in sensibility and so coarse in manner. What would she do with me, what would become of me if I persisted out of stubbornness and perversity in the disgusting ways they had taught me at home and on the streets?

To her the most offensive of these ways was the style in which I   11 dressed: a tee shirt, tightly pegged pants, and a red satin jacket with the legend "Cherokees, S.A.C." (social-athletic club) stitched in large white letters across the back. This was bad enough, but when on certain days I would appear in school wearing, as a particular ceremonial occasion required, a suit and tie, the sight of those immense padded shoulders and my white-on-white shirt would drive her to even greater heights of contempt and even lower depths of loving despair than usual. *Slum child, filthy little slum child.* I was beyond saving; I deserved no better than to wind up with all the other horrible little Jewboys in the gutter (by which she meant Brooklyn College). If only I would listen to her, the whole world could be mine: I could win a scholarship to Harvard, I could get to know the best people, I could grow up into a life of elegance and refinement and taste. Why was I so stupid as not to understand?

In those days it was very unusual, and possibly even against the   12 rules, for teachers in public high schools to associate with their students after hours. Nevertheless, Mrs. K. sometimes invited me to her home, a beautiful old brownstone located in what was perhaps the only section in the whole of Brooklyn fashionable enough to be intimidating. I would read her my poems and she would tell me about her family, about the schools she had gone to, about Vassar, about writers she had met, while her husband, of whom I was frightened to death and who to my utter astonishment turned out to be Jewish (but not, as Mrs. K. quite unnec-essarily hastened to inform me, *my* kind of Jewish), sat stiffly and silently in an armchair across the room, squinting at his newspaper through the first *pince-nez* I had ever seen outside the movies. He spoke to me but once, and that was after I had read Mrs. K. my tearful editorial for the school newspaper on the death of Roosevelt—an effusion which pro-voked him into a full five-minute harangue whose blasphemous contents would certainly have shocked me into insensibility if I had not been even more shocked to discover that he actually had a voice.

But Mrs. K. not only had me to her house; she also—what was even   13 more unusual—took me out a few times, to the Frick Gallery and the Metropolitan Museum, and once to the theater, where we saw a drama-tization of *The Late George Apley,* a play I imagine she deliberately chose with the not wholly mistaken idea that it would impress upon me the glories of aristocratic Boston.

One of our excursions into Manhattan I remember with particular   14 vividness because she used it to bring the struggle between us to rather a dramatic head. The familiar argument began this time on the subway. Why, knowing that we would be spending the afternoon together "in public," had I come to school that morning improperly dressed? (I was, as usual, wearing my red satin club jacket over a white tee shirt.) She realized, of course, that I owned only one suit (this said not in compassion but in derision) and that my poor parents had, God only knew where, picked up the idea that it was too precious to be worn except at one of those bar mitzvahs I was always going to. Though why, if my parents were so worried about clothes, they had permitted me to buy a suit which made me look like a young hoodlum she found it very difficult to imagine. Still, much as she would have been embarrassed to be seen in public with a boy whose parents allowed him to wear a zoot suit, she would have been somewhat less embarrassed than she was now by the ridiculous costume I had on. Had I no consideration for her? Had I no consideration for myself? Did I want everyone who laid eyes on me to think that I was nothing but an ill-bred little slum child?

My standard ploy in these arguments was to take the position that   15
such things were of no concern to me: I was a poet and I had more important matters to think about than clothes. Besides, I would feel silly coming to school on an ordinary day dressed in a suit. Did Mrs. K. want me to look like one of those "creeps" from Crown Heights who were all going to become doctors? This was usually an effective counter, since Mrs. K. despised her middle-class Jewish students even more than she did the "slum children," but probably because she was growing desperate at the thought of how I would strike a Harvard interviewer (it was my senior year), she did not respond according to form on that particular occasion. "At least," she snapped, "they reflect well on their parents."

I was accustomed to her bantering gibes at my parents, and   16
sensing, probably, that they arose out of jealousy, I was rarely troubled by them. But this one bothered me; it went beyond banter and I did not know how to deal with it. I remember flushing, but I cannot remember what if anything I said in protest. It was the beginning of a very bad afternoon for both of us.

We had been heading for the Museum of Modern Art, but as we got   17
off the subway, Mrs. K. announced that she had changed her mind about the museum. She was going to show me something else instead, just down the street on Fifth Avenue. This mysterious "something else" to which we proceeded in silence turned out to be the college department of an expensive clothing store, de Pinna. I do not exaggerate when I say that an actual physical dread seized me as I followed her into the store. I had never been inside such a store; it was not a store, it was enemy territory, every inch of it mined with humiliations. "I am," Mrs. K. declared in the coldest human voice I hope I shall ever hear, "going to buy you a suit that you will be able to wear at your Harvard interview." I had guessed, of course, that this was what she had in mind, and even at fifteen I understood what a fantastic act of aggression she was planning to commit against my parents and asking me to participate in. Oh no, I said in a panic (suddenly realizing that I *wanted* her to buy me that suit), I can't, my mother wouldn't like it. "You can tell her it's a birthday present. Or else I will tell her. If I tell her, I'm sure she won't object." The idea of Mrs. K. meeting my mother was more than I could bear: my mother, who spoke with a Yiddish accent and of whom, until that sickening moment, I had never known I was ashamed and so ready to betray.

To my immense relief and my equally immense disappointment, we   18
left the store, finally, without buying a suit, but it was not to be the end

of clothing or "manners" for me that day—not yet. There was still the ordeal of a restaurant to go through. Where I came from, people rarely ate in restaurants, not so much because most of them were too poor to afford such a luxury—although most of them certainly were—as because eating in restaurants was not regarded as a luxury at all; it was, rather, a necessity to which bachelors were pitiably condemned. A home-cooked meal was assumed to be better than anything one could possibly get in a restaurant, and considering the class of restaurants in question (they were really diners or luncheonettes), the assumption was probably correct. In the case of my own family, myself included until my late teens, the business of going to restaurants was complicated by the fact that we observed the Jewish dietary laws, and except in certain neighborhoods, few places could be found which served kosher food; in midtown Manhattan in the 1940's, I believe there were only two and both were relatively expensive. All this is by way of explaining why I had had so little experience of restaurants up to the age of fifteen and why I grew apprehensive once more when Mrs. K. decided after we left de Pinna that we should have something to eat.

The restaurant she chose was not at all an elegant one—I have, like   19 a criminal, revisited it since—but it seemed very elegant indeed to me: enemy territory again, and this time a mine exploded in my face the minute I set foot through the door. The hostess was very sorry, but she could not seat the young gentleman without a coat and tie. If the lady wished, however, something could be arranged. The lady (visibly pleased by this unexpected—or was it expected?—object lesson) did wish, and the so recently defiant but by now utterly docile young gentleman was forthwith divested of his so recently beloved but by now thoroughly loathsome red satin jacket and provided with a much oversized white waiter's coat and a tie—which, there being no collar to a tee shirt, had to be worn around his bare neck. Thus attired, and with his face supplying the touch of red which had moments earlier been supplied by his jacket, he was led into the dining room, there to be taught the importance of proper table manners through the same pedagogic instrumentality that had worked so well in impressing him with the importance of proper dress.

Like any other pedagogic technique, however, humiliation has its   20 limits, and Mrs. K. was to make no further progress with it that day. For I had had enough, and I was not about to risk stepping on another mine. Knowing she would subject me to still more ridicule if I made a point of my revulsion at the prospect of eating nonkosher food, I resolved to let her order for me and then to feign lack of appetite or possibly even illness when the meal was served. She did order—duck for both of us, undoubtedly because it would be a hard dish for me to manage without using my fingers.

The two portions came in deep oval-shaped dishes, swimming in a   21
brown sauce and each with a sprig of parsley sitting on top. I had not the
faintest idea of what to do—should the food be eaten directly from the
oval dish or not?—nor which of the many implements on the table to do
it with. But remembering that Mrs. K. herself had once advised me to
watch my hostess in such a situation and then to do exactly as she did, I
sat perfectly still and waited for her to make the first move. Unfortunately,
Mrs. K. also remembered having taught me that trick, and determined as
she was that I should be given a lesson that would force me to mend my
ways, she waited too. And so we both waited, chatting amiably, pretending not to notice the food while it sat there getting colder and colder by
the minute. Thanks partly to the fact that I would probably have gagged
on the duck if I had tried to eat it—dietary taboos are very powerful if
one has been conditioned to them—I was prepared to wait forever. And
in fact it was Mrs. K. who broke first.

"Why aren't you eating?" she suddenly said after something like   22
fifteen minutes had passed. "Aren't you hungry?" Not very, I answered.
"Well," she said, "I think we'd better eat. The food is getting cold."
Whereupon, as I watched with great fascination, she deftly captured the
sprig of parsley between the prongs of her serving fork, set it aside,
took up her serving spoon and delicately used those two esoteric
implements to transfer a piece of duck from the oval dish to her plate. I
imitated the whole operation as best I could, but not well enough to
avoid splattering some partly congealed sauce onto my borrowed coat
in the process. Still, things could have been worse, and having more or
less successfully negotiated my way around that particular mine, I now
had to cope with the problem of how to get out of eating the duck.
But I need not have worried. Mrs. K. took one bite, pronounced it
inedible (it must have been frozen by then), and called in quiet fury for
the check.

Several months later, wearing an altered but respectably conserva-   23
tive suit which had been handed down to me in good condition by a
bachelor uncle, I presented myself on two different occasions before
interviewers from Harvard and from the Pulitzer Scholarship Committee.
Some months after that, Mrs. K. had her triumph: I won the Harvard
scholarship on which her heart had been so passionately set. It was not,
however, large enough to cover all expenses, and since my parents could
not afford to make up the difference, I was unable to accept it. My
parents felt wretched but not, I think, quite as wretched as Mrs. K. For a
while it looked as though I would wind up in the "gutter" of Brooklyn
College after all, but then the news arrived that I had also won a Pulitzer
Scholarship which paid full tuition if used at Columbia and a small
stipend besides. Everyone was consoled, even Mrs. K.: Columbia was at
least in the Ivy League.

The last time I saw her was shortly before my graduation from   24
Columbia and just after a story had appeared in the *Times* announcing
that I had been awarded a fellowship which was to send me to
Cambridge University. Mrs. K. had passionately wanted to see me in
Cambridge, Massachusetts, but Cambridge, England was even better.
We met somewhere near Columbia for a drink, and her happiness over
my fellowship, it seemed to me, was if anything exceeded by her
delight at discovering that I now knew enough to know that the right
thing to order in a cocktail lounge was a very dry martini with lemon
peel, please.

Exercises

Some Important Words

imperceptible (paragraph 1), acculturated (1), idiosyncratic (4), attribute
(4), egalitarianism (5), genre (5), triviality (6), alienated (7), patrician (8),
dementedly (10), recalcitrant (10), intimidating (12), *pince-nez* (12),
effusion (12), harangue (12), blasphemous (12), insensibility (12), derision (14), zoot suit (14), bantering (16), gibes (16), pitiably (18), divested
(19), pedagogic (19), instrumentality (19).

Some of the Issues

1. Explain what kind of "journey" Podhoretz refers to in paragraph 1.
2. In paragraph 2 Podhoretz refers to his journey as "a kind of treason."
   What does he mean?
3. In Podhoretz's view, America is not a classless society (paragraph 5),
   but seems so at times because both the poor and the rich seem
   invisible. What would you say is the meaning of class in America? On
   what grounds do you place people in this class structure?
4. Reread the first sentence of paragraph 7; why is a link between class
   and literary ambition "inevitable"?
5. Where and how does Podhoretz make the transition from his general
   observations to the particular story he wants to tell?
6. Beginning with paragraph 14, Podhoretz focuses on one particular
   day he spent with Mrs. K. How exactly do these episodes show what
   Mrs. K. wants to change in Podhoretz?
7. Consider the title of the selection: "The Brutal Bargain." How does
   Podhoretz's story relate to that title?
8. In the struggle between Podhoretz and Mrs. K., who wins the battle?
   Who wins the war?

The Way We Are Told

9. Podhoretz opens his essay with the image of a journey. Examine how he uses the analogy in paragraphs 1 and 2.

10. When Podhoretz introduces Mrs. K., he widens the analogy of the journey; it becomes a journey into battle. Paragraphs 8 through 11 contain words and phrases that introduce the idea of combat. Find them.

11. In paragraph 14 Podhoretz begins his climactic, detailed story about the store and the restaurant. Show how he continues to develop his analogy of the journey here, both the journey into a new class and the journey into battle.

Some Subjects for Writing

12. Try to describe some basic change in your life, using a controlling image such as one of those Podhoretz uses: a journey, a series of battles, or a treasonable activity, or another image appropriate to your story. Subjects might be the changing or dropping of friends, going off to college, leaving a job.

13. Education can take many forms. School and college are not the only places where it occurs. In an essay describe and analyze three or four situations in which significant nonformal education takes place.

*14. John Tarkov ("Fitting In"), Harry Mark Petrakis ("Barba Nikos"), and Podhoretz all look back to their youth and to the tensions inherent in cultural change. All three react somewhat differently. Compare and contrast their reactions in an essay.

HAIR

Malcolm X

Malcolm X, born in Omaha, Nebraska, in 1925, changed his name from Malcolm Little when he joined Elijah Muhammad's Black Muslims, in which he eventually moved up to become second in command. He broke with the Muslims because of major differences in policy and established an organization of his own. Soon after that he was assassinated at a public meeting, on February 21, 1965. *The Autobiography of Malcolm X,* written with the help of Alex Haley (later more widely known as the author of *Roots*), was published in 1964. The selection reprinted here is from one of the early parts of the book and records an experience during his junior high school years in Michigan, in 1941. Malcolm X gives the reader what amounts to a recipe, but a recipe on two levels: he describes in detail the painful process of "conking," straightening hair, that he as a boy subjected himself to. On a more fundamental level it was, as he says, a "big step toward self-degradation."

Shorty soon decided that my hair was finally long enough to be conked. 1
He had promised to school me in how to beat the barbershop's three- and four-dollar price by making up congolene, and then conking ourselves.

I took the little list of ingredients he had printed out for me, and 2
went to a grocery store, where I got a can of Red Devil lye, two eggs, and two medium-sized white potatoes. Then at a drugstore near the pool-room, I asked for a large jar of vaseline, a large bar of soap, a large-toothed comb and a fine-toothed comb, one of those rubber hoses with a metal spray-head, a rubber apron and a pair of gloves.

"Going to lay on that first conk?" the drugstore man asked me. I 3
proudly told him, grinning, "Right!"

Shorty paid six dollars a week for a room in his cousin's shabby 4
apartment. His cousin wasn't at home. "It's like the pad's mine, he spends so much time with his woman," Shorty said, "Now, you watch me—"

He peeled the potatoes and thin-sliced them into a quart-sized 5
Mason fruit jar, then started stirring them with a wooden spoon as he gradually poured in a little over half the can of lye. "Never use a metal spoon; the lye will turn it black," he told me.

A jelly-like, starchy-looking glop resulted from the lye and potatoes, and Shorty broke in the two eggs, stirring real fast—his own conk and dark face bent down close. The congolene turned pale-yellowish. "Feel the jar," Shorty said. I cupped my hand against the outside, and snatched it away. "Damn right, it's hot, that's the lye," he said. "So you know it's going to burn when I comb it in—it burns *bad*. But the longer you can stand it, the straighter the hair." 6

He made me sit down, and he tied the string of the new rubber apron tightly around my neck, and combed up my bush of hair. Then, from the big vaseline jar, he took a handful and massaged it hard all through my hair and into the scalp. He also thickly vaselined my neck, ears and forehead. "When I get to washing out your head, be sure to tell me anywhere you feel any little stinging," Shorty warned me, washing his hands, then pulling on the rubber gloves, and tying on his own rubber apron. "You always got to remember that any congolene left in burns a sore into your head." 7

The congolene just felt warm when Shorty started combing it in. But then my head caught fire. 8

I gritted my teeth and tried to pull the sides of the kitchen table together. The comb felt as if it was raking my skin off. 9

My eyes watered, my nose was running. I couldn't stand it any longer; I bolted to the washbasin. I was cursing Shorty with every name I could think of when he got the spray going and started soap-lathering my head. 10

He lathered and spray-rinsed, lathered and spray-rinsed, maybe ten or twelve times, each time gradually closing the hot-water faucet, until the rinse was cold, and that helped some. 11

"You feel any stinging spots?" 12

"No," I managed to say. My knees were trembling. 13

"Sit back down, then. I think we got it all out okay." 14

The flame came back as Shorty, with a thick towel, started drying my head, rubbing hard. "*Easy, man, easy*" I kept shouting. 15

"The first time's always worst. You get used to it better before long. You took it real good, homeboy. You got a good conk." 16

When Shorty let me stand up and see in the mirror, my hair hung down in limp, damp strings. My scalp still flamed, but not as badly; I could bear it. He draped the towel around my shoulders, over my rubber apron, and began again vaselining my hair. 17

I could feel him combing, straight back, first the big comb, then the fine-tooth one. 18

Then, he was using a razor, very delicately, on the back of my neck. Then, finally, shaping the sideburns. 19

My first view in the mirror blotted out the hurting. I'd seen some pretty conks, but when it's the first time, on your *own* head, the transformation, after the lifetime of kinks, is staggering. 20

The mirror reflected Shorty behind me. We both were grinning and   21
sweating. And on top of my head was this thick, smooth sheen of shining
red hair—real red—as straight as any white man's.

How ridiculous I was! Stupid enough to stand there simply lost in   22
admiration of my hair now looking "white," reflected in the mirror in
Shorty's room. I vowed that I'd never again be without a conk, and I
never was for many years.

This was my first really big step toward self-degradation: when I   23
endured all of that pain, literally burning my flesh to have it look like a white
man's hair. I had joined that multitude of Negro men and women in America
who are brainwashed into believing that the black people are "inferior"—
and white people "superior"—that they will even violate and mutilate their
God-created bodies to try to look "pretty" by white standards.

Exercises

Some of the Issues

1. What is a conk and why did Malcolm X want it?
2. Why does Malcolm X describe the process of buying the ingredients
   and of applying them in such detail?
3. What is the thesis of this short selection? With what arguments,
   information, or assertions does Malcolm X support his thesis?

The Way We Are Told

4. The selection divides into two very different parts. What are they?
   How do they differ?
5. The main part of the selection is a description of a process. How is it
   arranged? What qualities of instruction, even of a recipe, has it? How
   and where does it differ from a recipe?

Some Subjects for Writing

6. Malcolm X describes a process that shows, among other things, that
   people will go to great lengths to conform. Develop a short essay
   describing, in a straightforward, neutral manner, some example of
   how people will subject themselves to pain, inconvenience, and
   embarrassment to conform to some fashion or idea.
7. Rewrite your previous essay, but take a strong stand indicating
   approval or disapproval of the process.
*8. Write an essay examining the rewards American society offers for
   conforming, or the penalties for not conforming. In addition to
   Malcolm X, you might read Podhoretz's "The Brutal Bargain."

THEIR MALCOLM,
MY PROBLEM

Gerald Early

Gerald Early was born in Philadelphia, Pennsylvania, in 1952. He graduated from the University of Pennsylvania and received his Ph.D. from Cornell in 1982. Early is the director of African and Afro-American Studies at Washington University in St. Louis, and the author of *Tuxedo Junction: Essays on American Culture* (1989) and a book of poems, *How the War in the Streets Is Won* (1993). He is also the editor of *Lure and Loathing* (1993), a collection of essays by 20 African-American intellectuals on the issue raised by the American historian and educator W. E. B. Du Bois nearly a century ago: "the double consciousness" of being Black and American.

In this essay from *Harper's* magazine, Early explains why his views toward the writings of Malcolm X have changed since the latter's assassination in 1965. He criticizes Malcolm X for preaching the necessity of being African at the complete expense of being American. In his view, African-Americans have given America its unique identity as a country dedicated to diversity, a nation of different peoples living together as one.

Late one afternoon last spring I sat at home on my couch, disheartened, 1
thumbing through an old copy of *The Autobiography of Malcolm X*.
Earlier that afternoon I'd had a lengthy meeting with black students from
my university, and although Malcolm X had been in the air on campus for
some time—the proliferation of X caps and T-shirts, gossip about the
Spike Lee movie, which would open at the end of the year—I suspect it
was mostly the passionate and angry tone of the black voices at the
meeting that prompted me to pull my copy of the book off the shelf.

I had reread *The Autobiography* many times, having taught it on 2
several occasions. A considerable literary accomplishment, it borrows
freely and innovatively from St. Augustine's *Confessions,* the slave
narrative tradition, and the bildungsroman tradition of Fielding and
Goethe. As a boy I felt it was the only book written expressly for me, a
young black American male. But over the years my view changed: the

book's rhetoric began to seem awkwardly out of date, and the energy of the man seemed contained in a vision that was as narrow as it was vivid; there was something about the nature of Malcolm's raillery that now left me unprovoked, something about his quest for humanity that left me unmoved.

But as I sat on the couch working my way through the narrative   3 that afternoon, I found much of what I'd been moved by so long ago coming back to me with remarkable force. I read again with revived interest how Malcolm was born in Omaha in 1925, the seventh child of a father who was an itinerant preacher, a fierce follower of Marcus Garvey, and of a mother so light-skinned that she was frequently mistaken for white. When Malcolm was six years old his father was murdered, presumably by white terrorists, because of his black-nationalist beliefs. It is this death, as well as the institutionalization of his mother—who suffered a breakdown as the result of her husband's murder and her struggle to support her family on welfare—that establishes the pattern of both the book and the life as a critique of racism and liberalism. As Malcolm claims angrily, "I am a creation of the Northern white man and of his hypocritical attitude toward the Negro."

After growing up in a detention home in Mason, Michigan, and   4 spending some time in Boston's Roxbury ghetto, living with his half sister, Malcolm, at age seventeen, settled in Harlem and became a petty hustler and dope pusher. He participated in a string of burglaries of rich white suburban homes but was caught, convicted, and sentenced to ten years in prison. While in jail Malcolm converted to Elijah Muhammad's Nation of Islam, embracing a strict religious but militantly racialist outlook and dedicating himself to telling "the truth about the white man." Once out of prison, Malcolm became Muhammad's most effective minister and proselytizer, attracting adherents and also the attention of the white media. In 1964 Malcolm was excommunicated from the Nation, ostensibly for describing the assassination of John Kennedy as the "chickens coming home to roost." But a schism had been brewing for some time: Muhammad had become increasingly jealous over Malcolm's media attention, Malcolm's stardom, while Malcolm had become disillusioned by Muhammad's extramarital affairs and the older man's reluctance to become more politically active.

After leaving the Nation, Malcolm tried, unsuccessfully, to found   5 two organizations, Muslim Mosque, Inc., and the Organization of Afro-American Unity, the latter patterned after the Organization of African Unity. During the last two years of his life, he traveled extensively in Africa and also made a pilgrimage to Mecca, during which he reconverted to a non-racialist Islam. He was assassinated in Harlem by members of the Nation of Islam in February 1965, just as he was about to give a speech. An angry end to an angry life.

Leafing through *The Autobiography*, I began to see that Malcolm X   6
was the ideological standard of Africanness now being offered up by my
students. His singular presence had been much in evidence at that
afternoon's meeting. I had agreed to sit down with a coalition of black
students—most of whom did not know me—soon after it was announced
that I was to become the new director of African and Afro-American
Studies at my university. In the weeks before we arranged to convene, I
had been furiously denounced and publicly pilloried for not being
sufficiently Afrocentric to head the department, a charge rather akin to
being "not black enough" in the 1960s.

What I found particularly baffling about these attacks was that I do   7
not possess any of the "social tokens" often associated with being
"insufficiently black": I do not have a white wife; I have served on most
of the university's affirmative-action committees; I am intellectually
engaged in the study of black subject matter; I have never publicly
criticized any black person connected with the campus during my entire
ten-year stay.

But in the eyes of these students, I had failed as a black man. I had   8
never led a protest march or even proposed that one be held. I had never
initiated or signed a petition. I had never attended any student meetings
that focused on black issues. I had never, in short, done anything
deemed heroic. And, for the young, a lack of demonstrable, outsized
heroism is a lack of commitment and a lack of commitment is a sign of
having sold out.

Some of this standard teacher-student strife is to be expected; I   9
suppose it is generational. Still, I was deeply pained to have been seen by
my black students as someone who compromised, who slouched, who
shuffled, someone who had not stood up and been counted, someone
who had never done anything heroic for the race.

When my ten-year-old daughter came home from school, she was   10
surprised to find me home, and more surprised to find me visibly upset.

"What's wrong?" she asked.   11

"The American Negro," I began sarcastically, as she made herself a   12
snack, "goes through periodic bouts of dementia when he romantically
proclaims himself an African, lost from his brothers and sisters. These
tides of benighted nationalism come and go, but this time it seems
particularly acute." By now my voice had become strident, my rage
nearly out of control.

"Never had I been subjected to more anti-intellectual, proto-fascistic   13
nonsense than what I have had to endure in the name of Afrocentrism.
And this man," I said, waving Malcolm's autobiography, "is the architect
of it all, the father of Afrocentrism. This idiot, this fool." I slumped at the
kitchen table, placing my forehead against the cool wood.

"But I thought you liked Malcolm X," she said.   14

Indeed, I was once keenly fond of Malcolm X. I first saw Malcolm on   15
television in 1963, when I was a ten-year-old boy living in Philadelphia;
three years later Malcolm, by now dead if not forgotten, left an indelible
mark on my life. That year my oldest sister, then a college student, joined
the local chapter of the Student Nonviolent Coordinating Committee
(SNCC), which at the time was becoming an increasingly Marxist and
militant group. Her conversation was now peppered with phrases like
"the white power structure," "the man," "black power," and "self-
determination for oppressed people." One day she brought home a
recorded Malcolm X speech entitled "Message to the Grass Roots."

Hearing it for the first time was a shock and a revelation. I had heard   16
men in barbershops say many of the same things but never in public. I
laughed and laughed at Malcolm's oratory, but I felt each word burn with
the brightness of a truth that was both utterly new and profoundly familiar.
Whenever I had the chance, I would play the record over and over. In a
few days I had memorized the entire speech, every word, every turn of
phrase, every vocal nuance. I could deliver the speech just as Malcolm
had. I never looked at the world in quite the same way again.

During the days of segregation, which continued, de facto, into the   17
Sixties, belonging to an all-black institution—anything from a church to a
social club to a Boy Scout troop—was like wearing a badge of inferiority.
Participation in these groups was not a choice made by blacks but a fiat,
decreed by whites, which clearly stated that blacks were not considered,
in any way, part of the white world—for most blacks, a world where what
happened, mattered. But Malcolm asserted blackness as a source of
honor and accomplishment, not degradation and shame.

Within months of the time I first heard Malcolm's "Message to the   18
Grass Roots," I not only had read his autobiography but had listened
carefully to other of his speeches, such as "The Ballot or the Bullet" and
"Malcolm X on Afro-American History." I had become knowledgeable
about the Congo, Patrice Lumumba, the Bandung Conference, and the
leadership of the American civil rights movement, topics that were hardly
of interest to other boys my age.

Not everyone I knew responded enthusiastically to Malcolm X. I   19
would often hear men in the barbershop making statements like: "All that
Malcolm X does is talk. In fact, that's what all them Muslims do is talk.
Just another nigger hustle." And one day, when I was fourteen, my friend
Gary became very angry with me when—with Malcolm X in mind—I
called him black.

"Don't call me black, man. I don't like that. I ain't black," he said   20
vehemently.

"We are all black people," I said. "You've been brainwashed by the   21
white man to hate your color. But you're black, and you've got to accept
that."

"I said don't call me black," he shouted. "What's wrong with you, anyway? You sound like you been hanging out with them Malcolm X guys. He was a phony just like all the rest of them Muslims. You sound like you snappin' out or something." 22

I was surprised at Gary's reaction. He was bigger and tougher than I was, and I assumed that he would view Malcolm as a hero, too. But when it became clear he didn't, I felt personally insulted. 23

"You're black, black, black," I said angrily. "Malcolm X was a great man who tried to free black people. What've you ever done to free black people? You're black and I'll call you black anytime I want to, you dumb nigger." 24

He hit me so hard in the chest that I fell down in the street, stunned and hurt by the blow. 25

"Don't call me that," he said, walking away. 26

It is unlikely that a young black person today would get swatted for defending Malcolm X. In fact, in many ways Malcolm's presence is more deeply felt in the black community now than at any time since his murder. The reasons for his enduring legacy are complex. Malcolm X does not remain an important figure in American cultural history simply because he was a charismatic black nationalist. Hubert H. Harrison, Henry McNeal Turner, Richard B. Moore, Martin Delany, David Walker, Elijah Muhammad, Alexander Crummell, Edward Wilmot Blyden, and Ron Karenga all were charismatic black nationalists of some sort in the nineteenth and twentieth centuries, and none is remembered as a distinct figure except by historians of African-American life and culture. 27

Malcolm was a fierce debater, a compelling public speaker, and a man of considerable intellectual agility. But, like Martin Luther King, he was hardly an original thinker: American blacks have been hearing some form of black nationalism—Ethiopianism, the back-to-Africa movement, Black Judaism, the Black Moors, Pan-Africanism, the Black Aesthetic, or Afrocentrism—for well over 200 years. Malcolm's basic idea—a vision of millenarian race-based cultural nationalism culminating in a worldwide race war that would overturn European dominance forever—was, like the Puritanism of Jonathan Edwards, already hoary with age even when it seemed most current. But just as Edwards brilliantly disseminated Calvinist ideas, Malcolm, with valor and wit, popularized ideas about black nationalism, black self-determination, and a universal African identity. 28

More important, however, than Malcolm's ideas—that is, his popularizing of black nationalism—was, and is, Malcolm the man. His life unfolded like a myth, a heroic tale. He had the imprimatur of both prison (the mark of a revolutionary) and the street (the mark of the proletariat), which lent him authenticity. But, as a Muslim, he was also a firm believer in the bourgeois ideals of diligence, discipline, and entrepreneurship. 29

Then there was Malcolm's youth. Although generational conflict 30
exists in many societies, it has a long and particularly intense history for
blacks. Each new generation views its elders with suspicion, thinking
them failures who compromised and accommodated themselves in order
to survive among the whites. And each generation, in some way, wishes
to free itself from the generation that produced it.

Malcolm's particular brand of youthfulness fed this desire. He em- 31
bodied a daring and a recklessness that young blacks, especially young
black men, have found compelling. At rallies I attended as a teenager in
the early 1970s, men older than myself would describe the inspiring
experience of having heard Malcolm live. They had, on several occasions
a decade earlier, attended Savior's Day rallies, annual Muslim conventions
during which Elijah Muhammad was scheduled to speak. But Malcolm
would always appear on the dais first. He was supposed to serve, simply,
as the warm-up act, but for these young men he always stole the show.
While black nationalist and separatist ideas coming from Elijah Muhammad seemed cranky, cult-like, backwaterish, and marginal, the same ideas
coming from Malcolm seemed revolutionary, hip, and vibrant.

Malcolm arrived on the scene during the age of Kennedy and King, 32
the blossoming of youth culture and the coming of rock and roll.
Flaunting his youth as a symbol of masculinity and magnetic power, he
exploited the generation gap among blacks. Because of Malcolm, the
leaders of the civil rights movement were made, through their comparative conservatism, to seem even older than they were, more cowardly
than they were, bigger sellouts than they were. He referred to them as
"Uncle Toms" or as "Uncles," associating them with the conflated
popular image of both Uncle Remus and Uncle Tom, fictional characters
created by white writers, aged black men who "loved their white folks."
Malcolm used this language even when talking about Martin Luther King,
who was, in fact, younger than he was. And Malcolm remains forever
young, having died at the age of thirty-nine. He—like the Kennedys and
King—died the tragic death of a political martyr.

Malcolm, the dead hero, has grown in stature in our black con- 33
sciousness even while other living former heroes are forgotten. It is
telling to compare the current view of Malcolm with that of another
important black figure of the 1960s, Muhammad Ali. Ali and Malcolm are
often yoked together in the black mind: two militant Muslims, public
troublemakers, disturbers of the peace. But today, those of us who lived
through the 1960s return to thinking about Malcolm not simply because
of his greater intellect but because we are unnerved by Ali now, by the
brain damage he has suffered in the ring, by the way he has aged.
Malcolm remains frozen forever in his stern youthfulness, almost immortal, like a saint, while Ali is a mirror of our own aging and mortality, a
busted-up, broken-down hero.

No doubt Malcolm's early death contributed to his enduring power   34
for young people today. But it is the existence of *The Autobiography* that
has mythologized him forever. If Malcolm—or Alex Haley (who assisted
in writing *The Autobiography*) or Malcolm's wife, Betty Shabazz (who is
said to have done extensive revisions on Haley's manuscript)—had not
written his story, he would have died a negligible curiosity on the
American political landscape in much the same way that, say, George
Lincoln Rockwell or Father Divine did. Today it is rare to come upon a
black student who has not read *The Autobiography of Malcolm X* or will
not read it at some point during his or her college career. It has sold more
than 3 million copies and is probably the most commonly taught and
most frequently recommended book written by a black American male.

Malcolm, frozen in time, stands before us as the lonely outsider, a   35
kind of bespectacled prince, estranged and embattled, holding a high-
noon posture of startling and doomed confrontation. It is this man who
has become for young blacks today the kind of figure that Thoreau, who
espoused the overturning of generations and the uselessness of the
elders in *Walden,* was for young whites in the late 1960s.

When I was growing up in the 1960s the goal for blacks was clear: 36
equality and integration. The civil rights movement, which provided an
arena for heroic political action aimed at destroying segregation, helped
forge this consensus among blacks. Today blacks, confused and angered
by the failure of "the dream," share little agreement about the future.
There is a sense that integration has been half-hearted and has been
achieved only at the expense of black identity.

To today's young, middle-class blacks in particular, Malcolm's   37
espousal of all-blackness—the idea that everything black is inherently
good and that blacks must purge themselves of white "contaminants"—
may be especially crucial; it is certainly more important than it was to my
generation. These young people have grown up, by and large, in an
integrated world. Most of the black students who attend the standard
prestigious, private, research-oriented university are the offspring of
either black professional parents or a mixed marriage, have lived most of
their lives in mixed or largely white neighborhoods, and have attended
white prep schools or predominantly white public schools. When they
arrive at a university that has an African or Afro-American Studies
program, these students expect to find, for the first time in their lives, an
all-black community, one that they have never experienced in the secular
world, a sort of intellectual "nation within a nation," to borrow W. E. B.
Du Bois's term. There they can be their "true" black selves. Yet in many
ways these black students share fundamentally the same values—a belief
in upward mobility and the rewards of hard work—as the whites who
surround them. These students are wholly neither inside nor outside of

the American mainstream, and they are unsure whether any ideal form of integration exists. But, like Malcolm, they wish to rid themselves of their feelings of ambiguity, their sense of the precariousness of their belonging. For many of them (and they are not entirely unjustified in feeling this way) integration is the badge of degradation and dishonor, of shame and inferiority, that segregation was for my generation.

I also have felt great shame in the era of integration because, as a   38
student and as a professor, I have taken the money of whites, been paid simply because I was black and was expected to make "black statements" in order to be praised by whites for my Negro-ness. I have felt much as if I were doing what James Baldwin described black domestics in white homes as doing: stealing money and items from whites that the whites expected them to take, wanted them to take, because it reinforced the whites' superiority and our own degradation. Allowing the whites to purchase my "specialness" through affirmative action has seemed not like reparations but like a new form of enslavement.

And I worry about my daughters, wondering whether they are   39
getting too cozy with whites at school and whether they seem too utterly middle class. So much are they protected from any blatant form of racism that I fear they are likely never to understand that it existed and continues to exist today. At these times I feel estranged from my children, knowing that I do not fully understand their experience, nor do they understand mine. For instance, when we moved to an affluent white suburb they clamored for a golden retriever, no doubt because a neighbor down the street had a very attractive one. I adamantly refused to consent, thinking that purchasing a friendly, suburban, sitcom-type dog was another concession to white, middle-class taste. "I don't like dogs," I said childishly before I finally relented.

On occasions like this, when I have wanted to instill in my   40
daughters a sense of "blackness," I tend to trot out a story about my boyhood. It is an anecdote that involves my friend Gary, and it took place about six months after our fight over Malcolm X. Think of my story as the black parent's jeremiad, a warning about the declension of the new generation. And once again Malcolm X seems central to it.

In order to get home from school each day, Gary and I had to walk   41
through an Italian neighborhood. Often during these trips home, several older Italian boys and their Doberman pinschers would chase Gary and me, or a group of us, for several blocks. Once we hit the border of our black Philadelphia neighborhood, around Sixth Street, they would retreat. The Italian boys called this game "chasing the coons" or "spooking the spooks," and it sometimes resulted in a black kid being bitten by one of their dogs. The black kids never fought back; we just ran, later cursing the Italian boys, rhetorically wreaking all manner of vengeance upon them.

On this particular afternoon, both Gary and I had bought sodas and 42
doughnuts, as we usually did, on our way home from school, and we
were strolling along when we suddenly heard some voices cry out, "Get
those niggers." We turned to see about five or six Italian boys and an
unleashed Doberman coming after us. We started running like beings
possessed. We were comfortably ahead and easily could have avoided
getting caught when Gary abruptly pulled up and caught my arm.

"I'm tired of running from them guys. I ain't running anymore and 43
neither are you."

"Hey, man," I said frantically. "Are you crazy or something? What 44
are we gonna do? Fight 'em? You must be crazy. I'm getting out of here."

"You ain't going nowhere," he said angrily through his teeth. "It's 45
time we stood up for ourselves. I'm tired of having them white bastards
chase me and laugh at me. If they beat us up, well, I guess that's one ass
whipping we got to take. But I ain't running."

Gary turned his soda bottle over in his hand like a weapon and I 46
reluctantly did the same. He picked up a brick from the street and I
followed; we waited for the Italian boys to catch up. When they did they
looked almost bewildered. They stood, perhaps twenty feet from us,
slowly comprehending that we were standing our ground. For several
moments, except for the growling dog, everyone was silent. Then one of
them spoke.

"What you niggers doing walking through our neighborhood? We 47
got a hunting season on jungle bunnies."

"We ain't causing no trouble," Gary said. "We just minding our own 48
business. And if you come another step closer, I guarantee I'll put your
ass in the hospital."

We all stood for what seemed the longest time, as if frozen in some 49
sort of still life. I was gripping the brick and bottle so hard my hands
ached. I felt ready, even eager, to fight, but I was also relieved when I
realized we wouldn't have to.

One Italian boy mumbled something about watching ourselves 50
"next time," and they all began to drift off.

As they were retreating, Gary shouted, "And we ain't no niggers. 51
We're black. Don't ever call us niggers again."

At this I was more than slightly startled, but I was very proud, as if I 52
had made a convert. I recalled at that instant something I had heard Malcolm
X say on television, something like, "The so-called Negro has to stop the
sit-in, the beg-in, the crawl-in, asking for something that is by rights already
his. The so-called Negro has to approach the white man as a man himself."
We felt like men, grown-up men, or what we thought grown-up men must
feel like when they have been tested and found themselves adequate.

Never once have I told this story in any way that impresses my 53
daughters. My youngest usually says, "Are you finished now, Daddy?"

They know the moral is something to the effect that it is good to be   54
black and that it is something for which we must all stand up. "Yeah," my
youngest says, "it's good to be black, but it's better not to have to spend
all your time thinking about how good it is to be black."

So here I am, caught between my daughters, who find my race lessons   55
tiresome, and my students, who think me somehow insufficiently black.
I need look no farther than Malcolm, old ally and new nemesis, to find
the source of this ambiguity. Malcolm embodied contradiction. He
preached the importance of Africa, yet he was the most American of men.
His autobiography is the quintessential Horatio Alger tale of the self-
created individual. Even Malcolm's turn toward Islam, his attempt to
embrace something explicitly non-Western, is itself classically American.
Americans have long been attracted to the East—in the form of
nineteenth-century orientalism, twentieth-century Egyptology, and the
current-day popularity, among many middle-class whites, of yoga and
Zen Buddhism. Even Afrocentrism itself can be seen as classically
American in its urge to romanticize and reinvent the past, much in the
way that Jay Gatsby did.

   And yet Fitzgerald's novel clearly warns against the temptation to   56
remake the past and the seduction of fraudulent identities. It is in its
defining of identity that Malcolm's thinking is uncomfortably rigid and
finally false. He developed two distinct but related beliefs about black
identity: that blacks are not Americans and that they are really Africans.
"We are just as much African today as we were in Africa four hundred
years ago, only we are a modern counterpart of it," Malcolm X said at
Harvard in 1964. "When you hear a black man playing music, whether it
is jazz or Bach, you still hear African music. In everything else we do we
still are African in color, feeling, everything. And we will always be that
whether we like it or not."

   By preaching a romantic reunification with mythological Africa as a   57
way of generating pride and racial unity, Malcolm advocated a single
identity for all black people, one that implicitly removed individual
distinctions among blacks. In Malcolm's view, individuality is a negligible
European creation, while the holy "community"—a creation of the
African and other dark-skinned peoples—is prized above everything
else. The idea of race as community, as invisible church, however, can
demand a stifling conformity; its popularity suggests that some aspects of
Afrocentrism, or all-blackness, as Malcolm popularized them and as they
are preached in some quarters today, far from being imaginative or
innovative, are utterly prosaic and philistine in their vision.

   Despite the unrealistic romanticism of Malcolm's back-to-   58
Africa preachings, he offers an important message for today's young
blacks: that blacks are, indeed, as Du Bois argues, a people of

"double-consciousness"; that both blackness and Americanness are real options, each having meaning only when measured against the other. Malcolm would not have argued with such passion and virulence against the validity of any kind of black *American* experience if he did not suspect that assimilation, that *being* American, was truly a rooted desire, if not a fulfilled reality, for most blacks. Yet he also knew that blacks in America cannot think about what their Americanness means without thinking about what it means to be of African descent: the two are inextricably bound together. As the historian Sterling Stuckey has argued, black people did not acquire a sense of what being African was until they came to America. They, like most people who came to this country, achieved their initial sense of identity through their clan—that is, slaves thought of themselves more as members of specific tribes or nations than as "Africans." Slavery compressed the diversity of African experience into one broad African identity, forcing blacks, in turn, to invent a collective sense of an African memory and an African self.

But Africanness is relevant to American blacks today only as a way 59 of helping us understand what it means to be American. While it is necessary that we recognize our African ancestry, and remember that it was, in varying degrees, stripped away by slavery, we must acknowledge, finally, that our story is one of remaking ourselves as Americans. My world is shaped by two indelible ideas: first, that I was once an African, that I grew, generations ago, from that ancestral soil; and, second, that I will never be African again, that I will, like Joseph, not be buried in the soil of my long-ago ancestors.

Malcolm preached the necessity of being African at the complete 60 expense of our American selves, a love of the misty past at the cost of our actual lives, our triumphs, our sufferings in the New World and as modern people. In this way, Malcolm merely increased our anxiety, further fueled our sense of inadequacy, and intensified our self-hatred and feelings of failure by providing us with a ready excuse: America is the white man's country, and the whites don't want you here and will never give you equal citizenship.

But it must always be remembered that our blood is here, our 61 names are here, our fate is here, in a land we helped to invent. By that I have in mind much more than the fact that blacks gave America free labor; other groups have helped build this and other countries for no or for nominal wages. We have given America something far more valuable: we have given her her particular identity, an identity as a country dedicated to diversity, a nation of different peoples living together as one. And no black person should care what the whites want or don't want in the realm of integration. The whites simply must learn to live as committed equals with their former slaves.

Our profound past of being African, which we must never forget, 62 must be balanced by the complex fate of being American, which we can never deny or, worse, evade. For we must accept who and what we are and the forces and conditions that have made us this, not as defeat or triumph, not in shame or with grandiose pride, but as the tangled, strange, yet poignant and immeasurable record of an imperishable human presence.

Exercises

Some Important Words

bildungsroman (paragraph 2), raillery (2), itinerant (3), racialist (4), prose-lytizer (4), schism (4), ideological (6), singular (6), pilloried (6), strife (9), dementia (12), benighted (12), strident (12), proto-fascistic (13), Afrocen-trism (13), keenly (15), indelible (15), oratory (16), nuance (16), de facto (17), fiat (17), degradation (17), the Congo (18), vehemently (20), snappin' out (22), charismatic (27), agility (28), millenarian (28), hoary (28), impri-matur (29), proletariat (29), bourgeois (29), diligence (29), entrepreneurship (29), compelling (31), dais (31), Uncle Remus (32), Uncle Tom (32), Mu-hammad Ali (33), negligible (34), estranged (35), embattled (35), espousal (37), secular (37), reparations (38), adamantly (39), jeremiad (40), nemesis (55), quintessential (55), prosaic (57), philistine (57), virulence (58), nominal (61), evade (62), gradiose (62), poignant (62).

Some of the Issues

1. Why did some of the Black students at Early's university react negatively to Early's appointment as the director of African and African-American Studies?
2. Describe Early's reaction to hearing Malcolm X's speech "Message to the Grass Roots" in 1963.
3. What was Malcolm's message (paragraph 28)?
4. Discuss the author's notion of the Black hero as represented by Malcolm X, Martin Luther King, and Muhammad Ali.
5. Why does Early say that it was the existence of the book *The Autobiography of Malcolm X* that mythologized Malcolm forever (paragraph 34)?
6. According to the author, how have African-American attitudes to-ward integration changed since the 1960s?
7. Explain Early's reasoning behind his claim that affirmative action programs may create a new form of enslavement (paragraph 38).
8. What dangers does Early perceive in becoming integrated into the middle class?
9. How would you characterize the attitude of the author's daughters toward his "blackness" tale (paragraphs 53 and 54)? What can you infer about their feelings toward race?

The Way We Are Told

10. Beginning in paragraph 56, the author argues against Malcolm X's definition of Black identity. What are his main objections?
11. How does Early support the assertion that Afrocentrism is based on "a romantic reunification with mythological Africa?"
12. What conclusion does Early draw regarding the issue of integration?

Some Subjects for Writing

13. Early envisions himself caught in a generation gap when talking to his college students and his young daughters. Do you sense that there is a lack of understanding between different generations today? Use your own experience and that of your peers to support your view.
*14. Read "The Brutal Bargain" by Norman Podhoretz, in which he describes becoming a member of the upper-middle class as being a kind of treason toward his family and friends. Is this the same or different from Early's reluctance to assimilate "white, middle-class taste"?
*15. Read "Hair" by Malcolm X. Examine the contrast in attitude toward white society between Malcolm X at fourteen and Early's young daughters. What conclusions can you draw to explain their differences?

BARBIE-Q

Sandra Cisneros

Sandra Cisneros was born to working-class Mexican-American parents on the South Side of Chicago in 1954. After graduating from Loyola University, she attended the Iowa Writers Workshop. Her novel *The House on Mango Street* (1989) won nomination for the American Book Award. She has also published a volume of poetry *My Wicked Wicked Ways* (1987), and *Woman Hollering Creek* (1991), from which this selection is taken, a collection of short stories and sketches that examine the condition of women.

"Barbie-Q" is a satirical glimpse at the ever popular Barbie doll. As the roles of women change in American society, the manufacturers of Barbie scramble to create new fashions to reflect the times: the 1992 preholiday sales featured "Desert Storm" Ken and Barbie attired in military uniform along with "Madison Avenue Shopper" Barbie with glossy shopping bag and black sunglasses as accessories.

Yours is the one with mean eyes and a ponytail. Striped swimsuit, 1
stilettos, sunglasses, and gold hoop earrings. Mine is the one with bubble hair. Red swimsuit, stilettos, pearl earrings, and a wire stand. But that's all we can afford, besides one extra outfit apiece. Yours, "Red Flair," sophisticated A-line coatdress with a Jackie Kennedy pillbox hat, white gloves, handbag, and heels included. Mine, "Solo in the Spotlight," evening elegance in black glitter strapless gown with a puffy skirt at the bottom like a mermaid tail, formal-length gloves, pink chiffon scarf, and mike included. From so much dressing and undressing, the black glitter wears off where her titties stick out. This and a dress invented from an old sock when we cut holes here and here and here, the cuff rolled over for the glamorous, fancy-free, off-the-shoulder look.

Every time the same story. Your Barbie is roommates with my 2
Barbie, and my Barbie's boyfriend comes over and your Barbie steals him, okay? Kiss kiss kiss. Then the two Barbies fight. You dumbbell! He's mine. Oh no he's not, you stinky! Only Ken's invisible, right! Because we don't have money for a stupid-looking boy doll when we'd both rather ask for a new Barbie outfit next Christmas. We have to make do with your mean-eyed Barbie and my bubblehead Barbie and our one outfit apiece not including the sock dress.

Until next Sunday when we are walking through the flea market on   3
Maxwell Street and *there!* Lying on the street next to some tool bits, and
platform shoes with the heels all squashed, and a fluorescent green
wicker wastebasket, and aluminum foil, and hubcaps, and a pink shag
rug, and windshield wiper blades, and dusty mason jars, and a coffee can
full of rusty nails. *There!* Where? Two Mattel boxes. One with the "Career
Gal" ensemble, snappy black-and-white business suit, three-quarter-
length sleeve jacket with kick-pleat skirt, red sleeveless shell, gloves,
pumps, and matching hat included. The other, "Sweet Dreams," dreamy
pink-and-white plaid nightgown and matching robe, lace-trimmed slippers, hairbrush and hand mirror included. How much? Please, please,
please, please, please, please, please, until they say okay.

On the outside you and me skipping and humming but inside we   4
are doing loopity-loops and pirouetting. Until at the next vendor's stand,
next to boxed pies, and bright orange toilet brushes, and rubber gloves,
and wrench sets, and bouquets of feather flowers, and glass towel racks,
and steel wool, and Alvin and the Chipmunks records, *there!* And *there!*
And *there!* And *there!* and *there!* and *there!* and *there!* Bendable Legs
Barbie with her new page-boy hairdo. Midge, Barbie's best friend. Ken,
Barbie's boyfriend. Skipper, Barbie's little sister. Tutti and Todd, Barbie
and Skipper's tiny twin sister and brother. Skipper's friends, Scooter and
Ricky. Alan, Ken's buddy. And Francie, Barbie's MOD'ern cousin.

Everybody today selling toys, all of them damaged with water and   5
smelling of smoke. Because a big toy warehouse on Halsted Street
burned down yesterday—see there?—the smoke still rising and drifting
across the Dan Ryan expressway. And now there is a big fire sale at
Maxwell Street, today only.

So what if we didn't get our new Bendable Legs Barbie and Midge   6
and Ken and Skipper and Tutti and Todd and Scooter and Ricky and Alan
and Francie in nice clean boxes and had to buy them on Maxwell Street,
all water-soaked and sooty. So what if our Barbies smell like smoke when
you hold them up to your nose even after you wash and wash and wash
them. And if the prettiest doll, Barbie's MOD'ern cousin Francie with real
eyelashes, eyelash brush included, has a left foot that's melted a
little—so? If you dress her in her new "Prom Pinks" outfit, satin splendor
with matching coat, gold belt, clutch, and hair bow included, so long as
your don't lift her dress, right?—who's to know.

Exercises

Some Important Words

stilettos (paragraph 1), pirouetting (4), clutch (6).

Some of the Issues

1. Who is the narrator addressing? Why do you think so? How can you account for the fact that the implied other character never responds?
2. What do you infer about the narrator and/or about the Barbie dolls from the line in paragraph 1, "But that's all we can afford, besides one extra outfit apiece."
3. Since Ken is "invisible" and "stupid-looking," (paragraph 2), why do they play the same story every time?
4. What physical and cultural images of women does Barbie represent?
5. How does the narrator justify buying the fire-damaged dolls? What seems to be the most important thing to her?

The Way We Are Told

6. What does the title suggest about the author's intent?
7. Approximately when does the story take place? What specific details does Cisneros use to place the time of the action in the past?
8. In paragraphs 3 and 4, notice the repetition of "*there!* And *there!* And *there!*" What effect does Cisneros intend? Does it work for you?
9. In the last paragraph, the words "So what," "So what," "so?" and "right?" could suggest an adversarial tone. Is this how you read it? If so, what could account for it?

Some Subjects for Writing

10. Many sociologists believe that childhood play is important to the development of identity. Through play, adult "scripts" are imitated and rehearsed. What messages about women's roles do the various Barbie themes such as "Red Flair," "Career Girl," "MOD'ern cousin," and so forth give to girls? Do you think the suggested roles are relevant models for young American women?
* 11. Read Jack G. Shaheen's "The Media's Image of Arabs," in which he asserts that Hollywood producers are partly responsible for the negative stereotypes of Arabs. In the same manner, do toy manufacturers perpetuate stereotypical gender identities? Defend your view with specific examples.

WE REAL COOL

Gwendolyn Brooks

Gwendolyn Brooks was born in Kansas in 1917 and has spent most of her life in Chicago. Her first volume of poetry, *A Street in Bronzeville,* was published in 1945. Many of her poems concern conditions in the African-American community, its feelings and attitudes. In 1950 she won the Pulitzer Prize for poetry. In 1972 she published her autobiography, *Report from Part One.* Other works include *The Near Johannesburg Boy* (1991); *Winnie* (1991); *Blacks* (1987), a volume of poetry; and *Selected Poems* (1963), from which this poem was taken.

The Pool Players
Seven at the Golden Shovel

We real cool. We
Left school. We

Lurk late. We
Strike straight. We

Sing sin. We
Thin gin. We

Jazz June. We
Die soon.

Rites of Passage in America

The photographs on the following pages reflect the astounding diversity of the American people and their ways of celebrating important events or rites of passage. Borrowed from the field of anthropology, the term *rites of passage* refers to social events that mark milestones in an individual's journey through the life cycle and serve to affirm his or her membership in a community. Participation in these ceremonies is universal.

In contemporary America, childhood rites of passage are observed at baptism, birthdays, the first day of school, and Little League tryouts. Coming-of-age events mark an individual's transition into adolescence and include confirmations, bar mitzvahs, first dates, sweet-sixteen or *quinceañera* parties, and obtaining a driver's license. Graduation, boot camp, fraternity pledging, voting and drinking rights, marriage, parenting, job promotions, and home ownership are rites of passage that take place in adulthood. Golden anniversaries, grandparenting, and retirement are celebrated as the rewards of advancing age. Finally, death and burial are observed by ceremonies that honor the spirit and memory of the deceased.

As seen in the photographs, the ways in which rites of passage are practiced in America vary according to an individual's ethnicity, religion, family, and community. For many Americans, the same rituals have been repeated for generations, while others are introduced to families through marriage, education, or participation in ethnic communities. Increasingly, many Americans want to preserve or renew customs that are both traditional and meaningful in a multicultural society.

This series of related photographs, or photo essay, is intended to be "read" as a visual text. Like other selections in this book, it raises issues and invites the reader's interpretation and powers of imagination.

Preparations for Chinese New Year's Celebrations in Chinatown, New York: A six-year-old boy will perform his first Lion's Dance on the streets of New York City.

Little League Pep Talk, Oakland, California

Coming of Age Sunrise Ceremony, White Mountain Apache Reservation, Arizona: This ceremony marks the transition of an Apache girl into womanhood. She is blessed with sacred yellow pollen and the eagle feather will be placed in her hair.

Teens at High School Prom in Hotel Ballroom, Austin, Texas

Cambodian-American Wedding, Philadelphia, Pennsylvania: During the ceremony, the couple lies on the pillow and guests tie strings for good luck around their wrists.

Artist Beatrice Wood turns 100. Ojai, California

Exercises

Some Ideas for Visual and Critical Thinking and Writing

1. Write down whatever first impressions, thoughts, or associations suggest themselves to you after seeing the photographs.
2. Select a single photograph from the essay and choose some of the following suggestions to respond to:
    a. What strikes you about the composition, the color, or the objects in the photograph?
    b. What associations, memories, or imaginings are called forth?
    c. Does the picture evoke a certain mood or tone? Can you point out details of the composition that reinforce this feeling?
    d. Choose a person who is the focus of the ceremony for you. What does the photograph suggest about that person's attitude?
    e. Choose other elements (individuals or objects) in the photograph that seem significant. How do they contribute to the entire composition?
    f. What does this photo say to you about the values (cultural, moral, communal) of the people and the event it portrays?
3. Look again at the photo essay as a whole. All of the pictures were taken in the United States in the 1980s and 1990s. Imagine that you have been asked to make a presentation at an international meeting on contemporary American life using these photographs to illustrate your talk. What themes or ideas would you focus on? What other photographs might you need to supplement your main idea?
4. Writing on photography, Susan Sontag said that "except for those situations in which the camera is used to document or to mark social rites, what moves people to take photographs is finding something beautiful." Would you classify any of the photographs in this essay as both social documents *and* works of art or beauty? Explain your answer.
5. Construct a photo essay composed of your personal photographs of rites of passage. Accompany each photo with a brief history of the event and its significance to you. You might also do this activity as a small group project and compare your experiences with others.

PART FIVE

Encounters

In the past, the United States was often referred to as a "melting pot," the idea that America functions as one vast container into which different ingredients—people, in this case—are amalgamated. The image of the melting pot does not do justice to another American ideal: the mosaic, or the belief that our various nationalities and races contribute important, unique ingredients to the total. More recently, there has been a shift toward recognition of and tolerance for our diversity.

We all know by the time we reach our teens, and sometimes much sooner, that difference is often viewed as threatening. Through ignorance and fear of the unknown, our worst selves can emerge. This section presents a variety of encounters that are the results of such fears. Some are simply personal; others occur as part of a historical event. Brent Staples, a tall African-American man, becomes a fearsome entity with whom pedestrians avoid making eye contact. Walter White describes how his family's house became a target of a mob during a race riot in Atlanta early in this century. In a selection at the end of the unit, Piri Thomas recalls being on "Alien Turf"—the new kid, a Puerto Rican—in an Italian neighborhood.

According to the traditional history books, the Pilgrims invited the Indians to our first Thanksgiving. Michael Dorris characterizes the account as an example of the conqueror's view of history, adding that later contacts between the two groups gave

215

Native Americans no cause for any further giving of thanks. Jeanne Wakatsuki Houston records her own experience in a historical event: the internment of Japanese-Americans on the West Coast at the beginning of World War II. Likewise, in the poem at the end of the unit, Dwight Okita recalls the irrational fears foisted on other Americans to justify the Japanese-American relocation policy.

NIGHT WALKER

Brent Staples

Brent Staples was born in 1951 in Chester, Pennsylvania. He holds a Ph.D. degree in psychology from the University of Chicago and is a member of the editorial board of the *New York Times* and the author of *Parallel Times: A Memoir* (1991). The selection reprinted here appeared originally in *Ms.* magazine in September 1986. In it Staples describes repeated experiences he had when he was taking walks at night. A tall African-American man, he aroused the fear of other pedestrians as well as drivers who saw him as the stereotypical mugger.

For Norman Podhoretz, whom Staples refers to in paragraph 11, read Podhoretz's essay "The Brutal Bargain."

My first victim was a woman—white, well dressed, probably in her early 1 twenties. I came upon her late one evening on a deserted street in Hyde Park, a relatively affluent neighborhood in an otherwise mean, impoverished section of Chicago. As I swung onto the avenue behind her, there seemed to be a discreet, uninflammatory distance between us. Not so. She cast back a worried glance. To her, the youngish black man—a broad six feet two inches with a beard and billowing hair, both hands shoved into the pockets of a bulky military jacket—seemed menacingly close. After a few more quick glimpses, she picked up her pace and was soon running in earnest. Within seconds she disappeared into a cross street.

That was more than a decade ago. I was 22 years old, a graduate 2 student newly arrived at the University of Chicago. It was in the echo of that terrified woman's footfalls that I first began to know the unwieldy inheritance I'd come into—the ability to alter public space in ugly ways. It was clear that she thought herself the quarry of a mugger, a rapist, or worse. Suffering a bout of insomnia, however, I was stalking sleep, not defenseless wayfarers. As a softy who is scarcely able to take a knife to a raw chicken—let alone hold it to a person's throat—I was surprised, embarrassed, and dismayed all at once. Her flight made me feel like an accomplice in tyranny. It also made it clear that I was indistinguishable from the muggers who occasionally seeped into the area from the

surrounding ghetto. That first encounter, and those that followed, signi-
fied that a vast, unnerving gulf lay between nighttime pedestrians—
particularly women—and me. And I soon gathered that being perceived
as dangerous is a hazard in itself. I only needed to turn a corner into a
dicey situation, or crowd some frightened, armed person in a foyer
somewhere, or make an errant move after being pulled over by a
policeman. Where fear and weapons meet—and they often do in urban
America—there is always the possibility of death.

In that first year, my first away from my hometown, I was to   3
become thoroughly familiar with the language of fear. At dark, shadowy
intersections in Chicago, I could cross in front of a car stopped at a traffic
light and elicit the *thunk, thunk, thunk, thunk* of the driver—black,
white, male, or female—hammering down the door locks. On less
traveled streets after dark, I grew accustomed to but never comfortable
with people who crossed to the other side of the street rather than pass
me. Then there were the standard unpleasantries with police, doormen,
bouncers, cab drivers, and others whose business it is to screen out
troublesome individuals *before* there is any nastiness.

I moved to New York nearly two years ago and I have remained an   4
avid night walker. In central Manhattan, the near-constant crowd cover
minimizes tense one-on-one street encounters. Elsewhere—visiting
friends in SoHo, where sidewalks are narrow and tightly spaced buildings
shut out the sky—things can get very taut indeed.

After dark on the warrenlike streets of Brooklyn where I live,   5
women seem to set their faces on neutral and, with their purse straps
strung across their chests bandolier style, they forge ahead as though
bracing themselves against being tackled. I understand, of course, that
the danger they perceive is not a hallucination. Women are particularly
vulnerable to street violence, and young black males are drastically
overrepresented among the perpetrators of that violence. Yet these truths
are no solace against the kind of alienation that comes of being ever the
suspect, against being set apart, a fearsome entity with whom pedestrians avoid making eye contact.

It is not altogether clear to me how I reached the ripe old age of 22   6
without being conscious of the lethality nighttime pedestrians attributed
to me. Perhaps it was because in Chester, Pennsylvania, the small, angry
industrial town where I came of age in the 1960s, I was scarcely
noticeable against a backdrop of gang warfare, street knifings, and
murders. I grew up one of the good boys, had perhaps a half-dozen fist
fights. In retrospect, my shyness of combat has clear sources.

Many things go into the making of a young thug. One of those   7
things is the consummation of the male romance with the power to
intimidate. An infant discovers that random flailings send the baby bottle
flying out of the crib and crashing to the floor. Delighted, the joyful babe

repeats those motions again and again, seeking to duplicate the feat. Just so, I recall the points at which some of my boyhood friends were finally seduced by the perception of themselves as tough guys. When a mark cowered and surrendered his money without resistance, myth and reality merged—and paid off. It is, after all, only manly to embrace the power to frighten and intimidate. We, as men, are not supposed to give an inch of our lane on the highway; we are to seize the fighter's edge in work and in play and even in love; we are to be valiant in the face of hostile forces.

Unfortunately, poor and powerless young men seem to take all this   8
nonsense literally. As a boy, I saw countless tough guys locked away; I have since buried several, too. They were babies, really—a teenage cousin, a brother of 22, a childhood friend in his mid-twenties—all gone down in episodes of bravado played out in the streets. I came to doubt the virtues of intimidation early on. I chose, perhaps even unconsciously, to remain a shadow—timid, but a survivor.

The fearsomeness mistakenly attributed to me in public places often   9
has a perilous flavor. The most frightening of these confusions occurred in the late 1970s and early 1980s when I worked as a journalist in Chicago. One day, rushing into the office of a magazine I was writing for with a deadline story in hand, I was mistaken for a burglar. The office manager called security and, with an ad hoc posse, pursued me through the labyrinthine halls, nearly to my editor's door. I had no way of proving who I was. I could only move briskly toward the company of someone who knew me.

Another time I was on assignment for a local paper and killing time   10
before an interview. I entered a jewelry store on the city's affluent Near North Side. The proprietor excused herself and returned with an enormous red Doberman pinscher straining at the end of a leash. She stood, the dog extended toward me, silent to my questions, her eyes bulging nearly out of her head. I took a cursory look around, nodded, and bade her good night. Relatively speaking, however, I never fared as badly as another black male journalist. He went to nearby Waukegan, Illinois, a couple of summers ago to work on a story about a murderer who was born there. Mistaking the reporter for the killer, police hauled him from his car at gunpoint and but for his press credentials would probably have tried to book him. Such episodes are not uncommon. Black men trade tales like this all the time.

In "My Negro Problem—And Ours" Podhoretz writes that the   11
hatred he feels for blacks makes itself known to him through a variety of avenues—one being his discomfort with that "special brand of paranoid touchiness" to which he says blacks are prone. No doubt he is speaking here of black men. In time, I learned to smother the rage I felt at so often being taken for a criminal. Not to do so would surely have led to madness—via that special "paranoid touchiness" that so annoyed Podhoretz at the time he wrote the essay.

I began to take precautions to make myself less threatening. I move   12
about with care, particularly late in the evening. I give a wide berth to
nervous people on subway platforms during the wee hours, particularly
when I have exchanged business clothes for jeans. If I happen to be
entering a building behind some people who appear skittish, I may walk
by, letting them clear the lobby before I return, so as not to seem to be
following them. I have been calm and extremely congenial on those rare
occasions when I've been pulled over by the police.

And on late-evening constitutionals along streets less traveled by, I   13
employ what has proved to be an excellent tension-reducing measure: I
whistle melodies from Beethoven and Vivaldi and the more popular classical composers. Even steely New Yorkers hunching toward nighttime
destinations seem to relax, and occasionally they even join in the tune.
Virtually everybody seems to sense that a mugger wouldn't be warbling
bright, sunny selections from Vivaldi's *Four Seasons*. It is my equivalent of
the cowbell that hikers wear when they know they are in bear country.

Exercises

Some Important Words

affluent (paragraph 1), impoverished (1), discreet (1), uninflammatory
(1), billowing (1), pace (2), unwieldy (2), alter (2), quarry (2), stalking
(2), insomnia (2), wayfarers (2), dismayed (2), accomplice (2), indistinguishable (2), elicit (3), avid (4), taut (4), warrenlike (5), bandolier style
(5), hallucination (5), vulnerable (5), perpetrators (5), solace (5), alienation (5), lethality (6), flailing (6), cowered (6), bravado (8), fearsomeness (9), perilous (9), ad hoc (9), posse (9), labyrinthine (9), cursory (10),
paranoid (11), wide berth (12), skittish (12), congenial (12), constitutionals (13), warbling (13).

Some of the Issues

1. How does Staples first discover his "ability to alter public space"
   (paragraph 2)?
2. What is Staples's reaction to the way he is perceived by strangers on
   his nightly walks? Does he show that he understands the feelings of
   some of those who fear him? Does he also show anger? Where?
3. What does Staples tell us about himself? About his childhood? How
   does this knowledge emphasize the contrast between his real self and
   the way he is often perceived by strangers?
4. How does Staples respond to Norman Podhoretz's contention that black
   men have a "special brand of paranoid touchiness" (paragraph 11)?

5. What has Staples learned to do to reduce the tension of passersby? Why does he choose the music he does? Does it solve his problem?

The Way We Are Told

6. Staples starts with an anecdote. Why does he use the word "victim" in the first sentence? Is there really a "victim"?
7. Identify examples drawn from Staples own experience. How are they used to support the generalizations he makes?

Some Subjects for Writing

8. Write telling about a time when someone misjudged you or something you did. What were the circumstances? How did you feel? What was the resolution? What did you learn from the experience?

I LEARN WHAT I AM

Walter White

Walter White was born in Atlanta, Georgia, in 1893. He joined the NAACP early in its development and served as its head from 1931 until his death in 1955. The following excerpt is taken from his autobiography, *A Man Called White* (1948).

The events White describes took place in his childhood, at the beginning of the twentieth century. The year was 1906 and he was living in Atlanta with his large family, near the line that separated the white community from his own. His father, an employee of the U.S. Postal Service, kept the house in immaculate repair, its white picket fence symbolizing the American Dream. When a race riot erupted in Atlanta, their house became a target of the mob. White tells the dramatic story of those two days.

There were nine light-skinned Negroes in my family: mother, father, five sisters, an older brother, George, and myself. The house in which I discovered what it meant to be a Negro was located on Houston Street, three blocks from the Candler Building, Atlanta's first skyscraper, which bore the name of the ex-drug clerk who had become a millionaire from the sale of Coca-Cola. Below us lived none but Negroes; toward town all but a very few were white. Ours was an eight room, two-story frame house which stood out in its surroundings not because of its opulence but by contrast with the drabness and unpaintedness of the other dwellings in a deteriorating neighborhood.

Only Father kept his house painted, the picket fence repaired, the board fence separating our place from those on either side white-washed, the grass neatly trimmed, and flower beds abloom. Mother's passion for neatness was even more pronounced and it seemed to me that I was always the victim of her determination to see no single blade of grass longer than the others or any one of the pickets in the front fence less shiny with paint than its mates. This spic-and-spanness became increasingly apparent as the rest of the neighborhood became more down-at-heel, and resulted, as we were to learn, in sullen envy among some of our white neighbors. It was the violent expression of that resentment against a Negro family neater than themselves which set the pattern of our lives.

On a day in September 1906, when I was thirteen, we were taught that there is no isolation from life. The unseasonably oppressive heat of an Indian summer day hung like a steaming blanket over Atlanta. My sisters and I had casually commented upon the unusual quietness. It seemed to stay Mother's volubility and reduced Father, who was more taciturn, to monosyllables. But, as I remember it, no other sense of impending trouble impinged upon our consciousness.

I had read the inflammatory headlines in the *Atlanta News* and the more restrained ones in the *Atlanta Constitution* which reported alleged rapes and other crimes committed by Negroes. But these were so standard and familiar that they made—as I look back on it now—little impression. The stories were more frequent, however, and consisted of eight-column streamers instead of the usual two- or four-column ones.

Father was a mail collector. His tour of duty was from three to eleven P.M. He made his rounds in a little cart into which one climbed from a step in the rear. I used to drive the cart for him from two until seven, leaving him at the point nearest our home on Houston Street, to return home either for study or sleep. That day Father decided that I should not go with him. I appealed to Mother, who thought it might be all right, provided Father sent me home before dark because, she said, "I don't think they would dare start anything before nightfall." Father told me as we made the rounds that ominous rumors of a race riot that night were sweeping the town. But I was too young that morning to understand the background of the riot. I became much older during the next thirty-six hours, under circumstances which I now recognize as the inevitable outcome of what had preceded. . . .

During the afternoon preceding the riot little bands of sullen, evil-looking men talked excitedly on street corners all over downtown Atlanta. Around seven o'clock my father and I were driving toward a mail box at the corner of Peachtree and Houston Streets when there came from near-by Pryor Street a roar the like of which I had never heard before, but which sent a sensation of mingled fear and excitement coursing through my body. I asked permission of Father to go and see what the trouble was. He bluntly ordered me to stay in the cart. A little later we drove down Atlanta's main business thoroughfare, Peachtree Street. Again we heard the terrifying cries, this time near at hand and coming toward us. We saw a lame Negro boot-black from Herndon's barber shop pathetically trying to outrun a mob of whites. Less than a hundred yards from us the chase ended. We saw clubs and fists descending to the accompaniment of savage shouting and cursing. Suddenly a voice cried, "There goes another nigger!" Its work done, the mob went after the new prey. The body with the withered foot lay dead in a pool of blood on the street.

Father's apprehension and mine steadily increased during the evening, although the fact that our skins were white kept us from attack. Another circumstance favored us—the mob had not yet grown violent enough to attack United States government property. But I could see Father's relief when he punched the time clock at eleven P.M. and got into the cart to go home. He wanted to go the back way down Forsyth Street, but I begged him, in my childish excitement and ignorance, to drive down Marietta to Five Points, the heart of Atlanta's business district, where the crowds were densest and the yells loudest. No sooner had we turned into Marietta Street, however, than we saw careening toward us an undertaker's barouche. Crouched in the rear of the vehicle were three Negroes clinging to the sides of the carriage as it lunged and swerved. On the driver's seat crouched a white man, the reins held taut in his left hand. A huge whip was gripped in his right. Alternately he lashed the horses and, without looking backward, swung the whip in savage swoops in the faces of members of the mob as they lunged at the carriage determined to seize the three Negroes.

There was no time for us to get out of its path, so sudden and swift was the appearance of the vehicle. The hub cap of the right rear wheel of the barouche hit the right side of our much lighter wagon. Father and I instinctively threw our weight and kept the cart from turning completely over. Our mare was a Texas mustang which, frightened by the sudden blow, lunged in the air as Father clung to the reins. Good fortune was with us. The cart settled back on its four wheels as Father said in a voice which brooked no dissent, "We are going home the back way and not down Marietta."

But again on Pryor Street we heard the cry of the mob. Close to us and in our direction ran a stout and elderly woman who cooked at a downtown white hotel. Fifty yards behind, a mob which filled the street from curb to curb was closing in. Father handed the reins to me and, though he was of slight stature, reached down and lifted the woman into the cart. I did not need to be told to lash the mare to the fastest speed she could muster.

The church bells tolled the next morning for Sunday service. But no one in Atlanta believed for a moment that the hatred and lust for blood had been appeased. Like skulls on a cannibal's hut the hats and caps of victims of the mob of the night before had been hung on the iron hooks of telegraph poles. None could tell whether each hat represented a dead Negro. But we knew that some of those who had worn the hats would never again wear any.

Late in the afternoon friends of my father's came to warn of more trouble that night. They told us that plans had been perfected for a mob to form on Peachtree Street just after nightfall to march down Houston Street to what the white people called "Darktown," three blocks or so below our house, "to clean out the niggers." There had never been a firearm in our house before that day. Father was reluctant even in those circumstances to violate the law, but he at last gave in at Mother's insistence.

We turned out the lights early, as did all our neighbors. No one removed his clothes or thought of sleep. Apprehension was tangible. We could almost touch its cold and clammy surface. Toward midnight the unnatural quiet was broken by a roar that grew steadily in volume. Even today I grow tense in remembering it.

12

Father told Mother to take my sisters, the youngest of them only six, to the rear of the house, which offered more protection from stones and bullets. My brother George was away, so Father and I, the only males in the house, took our places at the front windows of the parlor. The windows opened on a porch along the front side of the house, which in turn gave onto a narrow lawn that sloped down to the street and a picket fence. There was a crash as Negroes smashed the street lamp at the corner of Houston and Piedmont Avenue down the street. In a very few minutes the vanguard of the mob, some of them bearing torches, appeared. A voice which we recognized as that of the son of the grocer with whom we had traded for many years yelled, "That's where that nigger mail carrier lives! Let's burn it down! It's too nice for a nigger to live in!" In the eerie light Father turned his drawn face toward me. In a voice as quiet as though he were asking me to pass him the sugar at the breakfast table, he said, "Son, don't shoot until the first man puts his foot on the lawn and then—don't you miss!"

13

In the flickering light the mob swayed, paused, and began to flow toward us. In that instant there opened up within me a great awareness; I knew then who I was. I was a Negro, a human being with an invisible pigmentation which marked me a person to be hunted, hanged, abused, discriminated against, kept in poverty and ignorance, in order that those whose skin was white would have readily at hand a proof of their superiority, a proof patent and inclusive, accessible to the moron and the idiot as well as to the wise man and the genius. No matter how low a white man fell, he could always hold fast to the smug conviction that he was superior to two-thirds of the world's population, for those two-thirds were not white.

14

It made no difference how intelligent or talented my millions of brothers and I were, or how virtuously we lived. A curse like that of Judas was upon us, a mark of degradation fashioned with heavenly authority. There were white men who said Negroes had no souls, and who proved it by the Bible. Some of these now were approaching us, intent upon burning our house.

15

Theirs was a world of contrasts in values: superior and inferior, profit and loss, cooperative and noncooperative, civilized and aboriginal,

16

white and black. If you were on the wrong end of the comparison, if you were inferior, if you were noncooperative, if you were aboriginal, if you were black, then you were marked for excision, expulsion, or extinction. I was a Negro; I was therefore that part of history which opposed the good, the just, and the enlightened. I was a Persian, falling before the hordes of Alexander. I was a Carthaginian, extinguished by the Legions of Rome. I was a Frenchman at Waterloo, an Anglo-Saxon at Hastings, a Confederate at Vicksburg. I was the defeated, wherever and whenever there was a defeat.

Yet as a boy there in the darkness amid the tightening fright, I knew   17
the inexplicable thing—that my skin was as white as the skin of those who were coming at me.

The mob moved toward the lawn. I tried to aim my gun, wondering   18
what it would feel like to kill a man. Suddenly there was a volley of shots. The mob hesitated, stopped. Some friends of my father's had barricaded themselves in a two-story brick building just below our house. It was they who had fired. Some of the mobsmen, still blood-thirsty, shouted, "Let's go get the nigger." Others, afraid now for their safety, held back. Our friends, noting the hesitation, fired another volley. The mob broke and retreated up Houston Street.

In the quiet that followed I put my gun aside and tried to relax. But   19
a tension different from anything I had ever known possessed me. I was gripped by the knowledge of my identity, and in the depths of my soul I was vaguely aware that I was glad of it. I was sick with loathing for the hatred which had flared before me that night and come so close to making me a killer; but I was glad I was not one of those who hated; I was glad I was not one of those made sick and murderous by pride. I was glad I was not one of those whose story is in the history of the world, a record of bloodshed, rapine, and pillage. I was glad my mind and spirit were part of the races that had not fully awakened, and who therefore had still before them the opportunity to write a record of virtue as a memorandum to Armageddon.

It was all just a feeling then, inarticulate and melancholy, yet   20
reassuring in the way that death and sleep are reassuring, and I have clung to it now for nearly half a century.

Exercises

Some Important Words

opulence (paragraph 1), volubility (3), taciturn (3), impinged (3), apprehension (7), patent (14), degradation (15), enlightened (16), Carthaginian (16), Waterloo (16), Hastings (16), Armageddon (19).

Some of the Issues

1. In paragraph 1 White explains the location of his house in Atlanta. What is most important about the location?
2. In paragraph 2 White describes the appearance of the house and yard. Why is it important for him to stress the difference between it and its surroundings?
3. What does White mean when he says in paragraph 3, "we were taught that there is no isolation from life"?
4. In paragraph 4 White describes the headlines in the newspapers. How do they change in the days before the riot? Does he imply that his family believed what the papers said or not?
5. In paragraphs 5 through 13 there are indications that the riots are neither new nor isolated, unique occasions. Find these indicators.
6. In what ways do the actions of the mob differ between the first and second day of the rioting?
7. Where are the police?
8. In paragraphs 14 through 17 White interrupts his account of the mob's actions to describe his thoughts and feelings of bitterness. Contrast them to his thoughts in paragraphs 19 and 20, after the mob had fled and the danger was—temporarily—past.

The Way We Are Told

9. Why does White give his description of home and neighborhood in two paragraphs (1 and 2)? How do the paragraphs differ?
10. How does White begin to build suspense in paragraph 3? How do paragraphs 4 and 5 also prepare the reader for what is to come?
11. Paragraph 6 gives the first description of a specific event, using several words and phrases that have emotional impact. Cite four or five of these.
12. In paragraph 9 White describes another episode of rescue. See if there are any words here, like those in paragraph 6, that have emotional connotations.
13. How does White heighten the suspense in the final paragraphs of the essay?

Some Subjects for Writing

14. Have you ever felt yourself in real danger? If so, try to describe the circumstances in two ways: give an objective description of the events and then rewrite your essay, trying to heighten the effect by the careful use of emotionally effective words and phrases. (You will find that the overuse of emotional words diminishes rather than enhances the effect.)

15. White describes his experience in the Atlanta riots as a turning point in his life. Describe an experience in your own life that profoundly changed your values.

*16. Read Angelou's "Graduation." Both she and White record bad experiences that turned into a kind of victory in the end; both indicate that the victory is not final but needs to be fought for again and again. Write an essay in which you compare these experiences and their meaning to White and Angelou.

ARRIVAL AT MANZANAR

Jeanne Wakatsuki Houston
and James D. Houston

Like Walter White in the preceding selection, Jeanne Wakatsuki was
caught up in a historical event. The year was 1942, the place California. A few months before, the Japanese had attacked the United
States, bombing Pearl Harbor and overrunning U.S. possessions in the
Pacific. The war was going badly, the U.S. forces and those of its allies
were in retreat all over the area. Popular anger and fear turned against
the Japanese-Americans living on the West Coast. President Franklin D. Roosevelt signed an executive order to intern those thousands
of U.S. citizens—men, women, and children. They were rounded up
at short notice, had to leave their homes and businesses, either selling
them or abandoning them outright. They were shipped off to internment camps; Manzanar was one of them. They had to spend the war
years there, all except those men who volunteered for the army. The
battalion formed by these nisei, fighting in Italy, became the most
decorated U.S. Army unit in the war.

    The internment of Americans of Japanese descent increasingly
became a subject of controversy and criticism in the decades
following the war. In 1987 the U.S. Congress finally passed an act
that made some restitution to the former internees; it acknowledged
that what was done to them had been wrong and included a
payment of $20,000 to each of the survivors of the camps, that is, to
those who were still alive after more than 40 years.

    Jean Wakatsuki, born in California in 1935, was seven years
old when she, together with her family, was sent to the internment
camp at Manzanar. She remained there until age eleven. After high
school she studied sociology and journalism at San Jose State
College, where she met her husband, James D. Houston, a novelist.
Together they wrote *Farewell to Manzanar,* published in 1973, as a
record of life in the camp and of its impact on her and her family.
The following is a selection from it.

In December of 1941 Papa's disappearance didn't bother me nearly so   1
much as the world I soon found myself in.

229

He had been a jack-of-all-trades. When I was born he was farming   2
near Inglewood. Later, when he started fishing, we moved to Ocean Park,
near Santa Monica, and until they picked him up, that's where we lived,
in a big frame house with a brick fireplace, a block back from the beach.
We were the only Japanese family in the neighborhood. Papa liked it that
way. He didn't want to be labeled or grouped by anyone. But with him
gone and no way of knowing what to expect, my mother moved all of us
down to Terminal Island. Woody already lived there, and one of my older
sisters had married a Terminal Island boy. Mama's first concern now was
to keep the family together; and once the war began, she felt safer there
than isolated racially in Ocean Park. But for me, at age seven, the island
was a country as foreign as India or Arabia would have been. It was the
first time I had lived among other Japanese, or gone to school with them,
and I was terrified all the time.

This was partly Papa's fault. One of his threats to keep us younger   3
kids in line was "I'm going to sell you to the Chinaman." When I had
entered kindergarten two years earlier, I was the only Oriental in the
class. They sat me next to a Caucasian girl who happened to have very
slanted eyes. I looked at her and began to scream, certain Papa had sold
me out at last. My fear of her ran so deep I could not speak of it, even to
Mama, couldn't explain why I was screaming. For two weeks I had
nightmares about this girl, until the teachers finally moved me to the
other side of the room. And it was still with me, this fear of Oriental
faces, when we moved to Terminal Island.

In those days it was a company town, a ghetto owned and   4
controlled by the canneries. The men went after fish, and whenever the
boats came back—day or night—the women would be called to process
the catch while it was fresh. One in the afternoon or four in the morning,
it made no difference. My mother had to go to work right after we moved
there. I can still hear the whistle—two toots for French's, three for Van
Camp's—and she and Chizu would be out of bed in the middle of the
night, heading for the cannery.

The house we lived in was nothing more than a shack, a barracks   5
with single plank walls and rough wooden floors, like the cheapest kind
of migrant workers' housing. The people around us were hard-working,
boisterous, a little proud of their nickname, *yo-go-re,* which meant
literally *uncouth one,* or roughneck, or dead-end kid. They not only
spoke Japanese exclusively, they spoke a dialect peculiar to Kyushu,
where their families had come from in Japan, a rough, fisherman's
language, full of oaths and insults. Instead of saying *ba-ka-ta-re,* a
common insult meaning *stupid,* Terminal Islanders would say *ba-ka-ya-
ro,* a coarser and exclusively masculine use of the word, which implies
gross stupidity. They would swagger and pick on outsiders and persecute
anyone who didn't speak as they did. That was what made my own time

there so hateful. I had never spoken anything but English, and the other kids in the second grade despised me for it. They were tough and mean, like ghetto kids anywhere. Each day after school I dreaded their ambush. My brother Kiyo, three years older, would wait for me at the door, where we would decide whether to run straight home together, or split up, or try a new and unexpected route.

None of these kids ever actually attacked. It was the threat that frightened us, their fearful looks, and the noises they would make, like miniature Samurai, in a language we couldn't understand.

At the time it seemed we had been living under this reign of fear for years. In fact, we lived there about two months. Late in February the navy decided to clear Terminal Island completely. Even though most of us were American-born, it was dangerous having that many Orientals so close to the Long Beach Naval Station, on the opposite end of the island. We had known something like this was coming. But, like Papa's arrest, not much could be done ahead of time. There were four of us kids still young enough to be living with Mama, plus Granny, her mother, sixty-five then, speaking no English, and nearly blind. Mama didn't know where else she could get work, and we had nowhere else to move *to*. On February 25 the choice was made for us. We were given forty-eight hours to clear out.

The secondhand dealers had been prowling around for weeks, like wolves, offering humiliating prices for goods and furniture they knew many of us would have to sell sooner or later. Mama had left all but her most valuable possessions in Ocean Park, simply because she had nowhere to put them. She had brought along her pottery, her silver, heirlooms like the kimonos Granny had brought from Japan, tea sets, lacquered tables, and one fine old set of china, blue and white porcelain, almost translucent. On the day we were leaving, Woody's car was so crammed with boxes and luggage and kids we had just run out of room. Mama had to sell this china.

One of the dealers offered her fifteen dollars for it. She said it was a full setting for twelve and worth at least two hundred. He said fifteen was his top price. Mama started to quiver. Her eyes blazed up at him. She had been packing all night and trying to calm down Granny, who didn't understand why we were moving again and what all the rush was about. Mama's nerves were shot, and now navy jeeps were patrolling the streets. She didn't say another word. She just glared at this man, all the rage and frustration channeled at him through her eyes.

He watched her for a moment and said he was sure he couldn't pay more than seventeen fifty for that china. She reached into the red velvet case, took out a dinner plate and hurled it at the floor right in front of his feet.

The man leaped back shouting, "Hey! Hey, don't do that! Those are valuable dishes!"

Mama took out another dinner plate and hurled it at the floor, then   12
another and another, never moving, never opening her mouth, just
quivering and glaring at the retreating dealer, with tears streaming down
her cheeks. He finally turned and scuttled out the door, heading for the
next house. When he was gone she stood there smashing cups and
bowls and platters until the whole set lay in scattered blue and white
fragments across the wooden floor.

The name Manzanar meant nothing to us when we left Boyle   13
Heights. We didn't know where it was or what it was. We went because
the government ordered us to. And, in the case of my older brothers and
sisters, we went with a certain amount of relief. They had all heard stories
of Japanese homes being attacked, of beatings in the streets of California
towns. They were as frightened of the Caucasians as Caucasians were of
us. Moving, under what appeared to be government protection, to an
area less directly threatened by the war seemed not such a bad idea at all.
For some it actually sounded like a fine adventure.

Our pickup point was a Buddhist church in Los Angeles. It was very   14
early, and misty, when we got there with our luggage. Mama had bought
heavy coats for all of us. She grew up in eastern Washington and knew
that anywhere inland in early April would be cold. I was proud of my
new coat, and I remember sitting on a duffel bag trying to be friendly
with the Greyhound driver. I smiled at him. He didn't smile back. He was
befriending no one. Someone tied a numbered tag to my collar and to the
duffel bag (each family was given a number, and that became our official
designation until the camps were closed), someone else passed out box
lunches for the trip, and we climbed aboard.

I had never been outside Los Angeles County, never traveled more   15
than ten miles from the coast, had never even ridden on a bus. I was full
of excitement, the way any kid would be, and wanted to look out the
window. But for the first few hours the shades were drawn. Around me
other people played cards, read magazines, dozed, waiting. I settled
back, waiting too, and finally fell asleep. The bus felt very secure to me.
Almost half its passengers were immediate relatives. Mama and my older
brothers had succeeded in keeping most of us together, on the same bus,
headed for the same camp. I didn't realize until much later what a job
that was. The strategy had been, first, to have everyone living in the same
district when the evacuation began, and then to get all of us included
under the same family number, even though names had been changed
by marriage. Many families weren't as lucky as ours and suffered months
of anguish while trying to arrange transfers from one camp to another.

We rode all day. By the time we reached our destination, the shades   16
were up. It was late afternoon. The first thing I saw was a yellow swirl
across a blurred, reddish setting sun. The bus was being pelted by what
sounded like splattering rain. It wasn't rain. This was my first look at

something I would soon know very well, a billowing flurry of dust and sand churned up by the wind through Owens Valley.

We drove past a barbed-wire fence, through a gate, and into an 17 open space where trunks and sacks and packages had been dumped from the baggage trucks that drove out ahead of us. I could see a few tents set up, the first rows of black barracks, and beyond them, blurred by sand, rows of barracks that seemed to spread for miles across this plain. People were sitting on cartons or milling around, with their backs to the wind, waiting to see which friends or relatives might be on this bus. As we approached, they turned or stood up, and some moved toward us expectantly. But inside the bus no one stirred. No one waved or spoke. They just stared out the windows, ominously silent. I didn't understand this. Hadn't we finally arrived, our whole family intact? I opened a window, leaned out, and yelled happily "Hey! This whole bus is full of Wakatsukis!"

Outside, the greeters smiled. Inside there was an explosion of 18 laughter, hysterical, tension-breaking laughter that left my brothers choking and whacking each other across the shoulders.

We had pulled up just in time for dinner. The mess halls weren't 19 completed yet. An outdoor chow line snaked around a half-finished building that broke a good part of the wind. They issued us army mess kits, the round metal kind that fold over, and plopped in scoops of canned Vienna sausage, canned string beans, steamed rice that had been cooked too long, and on top of the rice a serving of canned apricots. The Caucasian servers were thinking the fruit poured over rice would make a good dessert. Among the Japanese, of course, rice is never eaten with sweet foods, only with salty or savory foods. Few of us could eat such a mixture. But at this point no one dared protest. It would have been impolite. I was horrified when I saw the apricot syrup seeping through my little mound of rice. I opened my mouth to complain. My mother jabbed me in the back to keep quiet. We moved on through the line and joined the others squatting in the lee of half-raised walls, dabbing courteously at what was, for almost everyone there, an inedible concoction.

After dinner we were taken to Block 16, a cluster of fifteen barracks 20 that had just been finished a day or so earlier—although finished was hardly the word for it. The shacks were built of one thickness of pine planking covered with tarpaper. They sat on concrete footings, with about two feet of open space between the floorboards and the ground. Gaps showed between the planks, and as the weeks passed and the green wood dried out, the gaps widened. Knotholes gaped in the uncovered floor.

Each barracks was divided into six units, sixteen by twenty feet, 21 about the size of a living room, with one bare bulb hanging from the ceiling and an oil stove for heat. We were assigned two of these for the twelve people in our family group; and our official family "number" was enlarged by three digits—16 plus the number of this barracks. We were issued steel army cots, two brown army blankets each, and some mattress covers, which my brothers stuffed with straw.

The first task was to divide up what space we had for sleeping. Bill 22 and Woody contributed a blanket each and partitioned off the first room: one side for Bill and Tomi, one side for Woody and Chizu and their baby girl. Woody also got the stove, for heating formulas.

The people who had it hardest during the first few months were 23 young couples like these, many of whom had married just before the evacuation began, in order not to be separated and sent to different camps. Our two rooms were crowded, but at least it was all in the family. My oldest sister and her husband were shoved into one of those sixteen-by-twenty-foot compartments with six people they had never seen before—two other couples, one recently married like themselves, the other with two teenage boys. Partitioning off a room like that wasn't easy. It was bitter cold when we arrived, and the wind did not abate. All they had to use for room dividers were those army blankets, two of which were barely enough to keep one person warm. They argued over whose blanket should be sacrificed and later argued about noise at night—the parents wanted their boys asleep by 9:00 P.M.—and they continued arguing over matters like that for six months, until my sister and her husband left to harvest sugar beets in Idaho. It was grueling work up there, and wages were pitiful, but when the call came through camp for workers to alleviate the wartime labor shortage, it sounded better than their life at Manzanar. They knew they'd have, if nothing else, a room, perhaps a cabin of their own.

That first night in Block 16, the rest of us squeezed into the 24 second room—Granny, Lillian, age fourteen, Ray, thirteen, May, eleven, Kiyo, ten, Mama, and me. I didn't mind this at all at the time. Being youngest meant I got to sleep with Mama. And before we went to bed I had a great time jumping up and down on the mattress. The boys had stuffed so much straw into hers, we had to flatten it some so we wouldn't slide off. I slept with her every night after that until Papa came back.

Exercises

Some Important Words

Caucasian (paragraph 3), Samurai (6), ominously (17), abate (23).

Some of the Issues

1. What do the first three paragraphs tell us about Houston's family?
2. Paragraphs 3 through 7 explain her fears. What are they? What would you imagine would be the mother's fears in this period?
3. What does the story about the secondhand dealer (paragraphs 8 through 12) tell us about the situation of Japanese-Americans at that time? What does it tell us about Houston's mother?
4. Examine the actions of the camp officials. To what extent can the authorities be said to be deliberately cruel? unthoughtful? or uninformed about cultural differences? Cite specific details to support your view.
*5. Read Maxine Hong Kingston's "Girlhood Among Ghosts." Both Kingston and Houston grew up in California at about the same time. In what way are the two experiences similar? How do they differ?

The Way We Are Told

6. In paragraphs 20 through 24 Houston gives a detailed description of the barracks. Does her description contain any words or phrases that express emotions? Justify their presence or absence.

Some Subjects for Writing

7. Jeanne Houston describes the bus ride to Manzanar from a child's point of view, as an adventure, almost fun, and not as a tragedy. Recall an incident of your childhood that would look different to you now (a fire, getting lost in a strange neighborhood). Describe it from a child's point of view and end with a paragraph explaining how you view the same incident as an adult.
8. Jeanne Wakatsuki Houston recalls her childhood just before internment and during its initial phase. Examine her attitude toward her experiences; how does it reflect her bicultural background?

FOR THE INDIANS,
NO THANKSGIVING

Michael Dorris

Michael Dorris, born in 1945, is a professor of anthropology at Dartmouth College. He is the author of several books, including *Native Americans 500 Years After* (1975) and the novel *A Yellow Raft in Blue Water* (1987). In 1989 Dorris published *The Broken Cord,* the story of Adam, a Sioux Indian boy born of an alcoholic mother whom Dorris adopted and tried to cure of Fetal Alcohol Syndrome. His most recent work, *Morning Girl,* was published in 1992.

The selection included here appeared in the *Chicago Tribune* at Thanksgiving 1988. With bitter humor Dorris, a member of the Modoc tribe, explains why Indians have no reason to give thanks on that Thursday in November. He describes how mainstream Americans have shaped the image of the Native American to suit their purpose.

King Philip's War, referred to in paragraph 2, was fought between the settlers in Massachusetts and the Wampanoags led by their chief Metacomet, who had taken the name Philip at a time when he befriended the colonists, and before he came to see them as enemies who would destroy his people. The Indians were defeated by the New England Confederation and Philip was killed.

Maybe those Pilgrims and Wampanoags actually got together for a November picnic, maybe not. It matters only as a facile, ironical footnote.

For the former group, it would have been a celebration of a precarious hurdle successfully crossed on the path to the political domination first of a continent and eventually of a planet. For the latter, it would have been, at best, a naïve extravaganza—the last meeting as equals with invaders who, within a few years, would win King Philip's War and decorate the city limits of their towns with rows of stakes, each topped with an Indian head.

The few aboriginal survivors of the ensuing violence were either sold into Caribbean slavery by their better armed, erstwhile hosts, or were ruthlessly driven from their Cape Cod homes. Despite the symbolic idealism of the first potluck, New England—from the emerging European point of view—simply wasn't big enough for two sets of societies.

An enduring benefit of success, when one culture clashes with   4
another, is that the victorious group controls the record. It owns not only
the immediate spoils but also the power to edit, embellish and concoct
the facts of the original encounter for the generations to come. Events,
once past, reside at the small end of the telescope, the vague and hazy
antecedents to accepted reality.

Our collective modern fantasy of Thanksgiving is a case in point. It   5
has evolved into a ritual pageant in which almost everyone of us, as
children, either acted or were forced to watch a 17th century vision that
we can conjure whole in the blink of an eye.

The cast of stock characters is as recognizable as those in any   6
Macy's parade: long-faced Pilgrim men, pre-N.R.A. muskets at their sides,
sitting around a rude outdoor table while their wives, dressed in long
dresses, aprons and linen caps, bustle about lifting the lids off steaming
kettles—pater and materfamilias of New World hospitality.

They dish out the turkey to a scattering of shirtless Indian invitees.   7
But there is no ambiguity as to who is in charge of the occasion, who
could be asked to leave, whose protocol prevails.

Only good Indians are admitted into this tableau, of course: those who   8
accept the manifest destiny of a European presence and are prepared to
adopt English dining customs and, by inference, English everything else.

These compliant Hollywood extras are, naturally enough, among   9
the blessings the Pilgrims are thankful for—and why not? They're
colorful, bring the food and vanish after dessert. They are something
exotic to write home about, like a visit to Frontierland. In the sound bite
of national folklore, they have metamorphosed into icons, totems of
America as evocative, and ultimately as vapid, as a flag factory.

And these particular Indians did not all repair to the happy hunting   10
grounds during the first Christmas rush. They lived on, smoking peace
pipes and popping up at appropriate crowd-pleasing moments.

They lost mock battles from coast to coast in Wild West shows. In   11
19th century art, they sat bareback on their horses and watched a lot of
sunsets. Whole professional teams of them take the home field every
Sunday afternoon in Cleveland or Washington.

They are the sources of merit badges for Boy Scouts and the   12
emblem of purity for imitation butter. They are, and have been from the
beginning, predictable, manageable, domesticated cartoons, inventions
without depth or reality apart from that bestowed by their creators.

These appreciative Indians, as opposed to the pesky flesh and   13
blood native peoples on whom they are loosely modeled, did not question
the enforced exchange of their territories for a piece of pie. They did not
protest when they died by the millions of European diseases.

They did not resist—except for the "bad" ones, the renegades—   14
when solemn pacts made with them were broken or when their religions

and customs were declared illegal. They did not make a fuss in courts in defense of their sovereignty. They never expected all the fixings anyway.

As for Thanksgiving 1988, the descendants of those first partygoers   15 sit at increasingly distant tables, the pretense of equity all but abandoned. Against great odds, native Americans have maintained political identity— hundreds of tribes have Federal recognition as "domestic, dependent nations."

But, in a country so insecure about heterogeneity that it votes its   16 dominant language as "official," this refusal to melt into the pot has been an expensive choice.

A majority of reservation Indians reside in among the most impov-   17 erished counties in the nation. They constitute the ethnic group at the wrong peak of every scale: most undernourished, most short-lived, least educated, least healthy.

For them, that long ago Thanksgiving was not a milestone, not a   18 promise. It was the last full meal.

Exercises

Some Important Words

Pilgrims (paragraph 1), Wampanoags (1), facile (1), ironical (1), precarious (2), naïve (2), extravaganza (2), aboriginal (3), ensuing (3), erstwhile (3), symbolic (3), idealism (3), potluck (3), emerging (3), enduring (4), spoils (4), edit (4), embellish (4), concoct (4), vague (4), antecedents (4), fantasy (5), ritual pageant (5), vision (5), conjure (5), stock characters (6), pre-N.R.A. muskets (6), rude (6), pater and materfamilias (6), scattering (7), ambiguity (7), protocol (7), prevails (7), tableau (8), manifest destiny (8), inference (8), compliant (9), Hollywood extras (9), exotic (9), sound bite (9), metamorphosed (9), icons (9), totems (9), evocative (9), vapid (9), happy hunting grounds (10), mock (11), emblem of purity (12), domesticated (12), bestowed (12), appreciative (13), pesky (13), loosely modeled (13), renegade (14), solemn pacts (14), sovereignty (14), equity (15), heterogeneity (16), undernourished (17), milestone (18).

Some of the Issues

1. What is the "November picnic"? If it did indeed take place, what does it signify for each group of participants?
2. What does Dorris mean by saying that the victor controls the record (paragraph 4)? How do the following paragraphs expand on that statement?
3. What, according to Dorris, is the definition of "good" Indians (paragraph 8)? What roles do they play? Who assigns them those roles?

4. In paragraphs 11–13 Dorris refers to various ways that the Indians' image has been used. What is his purpose?
5. What does Dorris mean in paragraph 15 when he says that the descendants of those first party-goers sit at increasingly distant tables?

The Way We Are Told

6. What kind of tone does the first paragraph set for the essay?
7. Dorris calls Thanksgiving "our collective modern fantasy" (paragraph 5). What terms does he use in the following paragraphs that amplify that idea of fantasy?
8. Consider the tone of the essay. Would you call it funny? Bitter? Angry? How does Dorris's language create that tone? Cite examples.

Some Subjects for Writing

9. In recent years Native American groups have raised objections to the use of Indian names for sports teams (Cleveland Indians, Atlanta Braves) and the use of Indian symbols such as the tomahawk in advertising. Find examples and discuss whether the objections are justified.

ALIEN TURF

Piri Thomas

Piri Thomas was born in Spanish Harlem in 1928 and grew up in its world of gangs, drugs, and petty crime. In his teens he became an addict, was convicted of attempted armed robbery, and served six years of a 15-year sentence. After his release, he began to work for drug rehabilitation programs in New York and Puerto Rico and developed a career as a writer. The autobiographical *Down These Mean Streets* (1967), from which the following selection is taken, was his first book. A sequel, *Savior, Savior, Hold My Hand,* was published in 1972.

Thomas tells the reader about an event in his childhood, one that many young people will have experienced: being the new kid on the block. But when the block is in a poor neighborhood and when, moreover, the new kid is from a background different from the prevailing culture, then the mix can turn explosive.

For some information about Puerto Rico, read the headnote for Jack Agueros's "Halfway to Dick and Jane."

Sometimes you don't fit in. Like if you're a Puerto Rican on an Italian 1 block. After my new baby brother, Ricardo, died of some kind of germs, Poppa moved us from 111th Street to Italian turf on 114th Street between Second and Third Avenue. I guess Poppa wanted to get Momma away from the hard memories of the old pad.

I sure missed 111th Street, where everybody acted, walked, and talked 2 like me. But on 114th Street everything went all right for a while. There were a few dirty looks from the spaghetti-an'-sauce cats, but no big sweat. Till that one day I was on my way home from school and almost had reached my stoop when someone called: "Hey, you dirty fuckin' spic."

The words hit my ears and almost made me curse Poppa at the same 3 time. I turned around real slow and found my face pushing in the finger of an Italian kid about my age. He had five or six of his friends with him.

"Hey, you," he said, "What nationality are ya?" 4

I looked at him and wondered which nationality to pick. And one 5 of his friends said, "Ah, Rocky, he's black enuff to be a nigger. Ain't that what you is, kid?"

My voice was almost shy in its anger. "I'm Puerto Rican," I said. "I 6
was born here." I wanted to shout it, but it came out like a whisper.

"Right here inna street?" Rocky sneered. "Ya mean right here inna 7
middle of da street?"

They all laughed. I hated them. I shook my head slowly from side 8
to side.

"Uh-uh," I said softly. "I was born inna hospital—inna bed." 9

"Umm, *paisan*—born inna bed," Rocky said. 10

I didn't like Rocky Italiano's voice. "Inna hospital," I whispered, 11
and all the time my eyes were trying to cut down the long distance from
this trouble to my stoop. But it was no good; I was hemmed in by Rocky's
friends. I couldn't help thinking about kids getting wasted for moving
into a block belonging to other people.

"What hospital, *paisan?*" Bad Rocky pushed. 12

"Harlem Hospital," I answered, wishing like all hell that it was 5 o'clock 13
instead of just 3 o'clock, 'cause Poppa came home at 5. I looked around for
some friendly faces belonging to grown-up people, but the elders were all
busy yakking away in Italian. I couldn't help thinking how much like Spanish
it sounded. Shit, that should make us something like relatives.

"Harlem Hospital?" said a voice. "I knew he was a nigger." 14

"Yeah," said another voice from an expert on color. "That's the 15
hospital where all them black bastards get born at."

I dug three Italian elders looking at us from across the street and I 16
felt saved. But that went out the window when they just smiled and went
on talking. I couldn't decide whether they had smiled because this new
whatever-he-was was gonna get his ass kicked or because they were
pleased that their kids were welcoming a new kid to their country. An
older man nodded his head at Rocky, who smiled back. I wondered if
that was a signal for my funeral to begin.

"Ain't that right, kid?" Rocky pressed. "Ain't that where all black 17
people get born?"

I dug some of Rocky's boys grinding and pushing and punching 18
closed fists against open hands. I figured they were looking to shake me
up, so I straightened up my humble voice and made like proud. "There's
all kinds of people born there. Colored people, Puerto Ricans like me,
an'—even spaghetti-benders like you."

"That's a dirty fuckin' lie"—*bash,* I felt Rocky's fist smack into my 19
mouth—"You dirty fuckin' spic."

I got dizzy and then more dizzy when fists started to fly from 20
everywhere and only toward me. I swung back, *splat, bish*—my fist hit
some face and I wished I hadn't, 'cause then I started getting kicked.

I heard people yelling in Italian and English and I wondered if 21
maybe it was 'cause I hadn't fought fair in having hit that one guy. But it
wasn't. The voices were trying to help me.

"Whas'sa matta, you no-good kids, leeva da kid alone," a man said.   22
I looked through a swelling eye and dug some Italians pushing their kids
off me with slaps. One even kicked a kid in the ass. I could have loved
them if I didn't hate them so fuckin' much.

"You all right, kiddo?" asked the man.   23

"Where you live, boy?" said another one.   24

"Is the *bambino* hurt?" asked a woman.   25

I didn't look at any of them. I felt dizzy. I didn't want to open my   26
mouth to talk, 'cause I was fighting to keep from puking up. I just hoped
my face was cool-looking. I walked away from the group of strangers. I
reached my stoop and started to climb the steps.

"Hey, spic," came a shout from across the street. I started to turn to   27
the voice and changed my mind. "Spic" wasn't my name. I knew that
voice, though. It was Rocky's. "We'll see ya again, spic," he said.

I wanted to do something tough, like spitting in their direction. But   28
you gotta have spit in your mouth in order to spit, and my mouth was
hurt dry. I just stood there with my back to them.

"Hey, your old man just better be the janitor in that fuckin'   29
building."

Another voice added, "Hey, you got any pretty sisters? We might let   30
ya stay onna block."

Another voice mocked, "Aw, fer Chrissake, where ya ever hear of   31
one of them black broads being pretty?"

I heard the laughter. I turned around and looked at them. Rocky   32
made some kind of dirty sign by putting his left hand in the crook of his
right arm while twisting his closed fist in the air.

Another voice said, "Fuck it, we'll just cover the bitch's face with   33
the flag an' fuck'er for old glory."

All I could think of was how I'd like to kill each of them two or   34
three times. I found some spit in my mouth and splattered it in their
direction and went inside.

Momma was cooking, and the smell of rice and beans was beating   35
the smell of Parmesan cheese from the other apartments. I let myself into
our new pad. I tried to walk fast past Momma so I could wash up, but she
saw me.

"My God, Piri, what happened?" she cried.   36

"Just a little fight in school, Momma. You know how it is, Momma,   37
I'm new in school an' . . ." I made myself laugh. Then I made myself say,
"But Moms, I whipped the living _____ outta two guys, an' one was
bigger'n me."

"*Bendito,* Piri, I raise my family in Christian way. Not to fight. Christ   38
says to turn the other cheek."

"Sure, Momma." I smiled and went and showered, feeling sore at   39
Poppa for bringing us into spaghetti country. I felt my face with easy

fingers and thought about all the running back and forth from school that was in store for me.

I sat down to dinner and listened to Momma talk about Christian   40
living without really hearing her. All I could think of was that I hadda go out in that street again. I made up my mind to go out right after I finished eating. I had to, shook up or not; cats like me had to show heart.

"Be back, Moms," I said after dinner, "I'm going out on the stoop."   41
I got halfway to the stoop and turned and went back to our apartment. I knocked.

"Who is it?" Momma asked.   42

"Me, Momma."   43

She opened the door. "*¿Qué pasa?*" she asked.   44

"Nothing, Momma, I just forgot something," I said. I went into the   45
bedroom and fiddled around and finally copped a funny book and walked out the door again. But this time I made sure the switch on the lock was open, just in case I had to get back real quick. I walked out on that stoop as cool as could be, feeling braver with the lock open.

There was no sign of Rocky and his killers. After awhile I saw   46
Poppa coming down the street. He walked like beat tired. Poppa hated his pick-and-shovel job with the WPA. He couldn't even hear the name WPA without getting a fever. *Funny,* I thought, *Poppa's the same like me, a stone Puerto Rican, and nobody in this block even pays him a mind. Maybe older people get along better'n us kids.*

Poppa was climbing the stoop. "Hi, Poppa," I said.   47

"How's it going, son? Hey, you sure look a little lumped up. What   48
happened?"

I looked at Poppa and started to talk it outta me all at once and   49
stopped, 'cause I heard my voice start to sound scared, and that was no good.

"Slow down, son," Poppa said. "Take it easy." He sat down on the   50
stoop and made a motion for me to do the same. He listened and I talked, I gained confidence. I went from a tone of being shook up by the Italians to a tone of being a better fighter than Joe Louis and Pedro Montanez lumped together, with Kid Chocolate thrown in for extra.

"So that's what happened," I concluded. "And it looks like only the   51
beginning. Man, I ain't scared, Poppa, but like there's nothin' but Italianos on this block and there's no me's like me except for me an' our family."

Poppa looked tight. He shook his head from side to side and   52
mumbled something about another Puerto Rican family that lived a coupla doors down from us.

I thought, *What good would that do me, unless they prayed over my*   53
dead body in Spanish? But I said, "Man! That's great. Before ya know it, there'll be a whole bunch of us moving in, huh?"

Poppa grunted something and got up. "Staying out here, son?"   54

"Yeah, Poppa, for a little while longer."   55

From that day on I grew eyes all over my head. Anytime I hit that   56
street for anything, I looked straight ahead, behind me and from side to
side all at the same time. Sometimes I ran into Rocky and his boys—the
cat was never without his boys—but they never made a move to snag
me. They just grinned at me like a bunch of hungry alley cats that could
get to their mouse anytime they wanted. That's what they made me feel
like—a mouse. Not like a smart house mouse but like a white house pet
that ain't got no business in the middle of cat country but don't know
better 'cause he grew thinking he was a cat—which wasn't far from
wrong 'cause he'd end up as part of the inside of some cat.

Rocky and his fellas got to playing a way-out game with me called   57
"One-finger-across-the-neck-inna-slicing-motion," followed by such gentle words as "It won't be long, spico." I just looked at them blank and
made it to wherever I was going.

I kept wishing those cats went to the same school I went to, a   58
school that was on the border between their country and mine, and I had
amigos there—and there I could count on them. But I couldn't ask two
or three *amigos* to break into Rocky's block and help me mess up his
boys. I knew 'cause I had asked them already. They had turned me down
fast, and I couldn't blame them. It would have been murder, and I guess
they figured one murder would be better than four.

I got through the days trying to play it cool and walk on by Rocky and   59
his boys like they weren't there. One day I passed them and nothing was
said. I started to let out my breath. I felt great; I hadn't been seen. Then
someone yelled in a high, girlish voice, "Yoo-hoo . . . Hey, *paisan* . . . we
see yoo . . ." And right behind that voice came a can of evaporated milk—
whoosh, clatter. I walked cool for ten steps then started running like mad.

This crap kept up for a month. They tried to shake me up. Every   60
time they threw something at me, it was just to see me jump. I decided
that the next fucking time they threw something at me I was gonna play
bad-o and not run. That next time came about a week later. Momma sent
me off the stoop to the Italian market on 115th Street and First Avenue,
deep in Italian country. Man, that was stompin' territory. But I went,
walking in the style which I had copped from the colored cats I had seen,
a swinging and stepping down hard at every step. Those cats were so
down and cool that just walking made a way-out sound.

Ten minutes later I was on my way back with Momma's stuff. I got   61
to the corner of First Avenue and 114th Street and crushed myself right
into Rocky and his fellas.

"Well-l, fellas," Rocky said, "Lookee who's here."   62

I didn't like the sounds coming out of Rocky's fat mouth. And I   63
didn't like the sameness of the shitty grins spreading all over the boys'
faces. But I thought, *No more! No more! I ain't gonna run no more.* Even

so, I looked around, like for some kind of Jesus miracle to happen. I was always looking for miracles to happen.

"Say, *paisan*," one guy said, "you even buying from us *paisans,* eh? Man, you must wantta be Italian."   64

Before I could bite that dopey tongue of mine, I said, "I wouldn't be a guinea on a motherfucking bet."   65

"Wha-at?" said Rocky, really surprised. I didn't blame him; I was surprised myself. His finger began digging a hole in his ear, like he hadn't heard me right. "Wha-at? Say that again?"   66

I could feel a thin hot wetness cutting itself down my leg. I had been so ashamed of being so damned scared that I had peed on myself. And then I wasn't scared any more; I felt a fuck-it-all attitude. I looked real bad at Rocky and said, "Ya heard me. I wouldn't be a guinea on a bet."   67

"Ya little sonavabitch, we'll kick the shit outta ya," said one guy, Tony, who had made a habit of asking me if I had any sen-your-ritas for sisters.   68

"Kick the shit outta me yourself if you got any heart, you mother fuckin' fucker," I screamed at him. I felt kind of happy, the kind of feeling that you get only when you got heart.   69

Big-mouth Tony just swung out, and I swung back and heard all of Momma's stuff plopping all over the street. My fist hit Tony smack dead in the mouth. He was so mad he threw a fist at me from about three feet away. I faked and jabbed and did fancy dance steps. Big-mouth put a stop to all that with a punch in my mouth. I heard the home cheers of "Yea, yea, bust that spic wide open!" Then I bloodied Tony's nose. He blinked and sniffed without putting his hands to his nose, and I remembered Poppa telling me, "Son, if you're ever fighting somebody an' you punch him in the nose, and he just blinks an' sniffs without holding his nose, you can do one of two things: fight like hell or run like hell—'cause that cat's a fighter."   70

Big-mouth came at me and we grabbed each other and pushed and pulled and shoved. *Poppa,* I thought, *I ain't gonna cop out. I'm a fighter, too.* I pulled away from Tony and blew my fist into his belly. He puffed and butted my nose with his head. I sniffed back. *Poppa, I didn't put my hands to my nose.* I hit Tony again in that same weak spot. He bent over in the middle and went down to his knees.   71

Big-mouth got up as fast as he could, and I was thinking how much heart he had. But I ran toward him like my life depended on it; I wanted to cool him. Too late. I saw his hand grab a fistful of ground asphalt which had been piled nearby to fix a pothole in the street. I tried to duck; I should have closed my eyes instead. The shitty-gritty stuff hit my face, and I felt the scrappy pain make itself a part of my eyes. I screamed and grabbed for two eyes with one hand, while the other I beat some kind of   72 helpless tune on air that just couldn't be hurt. I heard Rocky's voice shouting, "Ya scum bag, ya didn't have to fight the spic dirty; you could've fucked him up fair and square!" I couldn't see. I heard a fist hit a face, then Big-mouth's voice: "Whatta ya hittin' me for?" and then Rocky's voice: "*Putana!* I ought ta knock all your fuckin' teeth out."

I felt hands grabbing at me between my screams. I punched out.   73
I'm gonna get killed, I thought. Then I heard many voices: "Hold it, kid." "We ain't gonna hurt ya." "Je-*sus,* don't rub your eyes." "Ooooohhhh, shit, his eyes is fulla that shit."

You're fuckin' right, I thought, *and it hurts like* coño.   74

I heard a woman's voice now: "Take him to a hospital." And an old   75
man asked: "How did it happen?"

"Momma, Momma," I cried.   76

"Comon, kid," Rocky said, taking my hand. "Lemme take ya home."   77
I fought for the right to rub my eyes. "Grab his other hand, Vincent," Rocky said. I tried to rub my eyes with my eyelids. I could feel hurt tears cutting down my cheeks. "Come on, kid, we ain't gonna hurt ya," Rocky tried to assure me. "Swear to our mudders. We just wanna take ya home."

I made myself believe him, and trying not to make pain noises, I let   78
myself be led home. I wondered if I was gonna be blind like Mr. Silva, who went around from door to door selling dish towels and brooms, his son leading him around.

"You okay, kid?" Rocky asked.   79

"Yea n," what was left of me said.   80

"A-huh," mumbled Big-mouth.   81

"He got much heart for a nigger," somebody else said.   82

A *spic,* I thought.   83

"For anybody," Rocky said. "Here we are kid," he added. "Watch   84
your step."

I was like carried up the steps. "What's your apartment number?"   85
Rocky asked.

"One-B—inna back—ground floor," I said, and I was led there.   86
Somebody knocked on Momma's door. Then I heard running feet and Rocky's voice yelling back, "Don't rat, huh, kid?" And I was alone.

I heard the door open and Momma say, "*Bueno,* Piri, come in." I   87
didn't move. I couldn't. There was a long pause; I could hear Momma's fright. "My God," she said finally. "What's happened?" Then she took a closer look. "Aieeee," she screamed. "*¡Dios mío!*"

"I was playing with some kids, Momma," I said, "an' I got some dirt   88
in my eyes." I tried to make my voice come out without the pain, like a man.

"*Dios eterno*—your eyes!"   89

"What's the matter? What's the matter?" Poppa called from the   90
bedroom.

"*¡Está ciego!*" Momma screamed. "He is blind!"   91

I heard Poppa knocking things over as he came running. Sis began   92
to cry. Blind, hurting tears were jumping out of my eyes. "Whattya mean,
he's blind?" Poppa said as he stormed into the kitchen. "What happened?" Poppa's voice was both scared and mad.

"Playing, Poppa."   93

"Whatta ya mean, 'playing'?" Poppa's English sounded different   94
when he got warm.

"Just playing, Poppa."   95

"Playing? Playing got all that dirt in your eyes? I bet my ass. Them   96
damn Ee-ta-liano kids ganged up on you again." Poppa squeezed my
head between the fingers of one hand. "That settles it—we're moving
outta this damn section, outta this damn block, outta this damn shit."

Shit, I thought, *Poppa's sure cursin' up a storm.* I could hear him   97
slapping the side of his leg, like he always did when he got real mad.

"Son," he said, "you're gonna point them out to me."   98

"Point who out, Poppa? I was playin' an'—"   99

"Stop talkin' to him and take him to the hospital!" Momma   100
screamed.

"*Pobrecito,* poor Piri," cooed my little sister.   101

"You sure, son?" Poppa asked. "You was only playing?"   102

"Shit, Poppa, I said I was."   103

Smack—Poppa was so scared and mad, he let it out in the slap to   104
the side of my face.

"*¡Bestia!* ani-*mul!*" Momma cried. "He's blind, and you hit him!"   105

"I'm sorry, son, I'm sorry," Poppa said in a voice like almost crying.   106
I heard him running back into the bedroom yelling, "Where's my pants?"

Momma grabbed away fingers that were trying to wipe away the   107
hurt in my eyes. "*Caramba,* no rub, no rub," she said, kissing me. She
told Sis to get a rag and wet it with cold water.

Poppa came running back into the kitchen. "Let's go, son, let's go.   108
Jesus! I didn't mean to smack ya, I really didn't," he said, his big hand
rubbing and grabbing my hair gently.

"Here's the rag, Momma," said Sis.   109

"What's that for?" asked Poppa.   110

"To put on his eyes" Momma said.   111

I heard the smack of a wet rag, *blapt,* against the kitchen wall. "We   112
can't put nothing on his eyes. It might make them worse. Come on, son,"
Poppa said nervously, lifting me up in his big arms. I felt like a little baby,
like I didn't hurt so bad. I wanted to stay there, but I said, "Let me down,
Poppa, I ain't no kid."

"Shut up," Poppa said softly. "I know you ain't but it's faster this way."   113

"Which hospeetal are you taking him to?" Momma asked.   114

"Nearest one," Poppa answered as we went out the door. He   115
carried me through the hall and out into the street, where the bright

sunlight made a red hurting color through the crap in my eyes. I heard voices on the stoop and on the sidewalk: "Is that the boy?"

"A-huh. He's probably blinded."   116

"We'll get a cab, son," Poppa said. His voice loved me. I heard   117
Rocky yelling from across the street, "We're pulling for ya, kid. Remember what we . . ." The rest was lost to Poppa's long legs running down to the corner of Third Avenue. He hailed a taxi and we zoomed off toward Harlem Hospital. I felt the cab make all kinds of sudden stops and turns.

"How do you feel, *hijo?*" Poppa asked.   118

"It burns like hell."   119

"You'll be okay," he said, and as an afterthought added, "Don't   120
curse, son."

I heard cars honking and the Third Avenue el roaring above us. I   121
knew we were in Puerto Rican turf, 'cause I could hear our language.

"Son."   122

"Yeah, Poppa."   123

"Don't rub your eyes, fer Christ sake." He held my skinny wrists in   124
his one hand, and everything got quiet between us.

The cab got to Harlem Hospital. I heard change being handled and   125
the door opening and Poppa thanking the cabbie for getting here fast. "Hope the kid'll be okay," the driver said.

I will be, I thought, *I ain't gonna be like Mr. Silva.*   126

Poppa took me in his arms again and started running. "Where's   127
emergency mister?" he asked someone.

"To your left and straight away," said a voice.   128

"Thanks a lot," Poppa said, and we were running again.   129

"Emergency?" Poppa said when we stopped.   130

"Yes, sir," said a girl's voice. "What's the matter?"   131

"My boy's got his eyes full of ground-up tar an'—"   132

"What's the matter?" said a man's voice.   133

"Youngster with ground tar in his eyes, doctor."   134

"We'll take him, mister. You just put him down here and go with the   135
nurse. She'll take down the information. Uh, you the father?"

"That's right, doctor."   136

"Okay, just put him down here."   137

"Poppa, don't leave me," I cried.   138

"Sh, son, I ain't leaving you. I'm just going to fill out some papers,   139
an' I'll be right back."

I nodded my head up and down and was wheeled away. When the   140
rolling stretcher stopped, somebody stuck a needle in me and I got sleepy and started thinking about Rocky and his boys, and Poppa's slap, and how great Poppa was, and how my eyes didn't hurt no more . . .

I woke up in a room blind with darkness. The only lights were the   141
ones inside my head. I put my fingers to my eyes and felt bandages. "Let them be, sonny," said a woman's voice.

I wanted to ask the voice if they had taken my eyes out, but I didn't.   142
I was afraid the voice would say yes.

"Let them be, sonny," the nurse said, pulling my hand away from   143
the bandages. "You're all right. The doctor put the bandages on to
keep the light out. They'll be off real soon. Don't you worry none,
sonny."

I wished she would stop calling me sonny. "Where's Poppa?" I   144
asked cool like.

"He's outside, sonny. Would you like me to send him in?"   145

I nodded. "Yeah." I heard walking-away shoes, a door opening, a   146
whisper, and shoes walking back toward me. "How do you feel, *hijo?*"
Poppa asked.

"It hurts like shit, Poppa."   147

"It's just for awhile, son, and then off come the bandages. Every-   148
thing's gonna be all right."

I thought, *Poppa didn't tell me to stop cursing.*   149

"And son, I thought I told you to stop cursing," he added.   150

I smiled. Poppa hadn't forgotten. Suddenly I realized that all I had   151
on was a hospital gown. "Poppa, where's my clothes?" I asked.

I got them. I'm taking them home an'—"   152

"Whatta ya mean, Poppa?" I said, like scared. "You ain't leavin' me   153
here? I'll be damned if I stay." I was already sitting up and feeling my way
outta bed. Poppa grabbed me and pushed me back. His voice wasn't mad
or scared any more. It was happy and soft, like Momma's.

"Hey," he said, "get your ass back in bed or they'll have to put a   154
bandage there too."

"Poppa," I pleaded. "I don't care, wallop me as much as you want,   155
just take me home."

"Hey, I thought you said you wasn't no kid. Hell, you ain't scared of   156
being alone?"

Inside my head there was a running of *Yeah, yeah, yeah,* but I   157
answered, "Naw, Poppa, it's just that Momma's gonna worry and she'll
get sick an' everything, and—"

"Won't work, son," Poppa broke in with a laugh.   158

I kept quiet.   159

"It's only for a couple days. We'll come and see you an' every-   160
body'll bring you things."

I got interested but played it smooth. "What kinda things, Poppa?"   161

Poppa shrugged his shoulders and spread his big arms apart and   162
answered me like he was surprised that I should ask. "Uh . . . fruits and
. . . candy and ice cream. And Momma will probably bring you chicken
soup."

I shook my head sadly. "Poppa, you know I don't like chicken soup."   163

"So we won't bring chicken soup. We'll bring what you like.   164
Goddammit, whatta ya like?"

"I'd like the first things you talked about, Poppa," I said softly. "But 165
instead of soup I'd like"—I held my breath back, then shot it out—"some
roller skates!"

Poppa let out a whistle. Roller skates were about $1.50, and that 166
was rice and beans for more than a few days. Then he said, "All right,
son, soon as you get home, you got 'em."

But he had agreed too quickly. I shook my head from side to side. 167
Shit, I was gonna push all the way for the roller skates. It wasn't every
day you'd get hurt bad enough to ask for something so little like a pair of
roller skates. I wanted them right away.

"Fer Christ sakes," Poppa protested, "you can't use 'em in here. 168
Why, some kid will probably steal 'em on you." But Poppa's voice died
out slowly in a "you win" tone as I just kept shaking my head from side
to side. "Bring 'em tomorrow," he finally mumbled, "but that's it."

"Thanks, Poppa." 169

"Don't ask for no more." 170

My eyes were starting to hurt like mad again. The fun was starting 171
to go outta the game between Poppa and me. I made a face.

"Does it hurt, son?" 172

"Naw, Poppa. I can take it." I thought how I was like a cat in a 173
movie about Indians, taking it like a champ, tied to a stake and getting
like burned toast.

Poppa sounded relieved. "Yeah, it's only at first it hurts." His hand 174
touched my foot. "Well, I'll be going now . . ." Poppa rubbed my foot gently
and then slapped me the same gentle way on the side of my leg. "Be good,
son," he said and walked away. I heard the door open and the nurse telling
him about how they were gonna move me to the ward 'cause I was out of
danger. "Son," Poppa called back, "you're *un hombre*."

I felt proud as hell. 175

"Poppa." 176

"Yeah, son?" 177

"You won't forget to bring the roller skates, huh?" 178

Poppa laughed, "Yeah, son." 179

I heard the door close. 180

Exercises

Some Important Words

paisan—kid (paragraph 10), *bambino*—baby, child (25), *bendito*—stupid
(38), *¿Qué pasa?*—What's going on? (44), *putana*—whore (72), *¡Dios
mío!*—my God! (87), *Dios eterno*—eternal God (89), *está ciego*—he's
blind (91), *pobrecito*—you poor boy (101), *hijo*—son (118), *hombre*—
man (174).

Some of the Issues

1. How do the first two sentences set the scene?
2. Piri wants to project a certain self-image in front of the gang. Characterize it.
3. Until the climactic fight, the cat-and-mouse game that Rocky's gang plays goes through several stages. Determine what these stages are and how Piri reacts to them.
4. How do the grown-ups (those in the street as well as Piri's parents) react to the situation at the various stages? How does Piri deal with his parents' reactions in particular?
5. How does Rocky's attitude toward Piri change after one of the gang members throws the asphalt? What causes the change?
6. Explain Piri's reaction to "spic" and "nigger." Is Piri's desire to be identified as a Puerto Rican a matter of pride or practicality?
7. What is the importance of being "*un hombre*," of having "heart"? How does Piri prove himself a man? By whose standards?

The Way We Are Told

8. There is almost no description in this selection. It is all action and dialog. Thomas nevertheless manages to convey some strong impressions of individuals and their attitudes. How does he do it? Cite some examples.
*9. Both Angelou ("Graduation") and Thomas tell their stories from an adolescent's point of view. Apart from the content, how do the two stories differ? What causes the differences?

Some Subjects for Writing

10. Write about a conflict that you have had. Set the scene and then use mostly dialog to tell your story. See if you can make the voices authentic.
*11. *Rite de passage,* a French term, is usually used to indicate the ceremony marking the formal change of a young person from childhood to adulthood, such as a confirmation or *bar mitzvah.* Usually it is a religious ceremony. Write an essay arguing that Angelou's graduation and Thomas's big fight (or one or the other) were such rites of passage.
*12. Both Jack Agueros ("Halfway to Dick and Jane") and Thomas describe growing up Puerto Rican in New York City. Write an essay comparing and contrasting the way they talk about their childhoods.

IN RESPONSE TO EXECUTIVE ORDER 9066: ALL AMERICANS OF JAPANESE DESCENT MUST REPORT TO RELOCATION CENTERS

Dwight Okita

Dwight Okita was born in Chicago in 1958. A poet and playwright, he has had two plays—"The Salad Bowl Dance" and "The Rainy Season" produced. In 1992, he published a collection of poetry, *Crossing with the Light.*

Okita's mother was among the thousands of Japanese-Americans who were interned shortly after the United States entered World War II. This poem is written in his mother's voice.

To learn more about the internment of Japanese-Americans, read Jeanne Wakatsuki Houston and James D. Houston's "Arrival at Manzanar."

Dear Sirs:
Of course I'll come. I've packed my galoshes
and three packets of tomato seeds. Janet calls them
"love apples." My father says where we're going
they won't grow.

I am a fourteen-year-old girl with bad spelling
and a messy room. If it helps any, I will tell you
I have always felt funny using chopsticks
and my favorite food is hot dogs.
My best friend is a white girl named Denise—
we look at boys together. She sat in front of me
all through grade school because of our names:

252

O'Connor, Ozawa. I know the back of Denise's head very well.
I tell her she's going bald. She tells me I copy on tests.
We are best friends.

I saw Denise today in Geography class.
She was sitting on the other side of the room.
"You're trying to start a war," she said, "giving secrets away
to the Enemy, Why can't you keep your big mouth shut?"
I didn't know what to say.
I gave her a packet of tomato seeds
and asked her to plant them for me, told her
when the first tomato ripened
she'd miss me.

PART SIX

New Worlds

The New World—that designation for America has had a wider meaning than simply the name of the continent that Columbus ran into on his way to find the western passage to Asia. America has been an idea, or rather different ideas at different times. To the Spaniards, who were the first arrivals nearly 500 years ago, it was a source of unimagined wealth. Large-scale Spanish expeditions searched prairies and deserts for El Dorado and the Fountain of Youth. In some of the early English descriptions, often by writers who had never laid eyes on the New World, it resembled the Lost World—the Garden of Eden, Paradise, or the closest approach to it. Continuing the metaphor into the present, Bette Bao Lord, in the first selection of this section, describes her first glimpse of the Golden Gate as "more like the portals to Heaven than the arches of a man-made bridge."

Two of the selections in this section are about Columbus. The first traces Columbus's voyage and impressions of the inhabitants of the New World through his own journal; the second, subsequent impressions and interpretations of Christopher Columbus himself that have been passed down through 500 years. Nearly three centuries after the arrival of Columbus, Michel Guillaume St. Jean de Crèvecoeur came as a young man to the New World and settled in the French colony of Louisiane. In his *Letters from an American Farmer* (1782), written in French, he

255

imagines the pride of an enlightened Englishman when he first lands on the continent. He sees a prosperous agricultural society, virtually classless, in which persons can reach whatever position in life their abilities allow. This idea of America as a beacon of liberty and refuge for the poor extends into the late nineteenth century. America was the destination of "huddled masses yearning to breathe free," in the words of Emma Lazarus's poem inscribed at the foot of the newly installed Statue of Liberty. Alistair Cooke's description, which follows Crèvecoeur's, represents that picture of America, of the downtrodden poor leaving Old World Europe for a better life. What America "means" in a modern 1990s sense is illustrated by a list in a selection called "Recapture the Flag: 34 Reasons to Love America."

Often, the "better life" in the New World proved to be less than a Garden of Eden. Anzia Yezierska, in a semiautobiographical piece, recounts her struggle with those who had already "made it" in America and who tried to ensure their positions by keeping others out. Joseph Bruchac's poem at the end of this section tells more about the huddled masses that Cooke describes and reminds us that the masses who came seeking freedom and prosperity in America also eliminated the freedom of others.

WALKING IN LUCKY SHOES

Bette Bao Lord

Bette Bao Lord was born on November 3, 1938, in Shanghai, China, where her father worked as an official of the Nationalist Chinese government. She immigrated to the United States in 1946, attended Tufts University, and completed a law degree at Fletcher School of Law and Diplomacy in 1960. In 1963 she married Winston Lord, then president of the Council on Foreign Relations, and has worked to foster international goodwill as assistant to the director of the East–West Cultural Center in Hawaii and as advisor to the Fulbright Exchange Program in Washington, DC.

Bao Lord was awarded the American Book Award for her first novel, *Spring Moon* (1982). Bao Lord originally planned the book as a nonfiction account of her 1973 journey to China. However, fearing that her family in China might suffer reprisals from leaders of the Cultural Revolution, she decided to write a historical novel instead. The novel chronicles five generations of the Chang family, whose lives witness the eradication of the traditional Chinese family structure and the disappearance of the upper-middle class. Bao Lord's most recent book is *Legacies: A Chinese Mosaic* (1991).

In the following *Newsweek* guest editorial "My Turn," Bao Lord emphasizes that multiculturalism is a national strength that has the potential both to make us proud of our diverse ancestries and to bind us together. She believes Americans can be different as individuals, but all members of the same family.

I confess, Novelists have a fetish. We can't resist shoes. Indeed, we spend 1 our lives recalling the pairs we have shed and snatching others off unsuspecting souls. We're not proud. We're not particular. Whether it's Air Jordans or the clodhoppers of Frankenstein, Imelda's gross collection or one glass slipper, we covet them all. There's no cure for this affliction. To create characters, we must traipse around and around in our heads sporting lost or stolen shoes.

At 8, I sailed for America from Shanghai without a passing acquain- 2 tance of A, B or C, wearing scruffy brown oxfords. Little did I know then that they were as magical as those glittering red pumps that propelled Dorothy down the yellow brick road.

257

Only yesterday, it seems, resting my chin on the rails of the SS   3
Marylinx, I peered into the mist for *Mei Guo,* Beautiful Country. It refused
to appear. Then, in a blink, there was the Golden Gate, more like the
portals to Heaven than the arches of a man-made bridge.

Only yesterday, standing at PS 8 in Brooklyn, I was bewitched—   4
others, alas, were bothered and bewildered—when I proclaimed:

> *I pledge a lesson to the frog of*
> *the United States of America.*
> *And to the wee puppet for witch's hands.*
> *One Asian, in the vestibule,*
> *with little tea and just rice for all.*

Although I mangled the language, the message was not lost. Not on   5
someone wearing immigrant shoes.

Only yesterday, rounding third base in galoshes, I swallowed a   6
barrelful of tears wondering what wrong I had committed to anger my
teammates so. Why were they all madly screaming at me to go home, go
home?

Only yesterday, listening in pink cotton mules to Red Barber   7
broadcasting from Ebbetts Field, I vaulted over the Milky Way as my hero,
Jackie Robinson, stole home.

Only yesterday, enduring the pinch of new Mary Janes at my   8
grammar-school graduation, I felt as tall as the Statue of Liberty, reciting
Walt Whitman: "I hear America singing, the varied carols I hear . . . Each
singing what belongs to him or her and to none else. . . ."

Today I cherish every unstylish pair of shoes that took me up a   9
road cleared by the footfalls of millions of immigrants before me—to a
room of my own. For America has granted me many a dream, even one
that I never dared to dream—returning to the land of my birth in 1989 as
the wife of the American ambassador. Citizens of Beijing were astounded
to see that I was not a *yang guei ze,* foreign devil, with a tall nose and
ghostly skin and bumpy hair colored in outlandish hues, I looked
Chinese, I spoke Chinese, and after being in my company they accused
me of being a fake, of being just another member of the clan.

I do not believe that the loss of one's native culture is the price one   10
must pay for becoming an American. On the contrary, I feel doubly
blessed. I can choose from two rich cultures those parts that suit my
mood or the occasion best. And unbelievable as it may seem, shoes
tinted red, white and blue go dandy with them all.

Recently I spoke at my alma mater. There were many more Asian   11
faces in that one audience than there were enrolled at Tufts University
when I cavorted in white suede shoes to cheer the Jumbos to victory.
One asked, "Will you tell us about your encounters with racial prejudice?"
I had no ready answers. I thought hard. Sure, I had been roughed up at

school. Sure, I had failed at work. Sure, I had at times felt powerless. But had prejudice against the shade of my skin and the shape of my eyes caused these woes? Unable to show off the wounds I had endured at the hands of racists, I could only cite a scene from my husband's 25th reunion at Yale eight years ago. Throughout that weekend, I sensed I was being watched. But even after the tall, burly man finally introduced himself, I did not recognize his face or name. He hemmed and hawed, then announced that he had flown from Colorado to apologize to me. I could not imagine why. Apparently at a party in the early '60s, he had hectored me to cease dating his WASP classmate.

Someone else at Tufts asked, "How do you think of yourself? As a Chinese or as an American?" Without thinking, I blurted out the truth: "Bette Bao Lord." Did I imagine the collective sigh of relief that swept through the auditorium? I think not. Perhaps I am the exception that proves the rule. Perhaps I am blind to insult and injury. Perhaps I am not alone. No doubt I have been lucky. Others have not been as fortunate. They had little choice but to wear ill-fitting shoes warped by prejudice, to start down a less traveled road strewn with broken promises and littered with regrets, haunted by racism and awash with tears. Where could that road possibly lead? Nowhere but to a nation, divided, without liberty and no justice at all. 12

The Berlin wall is down, but between East Harlem and West Hempstead, between the huddled masses of yesterday and today, the walls go up and up. Has the cold war ended abroad only to usher in heated racial and tribal conflicts at home? No, I believe we shall overcome. But only when: 13

We engage our diversity to yield a nation greater than the sum of its parts. 14

We can be different as sisters and brothers are, and belong to the same family. 15

We bless, not shame, America, our home. 16

A home, no doubt, where skeletons nest in closets and the roof leaks, where foundations must be shored and rooms added. But a home where legacies conceived by the forefathers are tendered from generation to generation to have and to hold. Legacies not of gold but as intangible and inalienable and invaluable as laughter and hope. 17

We the people can do just that—if we clear the smoke of ethnic chauvinism and fears by braving our journey to that "City Upon a Hill" in each other's shoes. 18

Exercises

Some Important Words

fetish (paragraph 1), Air Jordans (1), clodhoppers (1), Imelda (1), covet (1), affliction (1), traipse (1), portals (3), galoshes (6), mules (7), Mary

Janes (8), Walt Whitman (8), cavorted (11), hectored (11), WASP (11), strewn (12), Berlin wall (13), tendered (17), intangible (17), inalienable (17), chauvinism (18).

Some of the Issues

1. How do you characterize Bao Lord's attitude and emotions toward America?
2. In paragraph 9, why did the Chinese accuse her of being a "a fake?" What point does she make by mentioning this experience?
3. In paragraph 11, what is significant about the man from Colorado's apology to her at her husband's 25th Yale reunion?
4. After she blurts out her name in the auditorium at Tufts University (paragraph 12) she perceives a "collective sigh of relief" from the audience. Why?

The Way We Are Told

5. The essay is structured chronologically. What stylistic device does Bao Lord use to mark time transitions?
6. In paragraph 1, Bao Lord introduces the shoe metaphor and then intersperses literal and figurative examples of shoes throughout the essay. Select instances of each use and show how they contribute to the thesis.
7. Give examples of Bao Lord's uses of humor in paragraphs 4–6. Do you find them funny? believable?

Some Subjects for Writing

8. In your opinion, is Bao Lord simply "walking in lucky shoes"? What role does luck play in her life? What other factors may have contributed to her success?
9. In the final paragraph, Bao Lord is optimistic that Americans will overcome racial conflicts. Are you hopeful that this will be accomplished in the near future? Why or why not?

JOURNAL OF DISCOVERY, OCTOBER 10TH TO 12TH, 1492

Christopher Columbus

Columbus's grand design was to reach Asia by sailing west across the Atlantic. His plan included not only the discovering Cipangu, or Japan, but also initiating dealings with the grand khan of Cathay (China) and establishing a direct trade route by sea with the Indies (India). Attempts to secure support for the voyage from King John of Portugal failed. While mediating an appeal to the king of France, Columbus went to Spain, where he proposed his plans to Queen Isabella. Columbus resolutely believed in his mission and asked boldly for the rank of "Admiral of the Ocean" in all those islands, seas, and continents that he might discover; the vice-royalty of all he should discover; and a tenth of the precious metals he should find. These conditions were rejected and his negotiations interrupted. After nearly five years of entreaties, Queen Isabella and King Ferdinand of Spain conceded to the expedition and an agreement was sealed between Columbus and their Catholic majesties on April 17, 1492. On August 3, at 8:00 in the morning, a small fleet of three ships and 88 crew members set out from Palos, Spain, for the Canary Islands.

Columbus's original shipboard journal has long been lost. However, an abstract of the admiral's diary survives in an early sixteenth-century version recopied by Bartolomé de las Casas, a priest whose primary interest in the journal may have been as supporting text for his work *Historia de las Indias*. Many researchers believe that long passages, including the entries below from October 10–12, were copied verbatim, without substantial omissions; thus many particulars may be obtained concerning this first voyage.

The selection starts just before the sighting of land, an island called Guanahani by the inhabitants (named San Salvador by Columbus). This voyage resulted in the discovery of the islands of Santa Maria de la Concepcion (Rum Cay), Fernandina (Long Island), Isabella (Crooked Island), Cuba (or Juana—named by Columbus in honor of the young prince of Spain), and Hispaniola (Haiti and Santo Domingo).

The translator of this selection, John Cummins, has newly restored and translated Columbus's journal on the basis of research from several sources, including the las Casas version, Columbus's son Fernando's biography of his father, legal records, and books from Columbus's own library.

You might also want to read the selection by David Gates entitled "Who Was Columbus?"

Wednesday, October 10, 1492

Sailed wsw at about eight knots, sometimes up to nine and a half, occasionally only five and a half. Sixty-two and a half leagues in the twenty-four hours; I told the men only forty-six and a half. They could contain themselves no longer, and began to complain of the length of the voyage. I encouraged them as best I could, trying to raise their hopes of the benefits they might gain from it. I also told them that it was useless to complain; having set out for the Indies I shall continue this voyage until, with God's grace, I reach them.   1

Thursday, October 11, and Friday, October 12, 1492

Course wsw. A heavy sea, the roughest in the whole voyage so far. We saw petrels, and a green reed close to the ship, and then a big green fish of a kind which does not stray far from the shoals. On the Pinta they saw a cane and a stick, and they picked up another little piece of wood which seemed to have been worked with an iron tool; also a piece of cane and another plant which grows on land, and a little board. On the Niña too they saw signs of land, and a thorn-branch laden with red fruits, apparently newly cut. We were all filled with joy and relief at these signs. Sailed twenty-eight and a half leagues before sunset. After sunset I resumed our original course westward, sailing at about nine knots. By two o'clock in the morning we had sailed about sixty-eight miles, or twenty-two and a half leagues.   2

When everyone aboard was together for the *Salve Regina,* which all seamen say or sing in their fashion, I talked to the men about the grace which God had shown us by bringing us in safety, with fair winds and no obstacles, and by comforting us with signs which were more plentiful every day. I urged them to keep a good watch and reminded them that in the first article of the sailing instructions issued to each ship in the Canaries I gave orders not to sail at night after we had reached a point seven hundred leagues from there; I was sailing on because of everyone's great desire to sight land. I warned them to keep a good lookout in the bows and told them that I would give a silk doublet to the man who first sighted land, as well as the prize of 10,000 *maravedis* promised by Your Majesties.   3

I was on the poop deck at ten o'clock in the evening when I saw a [4]
light.[1] It was so indistinct that I could not be sure it was land, but I called
Pedro Gutiérrez, the Butler of the King's Table, and told him to look at
what I thought was a light. He looked, and saw it. I also told Rodrigo
Sánchez de Segovia, Your Majesties' observer on board, but he saw
nothing because he was standing in the wrong place. After I had told
them, the light appeared once or twice more, like a wax candle rising
and falling. Only a few people thought it was a sign of land, but I was
sure we were close to a landfall.

Then the Pinta, being faster and in the lead, sighted land and made [5]
the signal as I had ordered. The first man to sight land was called Rodrigo
de Triana. The land appeared two hours after midnight, about two
leagues away. We furled all sail except the *treo*, the mainsail with no
bonnets, and jogged off and on[2] until Friday morning, when we came to
an island.[3] We saw naked people, and I went ashore in a boat with armed
men, taking Martín Alonso Pinzón and his brother Vicente Yáñez, captain
of the Niña. I took the royal standard, and the captains each took a
banner with the Green Cross which each of my ships carries as a device,
with the letters F and Y, surmounted by a crown, at each end of the cross.

When we stepped ashore we saw fine green trees, streams every- [6]
where and different kinds of fruit. I called to the two captains to jump
ashore with the rest, who included Rodrigo de Escobedo, secretary of the

[1]The mysterious light now described is a controversial subject. The uncharitable have
suggested that Columbus invented it because of his wish to be considered the first man to
make visual contact with the New World. Others have accepted that it was a light on shore,
sometimes with the aim of bolstering ideas on Columbus's landfall, or suggested that it was
a firebrand in an Indian canoe. The navigational details in this entry suggest that the source
of light must have been well out in the Atlantic, over thirty miles from the landfall. A strong
possibility is that what Columbus saw was part of the reproductive process of a marine
annelid of the genus *Odontosyllis*, whose evening or nocturnal courting procedure, on the
surface, involves the extrusion by the female of streams of brilliantly luminous matter along
with the ova. She does this several times over a period of a few minutes, the purpose of the
luminosity being to guide the males to the ova for fertilization. The display occurs in the
winter months, and is linked with the third quarter of the moon. For more details, see L. R.
Crawshay, "Possible Bearing of a Luminous Syllid on the Question of the Landfall of
Columbus," *Nature,* Vol. 136, 1935, p. 559.

[2]To jog off and on is to make short tacks towards and away from the coast. It was a
procedure commonly carried out at night off an unfamiliar coast which it would have been
dangerous to approach in the dark.

[3]Las Casas . . . inserts: "one of the Lucayos, which was called Guanahani in the Indians'
language." The first land sighted is generally thought to have been Watling Island, but the
landfall has been the subject of controversy. Recently a computer-generated reconstruction
of Columbus's course, taking into account magnetic variation, meteorological data, the
effect of currents and historical ship drift information led American scholars to the
conclusion that Guanahani was, after all, probably Watling Island (Philip L. Richardson and
Roger A. Goldsmith, "The Columbus Landfall: Voyage Track Corrected for Winds and
Currents," *Oceanus,* Vol. 30, 1987, pp. 3–10.

fleet, and Rodrigo Sánchez de Segovia, asking them to bear solemn witness that in the presence of them all I was taking possession of this land for their Lord and Lady the King and Queen, and I made the necessary declarations which are set down at greater length in the written testimonies.

Soon many of the islanders gathered round us. I could see that they were people who would be more easily converted to our Holy Faith by love than by coercion, and wishing them to look on us with friendship I gave some of them red bonnets and glass beads which they hung round their necks, and many other things of small value, at which they were so delighted and so eager to please us that we could not believe it. Later they swam out to the boats to bring us parrots and balls of cotton thread and darts, and many other things, exchanging them for such objects as glass beads and hawk bells. They took anything, and gave willingly whatever they had. 7

However, they appeared to me to be a very poor people in all respects. They go about as naked as the day they were born, even the women, though I saw only one, who was quite young. All the men I saw were quite young, none older than thirty, all well built, finely bodied and handsome in the face. Their hair is coarse, almost like a horse's tail, and short; they wear it short, cut over the brow, except a few strands of hair hanging down uncut at the back. 8

Some paint themselves with black, some with the colour of the Canary islanders,[4] neither black nor white, others with white, others with red, others with whatever they can find. Some have only their face painted, others their whole body, others just their eyes or nose. They carry no weapons, and are ignorant of them; when I showed them some swords they took them by the blade and cut themselves. They have no iron; their darts are just sticks without an iron head, though some of them have a fish tooth or something else at the tip. 9

They are all the same size, of good stature, dignified and well formed. I saw some with scars on their bodies, and made signs to ask about them, and they indicated to me that people from other islands nearby came to capture them and they defended themselves. I thought, and still think, that people from the mainland come here to take them prisoner. They must be good servants, and intelligent, for I can see that they quickly repeat everything said to them. I believe they would readily become Christians; it appeared to me that they have no religion. With God's will, I will take six of them with me for Your Majesties when I leave this place, so that they may learn Spanish. 10

I saw no animals on the island, only parrots. 11

---

[4]This is probably a reference to the Guanches, a people of African origin occupying the Canaries before the conquest by the Spanish.

Exercises

Some Important Words

knots (paragraph 1), leagues (1), petrels (2), shoals (2), *Salve Regina*—
devotional prayer to the Blessed Virgin Mary (3), doublet (3),
maravedis—an old Spanish coin (3), furled (5), coercion (7).

Some of the Issues

1. According to his own account, Columbus deliberately lied to his crew
   about the distance they had traveled on October 10. What do you
   believe was his motive for doing so?
2. What does Columbus's response to the complaints of his crew in the
   October 10 entry reveal about his nature?
3. What factors appear to have motivated the men to sail beyond the
   agreed-on point on October 11?
4. Which man was given credit in the journal entry for October 10
   (paragraph 5) as the first to sight land?
5. How would you describe the islanders' reaction to Columbus's
   landing (paragraph 7)? Speculate on what you would have done after
   seeing strange men and ships approach your land.
6. Columbus intends to take six islanders back to Spain. How does he
   justify this action? Contrast his view with a likely modern-day reaction
   to the abduction of these men.

The Way We Are Told

7. In paragraphs 8 and 9, do you think Columbus gives an *objective* or
   subjective description of the islanders? Defend your view with
   specific reference to the text.
8. What effect does the last line of the October 11 – 12 entry have on
   you?

Some Subjects for Writing

9. Imagine that you know nothing more about the original writer of this
   journal than what is written in these excerpts. How would you
   characterize him? Write a profile of his character in answer to the
   question, "Who was Columbus?" using examples from the journal to
   illustrate your ideas.

WHO WAS COLUMBUS?

David Gates

This article appeared in a special issue of *Newsweek* magazine in 1991, before the 500th anniversary of Columbus's voyages to the New World. A Quincentenary Commission, partly funded by Congress, had planned events around the nation to commemorate the occasion. However, the popular view of Columbus as hero was challenged by many after several groups ranging from the National Council of Churches to the American Indian Movement denounced the festivities. As a result, the National Endowment for the Humanities canceled federal funding.

David Gates writes book and music reviews for *Newsweek*. Before joining the magazine he lectured on English at the University of Virginia and was an instructor at Harvard University. He was educated at the University of Connecticut and now lives in New York City.

Read also "Journal of Discovery, October 10th to 12th, 1492" by Christopher Columbus.

Forget the lettering at the top of Sebastiano del Piombo's famous painting, identifying that pursed-lipped, peevish-looking character as Columbus. It was probably added, years after the fact, to a portrait of some long-forgotten Italian nobleman. And forget the yarns in which he has to persuade stubborn monarchs that the earth is round, and face down a mutinous crew terrified they're going to sail off the edge. In 1492 educated people already knew, in theory, that you could reach the East by sailing west; sailors had long ceased to smite their brows when ships and land masses popped into sight from below the horizon. And he probably never heard the name Columbus, a Latinizing of his likely birth name, Cristoforo Colombo; Richard Hakluyt's "Principall navigations" (1598) popularized this fancy-dan form among English speakers. He was generally called Cristóbal Colón, as he still is among Spanish speakers. He signed himself simply Xρο FERENS, a Greek-Latin hybrid clearly meant to suggest his self-assigned mission of bringing Christ to the naked people across the ocean. His son, who was also his biographer, called him Colonus.

Like heroes from Julius Caesar to John Kennedy, Christopher   2
Columbus has mostly been who people wanted him to be. To Renaissance humanists, he was the open-minded explorer, the arch-empiricist;
to North American revolutionaries, he was the Founding Fathers' father,
standing toe to toe with Old World monarchs and making them see
things his way. Even 20th-century historiography hasn't quite humanized
him—even when it's demythologized him. Samuel Eliot Morison's wor-
shipful "Admiral of the Ocean Sea" (1942) acknowledges Columbus's
slave trading and his disastrous stint as a colonial governor; still, his
Columbus is not only a master seaman—Morison traced the voyages
himself in a variety of boats—but a visionary "who carried Christian
civilization across the Ocean Sea." In Kirkpatrick Sale's hostile "The
Conquest of Paradise" (1990), Columbus becomes the embodiment of
every political, spiritual and ecological sin imaginable to a founder of the
New York Green Party: Eurocentrism, speciesism, capitalism, estrangement from both nature and self. "Perhaps most revealing of all," Sale
writes, "this is a man without a settled *name,* and it is hard not to believe
that a confusion, or at least inconstancy, of that kind reflects . . .
psychological instability." Oh, right: he's an incompetent sailor, too.

The real Columbus, according to people who had seen him in the   3
flesh, was a tall, red-faced man; he might've looked something like a
1512 portrait by Lorenzo Lotto, painted six years after Columbus's death.
(We're not dead certain *this* portrait was meant to be Columbus, either.)
He was probably born in Genoa, in 1451. His father was a wool weaver
and tavernkeeper. In his early 20s, Columbus went to Portugal, then the
most adventurous seafaring nation; at least once he sailed down the coast
of West Africa. He married, had a son and was widowed; later he had a
second son (Fernando, the biographer) by a woman he didn't marry.
(That and the miracles he didn't perform killed his proposed canonization in the 19th century.) At some point, for some reason, he made it his
life's goal to reach Asia by sailing west across the Atlantic. After years of
lobbying in the royal courts of both Portugal and Spain, he managed to
get funding from the Spanish monarchs Ferdinand and Isabella. On four
separate expeditions, he explored various Caribbean islands from which
he sent back plants, minerals and slaves. Once he claimed to have found
the Terrestrial Paradise: it was actually the mainland of South America.
Under his stewardship, the first permanent Spanish settlement in the New
World became so cruel and chaotic that he was returned to Europe in
chains. He made one final, anticlimactic voyage and died, embittered,
with plenty of money.

What was he like? Ambitious, obviously. Despite relatively humble   4
beginnings—Genoese wool weavers didn't have the prestige or political
clout of their Florentine or Venetian counterparts—he managed to marry
a Portuguese woman whose family had influence at court. (Only after

King João II turned him down did Columbus approach Spain's Ferdinand and Isabella.) He seems to have craved not just wealth but, as his first-name-only signature suggests, instant nobility. He campaigned, successfully, to be styled "Don," and Spain still honors his request to pass the title "Admiral of the Ocean Sea" on to his descendants. His ambition may or may not explain why he married Felipa Perestrello e Moniz, but it could well explain why he *didn't* marry Beatriz Enríquez de Arana, the mother of his son Fernando. "Marriage to a low-born orphan," write University of Minnesota historians William and Carla Phillips in the forthcoming "The Worlds of Christopher Columbus," "would do nothing to enhance his prestige and would surely impede his search for noble status."

If that seems distasteful—even after we've corrected for the 15th century's less enlightened views on both women and social class—consider that Columbus supported her in part with money he'd chiseled from the sailor who'd raised the cry of "*Tierra!*" on his 1492 voyage. Columbus had promised a 10,000-maravedi annuity (perhaps $1,400 today) to whoever first sighted land; at first he credited one Juan Rodríguez Bermejo, but he later argued that he himself should get the annuity, since he'd spotted, or thought he spotted, a distant light some hours earlier. Perhaps the real issue wasn't the money but the credit for being first: for Columbus, as for most people, money seems to have been mixed up with self-esteem. (Wealthy but neglected in his last days, he claimed to be "without a single blanca.") The Phillipses speculate that Columbus may have turned the annuity over to de Arana because he felt guilty about his treatment of Bermejo. It's possible—though it's equally possible he cheated the man to channel some money to his mistress. We'll never know.

One thing does seem certain: that Columbus sometimes exaggerated, misrepresented and just plain lied, particularly in overselling the islands he discovered. One often-cited instance of his deviousness may be a bum rap: the confession in his journal of the first voyage that he underreported the distance the ship made each day so as not to alarm the sailors. The Phillipses argue that this part of the journal may be garbled. (It doesn't exist in manuscript, but in a 16th-century paraphrase of an unreliable copy.) But there are enough other instances—like his forcing sailors on the second voyage to swear that Cuba was not an island—to justify Sale's claim that Columbus's indifference to the distinction between truth and falsehood sometimes verged on madness.

Yet where Columbus seems looniest to us, he's actually at his most orthodox. World maps in his day *did* place the Garden of Eden near Asia—where he always insisted his islands were—and he was sufficiently a man of the Middle Ages to deem the Bible a reliable (if sibylline) source of geographical knowledge. As the Phillipses show, Columbus's picture of the world was a collage of Scripture, Ptolemy, contemporary maps, his own observations and wishful thinking. Similarly, we should take seriously the stated purpose of his explorations: to bring the unconverted to Christ and to raise funds in order to capture Jerusalem, thereby ushering in the Second Coming. It's hard for moderns to ignore the dissonance between these pious aims and the reality: the Admiral of the Ocean Sea brutalizing and enslaving the "Indians" and enriching himself. It's safe to say he never saw it that way. Despite his posthumous status as empiricist exemplar, he put a lot of energy into *not* seeing things as they were.

It's become commonplace to regard Columbus as a representative man of his time, with one foot in the Middle Ages and one in the Renaissance. It's safer than making inferences about his personality, beyond such hard-to-miss traits as the grandiosity and self-pity he showed late in life. Consequently, today's Columbus is more "complex" than the imaginary hero who stood the egg on end, but also more remote. Only imagination can bring us close to him again: not by resurrecting discredited yarns, but by using the verifiable facts to reconstruct what his experience must have been like.   8

So put yourself in Columbus's shoes. You're 41—in those days, an old man—and at last your dream comes true. They've given you your ships, the winds are favorable, you reach the land you always knew was there. But it's not the way you thought it would be, and not what you promised when they put up the money. There's island after island after island, but you can't find Cipango (Japan), where the cities and the gold mines are, and you can't get a straight answer out of the locals. So you deliver what you can: a little gold, some plants you thought (mistakenly) you recognized and a few natives. You're vindicated; they give you more ships, more men. But something's not right, and your sponsors soon get suspicious. You should be dealing with Eastern potentates, not these naked people who've started to hate you. You try to keep order in your pitiful settlement, but things get out of hand. You wind up in chains, accused of brutality and, worse, incompetence. And you started out with the best intentions. You were going to get rich *and* save the world. You didn't see any contradiction there. You were the first American.   9

Exercises

Some Important Words

purse-lipped (paragraph 1), peevish (1), mutinous (1), smite (1), fancy-dan (1), arch-empiricist (2), historiography (2), demythologized (2), stint (2), Green Party (2), Eurocentrism (2), speciesism (2), inconstancy (2), canonization (3), impede (4), annuity (5), orthodox (7), sibylline (7),

Ptolemy (7), dissonance (7), posthumous (7), exemplar (7), grandiosity (8), vindicated (9), potentates (9).

Some of the Issues

1. What view of mid-fifteenth-century Europeans does Gates challenge in paragraph 1?
2. Compare two historians' interpretations of Columbus: Samuel Eliot Morison and Kirkpatrick Sale (paragraph 2).
3. According to Gates's account, what happened to the first permanent settlement that Columbus established in the New World (paragraph 3)?
4. According to the historians William and Carla Phillips, why didn't Columbus marry the mother of his second son, Fernando (paragraphs 4 and 5), since his first wife had died before he arrived in Spain? Based on your understanding of Columbus's character, is the Phillips' hypothesis consistent with your view of him?
5. In paragraph 6 what examples does Gates give to support the idea that Columbus often misrepresented the truth?
6. In paragraph 8, what method of investigation into the truth of Columbus's actual character does Gates advocate?

The Way We Are Told

7. What is Gates's intent in paragraph 1? What writing strategy does he use throughout the opening two paragraphs to introduce the main idea?
8. How would you characterize the tone of the last sentence in paragraph 2? Does Gates continue this tone throughout the essay, or does his attitude change? Support your view with direct reference to the text.
9. In paragraph 9, what effect does Gates hope to achieve by inviting the reader to step into Columbus's shoes?

Some Subjects for Writing

*10. Read the selection from Columbus's journal. Based on the information in the two selections, has your original view of Christopher Columbus been challenged? In what ways? What specific information led you to reevaluate your thinking?
11. Gates says in paragraph 2 that heroes such as Julius Caesar, John Kennedy, and Christopher Columbus have "mostly been who people wanted [them] to be," suggesting that history sheds a different light on their personalities and accomplishments. Consider your definition of *hero*. According to your own criteria, was Columbus a hero? What other people might you include in this category?

WHAT IS AN AMERICAN?

Michel Guillaume St. Jean de Crèvecoeur

Michel Guillaume St. Jean de Crèvecoeur (1735–1813) came as a young man to the New World, settling at first in the French colony of Louisiane, which at that time stretched in a huge arc from the mouth of the St. Lawrence River in the north to the mouth of the Mississippi in the south. In the Seven Years War (1756–1763), called the French and Indian Wars in America, he fought under Montcalm against the British. When the colonies passed into British hands, he remained and settled as a farmer in Vermont. The Revolutionary War found him on the side of the loyalists. Crèvecoeur returned to France permanently in 1790. His *Letters from an American Farmer,* written in French, was published in 1782 and is among the earliest descriptions of life in America.

Crèvecoeur defines and describes what he sees as the virtues and advantages America possesses as compared to the Europe of his day. He sees a prosperous agricultural society, virtually classless, in which persons can reach whatever position in life their abilities allow. He contrasts this to the Old World with its ingrained class structure, where a man (or woman) is born to wealth and high status or to poverty and lifelong drudgery, with no way to escape. He sees America as a young, mobile society in contrast to the static world from which the new man, the American, has made his escape.

I wish I could be acquainted with the feelings and thoughts which must   1
agitate the heart and present themselves to the mind of an enlightened Englishman, when he first lands on this continent. He must greatly rejoice, that he lived at a time to see this fair country discovered and settled; he must necessarily feel a share of national pride, when he views the chain of settlements which embellishes these extended shores. When he says to himself, this is the work of my countrymen, who, when convulsed by factions, afflicted by a variety of miseries and wants, restless and impatient, took refuge here. They brought along with them their national genius, to which they principally owe what liberty they enjoy, and what substance they possess. Here he sees the industry of his

271

native country, displayed in a new manner, and traces in their works the embryos of all the arts, sciences, and ingenuity which flourish in Europe. Here he beholds fair cities, substantial villages, extensive fields, an immense country filled with decent houses, good roads, orchards, meadows, and bridges, where an hundred years ago all was wild, woody, and uncultivated!

What a train of pleasing ideas this fair spectacle must suggest! It is a prospect which must inspire a good citizen with the most heartfelt pleasure. The difficulty consists in the manner of viewing so extensive a scene. He is arrived on a new continent; a modern society offers itself to his contemplation, different from what he had hitherto seen. It is not composed, as in Europe, of great lords who possess every thing, and of a herd of people who have nothing. Here are no aristocratical families, no courts, no kings, no bishops, no ecclesiastical dominion, no invisible power giving to a few a very visible one; no great manufacturers employing thousands, no great refinements of luxury. The rich and the poor are not so far removed from each other as they are in Europe. 2

Some few towns excepted, we are all tillers of the earth, from Nova Scotia to West Florida. We are a people of cultivators, scattered over an immense territory, communicating with each other by means of good roads and navigable rivers, united by the silken bands of mild government, all respecting the laws without dreading their power, because they are equitable. We are all animated with the spirit of industry, which is unfettered, and unrestrained, because each person works for himself. If he travels through our rural districts, he views not the hostile castle, and the haughty mansion, contrasted with the clay-built hut and miserable cabin, where cattle and men help to keep each other warm, and dwell in meanness, smoke, and indigence. A pleasing uniformity of decent competence appears throughout our habitations. The meanest of our log-houses is a dry and comfortable habitation. Lawyer or merchant are the fairest titles our towns afford; that of a farmer is the only appellation of the rural inhabitants of our country. It must take some time ere he can reconcile himself to our dictionary, which is but short in words of dignity, and names of honour. There, on a Sunday, he sees a congregation of respectable farmers and their wives, all clad in neat homespun, well mounted, or riding in their own humble waggons. There is not among them an esquire, saving the unlettered magistrate. There he sees a parson as simple as his flock, a farmer who does not riot on the labour of others. We have no princes, for whom we toil, starve, and bleed: we are the most perfect society now existing in the world. Here man is free as he ought to be; nor is this pleasing equality so transitory as many others are. Many ages will not see the shores of our great lakes replenished with inland nations, nor the unknown bounds of North America entirely peopled. Who can tell how far it extends? Who can tell the millions of men whom 3 it will feed and contain? for no European foot has as yet travelled half the extent of this mighty continent?

The next wish of this traveller will be to know whence came all 4 these people? They are a mixture of English, Scotch, Irish, Dutch, Germans, and Swedes. From this promiscuous breed, the race now called Americans have arisen. The eastern provinces must indeed be excepted, as being the unmixed descendants of Englishmen. I have heard many wish they had been more intermixed also: for my part, I am no wisher; and think it much better as it has happened. They exhibit a most conspicuous figure in this great and variegated picture; they too enter for a great share in the pleasing perspective displayed in these thirteen provinces. I know it is fashionable to reflect on them; but I respect them for what they have done; for the accuracy and wisdom with which they have settled their territory; for the decency of their manners; for their early love of letters; their ancient college, the first in this hemisphere; for their industry, which to me, who am but a farmer, is the criterion of every thing. There never was a people, situated as they are, who, with so ungrateful a soil, have done more in so short a time. Do you think that the monarchical ingredients which are more prevalent in other govern-ments, have purged them from all foul stains? Their histories assert the contrary.

In this great American asylum, the poor of Europe have by some 5 means met together, and in consequence of various causes; to what purpose should they ask one another, what countrymen they are? Alas, two thirds of them had no country. Can a wretch who wanders about, who works and starves, whose life is a continual scene of sore affliction of pinching penury; can that man call England or any other kingdom his country? A country that had no bread for him, whose fields procured him no harvest, who met with nothing but the frowns of the rich, the severity of the laws, with jails and punishments; who owned not a single foot of the extensive surface of this planet? No! Urged by a variety of motives, here they came. Everything has tended to regenerate them; new laws, a new mode of living, a new social system; here they are become men: in Europe they were as so many useless plants, wanting vegetative mould, and refreshing showers; they withered, and were mowed down by want, hunger, and war: but now, by the power of transplantation, like all other plants, they have taken root and flourished! Formerly they were not numbered in any civil list of their country, except in those of the poor; here they rank as citizens. By what invisible power has this surprizing metamorphosis been performed? By that of the laws and that of their industry. The laws, the indulgent laws, protect them as they arrive, stamping on them the symbol of adoption; they receive ample rewards for their labours; these accumulated rewards procure them lands; those lands confer on them the title of freemen; and to that title every benefit is affixed which men can possibly require. This is the great operation daily performed by our laws. From whence proceed these laws? From our government. Whence that government? It is derived from the original genius and strong desire of the people, ratified and confirmed by government. This is the great chain which links us all, this is the picture which every province exhibits.

What attachment can a poor European emigrant have for a country   6 where he had nothing? The knowledge of the language, the love of a few kindred as poor as himself, were the only cords that tied him: his country is now that which gives him land, bread, protection, and consequence: *Ubi panis ibi patria,* is the motto of all emigrants. What then is the American, this new man? He is either an European, or the descendant of an European; hence that strange mixture of blood, which you will find in no other country. I could point out to you a man, whose grandfather was an Englishman, whose wife was Dutch, whose son married a French woman, and whose present four sons have now four wives of different nations. *He* is an American, who, leaving behind him all his ancient prejudices and manners, receives new ones from the new mode of life he has embraced, the new government he obeys, and the new rank he holds. He becomes an American by being received in the broad lap of our great *Alma Mater.*

Here individuals of all nations are melted into a new race of men,   7 whose labours and posterity will one day cause great change in the world. Americans are the western pilgrims, who are carrying along with them that great mass of arts, sciences, vigour, and industry, which began long since in the east; they will finish the great circle. The Americans were once scattered all over Europe; here they are incorporated into one of the finest systems of population which has ever appeared, and which will hereafter become distinct by the power of the different climates they inhabit. The American ought, therefore, to love this country much better than that wherein either he or his forefathers were born. Here the rewards of his industry follow with equal steps the progress of his labour; his labour is founded on the basis of nature, *self-interest;* can it want a stronger allurement? Wives and children, who before in vain demanded of him a morsel of bread, now, fat and frolicsome, gladly help their father to clear those fields whence exuberant crops are to arise to feed and to clothe them all; without any part being claimed, either by a despotic prince, a rich abbot, or a mighty lord. Here religion demands but little of him; a small voluntary salary to the minister, and gratitude to God; can he refuse these? The American is a new man, who acts upon new principles; he must therefore entertain new ideas, and form new opinions. From involuntary idleness, servile dependence, penury, and useless labour, he has passed to toils of a very different nature, rewarded by ample subsistence.—This is an American.

Exercises

Some Important Words

enlightened (paragraph 1), factions (1), ecclesiastical (2), dominion (2), unfettered (3), indigence (3), habitation (3), homespun (3), replenished (3), variegated (4), monarchical (4), metamorphosis (5), *ubi panis ibi patria*—where bread is, there is my country (6), frolicsome (7), exuberant (7), penury (7).

Some of the Issues

1. Why should the "enlightened Englishman" rejoice at landing in America?
2. What is the central idea of the second paragraph? How does it relate to the first? How does it carry Crèvecoeur's ideas beyond the first paragraph?
3. Consider the last sentence in paragraph 2 and explain how it is expanded upon in paragraph 3.
4. Paragraph 3 makes its point by means of contrasts. What are they?
5. Paragraphs 4 and 5 classify the people who came to America, but in two different ways. Paragraph 4 discusses national origins. How are Americans described in paragraph 5?
6. In paragraphs 6 and 7 Crèvecoeur asserts that these diverse Europeans are "melted into a new race of men"—Americans. How does that process take place? (Note the word "melted.")
7. Make a list of the contrasts Crèvecoeur makes or clearly implies between Europe and America. Then attempt to organize and classify them into major groupings.
8. Crèvecoeur omits two groups of inhabitants of America. Who are they? Why do you think he omits them when he is clearly concerned about the well-being of ordinary people?

The Way We Are Told

9. Why does Crèvecoeur create the character of the "enlightened Englishman" to report on America in paragraph 1, instead of continuing to use the first person singular, as he does in the opening sentence?
10. Crèvecoeur tries to convince the reader of the superiority of Americans and their institutions. Who, would you say, are his readers? What are their likely beliefs? How does Crèvecoeur respond to these beliefs?
11. Crèvecoeur uses rhetorical questions, exclamations, and repetition of words and phrases to strengthen his case. Find examples of each.

Some Subjects for Writing

12. Write an essay in praise of some institution that you admire. Select those aspects that seem important to you, organize them in some logical order, and write your description, stressing the favorable facts rather than giving your opinions.
13. Crèvecoeur presents the American as an ideal "new man," free of the shackles of history imposed on him in Europe. In an essay examine the extent to which the American can still be described in Crèvecoeur's terms today.
14. Crèvecoeur may have been the first to use the word *melt* to describe the fusion of people of different nationalities into a new "race of men"—Americans. The term *melting pot* has become a cliché representing that process. More recently some observers have cast doubts on the extent of that process and preferred the analogy of the salad bowl to the melting pot. Write an essay "American Society—Melting Pot or Salad Bowl?"

THE HUDDLED MASSES

Alistair Cooke

Alistair Cooke is probably best known as the former host of the PBS television series "Masterpiece Theater," a function he fulfilled from 1971 to early 1993. In the 1970s he also hosted "Alistair Cooke's America" on PBS, a narrative history of the growth of the United States. The following selection is taken from the book based on that series, and describes immigration to the United States at the height of the influx of Europeans in the late nineteenth and early twentieth centuries.

Cooke, born in Manchester, England, in 1908, is himself an immigrant, having left his native England for America in 1937. As a broadcaster, journalist, and commentator he has concentrated his attention on interpreting America, its culture and institutions, to the world. He has written a number of books in that field and holds honorary degrees from several universities, including Edinburgh, Manchester, and St. Andrews.

For more on the history and subsequent restoration of Ellis Island as a national landmark and museum of immigration, read Joseph Bruchac's "Ellis Island."

"We call England the Mother country," Robert Benchley once remarked, "because most of us come from Poland or Italy." It's not quite as drastic as that, but today the chances of an American being of wholly English stock are, outside the South, no more than one in four. Only the English visitor is still surprised by this palpable fact. When a German makes his first trip across the Atlantic, he can go into almost any large city between southern Pennsylvania and the Great Lakes, and on across the prairie into the small towns of Kansas, and he will find himself among people whose physique is familiar, who share many of his values and his tastes in food and drink. The Scandinavian will be very much at home with the landscape and the farming of Minnesota, and he will not be surprised to hear that the state is represented in Congress by men named Langen and Olson and Nelsen. A Polish Catholic would easily pass as a native among the sandy potato fields, the lumbering wooden churches, and the Doroskis and Stepnoskis of eastern Long Island.

For three quarters of the population that hears itself so often hailed   2
as "the American people" are the descendants of immigrants from Asia
and Africa and, most of all, from the continent of Europe. They brought
over with them their religions and folkways and their national foods, not
least their national prejudices, which for a long time in the new country
turned the cities of the Northeast and the Midwest into adjoining
compounds of chauvinists, distrustful not only of immigrants from other
nations everywhere but too often of their neighbors three or four blocks
away.

But even the most clannish of them sooner or later had to mix with   3
the peoples already there and learn among other things a new kind of
politics, in which the dominant power went to men who knew how to
balance the needs of one national group against another. The American
delicatessen became an international store for the staples that the old
immigrant could not do without. Few American children, certainly in the
cities, need to be told that goulash comes from Hungary, liverwurst from
Germany, borscht from Russia, and lasagne from Italy. And even Gentiles
who never tasted the combination probably know that lox—smoked
salmon—and the doughnut-shaped rolls called bagels are as inseparable,
in Jewish households of any nationality, as an Englishman's—and an
Anglo-Saxon American's—bacon and eggs.

Why did they come? Why do they still come? For a mesh of reasons   4
and impulses that condition any crucial decision in life. But the most
powerful was one common to most of the immigrants from the 1840s
on—hard times in the homeland. They chose America because, by the
early nineteenth century, Europeans, especially if they were poor, had
heard that the Americans had had a revolution that successfully over-
threw the old orders of society. Madame de Staël could tell a Boston
scholar, in 1817, "You are the advance guard of the human race." And
Goethe, ten years later, wrote for anybody to read: "Amerika, du hast es
besser als unser Kontinent" (which may be loosely translated as: "America, you have things better over there.") He was thinking of the freedom
from the binding force of "useless traditions." But people who had never
heard of Madame de Staël and Goethe picked up the new belief that
there was a green land far away preserved "from robbers, knights and
ghosts affrighting." Whenever life could hardly be worse at home, they
came to believe that life was better in America.

In Ireland in the middle 1840s human life had touched bottom.   5
Ironically, two causes of the Irish plight came *from* America. The rising
competition of American agriculture made thousands of very small
farmers (300,000 of Ireland's 685,000 farms had less than three acres) shift
from tillage to grazing, on barren ground. And the potato blight, which
was to putrefy vast harvest in a few weeks, had crossed the Atlantic from
America in 1845. Within five years the potato famine had claimed almost

a million Irish lives, over twenty thousand of them dropping in the fields from starvation.

The young Queen Victoria was informed that the state of Ireland 6 was "alarming" and that the country was so full of "inflammable matter" that it could explode in rebellion. So she paid a royal visit, serenely admired the beauty of the scenery, and was relieved that the people "received us with the greatest enthusiasm." Nevertheless, at Kingston and at Cork she noted: "You see more ragged and wretched people here than I ever saw anywhere else." One of those ragged people could well have been a bankrupt farmer from Wexford County who had gone to Cork. Most such, with any energy left over after the famine, retreated to the towns and either joined sedition societies or headed for America. This one chose America, and, like very many of the Irish who came after, his destination was chosen for him by the simple fact that Boston was the end of the Cunard line. His name was Patrick Kennedy, great-grandfather of the thirty-fifth President of the United States. He was one of the 1,700,000 Irish—a little less than one quarter of the whole population when the famine began—who left for America in the 1840s and 1850s.

Hunger, then, was the spur in Ireland. There were other, equally 7 fearful incentives. In the single year of 1848 political storms swept across Europe—in Austria, an abdication, arrests, and executions; in Italy, a revolution and a declaration of war by the Pope against Austria; in Sicily, an uprising against the King of Naples; in Germany, a liberal revolution that failed. Both then and throughout the rest of the century and on into our own, in any troubled country, whether or not its mischief could be laid to known culprits, there was always the ancient scapegoat of the Jew. In eastern and central Europe the ghettos had long been routine targets for the recruiting sergeant and the secret police, and their inhabitants were acquainted from childhood with what one of them called "the stoniest sound in the world: the midnight knock on the door." It would be hard to calculate but easy to guess at the millions of American Jews whose forefathers were harried and haunted by these persecutors. It is something hardly thought of by most of us who came here by free choice, or were born here without ever having to make a choice.

In some cities of Europe, Jews were permitted to practice their 8 religion in compounds. But in many more places, where the Jews had been systematically vilified for fifteen hundred years, authorities considered their rituals to be as sinister as black magic, and the more daring or devout worshiped in stealth. In America, they had heard, they could worship openly in their own fashion, Orthodox, Reform, Conservative— or, as radical Reconstructionists, they could look to the United States as a permitted rallying ground on which to muster the faithful for the return to Palestine. I dwell on the Jews because, in the great tidal wave of the late nineteenth- and early twentieth-century immigration, they were the most numerous of those who saw America as the Land of Canaan; because their story offers the most dramatic and arduous exercise in the struggle to assimilate; and because, as much or more than other peoples, they created the American polyglot metropolis against which, in 1924, the Congress protested with restrictive legislation that tried, too late, to restore the United States to its northern European origins.

So late as 1880, there were only a quarter of a million Jews in the United States. By 1924 there were four and a half million, the product of a westward movement that started in the early nineteenth century with their exodus from the ghettos of eastern Europe into the new factories of western Europe. They had moved in that direction earlier throughout the Thirty Years War and then after the later Cossack massacres and peasant revolts. But the factory system provided them with a legal right to flee from their inferior citizenship in Germany and from pogroms in Russia, Poland, and Romania. In the last quarter of the nineteenth century, both city and rural Jews were the willing quarry of emigration agents from America carrying glowing broadsides from house to house about the high wages, good clothes, abundant food, and civil liberties available in the New World. The sweet talk of these promoters might be sensibly discounted, but not the bags of mail containing "America letters" from relatives who had made the voyage and whose more practical accounts of an attainable decent life were read aloud in cottages, markets, and factories. 9

The word spread beyond the factories and the ghettos to the farmers of southern and central Europe. And whereas before 1890 the immigrant stream had flowed out of Scandinavia, Germany, Ireland, England, and Canada, in the next thirty years the mass of immigrants came from Italy, Austria-Hungary, Russia, and again and always Ireland. 10

The Germans formed a strong and special current in the mainstream of immigration. There were already a quarter of a million of them in the United States at the time of the Declaration of Independence, and in the thirty years between 1860 and 1890 they contributed more refugees than any other nation. among them more varied social types, more professionals, and more scholars than the others. They also settled far and wide. The German Jews, beginning as small merchants, prospered more conspicuously and founded many of the great banking families of New York. Wherever the Germans went, they tended to establish themselves, both by superiority of talent and a marked gift of clannishness, at the head of the social hierarchy of Jewry. The Sephardic Jews and the German Jews were at the top, and at the bottom were the Lithuanians and the Hungarians, elements in a social system that discouraged intermarriage between its upper and lower strata the defiance of which has probably caused as much snobbish anguish as the love matches of Jews and Gentiles in other immigrant families. 11

All told, in the first two decades of this century, an unbelievable   12
fourteen and a half million immigrants arrived. They were mostly the
persecuted and the poor, "the wretched refuse of your teeming shore"
apostrophized by Emma Lazarus, a wealthy and scholarly young lady
whose poetic dramas and translations of Heine are forgotten in the
thunder of five lines inscribed on the Statue of Liberty. These unlettered
millions were, for the most part, to become the "huddled masses" who,
in the tenements of the American cities, would have quite a time of it
"yearning to breathe free." They had never heard of Thomas Jefferson or
George Washington. But they were the easy victims of the absurd myth
that the streets of America were paved with gold—not much, perhaps,
but enough to offer striking proof, in sepia photographs sent back to
Poland or Hungary, of well-fed families who looked you in the eye, of a
father or a cousin wearing a suit and shiny shoes, just like a doctor or a
merchant in the old country.

Long before they arrived at the ports of embarkation—Constantinople,   13
Piraeus, Antwerp, Bremen—emigrant trains had started deep inside
Russia. Most of them were linked box cars, sometimes with benches, the
men in one car, the women and children in another. Every few hundred
miles the train would be shunted on to a siding in order to pick up other
new armies, of Austrians, Hungarians, Lithuanians, and finally a troop of
Germans, before they came to, say, Hamburg. There they were corralled
and checked to see of they had the three essential passports to America:
an exit paper, twenty-five spare dollars to prevent their becoming a
public charge, and the price of the passage. By the 1890s lively rate wars
between steamship lines had halved the steerage fare from about twenty
dollars to ten. In an enclosure outside Hamburg they would be bathed,
de-loused, and fed, and their baggage and clothes fumigated. Then they
were ferried out to the big ship and stowed aboard, as many as nine
hundred in steerage.

In the floating commune of the emigrant ship, the status symbols   14
were few but well defined. A suitcase, however battered, was most likely
the mark of a city man. To a poor peasant, a wicker basket was elegance
enough. Most people tied everything up in a blanket or a sheet. They
had brought with them what they thought to be indispensable to a
decent life afloat. First, the necessity of a pillow, goose-feather, if they
were lucky—a point of pride, a relic, and a symbol that some families
kept throughout their lives. Village girls took along their only certain
dowry, a special extra petticoat and, for formal occasions, a corset. Many
of the young women were engaged to men from the home town on the
other side of the Atlantic. It was well understood that the ambitious male,
engaged or already married, went on ahead to stake out the fortune,
which was more often the bare living that could sustain a family. Many of

these engagements were broken once for all on the way over by the rude proximity of the males in steerage.

Like all travelers, both simple and sophisticated, they were deeply   15 suspicious of the other nation's food. It was a common thing to take along a cooking pot, a few raw vegetables, and a hunk of sausage or some other final reminder of the favorite snack. The religious invariably took with them the tokens of their faith, a cross or a prayer book or phylacteries; and a member of a closely-knit family would cherish an heirloom yielded up in the moment of parting. It could be nothing more pretentious than a brass candlestick or a lock of hair.

For two weeks or eight days, depending on the size of the ship,   16 they sewed, played cards, sang to harmonicas or tin whistles, counted their savings, continually checked their exit papers, complained about the atrocious food and the ubiquity of the rats. The ones who could read, probably less than half the flock, recited the cheering promise of the emigrant agents' broadsides and pamphlets. The young women nursed the elders and the chronically seasick and resisted, or succumbed to, the advances of spry bachelors. There was no possibility of privacy in the swarm of steerage.

But as America came nearer, some of them suffered from nervous   17 recall of the stratagems that had got them this far. Bright youngsters who had carefully failed their high school examinations in order to prove their unfitness for military service. Oldsters who began to mask a fever with massive doses of medicine. Embezzlers, petty criminals, and betrothed men skipping breach-of-promise suits who had obviously had the wit to fake an exit pass or steal the passage money. A lot of people had a lot to hide.

Far down in the lower bay of New York City, they crowded to the   18 rail to eye their first Americans in the persons of the immigration inspectors, two men and a woman in uniform clambering up a ladder from a cutter that had nosed alongside. The captain was required to note on the ship's manifest the more flagrant cases of contagious disease, for only seventy years ago they were still on the lookout for yellow fever and leprosy. The unlucky victims of such ailments were taken off in a quarantine boat to a special island to be deported as soon as possible.

The harbor was sometimes choked with ships at anchor. In the   19 early 1900s there could be as many as fifteen thousand immigrants arriving in one day, and the ships had to drop anchor and wait. But eventually the engines would rumble again, and there, like a battleship on the horizon, stood what the song calls "Manhattan, an isle of joy." Closer, it grew into a cluster of pinnacles known as skyscrapers. And then the midtown skyscrapers topped the ones first seen. It was unlike any other city, and to the European it was always audacious and magical, and threatening.

Soon the newcomers would be on the docks sorting their bundles   20
and baggage in a babble of languages, and when that was done they
were tagged with numbers. Until 1892 they were cleared for entry at
Castle Garden, once a fort, then a theater and a public amusement place
down at the Battery. However, the volume of immigrants grew so great,
and so many of them managed to disappear into Manhattan before being
"processed," that a larger and more isolated sorting point had to be
found. So, from 1892 on, once the immigrants had been tagged with
numbers they were shipped aboard a ferry or a barge to what was to be
known in several languages as "the isle of tears," the clearing station, Ellis
Island.

It had been used by the early Dutch as a picnic ground. Much later   21
its three acres were increased by landfill into twenty-seven, and it
became a government arsenal. Today, it looks like a rather imposing
college recently gutted by fire. It is totally derelict, a frowzy monument to
the American habit of junking and forgetting whatever wears out. But
wandering through its great central hall and tattered corridors, seeing the
offices with their rusting files, the broken lavatories, and upturned dining
tables, one can imagine the bedlam of its heyday, when the milling
swarm of strangers was served and interrogated by hundreds of inspectors, wardens, interpreters, doctors, nurses, waiters, cooks, and agents of
immigrant aid societies; and all the while a guerilla army of con men,
land swindlers, and hackmen passed out fresh broadsides boosting the
heavenly prospects of the inland towns and unheard-of settlements on
the prairie.

The newcomers crowded into the main building and the first thing   22
they heard over the general bedlam were the clarion voices of inspectors
bellowing out numbers in Italian, German, Polish, Hungarian, Russian,
and Yiddish. According to assigned numbers they were herded into
groups of thirty and led through long tiled corridors up a wide staircase
into the biggest hall most of them had ever seen. Its dimensions, its
pillars, its great soaring windows still suggest the grand ballroom of some
abdicated monarch. Once they were assembled there in their thousands,
the clearance procedure began. I recently pressed an aged immigrant to
describe it. "Procedure?" he squealed incredulously. "Din, confusion,
bewilderment, madness!"

They moved in single file through a stockyard maze of passage-   23
ways and under the eye of a doctor in a blue uniform who had in his
hand a piece of chalk. He was a tough instant diagnostician. He would
look at the hands, the hair, the faces and rap out a few questions. He
might spot a panting old man with purple lips, and he would chalk on his
back a capital "H" for suspected heart disease. Any facial blotches, a hint
of gross eczema brought forth a chalked "F," for facial rash. Children in
arms were made to stand down to see if they rated an "L" for the limp of

rickets or some other deficiency disease. There was one chalk mark that every family dreaded, for it guaranteed certain deportation. It was a circle with a cross in the middle, and it indicated "feeble-minded."

Next they moved on to two doctors dipping into bowls of disinfectant and snapping back the eyelids of suspects, usually with a buttonhook. They were looking for a disease very common then in southern and eastern Europe, trachoma. If you had it, an "E" was chalked on your back, and your first days in the New World were surely your last.

About eight in ten survived this scrutiny and passed to the final ordeal, the examination before an immigration inspector standing with an interpreter. Not noticeably gracious types, for they worked ten hours a day, seven days a week, they droned out an unchanging catechism: Who paid your passage? How many dependents? Ever been in prison? Can you read and write? (There was for a long time no legal obligation to be able to do either.) Is there a job waiting for you? (This was a famous catch, since a law called the Contract Labor Law forbade immigrants from signing up abroad for any work at all.) Finally, your name was checked against the ship's manifest. Many people were lucky to emerge into the new life with their old name. An Irish inspector glancing down at what to him was the gobbledygook of "Ouspenska" wrote on the landing card "Spensky." A Norwegian with an unpronounceable name was asked for the name of the town he had left. It was Dröbak. The inspector promptly wrote down what he thought he'd heard. Another Norwegian standing nearby philosophically realized that his own name was just as unmanageable and decided that what was good enough for his friend was good enough for him. To this day the progeny of both families rejoice in the name of Robeck.

But a new identity was better than none, and it gave you a landing card. With it you were now ready to pay a visit to a currency booth to change your lire or drachmas, or whatever, into dollars. This exchange could entail prolonged haggling and not a few fist fights with the cashiers, who for many years were short-change artists. But at last you were handed over to the travel agent or the railroad men, if you were going far afield, or you sought the help of an aid society or a beckoning politician, if New York was to be the end of the line. Most immigrants could speak hardly a word of English except the one they had memorized as the town of their destination. A man would unfold a scrap of paper and point to a block-printed word: "Pringvilliamas." Maybe he eventually arrived in Springfield, Massachusetts, and maybe he didn't. But at this point the immigrants' only concern was to get off Ellis Island. All of them looked in relief for the door that was marked "Push to New York." And they pushed.

Exercises

Some Important Words

palpable (paragraph 1), chauvinists (2), Gentiles (3), Anglo-Saxon (3), Madame de Staël (4), Goethe (4), tillage (5), putrefy (5), Queen Victoria (6), sedition (6), abdication (7), ghettos (7), vilified (8), Land of Canaan (8), polyglot (8), metropolis (8), exodus (9), Thirty Years War (9), Cossack (9), pogroms (9), quarry (9), broadsides (9), clannishness (11), social hierarchy (11), Sephardic Jews (11), strata (11), apostrophized (12), Emma Lazarus (12), Heinrich Heine (12), tenements (12), sepia (12), steerage (13), fumigated (13), relic (14), dowry (14), phylacteries (15), ubiquity (16), swarm (16), stratagem (17), embezzlers (17), betrothed (17), breech-of-promise (17), clambering (18), ship's manifest (18), flagrant (18), quarantine (18), pinnacles (19), babble (20), Ellis Island (20), derelict (21), bedlam (21), guerrilla army (21), clarion (22), trachoma (24), catechism (25), gobbledygook (25), progeny (25).

Some of the Issues

1. In paragraphs 2 and 3 Cooke singles out several consequences of Americans' diverse origins. What are the most significant ones?
2. What according to Cooke was the most powerful reason for immigrants to come to the United States in the nineteenth and early twentieth centuries?
3. The author singles out two groups in particular, the Irish and the Jews. What reasons for coming did they have? In what ways did their reasons differ?
4. In the first 12 paragraphs the topic is: who came from Europe and why? What is the major topic in the second part of the essay (paragraphs 13–26)?
5. What obstacles did prospective immigrants have to cope with in order to be admitted to the United States?

The Way We Are Told

6. The first three paragraphs are all concerned with the diversity of the origins of Americans. Each paragraph has a specific subtopic, however. What is the logic of their sequence?
7. Examine paragraph 6. What do you think was the author's purpose in telling the reader about Queen Victoria and Patrick Kennedy? What contrasts does he try to evoke by pairing them in the same paragraph?
8. In paragraphs 3 and 15, the author refers to food. How would you say he uses those references to demonstrate the effects of diversity?

Some Subjects for Writing

9. In the last 20 to 30 years the pattern of immigration has increasingly deviated from the one Cooke describes. A majority of immigrants now come from Asia and Latin America. Using newspapers and magazines as resources, discuss the countries of origin of these more recent immigrants and examine what causes them to come. Do you see any similarities to the earlier waves of immigrants whom Cooke discusses?

RECAPTURE THE FLAG: 34 REASONS TO LOVE AMERICA

This list was selected from a longer one that appeared in the Minneapolis/St. Paul *City Pages* on the day before Independence Day, July 3, 1991. Some of the items on the list might be considered to be traditional, whereas others are quite unconventional; together they attempt to capture the American mosaic.

1. The hometown team on a winning streak
2. Pancakes (not crepes)
3. *Roe v. Wade*
4. Thurgood Marshall
5. American cranks—quirky thinkers with transformative visions: Gertrude Stein, William Burroughs, Howlin' Wolf, Henry Thoreau, R. Crumb, Charlie Parker, Abbie Hoffman, Charlotte Perkins Gilman, Lester Bangs, Jill Johnston, Dorothy Parker, Emma Goldman, Hunter S. Thompson, Josephine Baker, Whitman, Lenny Bruce
6. Corn on the cob
7. The idea of the road as a place to reinvent yourself, a train of thought running from Robert Johnson through Kerouac to *Thelma & Louise*
8. Cool, dark bars where the bartender knows your name
9. Computer hackers
10. Dairy Queen
11. Soul food, po' boy sandwiches: Cuisine made from the cheap and unwanted
12. Elvis Presley. He had to invent himself first, because what he chased after—an amped-up fusion of black and white musics with deep, surreptitious roots—wasn't supposed to exist at all. When Elvis happened, the pitched reaction didn't portend only rock & roll; it foreshadowed a chain of events from the Selma marches to the Reagan backlash
13. Pioneers of social frontiers: Jackie Robinson, Queer Nation, AIM, Malcolm X, Angela Davis, Harriet Tubman, the Radical Faeries, Betty Friedan, Sojourner Truth, C.O.Y.O.T.E., Elizabeth Cady Stanton, Martin Luther King Jr.

14. The front porch or stoop: Gossip, swings, neighbor-spying, gin & tonics

15. The way immigration transforms the nation's eating habits: Wieners, potatoes, pizza, chow mein, spaghetti, tacos, egg rolls, curry, mock duck, pad thai

16. The phenomenal growth of popular literature written by women over the last 30 years: Adrienne Rich, Anne Tyler, Marge Piercy, Toni Morrison, Ursula LeGuin, Alice Hoffman, Maxine Hong Kingston, Audre Lorde, Gloria Naylor, Amy Tan, Kay Gibbons, Louise Erdrich, Terry Macmillan, Alice Walker, etc., etc., etc.

17. People who don't force you to love America

18. Blues, gospel, country & western, jazz, rock, bluegrass, soul, disco, rap, zydeco . . . strains from different cultures tossed together on the long, long road from Memphis to Chicago, Abliene to Hoboken, Detroit to L.A.

19. The land

20. Roadside diners with biscuits and gravy and bottomless glasses of iced tea

21. The richness of speech as you cross from state to state, region to region, sometimes city block to city block

22. All the highways in the Great Plains that curve into extravagant, sprawling space

23. The desperate courage of AIDS activists in the 1980s

24. Louis Armstrong, William Faulkner, Duke Ellington, Billie Holiday, Raymond Chandler, Ray Charles, John Ford and John Wayne, Alfred Stieglitz, Georgia O'Keeffe, Flannery O'Connor, Jimmie Rodgers, Aretha Franklin, Babe Ruth, Hank Williams, Muddy Waters, Robert Frank, Allen Ginsberg, Ishmael Reed, James Brown, Orson Welles, Jackson Pollock: While too much of white America still looked nervously to Europe, they helped shape a culture of breathtaking scope, vibrancy, and vulgar energy

25. Michael Jordan

26. The Vietnam War Memorial, for the lesson it takes to heart: Its egalitarianism, the air of loss, the way it ennobles war deaths without glorifying them

27. The verse of Woody Guthrie's "This Land Is Your Land" that most people never heard, which captured the spirit of the whole song: "Was a big high wall there that tried to stop me/A sign was painted said: Private Property/But on the back side it didn't say nothing/This land was made for you and me"

28. James Baldwin, the best thinker on race in the second half of this century, maybe the best essayist of his age, period: the writer most committed to working out his horrific ambivalence toward his motherland: America, not Africa

29. Earth First!

30. The Ramones: At a time when American rock & roll was becoming unbearably ponderous (Eagles, America, Jackson Browne), they melded '60s girl-group singing with Bay City Rollers pop chants, surf licks, and MC5 buzzsaw guitars, to create a whole new genre—cartoon rock. Gabba gabba hey

31. All-night grocery stores

32. Roadside monuments: Driving down the highway you spot something unusual on the horizon. It doesn't look like a tree exactly; it's definitely not a billboard. As you get closer, you figure it out—a 30-foot-high talking cow

33. Backyard barbecues: Swat the flies. Drop a burger in the dirt. Serve it anyway

34. Avon ladies, door-to-door encyclopedia salesmen, and Mary Kay pink Cadillacs

Exercises

Words to Know

Note that in this selection, proper names are omitted. The numerals after each word refer to the number of the reason, rather than the paragraph. surreptitious (12), portend (12), foreshadowed (12), backlash (12), egalitarianism (26), ennobles (26), horrific (28), ponderous (30).

Some of the Issues

1. Say which reasons are your favorites and why.
2. Cite the positive and negative qualities in the list.
3. Classify. Group similar reasons together and give a label to each category.
4. Consensus. Meet with others in a small group and share your categories. Try to reach a consensus on at least three or four common categories.

The Way We Are Told

5. What can you infer about the composers of this list? What values and beliefs are inherent in their choices?
6. Do you think this list was generated by people your age? Justify your answer.

Some Topics for Writing

7. In a small group, brainstorm your own list of reasons to love (or not love) America. Again, see if you can come to a consensus on which categories to add or to expand.

8. Use your own list or the one provided here to write about one representative trait that you think Americans can be proud of.

SOAP AND WATER

Anzia Yezierska

Anzia Yezierska was born in Pinsk in the Russian-controlled part of Poland, circa 1885. At age 16, she immigrated to the United States with her family. A Talmudic scholar, her father depended on his wife and children to support the household. For three years Anzia worked as a seamstress, a domestic, and a factory worker before earning a scholarship to study at Columbia University. After graduation, she taught domestic science at an elementary school. In 1917 she met the American educator and philosopher John Dewey, who became her mentor and encouraged her literary pursuits. She published several novels, including *Salome of the Tenements* (1923); *Bread Givers: A Struggle Between a Father of the Old World, and a Daughter of the New* (1925); *Arrogant Beggar* (1927); and an autobiographical novel *Red Ribbon on a White Horse* (1950). Some of her stories are collected in *How I Found America: Collected Stories of Anzia Yezierska* (1991). Much of her writing focuses on the Jewish immigrant experience seen from a woman's point of view.

The Following selection is taken from her first volume of stories, *Hungry Hearts,* published in 1920. With the dream of America as a land of unlimited opportunities, the young immigrant struggles to find acceptance and self-expression in a hostile new world.

1 What I so greatly feared, happened! Miss Whiteside, the dean of our college, withheld my diploma. When I came to her office, and asked her why she did not pass me, she said that she could not recommend me as a teacher because of my personal appearance.

2 She told me that my skin looked oily, my hair unkempt, and my fingernails sadly neglected. She told me that I was utterly unmindful of the little niceties of the well-groomed lady. She pointed out that my collar did not set evenly, my belt was awry, and there was a lack of freshness in my dress. And she ended with: "Soap and water are cheap. Anyone can be clean."

3 In those four years while I was under her supervision, I was always timid and diffident. I shrank and trembled when I had to come near her. When I had to say something to her, I mumbled and stuttered, and grew red and white in the face with fear.

Every time I had to come to the dean's office for a private   4
conference, I prepared for the ordeal of her cold scrutiny, as a patient
prepares for a surgical operation. I watched her gimlet eyes searching for
a stray pin, for a spot on my dress, for my unpolished shoes, for my
uncared-for fingernails, as one strapped on the operating table watches
the surgeon approaching with his tray of sterilized knives.

She never looked into my eyes. She never perceived that I had a   5
soul. She did not see how I longed for beauty and cleanliness. How I
strained and struggled to lift myself from the dead toil and exhaustion
that weighed me down. She could see nothing in people like me, except
the dirt and the stains on the outside.

But this last time when she threatened to withhold my diploma,   6
because of my appearance, this last time when she reminded me that
"Soap and water are cheap. Anyone can be clean," this last time,
something burst within me.

I felt the suppressed wrath of all the unwashed of the earth break   7
loose within me. My eyes blazed fire. I didn't care for myself, nor the
dean, nor the whole laundered world. I had suffered the cruelty of
their cleanliness and the tyranny of their culture to the breaking point.
I was too frenzied to know what I said or did. But I saw clean,
immaculate, spotless Miss Whiteside shrivel and tremble and cower
before me, as I had shriveled and trembled and cowered before her for
so many years.

Why did she give me my diploma? Was it pity? Or can it be that in   8
my outburst of fury, at the climax of indignities that I had suffered, the
barriers broke, and she saw into the world below from where I came?

Miss Whiteside had no particular reason for hounding and perse-   9
cuting me. Personally, she didn't give a hang if I was clean or dirty. She
was merely one of the agents of clean society, delegated to judge who is
fit and who is unfit to teach.

While they condemned me as unfit to be a teacher, because of my   10
appearance, I was slaving to keep them clean. I was slaving in a laundry
from five to eight in the morning, before going to college, and from six to
eleven at night, after coming from college. Eight hours of work a day,
outside my studies. Where was the time and the strength for the "little
niceties of the well-groomed lady"?

At the time when they rose and took their morning bath, and put   11
on their fresh-laundered linen that somebody had made ready for them,
when they were being served with their breakfast, I had already toiled
for three hours in a laundry.

When the college hours were over, they went for a walk in the fresh   12
air. They had time to rest, and bathe again, and put on fresh clothes for
dinner. But I, after college hours, had only time to bolt a soggy meal, and
rush back to the grind of the laundry till eleven at night.

At the hour when they came from the theater or musicale, I came   13
from the laundry. But I was so bathed in the sweat of exhaustion that I
could not think of a bath of soap and water. I had only strength to drag
myself home, and fall down on the bed and sleep. Even if I had had the
desire and the energy to take a bath, there were no such things as
bathtubs in the house where I lived.

Often as I stood at my board at the laundry, I thought of Miss   14
Whiteside, and her clean world, clothed in the snowy shirtwaists I had
ironed. I was thinking—I, soaking in the foul vapors of the steaming
laundry, I, with my dirty, tired hands, I am ironing the clean, immaculate
shirtwaists of clean, immaculate society. I, the unclean one, am actually
fashioning the pedestal of their cleanliness, from which they reach down,
hoping to lift me to the height that I have created for them.

I look back at my sweatshop childhood. One day, when I was about   15
sixteen, someone gave me Rosenfeld's poem "The Machine" to read. Like
a spark thrown among oil rags, it set my whole being aflame with
longing for self-expression. But I was dumb. I had nothing but blind,
aching feeling. For days I went about with agonies of feeling, yet utterly
at sea how to fathom and voice those feelings—birth-throes of infinite
worlds, and yet dumb.

Suddenly, there came upon me this inspiration. I can go to   16
college! There I shall learn to express myself, to voice my thoughts. But
I was not prepared to go to college. The girl in the cigar factory, in the
next block, had gone first to a preparatory school. Why shouldn't I find
a way, too?

Going to college seemed as impossible for me, at that time, as for   17
an ignorant Russian shop-girl to attempt to write poetry in English. But I
was sixteen then, and the impossible was a magnet to draw the dreams
that had no outlet. Besides, the actual was so barren, so narrow, so
strangling, that the dream of the unattainable was the only air in which
the soul could survive.

The ideal of going to college was like the birth of a new religion in   18
my soul. It put new fire in my eyes, and new strength in my tired arms
and fingers.

For six years I worked daytimes and went at night to a preparatory   19
school. For six years I went about nursing the illusion that college was a
place where I should find self-expression, and vague, pent-up feelings
could live as thoughts and grow as ideas.

At last I came to college. I rushed for it with the outstretched arms   20
of youth's aching hunger to give and take of life's deepest and highest,
and I came against the solid wall of the well-fed, well-dressed world—
the frigid whitewashed wall of cleanliness.

Until I came to college I had been unconscious of my clothes.   21
Suddenly I felt people looking at me at arm's length, as if I were crooked

or crippled, as if I had come to a place where I didn't belong, and would never be taken in.

How I pinched, and scraped, and starved myself, to save enough to   22
come to college! Every cent of the tuition fee I paid was drops of sweat and blood from underpaid laundry work. And what did I get for it? A crushed spirit, a broken heart, a stinging sense of poverty that I never felt before.

The courses of study I had to swallow to get my diploma were   23
utterly barren of interest to me. I didn't come to college to get dull learning from dead books. I didn't come for that dry, inanimate stuff that can be hammered out in lectures. I came because I longed for the larger life, for the stimulus of intellectual associations. I came because my whole being clamored for more vision, more light. But everywhere I went I saw big fences put up against me, with the brutal signs: "No trespassing. Get off the grass."

I experienced at college the same feeling of years ago when I came   24
to this country, when after months of shut-in-ness, in dark tenements and stifling sweatshops, I had come to Central Park for the first time. Like a bird just out from a cage, I stretched out my arms, and then flung myself in ecstatic abandon on the grass. Just as I began to breathe in the fresh-smelling earth, and lift up my eyes to the sky, a big, fat policeman with a club in his hand, seized me, with: "Can't you read the sign? Get off the grass!" Miss Whiteside, the dean of the college, the representative of the clean, the educated world, for all her external refinement, was to me like that big, brutal policeman, with the club in his hand, that drove me off the grass.

The death-blows to all aspiration began when I graduated from   25
college and tried to get a start at the work for which I had struggled so hard to fit myself. I soon found other agents of clean society, who had the power of giving or withholding the positions I sought, judging me as Miss Whiteside judged me. One glance at my shabby clothes, the desperate anguish that glazed and dulled my eyes and I felt myself condemned by them before I opened my lips to speak.

Starvation forced me to accept the lowest-paid substitute position.   26
And because my wages were so low and so unsteady, I could never get the money for the clothes to make an appearance to secure a position with better pay. I was tricked and foiled. I was considered unfit to get decent pay for my work because of my appearance, and it was to the advantage of those who used me that my appearance should damn me, so as to get me to work for the low wages I was forced to accept. It seemed to me the whole vicious circle of society's injustices was thrust like a noose around my neck to strangle me.

The insults and injuries I had suffered at college had so eaten into   27
my flesh that I could not bear to get near it. I shuddered with horror

whenever I had to pass the place blocks away. The hate which I felt for Miss Whiteside spread like poison inside my soul, into hate for all clean society. The whole clean world was massed against me. Whenever I met a well-dressed person, I felt the secret stab of a hidden enemy.

I was so obsessed and consumed with my grievances that I could   28
not get away from myself and think things out in the light. I was in the grip of that blinding, destructive, terrible thing—righteous indignation. I could not rest. I wanted the whole world to know that the college was against democracy in education, that clothes form the basis of class distinctions, that after graduation the opportunities for the best positions are passed out to those who are best-dressed, and the students too poor to put up a front are pigeon-holed and marked unfit and abandoned to the mercy of the wind.

A wild desire raged in the corner of my brain. I knew that the dean   29
gave dinners to the faculty at regular intervals. I longed to burst in at one of those feasts, in the midst of their grand speech-making, and tear down the fine clothes from these well-groomed ladies and gentlemen, and trample them under my feet, and scream like a lunatic: "Soap and water are cheap! Soap and water are cheap! Look at me! See how cheap it is!"

There seemed but three avenues of escape to the torments of my   30
wasted life: madness, suicide, or a heart-to-heart confession to someone who understood. I had not energy enough for suicide. Besides, in my darkest moments of despair, hope clamored loudest. Oh, I longed so to live, to dream my way up on the heights, above the unreal realities that ground me and dragged me down to earth.

Inside the ruin of my thwarted life, the *unlived* visionary immigrant   31
hungered and thirsted for America. I had come a refugee from the Russian pogroms, aflame with dreams of America. I did not find America in the sweatshops, much less in the schools and colleges. But for hundreds of years the persecuted races all over the world were nurtured on hopes of America. When a little baby in my mother's arms, before I was old enough to speak, I saw all around me weary faces light up with thrilling tales of the far-off "golden country." And so, though my faith in this so-called America was shattered, yet underneath, in the sap and roots of my soul, burned the deathless faith that America is, must be, somehow, somewhere. In the midst of my bitterest hates and rebellions, visions of America rose over me, like songs of freedom of an oppressed people.

My body was worn to the bone from overwork, my footsteps   32
dragged with exhaustion, but my eyes still sought the sky, praying, ceaselessly praying, the dumb, inarticulate prayer of the lost immigrant: "America! Ach, America! Where is America?"

It seemed to me if I could only find some human being to whom I   33
could unburden my heart, I would have new strength to begin again my insatiable search for America.

But to whom could I speak? The people in the laundry? They never 34 understood me. They had a grudge against me because I left them when I tried to work myself up. Could I speak to the college people? What did these icebergs of convention know about the vital things of the heart?

And yet, I remembered, in the freshman year, in one of the courses 35 in chemistry, there was an instructor, a woman, who drew me strangely. I felt she was the only real teacher among all the teachers and professors I met. I didn't care for the chemistry, but I liked to look at her. She gave me life, air, the unconscious emanation of her beautiful spirit. I had not spoken a word to her, outside the experiments in chemistry, but I knew her more than the people around her who were of her own class. I felt in the throb of her voice, in the subtle shading around the corner of her eyes, the color and texture of her dreams.

Often in the midst of our work in chemistry I felt like crying out to 36 her: "Oh, please be my friend. I'm so lonely." But something choked me. I couldn't speak. The very intensity of my longing for her friendship made me run away from her in confusion the minute she approached me. I was so conscious of my shabbiness that I was afraid maybe she was only trying to be kind. I couldn't bear kindness. I wanted from her love, understanding, or nothing.

About ten years after I left college, as I walked the streets bowed 37 and beaten with the shame of having to go around begging for work, I met Miss Van Ness. She not only recognized me, but stopped to ask how I was, and what I was doing.

I had begun to think that my only comrades in this world were the 38 homeless and abandoned cats and dogs of the street, whom everybody gives another kick, as they slam the door on them. And here was one from the clean world human enough to be friendly. Here was one of the well-dressed, with a look in her eyes and a sound in her voice that was like healing oil over the bruises of my soul. The mere touch of that woman's hand in mine so overwhelmed me, that I burst out crying in the street.

The next morning I came to Miss Van Ness at her office. In those 39 ten years she had risen to a professorship. But I was not in the least intimidated by her high office. I felt as natural in her presence as if she were my own sister. I heard myself telling her the whole story of my life, but I felt that even if I had not said a word she would have understood all I had to say as if I had spoken. It was all so unutterable, to find one from the other side of the world who was so simply and naturally that miraculous thing—a friend. Just as contact with Miss Whiteside had tied and bound all my thinking processes, so Miss Van Ness unbound and freed me and suffused me with light.

I felt the joy of one breathing on the mountain-tops for the first time. 40 I looked down at the world below. I was changed and the world was changed. My past was the forgotten night. Sunrise was all around me.

I went out from Miss Van Ness's office, singing a song of new life: 41
"America! I found America."

Exercises

Some Important Words

unkempt (paragraph 2), awry (2), diffident (3), gimlet (4), suppressed (7), wrath (7), cower (7), persecuting (9), immaculate (14), sweatshop (15), fathom (15), barren (23), inanimate (23), foiled (26), righteous (28), thwarted (31), pogroms (31), insatiable (33), emanation (35).

Some of the issues

1. "What I so greatly feared, happened!" says Anzia in the opening line. What made her suspect that she would not be given her diploma?
* 2. In paragraph 7, Anzia protests against the tyranny of the dean and the "whole laundered world." Which social group in America is she referring to? Compare Anzia's perceptions to Michael Novak's description of the "power elite" in "In Ethnic America" (paragraph 13).
3. What was the turning point that motivated her to seek a college education?
4. Do you think her hatred and "righteous indignation" (paragraph 28) are justified?
5. In paragraphs 37–40, the meeting with Miss Van Ness changes Anzia's outlook. How do you explain her sudden transformation?
6. In the last lines, Anzia exclaims that she has found America. What does she mean?

The Way We Are Told

7. Yezierska's style is characterized by language that is intended to provoke an emotional response. Can you find examples? Does the language seem overly dramatized or old-fashioned? If so, where?
8. Why is it ironic that Miss Whiteside points out to Anzia, "Soap and water are cheap. Anyone can be clean"?
9. How does Yezierska portray Miss Van Ness? Is the character convincing?

Some Subjects for Writing

10. After six years of hard work and anticipation, Anzia is disillusioned that college is not what she had expected. Reflect on your own experience. Was there ever a time when you felt disenchanted or disappointed in your college education?

11. In paragraph 28, Anzia says "clothes form the basis of class distinctions." Do you agree that social class is reflected by a person's apparel? (You may want to include names of department stores; brand names; and descriptions of styles, colors, and fashions that Americans wear to defend your view.)

*12. The poet Stephen Spender once wrote that "Despair and hope, sacrifice and promise exist side by side in Jewish history, each equally real, irreconcilable opposites." Read "The German Refugee" by Bernard Malamud and show how Oskar Gassner's story and Anzia Yezierska's story illustrate these opposites.

ELLIS ISLAND

Joseph Bruchac

Joseph Bruchac, born in 1942, is of mixed immigrant and native American ancestry. He teaches English at Hamilton College in Clinton, New York. He has written poetry and fiction and translated West African and Iroquois literature. He is the editor of *Breaking Silence,* a collection of Asian-American poetry, *Turtle Men and Other Stories* (1993), *Native American Stories* (1991), and *Survival This Way: Interviews with Native American Poets* (1990).

Ellis Island in New York harbor became the main point of entry for immigrants to the United States in 1892. As many as a million people a year passed through its vast sheds in the early twentieth century, up to fifteen thousand being herded through in one day. (For more on the immigrants and the immigration procedures at Ellis Island, read Alistair Cooke's "The Huddled Masses.") Finally closed in 1954, it was abandoned and allowed to decay. In 1965 Ellis Island was declared a national landmark, but it was not until the 1980s that interest in its place in history became sufficiently strong to encourage moves toward its restoration. Work on it was begun in earnest at the time the Statue of Liberty, its neighbor, was being restored. In 1990 Ellis Island, partially restored as a museum of immigration and a national monument, was reopened to the public.

In his poem Joseph Bruchac concerns himself not only with the waves of immigration but with one of its results: the displacement of Native Americans from their ancestral lands.

Beyond the red brick of Ellis Island
Where the two Slovak children
who became my grandparents
waited the long days of quarantine,
after leaving the sickness,
the old Empires of Europe,
a Circle Line ship slips easily
on its way to the island
of the tall woman, green
as dreams of forests and meadows

waiting for those who'd worked
a thousand years
yet never owned their own.

Like millions of others,
I too come to this island,
nine decades the answerer
of dreams.

Yet only one part of my blood loves that memory.
another voice speaks
of native lands
within this nation.
Lands invaded
when the earth became owned.
Lands of those who followed
The changing Moon,
knowledge of the season
in their veins.

PART SEVEN

Other Worlds

The selections in Part Seven take the reader to other parts of the globe. Knowledge of widely varied cultures can sharpen our awareness and appreciation of cultural differences. Unfortunately, it is too often the case that people will tolerate the *idea* of cultural difference as long as it remains an idea. Americans may not mind, for example, the fact that some people in France consider horses desirable to eat. Eating horses, defined as a custom, may seem strange, even offensive, but not of central concern as long as one is not obliged to participate. However, when cultural differences touch on values we consider central, we may find them harder to accept. We are likely to judge another culture as simple or backward simply because we do not know very much about it. Further, we are likely to believe that our way of looking at the world is the right way and the only way. These attitudes are forms of ethnocentricity—the view that our culture is at the center of things.

Because we are beginning to recognize the vital importance of a global economy, a global environment, and global interrelations, the notion of ethnocentrism is not only misguided, but also outdated. A more enlightened view respects cultural differences out of a concern for a more harmonious world and, ultimately, for the future survival of our planet. All nations need to understand that different cultures may have different answers to the same questions and that these answers may be as logical as the ones they are accustomed to hearing.

301

Some of the selections in Part Seven illustrate transforming personal insights that can be gained by confronting cultural differences. Two of these observations are made by Americans. Mark Salzman, teaching English in China, encounters a new perspective on history and governmental politics. The Tiv in Africa show Laura Bohannan that a story she considers universal can be seen from a very different angle. George Orwell, a British colonial officer in Burma, discovers, as he says, "the real motives for which despotic governments act." In an essay on Japan, Ian Buruma cites two detailed examples taken from Japanese work situations that demonstrate some basic differences in attitude toward individuality and creativity between that culture and accepted notions of behavior in the West. In the fictional piece at the end of this section, "Living in a Japanese Home," John David Morley's main character discovers analogies between the concept of a Japanese house and the Japanese concept of self.

Three of the essays in Part Seven challenge controversial beliefs about the presence and influence of a dominant power in other less powerful countries. Margaret Atwood casts doubt on one assumption held by many Americans that Canada is a country much like ours—a friendly neighbor, trading partner, and fellow democracy—and reveals that many Canadians are concerned about economic and cultural dominance by their much more powerful neighbor. Barbara Ehrenreich and Annette Fuentes challenge a second assumption that foreign investment and industrialization of Third World countries are beneficial because they free people from backbreaking labor in the fields and provide them with better jobs in factories and workshops. Their research examines substandard working conditions and the resultant social and cultural problems created by corporate development in the Third World. In an essay that reaches back 250 years, Jonathan Swift, a clergyman, suggests rather brutally to his fellow Englishmen of the mid-eighteenth century that they need to reflect on the consequences of the way they treat the Irish people.

Part Seven concludes with Nikki Giovanni's poem "They Clapped," in which she comments on the unexpected reactions of a group of African-Americans who travel to Africa in search of their roots.

TEACHER MARK

Mark Salzman

Mark Salzman, scholar of Chinese language and literature, screen-writer, actor, and martial arts expert, was born in Greenwich, Connecticut, in 1959. Not long after his graduation from Yale University in 1982, he took a job teaching English in Changsha, the capital of Hunan province in China. The following selection is taken from his memoir of that experience, *Iron and Silk: A Young American Encounters Swordsmen, Bureaucrats, and Other Citizens of Contemporary China* (1987). He is also the author of a novel, *The Laughing Sutra* (1991).

The early and mid-1980s were marked by rapid changes in the People's Republic of China. The country, with more than one billion people—by far the most populous on earth—was rapidly opening up to the outside world, particularly the industrialized West. Tens of thousands of Chinese university students were coming to study in Western countries, including the United States. Western corporations were encouraged to develop commerce and industry with, and in, China. The communist government that had ruled the country since the revolution in 1949 was experimenting with capitalist incentives for economic development. The country seemed to be moving from a rigidly socialist system under a dictatorial regime to an intellectual opening up that promised changes in a democratic direction. In 1989 the impatience with the slow pace of that opening-up process, as well as anger about corruption and favoritism in the government, led to huge protest demonstrations led by hundreds of thousands of students. In the late spring of 1989 these movements were harshly suppressed.

Mark Salzman describes a time when the opening-up seemed in full flower and likely to continue. The teachers he talks about may be less willing to talk freely in the 1990s than they were in the mid-1980s, but they may also be less willing to trust their own news media as they did then. But that, it must be understood, is merely a conjecture.

The Cultural Revolution referred to in paragraph 41 was a time of great upheaval and destruction in the 1960s. Bands of young women and men, called the Red Guards, roamed the country out of

303

control, dispensing what they considered justice. Education came to a standstill as millions of teachers, students, and professionals were sent to work as peasants in the countryside under the harshest conditions.

The Gulag Archipelago (paragraph 50) by the Russian novelist Aleksandr Solzhenitsyn is a description —and severe indictment—of the concentration camps in the Soviet Union under Josef Stalin, in which millions of people lived and died. Its author lives in exile in the United States. The camps themselves, however, have essentially disappeared.

In 1982, I graduated from Yale University as a Chinese literature major. I was fluent in Mandarin and nearly so in Cantonese, had struggled through a fair amount of classical Chinese and had translated the works of Huang Po-Fei, a modern poet. Oddly, though, I had no real desire to go to China; it sounded like a giant penal colony to me, and besides, I have never liked traveling much. I applied to the Yale-China Association because I needed a job, and was assigned to teach English at Hunan Medical College in Changsha, a sooty, industrial city of more than a million people and the capital of the southern province of Hunan.

When I arrived in Changsha, the temperature was above 100 degrees. I was 22 years old and homesick. The college assigned three classes to me: 26 doctors and teachers of medicine; four men and one woman identified as "the Middle-Aged English Teachers," and 25 medical students, ages 22 to 28. I was entirely unsure what to expect from them; the reverse, I would learn, was also true.

Their English ability ranged from nearly fluent to practically hopeless. At the end of the first week the Class Monitor for the class of doctors read aloud the results of their "Suggestions for Better Study" meeting: "Dear Teacher Mark. You are an active boy! Your lessons are very humorous and very wonderful. To improve our class, may we suggest that in the future, we (1) spend more time reading (2) spend more time listening (3) spend more time writing, and (4) spend more time speaking. Also, some students feel you are moving too quickly through the book. However, some students request that you speed up a little, because the material is too elementary. We hope we can struggle together to overcome these contradictions! Thank you, our dear teacher."

On the first day of class, when I asked the Middle-Aged English Teachers to introduce themselves to me, each chose instead to introduce the person sitting next to him. Teacher Xu began: "Teacher Cai was a wonderful dancer when he was a young man. He is famous in our college because he has a beautiful wife." Teacher Cai hit Teacher Xu and said, "Teacher Xu is always late to class, and he is afraid of his wife!"

"I am not!"   5

"Oh, but you are!"   6

Teacher Zhang pointed to Teacher Zhu. "Teacher Zhu was a navy   7
man," he said. "But he can't swim! And Teacher Du is very fat. So we call
her Fatty Du—she has the most powerful voice in our college!" Fatty Du
beamed with pride and said, "And Teacher Zhang's special characteristic
is that he is afraid of me!"

"I am not!"   8

"Oh, but you are!"   9

On an afternoon some weeks later, I asked them to open their text-   10
books to a chapter entitled "War," which contained photographs of World
War II, including one of the atomic bomb explosion over Hiroshima.

"Teacher Zhu," I said, "Can you tell us something about your   11
experiences during the war?"

Teacher Zhu, an aspiring Communist Party member, stood up and   12
smiled.

"Yes," he said. Then he hesitated. "This is a picture of the atom   13
bomb, isn't it?"

"Yes."   14

He smiled stiffly. "Teacher Mark—how do you feel, knowing your   15
country dropped an atom bomb on innocent people?"

My face turned red with embarrassment at having the question put   16
so personally, but I tried to remain detached.

"This is a good question, Teacher Zhu. I can tell you that in   17
America, many people disagree about this. Not everyone thinks it was
the right thing to do, although most people think that it saved lives."

"How did it save lives?"   18

"Well, by ending the war quickly."   19

Here, Teacher Zhu looked around the room at his classmates.   20

"But Teacher Mark. It is a fact that the Japanese had already   21
surrendered to the Communist Eighth Route Army of China. America put
the bomb on Japan to make the world think America was the . . ."

"The victor!" shouted Fatty Du.   22

"Yes, the victor," said Teacher Zhu.   23

I must have stood gaping for a long time, for the other students   24
began to laugh.

"Teacher Zhu," I asked, "how do you know this is a fact?"   25

"Because that is what our newspapers say!"   26

"I see. But our newspapers tell a different story. How can we know   27
which newspaper has told the truth?"

Here he seemed relieved.   28

"That is easy! Our newspapers are controlled by the people, but   29
your newspapers are owned by capitalist organizations, so of course they
make things up to support themselves."

My mouth opened and closed a few times. Fatty Du, apparently   30
believing that the truth had been too much for me, came to my aid.

"It doesn't matter! Any capitalist country would do that. It is not just   31
your country!"

My head swimming, I asked her if she thought only capitalist   32
countries lied in the papers.

"Oh, of course not! The Russians do it, too. But here in China, we   33
have no reason to lie in the papers. When we make a mistake, we admit
it! As for war, there is nothing to lie about. China has never attacked a
nation. It has only defended its borders. We love peace. If we were the
most powerful country in the world, think how peaceful the world
would be!"

I agreed that war was a terrible thing and said I was glad that China   34
and the United States had become friendly. The class applauded my
speech.

"Teacher Mark—can I trouble you? I have a relative. She is my wife's   35
cousin. She is a doctor visiting from Harbin. She speaks very good
English and is very interested in learning more. Could I take her here to
practice with you? It would only be once or twice."

Because of the overwhelming number of relatives and friends of   36
students, not to mention perfect strangers, who wanted to learn English,
I had to be protective of my time. I explained this to my student and
apologized for not being able to help him.

"This is terrible," he said, smiling sheepishly.   37

"Why?" I asked.   38

"Because . . . I already told her you would."   39

I tried to let my annoyance show, but the harder I frowned, the   40
more broadly he smiled, so at last I agreed to meet with her once.

"Her name is Little Mi," he said, much relieved. "She is very smart   41
and strong-willed. She was always the leader of her class and was even
the head of the Communist Youth League in her school. During the
Cultural Revolution, she volunteered to go to the countryside. There she
almost starved to death. At last she had a chance to go to medical school.
She was the smartest in her class."

Little Mi sounded like a terrific bore; I cleared my throat, hoping that   42
my student would simply arrange a time and let me be, but he continued.
"Her specialty was pediatrics. She wanted to work with children. When the
time came for job assignments after graduation, though, some people
started a rumor that she and some of the other English students read Western
literature in their spare time instead of studying medicine. They were accused of *fang yang pi*!"—imitating Westerners.

"So instead of being sent to a good hospital, she was sent to a small   43
family planning clinic outside of the city. There she mostly assists doctors

with abortions. That is how she works with children. But saddest of all, she has leukemia. Truly, she has eaten bitter all her life. When can I bring her?"

I told him they could come to my office in the Foreign Languages   44
Building that evening. He thanked me extravagantly and withdrew.

At the appointed time someone knocked. I braced myself for an   45
hour of grammar questions and opened the door. There stood Little Mi, who could not have been much older than I, with a purple scarf wrapped around her head like a Russian peasant woman. She was petite, unsmiling and beautiful. She looked at me without blinking.

"Are you Teacher Mark?" she asked in an even, low voice.   46

"Yes—please come in." She walked in, sat down and said in fluent   47
English, "My cousin's husband apologizes for not being able to come. His adviser called him in for a meeting. Do you mind that I came alone?"

"Not at all. What can I do for you?"   48

"Well," she said, looking at the bookshelf next to her, "I love to   49
read, but it is difficult to find good books in English. I wonder if you would be so kind as to lend me a book or two, which I can send back to you from Harbin as soon as I finish them." I told her to pick whatever she liked from my shelf. As she went through the books she talked about the foreign novels she had enjoyed; "Of Mice and Men," "From Here To Eternity" and "The Gulag Archipelago."

"How did you get 'The Gulag Archipelago'?" I asked her.   50

"It wasn't easy," she answered. "I hear that Americans are shocked   51
by what they read in it. Is that true?"

"Yes, weren't you?"   52

"Not really," she answered quietly.   53

I remembered the story of her life my student had told. "You are a   54
pretty tough girl, aren't you?" I said.

She looked up from the magazine she had been leafing through   55
with a surprised expression, then covered her mouth with her hand and giggled nervously. "How terrible! I'm not like that at all!"

We talked for over an hour, and she picked a few books to take   56
with her. When she got up to leave, I asked her when she would return to Harbin.

"The day after tomorrow."   57

Against all better judgment I asked her to come visit me again the   58
next evening. She eyed me closely, said "Thank you—I will," then disappeared into the unlit hallway. I listened to her footsteps as she made her way down the stairs and out of the deserted building. Then from the window I watched her shadowy figure cross the athletic field.

She came the next night at exactly the same time. I had brought for   59
her a few books of photographs of the United States, and she marveled at the color pictures taken in New England during the fall. "How beautiful," she said. "Just like a dream."

I could not openly stare at her, so I gazed at her hand as she turned   60
the pages of the book, listened to her voice, and occasionally glanced at
her face when she asked me something.

We talked and talked, then she seemed to remember something   61
and looked at her watch. It was after 10 o'clock—nearly two hours had
passed. She gasped, suddenly worried. "I've missed the last bus!"

She was staying in a hospital on the other side of the river, at least   62
a two-hour walk. It was a bitter cold night. On foot, she would get back
after midnight and arouse considerable suspicion. The only thing to do
was put her on the back of a bicycle and ride her. That in itself would not
attract attention, since that is how most Chinese families travel around
town. I had seen families of five on one bicycle many times, and young
couples ride this way for want of anything else to do at night. The woman
usually rides sidesaddle on the rack over the rear wheel with her arms
around the man's waist, leaning her shoulder and face against his back.

A Chinese woman riding that way on a bicycle powered by a   63
Caucasian male would attract attention, however. I put on my thick
padded Red Army coat, tucked my hair under a Mao hat, wore a surgical
mask (as many Chinese do, to keep dust out of their lungs), and put on
a pair of Chinese sunglasses, the kind that *liumang*—young punks—
wear. Little Mi wrapped her scarf around her head and left the building
first.

Five minutes later, I went out, rode fast through the gate of our   64
college, and saw her down the street, shrouded in the haze of dust
kicked up by a coal truck. I pulled alongside her and she jumped on
before I stopped.

The street was crowded. Neither of us said a word. Trucks, buses   65
and jeeps flung themselves madly through the streets, bicycles wove
around us, and pedestrians darted in front of us, cursing the *liumang*.
Finally I turned onto the road that ran along the river, and the crowd
thinned out. It was a horrible road, with potholes everywhere that I
could not see in time to avoid. She, too shy to put her arms around my
waist, had been balancing herself across the rack, but when we hit an
especially deep rut I heard her yelp and felt her grab on to me. Regaining
her balance, she began to loosen her grip, but I quickly steered into
another pothole and told her to hold on. Very slowly, I felt her leaning
her shoulder against my back. When at last her face touched my coat, I
could feel her cheek through it.

We reached the steep bridge and I started the climb. About halfway   66
up she told me to stop riding, that we could walk up the bridge to give
me a rest. At the top, we stopped to lean against the rail and look at the
lights of the city. Trucks and jeeps were our only company.

"Does this remind you of America?" she asked, gesturing toward the   67
city lights with her chin.

"Yes, a little."   68

"Do you miss home?"   69

"Very much. But I'll be home very soon. And when I get home, I   70
will miss Changsha."

"Really? But China is so . . . no you tell me—what is China like?"   71

"The lights are dimmer here."   72

"Yes," she said quietly, "and we are boring people, aren't we?" Only   73
her eyes showed above the scarf wrapped around her face. I asked her if
she thought she was boring, and her eyes wrinkled with laughter.

"I am not boring. I believe I am a very interesting girl. Do you think   74
so?"

"Yes, I think so." She had pale skin, and I could see her eyelids   75
blush.

"When you go back to America, will you live with your parents?"   76

"No."   77

"Why not?"   78

"I'm too old! They would think it was strange if I didn't live on my   79
own."

"How wonderful! I wish my parents felt that way. I will have to live   80
with them forever."

"Forever?"   81

"Of course! Chinese parents love their children, but they also think   82
that children are like furniture. They own you, and you must make them
comfortable until they decide to let you go. I cannot marry, so I will have
to take care of them forever. I am almost 30 years old, and I must do
whatever they say. So I sit in my room and dream. In my imagination I am
free, and I can do wonder things!"

"Like what?"   83

She cocked her head to one side and raised one eyebrow.   84

"Do you tell people your dreams?"   85

"Yes, sometimes."   86

She laughed and said, "I'm not going to tell you my dreams."   87

We were silent awhile, then she suddenly asked me if I was a sad   88
man or a happy man.

"That's hard to say—sometimes I'm happy, sometimes I'm sad.   89
Mostly, I just worry."

"Worry? What do you worry about?"   90

"I don't know—everything, I guess. Mostly about wasting time."   91

"How strange! My cousin's husband says that you work very hard."   92

"I like to keep busy. That way I don't have time to worry."   93

"I can't understand that. You are such a free man—you can travel all   94
over the world as you like, make friends everywhere. You are a fool not
to be happy, especially when so many people depend on it."

"What do you mean?"   95

"My relative says that your nickname in the college is *huo-*   96
shenxian—an immortal in human form—because you are so . . . different. Your lectures make everyone laugh, and you make people feel
happy all the time. This is very unusual."

I asked her if she was happy or sad. She raised one eyebrow again,   97
looking not quite at me.

"I don't have as many reasons to be happy as you." She looked at her   98
watch and shook her head. "I must get back—we have to hurry." As I turned
toward the bicycle she leaned very close to me, almost touching her face
against mine, looking straight into my eyes, and said, "I have an idea."

I could feel her breath against my throat.   99

"Let's coast down the bridge," she said. "Fast! No brakes!"   100

I got on the bicycle.   101

"Are you getting on?" I asked her.   102

"Just a minute. At the bottom I'll get off, so I'll say goodbye now."   103

"I should at least take you to the gate of the hospital."   104

"No, that wouldn't be a good idea. Someone might see me and ask   105
who you were. At the bottom of the bridge I'll hop off, and you turn
around. I won't see you again, so thank you. It was fun meeting you. You
should stop worrying." She jumped on, pressed her face against my back,
held me like a vice, and said, "Now—go! As fast as you can!"

Exercises

Some Important Words

Mandarin (paragraph 1), Cantonese (1), penal colony (1), detached (16),
gaping (24), capitalist (29), sheepishly (37), Cultural Revolution (41),
pediatrics (42), leukemia (43), extravagantly (44), petite (45), *The Gulag
Archipelago* (49), sidesaddle (62), Caucasian (63), shrouded (64), immortal (96).

Some of the Issues

1. How did Salzman feel about going to China before traveling there?
   What was his preparation for the job of teaching English?
2. Describe Salzman's English classes. How appropriate are the doctors'
   suggestions? How did the middle-aged English teachers introduce
   one another?
3. What differing views of history are revealed in paragraphs 13–34?
4. What impression did Salzman have of Little Mi before meeting her?
   What do you learn about her past? About the effects of the Cultural
   Revolution?

5. What is Salzman's reaction when he finds out that Little Mi has read *The Gulag Archipelago*?
6. How is Little Mi's personality revealed to us? What indications are there of a change in Salzman's feelings?
7. The final conversation between Salzman and Little Mi reveals many differences in their lives and attitudes toward living. What are they? Do you think Salzman and Little Mi understand each other in spite of their differences?

The Way We Are Told

8. At first sight Salzman seems simply to be recording his conversations and impressions. Yet, in doing so, he lets the reader know quite clearly what he feels. How does Salzman express his point of view? Try to find some examples.
9. In paragraph 15 Teacher Zhu confronts Salzman with a question about dropping the atom bomb on Hiroshima. Examine the rest of the discussion between Salzman and the teachers. How does Salzman show that they, far from wanting a confrontation on that topic, go out of their way to "help" him understand?

Some Subjects for Writing

10. Salzman and Little Mi lead lives that are very far apart. Before their meeting Salzman expects her to be a bore. Yet, in the few hours they spend together, they bridge the wide gap between them. Describe a situation in which your own anticipation or first impression of someone turned out to be wrong.

CANADIANS:
WHAT DO THEY WANT?

Margaret Atwood

Margaret Atwood is one of Canada's foremost contemporary writers. She was born in Ottawa in 1939 and holds a B.A. degree from the University of Toronto and an M.A. from Radcliffe (Harvard). She has served as writer in residence at several universities and has received a number of honorary degrees and prizes for her writing. Poet, novelist, and essayist, she is best known for her novels, among them *The Edible Woman* (1970), *Lady Oracle* (1976), *Life Before Man* (1980), *The Handmaid's Tale* (1985), *Cat's Eye* (1988), and *Wilderness Tips* (1992).

With its 10 provinces and vast Northern and Yukon Territories stretching toward the North Pole, Canada is larger than the United States. But with some 24 million inhabitants, the size of its population is just 10 percent of that of its southern (and only) neighbor. Canadians often complain that Americans know far too little about Canada, taking it for granted as an ally, a trading partner, and a fellow democracy. Canadians are concerned about dominance by their much more powerful neighbor, not only economic but cultural dominance as well.

About one in four Canadians is French-speaking, most of them living in the province of Quebec, north of New York State and New England. Just as Canadians in general are concerned about being dominated by the United States, so French Canadians are concerned about being deprived of their culture by the English-speaking majority, which has led to a separatist movement and some legislation restricting the use of English in Quebec.

Last month, during a poetry reading, I tried out a short prose poem called 1 "How to Like Men." It began by suggesting that one start with the feet. Unfortunately, the question of jackboots soon arose, and things went on from there. After the reading I had a conversation with a young man who thought I had been unfair to men. He wanted men to be liked totally, not just from the heels to the knees, and not just as individuals but as a group; and he thought it negative and inegalitarian of me to have alluded to war and rape. I pointed out that as far as any of us knew these were two activities not widely engaged in by women, but he was still upset. "We're both in this together," he protested. I admitted that this was so; but could he, maybe, see that our relative positions might be a little different.

This is the conversation one has with Americans, even, uh, *good*   2 Americans, when the dinner-table conversation veers round to Canadian-American relations. "We're in this together," they like to say, especially when it comes to continental energy reserves. How do you *explain* to them, as delicately as possible, why they are not categorically beloved? It gets like the old Lifebuoy ads: even their best friends won't tell them. And Canadians are supposed to be their best friends, right? Members of the family?

Well, sort of. Across the river from Michigan, so near and yet so far,   3 there I was at the age of eight, reading *their* Donald Duck comic books (originated however by one of *ours;* yes, Walt Disney's parents were Canadian) and coming at the end to Popsicle Pete, who promised me the earth if only I would save wrappers, but took it all away from me again with a single asterisk: Offer Good Only in the United States. Some cynical members of the world community may be forgiven for thinking that the same asterisk is there, in invisible ink, on the Constitution and the Bill of Rights.

But quibbles like that aside, and good will assumed, how does one   4 go about liking Americans? Where does one begin? Or, to put it another way, why did the Canadian women lock themselves in the john during a '70s "international" feminist conference being held in Toronto? Because the American sisters were being "imperialist," that's why.

But then, it's always a little naive of Canadians to expect that   5 Americans, of whatever political stamp, should stop being imperious. How can they? The fact is that the United States is an empire and Canada is to it as Gaul was to Rome.

It's hard to explain to Americans what it feels like to be a Canadian.   6 Pessimists among us would say that one has to translate the experience into their own terms and that this is necessary because Americans are incapable of thinking in any other terms—and this in itself is part of the problem. (Witness all those draft dodgers who went into culture shock when they discovered to their horror that Toronto was not Syracuse.)

Here is a translation: Picture a Mexico with a population ten times   7 larger than that of the United States. That would put it at about two billion. Now suppose that the official American language is Spanish, that 75 percent of the books Americans buy and 90 percent of the movies they see are Mexican, and that the profits flow across the border to Mexico. If an American does scrape it together to make a movie, the

Mexicans won't let him show it in the States, because they own the distribution outlets. If anyone tries to change this ratio, not only the Mexicans but many fellow Americans cry "National chauvinism," or, even more effectively, "National socialism." After all, the American public prefers the Mexican product. It's what they're used to.

Retranslate and you have the current American-Canadian picture. 8 It's changed a little recently, not only on the cultural front. For instance, Canada, some think a trifle late, is attempting to regain control of its own petroleum industry. Americans are predictably angry. They think of Canadian oil as *theirs*.

"What's mine is yours," they have said for years, meaning exports: 9 "What's yours is mine" means ownership and profits. Canadians are supposed to do retail buying, not controlling, or what's an empire for? One could always refer Americans to history, particularly that of their own revolution. They objected to the colonial situation when they themselves were a colony; but then, revolution is considered one of a very few homegrown American products that definitely are not for export.

Objectively, one cannot become too self-righteous about this state 10 of affairs. Canadians owned lots of things, including their souls, before World War II. After that they sold, some say because they had put too much into financing the war, which created a capital vacuum (a position they would not have been forced into if the Americans hadn't kept out of the fighting for so long, say the sore losers). But for whatever reason, capital flowed across the border in the '50s, and Canadians, traditionally sock-under-the-mattress hoarders, were reluctant to invest in their own country. Americans did it for them and ended up with a large part of it, which they retain to this day. In every sellout there's a seller as well as a buyer, and the Canadians did a thorough job of trading their birthright for a mess.

That's on the capitalist end, but when you turn to the trade union 11 side of things you find much the same story, except that the sellout happened in the '30s under the banner of the United Front. Now Canadian workers are finding that in any empire the colonial branch plants are the first to close, and what could be a truly progressive labor movement has been weakened by compromised bargains made in international union headquarters south of the border.

Canadians are sometimes snippy to Americans at cocktail parties. 12 They don't like to feel owned and they don't like having been sold. But what really bothers them—and it's at this point that the United States and Rome part company—is the wide-eyed innocence with which their snippiness is greeted.

Innocence becomes ignorance when seen in the light of interna- 13 tional affairs, and though ignorance is one of the spoils of conquest—the

Gauls always knew more about the Romans than the Romans knew about them—the world can no longer afford America's ignorance. Its ignorance of Canada, though it makes Canadians bristle, is a minor and relatively harmless example. More dangerous is the fact that individual Americans seem not to know that the United States is an imperial power and is behaving like one. They don't want to admit that empires dominate, invade and subjugate—and live on the proceeds—or, if they do admit it, they believe in their divine right to do so. The export of divine right is much more harmful than the export of Coca-Cola, though they may turn out to be much the same thing in the end.

Other empires have behaved similarly (the British somewhat better,   14
Genghis Khan decidedly worse); but they have not expected to be *liked* for it. It's the final Americanism, this passion for being liked. Alas, many Americans are indeed likable; they are often more generous, more welcoming, more enthusiastic, less picky and sardonic than Canadians, and it's not enough to say it's only because they can afford it. Some of that revolutionary spirit still remains: the optimism, the 18th-century belief in the fixability of almost anything, the conviction of the possibility of change. However, at cocktail parties and elsewhere one must be able to tell the difference between an individual and a foreign policy. Canadians can no longer afford to think of Americans as only a spectator sport. If Reagan blows up the world, we will unfortunately be doing more than watching it on television. "No annihilation without representation" sounds good as a slogan, but if we run it up the flagpole, who's going to salute?

We *are* all in this together. For Canadians, the question is how to   15
survive it. For Americans there is no question, because there does not have to be. Canada is just that vague, cold place where their uncle used to go fishing, before the lakes went dead from acid rain.

How do you like Americans? Individually, it's easier. Your average   16
American is no more responsible for the state of affairs than your average man is for war and rape. Any Canadian who is so narrow-minded as to dislike Americans merely on principle is missing out on one of the good things in life. The same might be said, to women, of men. As a group, as a foreign policy, it's harder. But if you like men, you can like Americans. Cautiously. Selectively. Beginning with the feet. One at a time.

Exercises

Some Important Words

jackboots (paragraph 1), inegalitarian (1), alluded (1), veers (2), categorically (2), asterisk (3), cynical (3), quibbles (4), imperious (5), Gaul (5), pessimists (6), draft dodgers (6), culture shock (6), chauvinism (7), self-righteous (10), progressive (11), compromised (11), snippy (12) spoils (13), subjugate (13), divine right (13), Genghis Khan (14), sardonic (14), annihilation (14), acid rain (15).

Some of the Issues

1. How does Atwood answer the young man who asserts that men and women are "in this together"? How does she respond as a Canadian when Americans tell her the same thing?
2. Why is it hard to explain to Americans what it feels like to be Canadian?
3. Atwood accuses Americans of being imperialists. Does she support that claim? How? Do you think most Americans would be surprised by her accusation? Do you agree with it? Why or why not?
4. Explain the analogy Atwood makes (paragraphs 7 and 8) to help Americans understand Canada's attitudes toward American dominance.
5. What according to Atwood is "one of a very few homegrown American products that definitely are not for export"?
6. In paragraphs 10 and 11 Atwood concedes that Canadians must share some blame for American domination. What specific examples does she give?
7. Atwood accuses Americans of ignorance. Of what in particular? What, according to Atwood, accounts for this ignorance?
8. Atwood admits that many Americans are likeable as individuals. Why is this not enough for her?

The Way We Are Told

9. Who is Atwood's audience? Can she afford to be critical of it? Does she make any concessions to her audience's sense of patriotism?
10. Consider Atwood's style. Does it often resemble speech? Make note of the use of italics, the phrase "even, uh, *good* Americans" and the choice of vocabulary.
11. How would you characterize the tone of Atwood's article? How does she use humor? Does humor help her to disarm the reader?
12. Atwood makes several references to slogans; for example, "even their best friends won't tell them" (paragraph 2). What is the effect? What is she referring to when she says "No annihilation without representation"?
13. In the last paragraph Atwood returns to a comment she made at the very beginning of the essay. What is the advantage of beginning and ending in this way?

Some Subjects for Writing

14. Atwood accuses the United States of being an imperialist power in certain ways. Examine her claim. Do you agree or disagree?
*15. Read Ngugi wa Thiong'o's "The Politics of Language." Both Ngugi and Atwood are concerned with imperialist pressures on their respective cultures exerted by much more formidable powers. Examine what these pressures consist of in each case, and compare their impact.

SHOOTING AN ELEPHANT

George Orwell

In Orwell's time, Burma, where he was stationed, was a part of the Indian Empire under British rule. When India gained independence in 1947, Burma became a separate, sovereign state. About the size of Texas with a population of 40 million, this country, now called Myanmar, is ruled by a heavy-handed military dictatorship, and is largely closed off from the rest of the world.

In 1988, under international pressure, free elections were held, but the party winning 80 percent of the vote was not allowed to take power. The following year a pro-democracy uprising was brutally put down. One of the leaders of the uprising was Aung San Suu Kyi, winner of the Nobel Peace Prize in 1991.

After leaving India, Orwell turned to writing but with little success. He lived in great poverty for some time, as described in his first published book, *Down and Out in Paris and London* (1933). In the mid-1930s he fought on the side of the Republic in the Spanish Civil War, was wounded and wrote of his experience in *Homage to Catalonia* (1938). Success finally came late in his life with *Animal Farm* (1945) and *1984,* both of which expressed his disillusionment with communism. *1984* was published in 1949, the year before his death from tuberculosis.

In Moulmein, in lower Burma, I was hated by large numbers of people—the only time in my life that I have been important enough for this to happen to me. I was sub-divisional police officer of the town, and in an aimless, petty kind of way anti-European feeling was very bitter. No one had the guts to raise a riot, but if a European woman went through the bazaars alone somebody would probably spit betel juice over her dress. As a police officer I was an obvious target and was baited whenever it seemed safe to do so. When a nimble Burman tripped me up on the football field and the referee (another Burman) looked the other way, the crowd yelled with hideous laughter. This happened more than once. In the end the sneering yellow faces of young men that met me everywhere, the insults hooted after me when I was at a safe distance, got badly on my nerves. The young Buddhist priests were the worst of

1

all. There were several thousands of them in the town and none of them seemed to have anything to do except stand on street corners and jeer at Europeans.

All this was perplexing and upsetting. For at that time I had already made up my mind that imperialism was an evil thing and the sooner I chucked up my job and got out of it the better. Theoretically—and secretly, of course—I was all for the Burmese and all against their oppressors, the British. As for the job I was doing, I hated it more bitterly than I can perhaps make clear. In a job like that you see the dirty work of Empire at close quarters. The wretched prisoners huddling in the stinking cages of the lockups, the grey, cowed faces of the long-term convicts, the scarred buttocks of the men who had been flogged with bamboos—all these oppressed me with an intolerable sense of guilt. But I could get nothing into perspective. I was young and ill-educated and I had had to think out my problems in the utter silence that is imposed on every Englishman in the East. I did not even know that the British Empire is dying, still less did I know that it is a great deal better than the younger empires that are going to supplant it. All I knew was that I was stuck between my hatred of the empire I served and my rage against the evil-spirited little beasts who tried to make my job impossible. With one part of my mind I thought of the British Raj as an unbreakable tyranny, as something clamped down, in *saecula saeculorum,* upon the will of prostrate peoples; with another part I thought that the greatest joy in the world would be to drive a bayonet into a Buddhist priest's guts. Feelings like these are the normal by-products of imperialism; ask any Anglo-Indian official, if you can catch him off duty.

One day something happened which in a roundabout way was enlightening. It was a tiny incident in itself, but it gave me a better glimpse than I had had before of the real nature of imperialism—the real motives for which despotic governments act. Early one morning the sub-inspector at a police station the other end of the town rang me up on the 'phone and said that an elephant was ravaging the bazaar. Would I please come and do something about it? I did not know what I could do, but I wanted to see what was happening and I got on to a pony and started out. I took my rifle, an old .44 Winchester and much too small to kill an elephant, but I thought the noise might be useful *in terrorem.* Various Burmans stopped me on the way and told me about the elephant's doings. It was not, of course, a wild elephant, but a tame one which had gone "must." It had been chained up, as tame elephants always are when their attack of "must" is due, but on the previous night it had broken its chain and escaped. Its mahout, the only person who could manage it when it was in that state, had set out in pursuit, but had taken the wrong direction and was now twelve hours' journey away, and in the morning the elephant had suddenly reappeared in the town. The

Burmese population had no weapons and were quite helpless against it. It had already destroyed somebody's bamboo hut, killed a cow and raided some fruit-stalls and devoured the stock; also it had met the municipal rubbish van and, when the driver jumped out and took to his heels, had turned the van over and inflicted violences upon it.

The Burmese sub-inspector and some Indian constables were waiting for me in the quarter where the elephant had been seen. It was a very poor quarter, a labyrinth of squalid bamboo huts, thatched with palm-leaf, winding all over a steep hillside. I remember that it was a cloudy, stuffy morning at the beginning of the rains. We began questioning the people as to where the elephant had gone and, as usual, failed to get any definite information. That is invariably the case in the East; a story always sounds clear enough at a distance, but the nearer you get to the scene of events the vaguer it becomes. Some of the people said that the elephant had gone in one direction, some said that he had gone in another, some professed not even to have heard of any elephant. I had almost made up my mind that the whole story was a pack of lies, when we heard yells a little distance away. There was a loud, scandalized cry of "Go away, child! Go away this instant!" and an old woman with a switch in her hand came round the corner of a hut, violently shooing away a crowd of naked children. Some more women followed, clicking their tongues and exclaiming; evidently there was something that the children ought not to have seen. I rounded the hut and saw a man's dead body sprawling in the mud. He was an Indian, a black Dravidian coolie, almost naked, and he could not have been dead many minutes. The people said that the elephant had come suddenly upon him round the corner of the hut, caught him with its trunk, put its foot on his back and ground him into the earth. This was the rainy season and the ground was soft; and his face had scored a trench a foot deep and a couple yards long. He was lying on his belly with arms crucified and head sharply twisted to one side. His face was coated with mud, the eyes wide open, the teeth bared and grinning with an expression of unendurable agony. (Never tell me, by the way, that the dead look peaceful. Most of the corpses I have seen looked devilish.) The friction of the great beast's foot had stripped the skin from his back as neatly as one skins a rabbit. As soon as I saw the dead man I sent an orderly to a friend's house nearby to borrow an elephant rifle. I had already sent back the pony, not wanting it to go mad with fright and throw me if it smelt the elephant.

The orderly came back in a few minutes with a rifle and five cartridges, and meanwhile some Burmans had arrived and told us that the elephant was in the paddy fields below, only a few hundred yards away. As I started forward practically the whole population of the quarter flocked out of the houses and followed me. They had seen the rifle and were all shouting excitedly that I was going to shoot the elephant. They had not shown much interest in the elephant when he was merely ravaging their homes, but it was different now that he was going to be shot. It was a bit of fun to them, as it would be to an English crowd; besides they wanted the meat. It made me vaguely uneasy. I had no intention of shooting the elephant—I had merely sent for the rifle to defend myself if necessary—and it is always unnerving to have a crowd following you. I marched down the hill, looking and feeling a fool, with the rifle over my shoulder and an ever-growing army of people jostling at my heels. At the bottom, when you got away from the huts, there was a metalled road and beyond that a miry waste of paddy fields a thousand yards across, not yet ploughed but soggy from the first rains and dotted with coarse grass. The elephant was standing eight yards from the road, his left side towards us. He took not the slightest notice of the crowd's approach. He was tearing up bunches of grass, beating them against his knees to clean them and stuffing them into his mouth.

I had halted on the road. As soon as I saw the elephant I knew with   6
perfect certainty that I ought not to shoot him. It is a serious matter to shoot a working elephant—it is comparable to destroying a huge and costly piece of machinery—and obviously one ought not to do it if it can possibly be avoided. And at that distance, peacefully eating, the elephant looked no more dangerous than a cow. I thought then and I think now that his attack of "must" was already passing off; in which case he would merely wander harmlessly about until the mahout came back and caught him. Moreover, I did not in the least want to shoot him. I decided that I would watch him for a little while to make sure that he did not turn savage again, and then go home.

But at that moment I glanced round at the crowd that had followed   7
me. It was an immense crowd, two thousand at the least and growing every minute. It blocked the road for a long distance on either side. I looked at the sea of yellow faces above the garish clothes—faces all happy and excited over this bit of fun, all certain that the elephant was going to be shot. They were watching me as they would watch a conjurer about to perform a trick. They did not like me, but with the magical rifle in my hands I was momentarily worth watching. And suddenly I realized that I should have to shoot the elephant after all. The people expected it of me and I had got to do it; I could feel their two thousand wills pressing me forward, irresistibly. And it was at this moment, as I stood there with the rifle in my hands, that I first grasped the hollowness, the futility of the white man's dominion in the East. Here was I, the white man with his gun, standing in front of the unarmed native crowd—seemingly the leading actor of the piece; but in reality I was only an absurd puppet pushed to and fro by the will of those yellow faces behind. I perceived in this moment that when the white man turns tyrant it is his own freedom that he destroys. He becomes a sort of hollow, posing dummy, the

conventionalized figure of a sahib. For it is the condition of his rule that he shall spend his life in trying to impress the "natives," and so in every crisis he has got to do what the "natives" expect of him. He wears a mask, and his face grows to fit it. I had got to shoot the elephant. I had committed myself to doing it when I sent for the rifle. A sahib has got to act like a sahib; he has got to appear resolute, to know his own mind and do definite things. To come all that way, rifle in hand, with two thousand people marching at my heels, and then to trail feebly away, having done nothing—no, that was impossible. The crowd would laugh at me. And my whole life, every white man's life in the East, was one long struggle not to be laughed at.

But I did not want to shoot the elephant. I watched him beating his   8
bunch of grass against his knees, with that preoccupied grandmotherly air that elephants have. It seemed to me that it would be murder to shoot him. At that age I was not squeamish about killing animals, but I had never shot an elephant and never wanted to. (Somehow it always seems worse to kill a *large* animal.) Besides, there was the beast's owner to be considered. Alive, the elephant was worth at least a hundred pounds; dead, he would only be worth the value of his tusks, five pounds, possibly. But I had got to act quickly. I turned to some experienced-looking Burmans who had been there when we arrived, and asked them how the elephant had been behaving. They all said the same thing: he took no notice of you if you left him alone, but he might charge if you went too close to him.

It was perfectly clear to me what I ought to do. I ought to walk up   9
to within, say, twenty-five yards of the elephant and test his behavior. If he charged, I could shoot; if he took no notice of me, it would be safe to leave him until the mahout came back. But also I knew that I was going to do no such thing. I was a poor shot with a rifle and the ground was soft mud into which one would sink at every step. If the elephant charged and I missed him, I should have about as much chance as a toad under a steam-roller. But even then I was not thinking particularly of my own skin, only of the watchful yellow faces behind. For at that moment, with the crowd watching me, I was not afraid in the ordinary sense, as I would have been if I had been alone. A white man mustn't be frightened in front of "natives"; and so, in general, he isn't frightened. The sole thought in my mind was that if anything went wrong those two thousand Burmans would see me pursued, caught, trampled on and reduced to a grinning corpse like that Indian up the hill. And if that happened it was quite probable that some of them would laugh. That would never do. There was only one alternative. I shoved the cartridges into the magazine and lay down on the road to get a better aim.

The crowd grew very still, and a deep, low, happy sigh, as of   10
people who see the theatre curtain go up at last, breathed from

innumerable throats. They were going to have their bit of fun after all. The rifle was a beautiful German thing with cross-hair sights. I did not then know that in shooting an elephant one would shoot to cut an imaginary bar running from ear-hole to ear-hole. I ought, therefore, as the elephant was sideways on, to have aimed straight at his ear-hole; actually I aimed several inches in front of this, thinking the brain would be further forward.

When I pulled the trigger I did not hear the bang or feel the kick— one never does when a shot goes home—but I heard the devilish roar of glee that went up from the crowd. In that instant, in too short a time, one would have thought, even for the bullet to get there, a mysterious, terrible change had come over the elephant. He neither stirred nor fell, but every line of his body had altered. He looked suddenly stricken, shrunken, immensely old, as though the frightful impact of the bullet had paralysed him without knocking him down. At last, after what seemed a long time—it might have been five seconds, I dare say—he sagged flabbily to his knees. His mouth slobbered. An enormous senility seemed to have settled upon him. One could have imagined him thousands of years old. I fired again into the same spot. At the second shot he did not collapse but climbed with desperate slowness to his feet and stood weakly upright, with legs sagging and head drooping. I fired a third time. That was the shot that did for him. You could see the agony of it jolt his whole body and knock the last remnant of strength from his legs. But in falling he seemed for a moment to rise, for as his hind legs collapsed beneath him he seemed to tower upward like a huge rock toppling, his trunk reaching skywards like a tree. He trumpeted, for the first and only time. And then down he came, his belly towards me, with a crash that seemed to shake the ground even where I lay.

I got up. The Burmans were already racing past me across the mud. It was obvious that the elephant would never rise again, but he was not dead. He was breathing very rhythmically with long rattling gasps, his great mound of a side painfully rising and falling. His mouth was wide open—I could see far down into caverns of pale pink throat. I waited a long time for him to die, but his breathing did not weaken. Finally I fired my two remaining shots into the spot where I thought his heart must be. The thick blood welled out of him like red velvet, but still he did not die. His body did not even jerk when the shots hit him, the tortured breathing continued without a pause. He was dying, very slowly and in great agony, but in some world remote from me where not even a bullet could damage him further. I felt that I had got to put an end to that dreadful noise. It seemed dreadful to see the great beast lying there, powerless to move and yet powerless to die, and not even to be able to finish him. I send back for my small rifle and poured shot after shot into his heart and down his throat. They seemed to make no impression. The tortured gasps continued as steadily as the ticking of a clock.

In the end I could not stand it any longer and went away. I heard   13
later that it took him half an hour to die. Burmans were bringing dahs
and baskets even before I left, and I was told they had stripped his body
almost to the bones by the afternoon.

Afterwards, of course, there were endless discussions about the   14
shooting of the elephant. The owner was furious, but he was only an
Indian and could do nothing. Besides, legally I had done the right thing,
for a mad elephant has to be killed, like a mad dog, if its owner fails to
control it. Among the Europeans opinion was divided. The older men
said I was right, the younger men said it was a damn shame to shoot an
elephant for killing a coolie, because an elephant was worth more than
any damn Coringhee coolie. And afterwards I was very glad that the
coolie had been killed; it put me legally in the right and it gave me a
sufficient pretext for shooting the elephant. I often wondered whether
any of the others grasped that I had done it solely to avoid looking a fool.

Exercises

Some Important Words

perplexing (paragraph 2), imperialism (2), supplant (2), British Raj (2),
saecula saeculorum—for all time (2), prostrate (2), ravaging (3), bazaar
(3), *in terrorem*—to spread terror (3), mahout (3), rubbish (3), Dravidian
(4), jostling (5), conjurer (7), conventionalized (7), sahib (7), flabbily (11),
senility (11), dahs (13).

Some of the Issues

1. Before Orwell begins to tell the story of the shooting of the elephant,
   he uses two paragraphs to talk about feelings: the feelings of the
   Burmese toward him as a colonial officer, and his own "perplexing
   and upsetting" feelings toward the Burmese. Why are Orwell's
   feelings complex and contradictory? How does this discussion of
   attitudes set the scene for the narrative that follows?
2. The main topic or theme of the essay is stated in the first few
   sentences of paragraph 3. After reading the whole essay, explain why
   the incident Orwell describes gave him "a better glimpse . . . of the
   real nature of imperialism." What, according to Orwell, are "the real
   motives for which despotic governments act"?
3. In paragraph 7 Orwell says, "I perceived in this moment that when
   the white man turns tyrant it is his own freedom that he destroys."
   Explain the meaning of this sentence; how does it apply to the story
   Orwell tells?

The Way We Are Told

4. When Orwell begins to tell the story of the elephant, in paragraph 3, he continues to reveal his attitude toward the Burmese in various indirect ways. Try to show how he does this.
5. In paragraph 4 Orwell describes the dead coolie in considerable detail. Compare that description to the one of the elephant's death. How do the descriptions differ? What are some of the words and phrases that show the difference?
6. In paragraphs 5-9 Orwell discusses his plans and options regarding the elephant. Paragraphs 5 and 6, however, differ greatly from 7, 8, and 9, both in content and treatment. Characterize the difference.

Some Subjects for Writing

7. Have you ever been placed in a situation in which you were forced to do something that you did not entirely agree with? For example, an employee must often carry out the policies of his or her employer even while disagreeing with them. Write an essay describing such an incident and detail your feelings before, during, and after.
8. Orwell is placed in a position of authority but finds that it restricts his scope of action rather than expands it. Write an essay that asserts the truth of this apparent contradiction. Try to find examples of other situations in which the possession of power limits the possessor.

CONFORMITY AND INDIVIDUALITY IN JAPAN

Ian Buruma

Ian Buruma is the author of *Playing the Game* (1991); *Behind the Mask*, a study of contemporary Japanese culture; and *God's Dust: A Modern Asian Journey* (1989). He is the cultural editor of the *Far Eastern Review* in Hong Kong, and a frequent contributor to American magazines.

The selection below was first published in *Tokyo: Form and Spirit* (1986), edited by Mildred Friedman. Buruma uses two examples, an elevator operator and a "salaryman" (middle rank businessman), to demonstrate the impact of conformity and "human relations based on hierarchy" in the Japanese workplace. Buruma goes on to discuss the role of talent, the obstacles to its rise, and the loneliness that the talented are likely to face. Nevertheless, "originality and creativity do exist in Japan." However, as Buruma points out, the Japanese preference for skill over originality results in pride being taken in routine work.

To learn more about Japan, read John David Morley's "Living in a Japanese Home."

The repetitive zeal with which Japanese go about honing their skills 1 makes them seem obsessed with form, with mechanics rather than content. A rather touching example of this is the first reaction of Japanese audiences to moving pictures: they turned round their chairs to watch the projector, a source of much more fascination than the images flickering on the screen. Added to their reputation as copycats is their image as robots. This, too, is missing the point. The preoccupation with style does not necessarily mean the lack of a soul; just as Japanese do not feel that good manners make a human being less "real," "himself," "natural" or whatever term one wishes to use for that elusive inner core of man. Style, in the post-romantic West, is largely an extension of man's ego; traditional style in Japan—and China, for that matter—is more a transformation of the ego: to acquire a perfect technique, one eliminates, as it were, one's individuality, only to regain it by transcending the skill. This new

326

individuality is not the expression of one's real private life, but an individual interpretation of something already there and thus in the public domain.

Private life in Japan is just that: private. An artist or, for that matter, 2 a waitress, is not expected to reveal his—or her—private "self," but his public one. The borderline between public and private worlds is much clearer in Japan than it is in the West (as in China, many Japanese houses have walls around them). Thus, the public self is not seen as a humiliating infringement on the "real" self. Of course, in certain periods, Japanese artists have rebelled against this division and the rigidity of style by going to the opposite extreme: writers of the "natural" school saw it as their vocation to burden the reader with the minutest details of their private lives. One key, I think, to the public aesthetic is the skill of an elevator girl.

Yoko Sato is nineteen and she is being trained to be an elevator girl 3 in a department store. She lives at home with her parents but needs the extra money she earns to buy clothes and go to discos on Saturday nights. It's hard being an elevator girl for, as Yoko is ceaselessly told, she is the face of the store. If she does something wrong or displeases a customer, the company loses face.

Yoko does not much enjoy the lectures on company loyalty or 4 philosophy written in fussy Chinese characters by the owner of the store, who likes to expound at length on the uniqueness of his firm. Still, Yoko learned all the lines by heart and recites them every morning with her colleagues. It may be a lot of boring nonsense, but this is the way things are done, and Yoko wants to do a good job.

The voice and bowing lessons are a little more interesting. Yoko 5 always prides herself on being a good mimic—her imitations of the pompous section chief make her friends laugh. The perfect elevator girl's voice is high-pitched, on the verge of falsetto, and seeming to bubble over into merry laughter, without actually doing so. This is not an easy effect to achieve and it takes hours of drilling. Yoko's name was called out by the teacher, asking her to come forward. She was told to speak the following lines: this lift is going up, this lift is going down; and again: this lift is going up . . . and again. Her pitch was too low and her delivery not quite sprightly enough. The teacher told her to practice at home.

Bowing lessons are a more mechanical exercise. An inventive 6 young engineer in the design department devised a bowing machine. It is a steel contraption a bit like those metal detectors through which one must pass at international airports. An electronic eye, built into the machine, registers exactly the angle of the bow and lights flicker on at fifteen degrees, thirty degrees and forty-five degrees. The teacher of the bowing class explained that the "fifteen bow" was for an informal greeting to colleagues. The "thirty bow" was appropriate for meeting senior members of the store, and the deepest bow essential when welcoming clients, shoppers and other visitors. Much of the average day of an elevator girl is spent at a perfect forty-five degree angle.

Yoko does not find this in the least humiliating, or even dull. Learning a skill like this is a challenge, and she is eager to get it just right. The girls were lined up in front of the machine and one by one, like pupils at a gymnastics class, they walked up to make three bows. Yoko missed the first one by several degrees; the disapproving noise of an electronic buzzer told her so. She blushed. The second, thirty degrees, she got wrong again, by inches. Determined to get it right the next time, she bent down, back straight, fingers together and eyes trained to the floor about three feet from her toes—the light flashed, she did it, a smile of contentment spread across her face.   7

This is an extreme—though in Japan by no means despised— example of the insistence on form and of the way it is taught. The training of elevator girls also points to another constant factor in Japanese attitudes to work: form in human relations. The importance of etiquette and ritual in Japanese work is vital. When male bosses tell their female staff that serving tea, bowing to clients and other such ceremonial functions are as necessary as the jobs usually reserved for men, they are only being partly hypocritical. To be sure, many men would feel threatened if too many women encroached on their traditional domains. It is much safer to insist that women should stick to the home after marriage or, in the case of unmarried "office ladies" (OLs), stick to making tea or other ceremonies. But, at the same time, Japanese do attach far more importance to such decorative functions than Westerners tend to do; and they genuinely feel that women do them best. Although some Western tourists might find the artificial ways of elevator girls grating, humiliating or, at best, quaint, Japanese feel comfortable with them and indeed miss such service when it is not provided.   8

Men, too, spend much of their time on the rites of human relations. Although Japanese have a strong sense of hierarchy, decisions are based upon at least a show of consensus. This makes it difficult to take individual initiatives, and passing the buck is therefore a national sport. Consensus, as indeed all forms of Japanese business, is built on personal relations. These relations are based on mutual obligations: if I do this for you, you do that for me. Such favors are rarely expressed directly and relations take much time and effort to cement. This is where most salarymen—the middle-ranking samurai of today—come in. Because there are so many salarymen and so many relations to cement, many hours are spent in coffee shops during the day and bars and restaurants at night. This may seem inconsequential or even parasitic to the Western mind. It certainly does not make for efficiency. But just as the trade of   9 rugs in the Middle East cannot proceed without endless cups of tea, the coffee shop workers are the backbone of the Japanese miracle. Let us turn again to an example.

Every table at the Café L'Etoile, a coffee shop in the Ginza, was occupied. Through the thick screen of cigarette smoke one could just discern Kazuo Sasaki, a young employee of one of the largest advertising companies. He was exchanging *meishi* (name cards) with three men from a small public relations firm. All four of them studied the cards carefully, made polite hissing noises and sat down. Sasaki ordered his tenth cup of coffee and lit his thirteenth filter-tipped cigarette.   10

His order was taken by a uniformed young waiter who yelled out the command to another waiter, who shouted it to another link in the chain. The effect was highly theatrical—a spectacle of work, as it were. This particular gimmick was unique to L'Etoile and new waiters were drilled endlessly until they got it just right.   11

So much of Sasaki's day was spent meeting people in coffee shops that it was easier to reach him at Café L'Etoile than at his office. He has been working for his company for four years. His main job is to delegate commissions taken by his company to smaller companies, who then often delegate them to even smaller firms.   12

Business was not much discussed at Café L'Etoile. It would be indelicate to come directly to the point. Instead, Sasaki had become expert at discussing golf handicaps—the nearest he got to a golf course himself was one of those practicing ranges where one spent hours hitting balls into a giant net. He also had an endless supply of jokes about last night's hangover, or jocular comments on his client's sexual prowess. He always knew the latest baseball results and could talk for hours about television programs. On those rare occasions when an eccentric client insisted on talking about politics or books, Sasaki was at least a good listener. He has, in short, the social graces of a very superior barber.   13

In a country where so much depends on social graces, this is not to be despised. It is, I think rightly, argued that human relationships in Japan transcend abstract ideals of right and wrong. This is not true, for instance, in the Judeo-Christian tradition, where God is the final arbiter, in whose eyes we shall be judged. To commit perjury in a Japanese court, to protect one's boss, is the moral thing to do. Loyalty transcends a mere law.   14

Human relations based on hierarchy are a comfort to many, especially in a highly competitive world. In most Japanese companies seniority counts for more than competence and, ideally, one's job is forever assured. This works best for mediocrity—which, for face-saving reasons, is rarely exposed—and worst for talented mavericks.   15

Talent, being highly individualistic and thus socially troublesome, is not always highly regarded in Japan. Hard work and skill, especially in   16 the sense of dexterity (*kiyō*), are the two qualities Japanese pride themselves on as a people. The traditional Japanese stress on refining and miniaturizing everything—the Korean critic Yi O Ryong argues that this is the key to Japanese culture—may explain the modern success in transistor, microchip or camera making. But although manual dexterity, the appearance of consensus and the discipline—not to say docility—of the Japanese rank and file account for some of Japan's success story, no country can succeed without talented mavericks. Despite the Japanese saying that nails that stick out must be hammered in, there are those odd, talented exceptions, even in Japan, who refuse to be hammered in. Though sometimes respected, such people are rarely liked. The great Japanese filmmaker Akira Kurosawa, known in Japan as The Emperor, is a case in point. He is undoubtedly one of the greatest artists of the century, but Japanese critics have consistently tried to pull him off his pedestal, often in snide personal attacks. He has consistently refused to toe the social line; he has neither masters nor pupils; the ritual of human relations is less important to him than his talent. He is, in short, a loner, as is almost every truly gifted man or woman in this collectivist society.

But the creative force in Japan comes from these loners. They tend 17 to come to the fore mostly in periods of social instability. The immediate aftermath of World War II seems to have been especially congenial to nonconformist entrepreneurs. Akio Morita, founder of Sony, Konosuke Matsushita of Matsushita and Soichirō Honda, the grand old man behind the motor cars, immediately come to mind. The interesting thing about such creative oddballs is that once they make it to the top, they almost invariably become traditional masters, laying down the rules for the young to follow. They are more than teachers of technical skills or business methods, in the manner of such figures as Lee Iacocca. In fact, they conform more closely to the image of the classical Confucian sage, concerned with ethics and moral philosophy rather than technique. Matsushita wrote a kind of bible, expounding his philosophy; and Honda's autobiography has an equally lofty tone.

Recently the enormous success of high technology industries has 18 spurred a new generation of mavericks—whiz kids, laying the paths to Japanese versions of Silicon Valley. Such people are especially interesting as they combine the old Japanese penchant for miniature refinement and uncommon individualism. They often get their start in research and development departments of large companies, but proceed to break with the time-honored tradition of company loyalty to start their own firms. According to an official at the Ministry of International Trade and Industry there are now about five thousand "highly innovative" small companies with the potential to emerge as future Sonys or Hondas. No doubt their leaders, too, will one day write their books and become masters.

Although the difference between artist and craftsman has never 19 been as clear in Japan as in the post-romantic West, there have always been mavericks in the arts as well. But those who do not follow masters often pay a heavy price. The number of suicides among Japanese writers in this century cannot be a mere romantic aberration. Such artists, like the gung-ho entrepreneurs, also thrive in times of unrest. The turbulent early nineteenth century produced such highly eccentric playwrights as Tsuruya Namboku and artists such as Ekin, who rejected every traditional school and persisted in a highly individualistic style. Two famous eccentric geniuses of our own time are Kurosawa and the author Yukio Mishima (1925–1970), Japan's most celebrated twentieth-century novelist, who ended his life at forty-five in a dramatic suicide.

Creative loners are by no means limited to men. In some periods of   20
Japanese history women had more freedom to express themselves than men, paradoxically because they had less freedom to engage in other public pursuits. Perhaps the greatest period for Japanese literature was the Heian (794–1185), particularly the tenth century, when the *kana* syllabary, a truly indigenous script, was developed. While educated men—virtually restricted to the aristocracy—still wrote in literary Chinese, talented women expressed themselves in the vernacular; the obvious example being Murasaki Shikibu (978–1015/31?), the author of *Genji monogatari* (*The Tale of Genji*). One of the greatest writers of modern Japan was also a woman: Higuchi Ichiyō (1872–1896), who lived and died—very young—at the end of the nineteenth century. Both women wrote mostly about loneliness—a common theme in literature and a usual fate of writers anywhere, to be sure, but especially in Japan, where isolation from the common herd is particularly keenly felt.

So originality and creativity do exist in Japan. But they are all too often   21
stifled by the pressure to conform. It takes tremendous courage to continue on in one's individual course. Let us be thankful for those few who do. But while such gifted eccentrics are rarer than in countries where individualism is fostered, there is an advantage to the Japanese preference for skill over originality. In places where everyone wants to be a star, but mediocrity necessarily prevails, there is a disturbing lack of pride in an ordinary job well done. In Western Europe there is even a perverse tendency to be proud of sloppiness. Japan may have fewer Nobel Prize winners than, say, Britain, but to see a shop girl wrap a package or a factoryworker assemble a bike is to see routine work developed to a fine art. This, the lack of Nobel Prizes not withstanding, may be Japan's grandest tradition.

Exercises

Some Important Words

repetitive (paragraph 1), zeal (1), honing (1), preoccupation (1), elusive (1), ego (1), transcending (1), public domain (1), infringement (2), minutest (2), aesthetic (2), pompous (5), falsetto (5), sprightly (5), hypocritical (8), encroached (8), domains (8), quaint (8), hierarchy (9), consensus (9), initiatives (9), passing the buck (9), samurai (9), parasitic (9), indelicate (13), jocular (13), eccentric (13), Judeo-Christian tradition (14), arbiter (14), perjury (14), transcends (14), seniority (15), mediocrity (15), mavericks (15), dexterity (16), miniaturizing (16), docility (16), pedestal (16), collectivist society (16), social instability (17), entrepreneurs (17), Confucian sage (17), expounding (17), spawned (18), Silicon Valley (18), penchant (18), post-romantic West (19), aberration (19), gung-ho entrepreneurs (19), eccentric (19), paradoxically (20), syllabary (20), indigenous (20), fostered (21), perverse (21).

Some of the Issues

1. In paragraph 1 Buruma cites two character traits commonly attributed to the Japanese. What are they?
2. In what way does the traditional Japanese notion of a personal style differ from that in the West?
3. How do private and public selves differ from each other in Japan, according to the author?
4. What, according to Buruma, is the particular importance of being an elevator girl?
5. Describe the process of training an elevator girl. Why would Yoko find it challenging? How does the author relate the challenge to the importance of style in human relations in Japan?
6. The story about the salaryman Kazuo Sasaki also concerns personal style. What leads Buruma to say that Sasaki has "the social graces of a very superior barber"? Why are such social graces valuable in Japanese culture?
7. How does Buruma account for the rise of the great entrepreneurs? What is the general attitude toward them?
8. What according to Buruma are the results of the Japanese preference for skill over originality?
9. Why would loneliness be a persistent theme in Japanese literature?
10. In paragraph 21 Buruma cites the advantages of the Japanese outlook on work. What are they?
* 11. Read John David Morley's "Living in a Japanese Home." What do you learn about Japanese style there that relates to Buruma's views?

The Way We Are Told

12. How does the author try to show that Yoko's training is not viewed as humiliating or at least boring, but as challenging?
13. In the description of Kazuo Sasaki at the Café L'Etoile, how does Buruma demonstrate the importance of style over substance?

14. How does Buruma show the ambivalent attitude toward the person of talent, the loner? How does he distinguish him or her from the American type?

Some Subjects for Writing

15. If you have ever been trained for a job, describe the training. What would you say was its aim? How did it differ in its purpose from the training given to Yoko?

*16. Read John David Morley's "Living in a Japanese Home." In what respects, would you say, does the Japanese home reflect, as well as contribute, to the ambivalent attitude toward the person who stands out from the crowd?

SHAKESPEARE IN
THE BUSH

Laura Bohannan

Laura Bohannan, born in New York City in 1922, was a professor of anthropology at the University of Illinois in Chicago. She received her doctorate from Oxford University and later did field work with various peoples in Africa, including the Tiv, a tribe in central Nigeria, with whom this story is concerned. Under the pseudonym Elenore Smith Bowen, she has published a novel about anthropological field work, *Return to Laughter*.

The Tiv, who have a tradition of storytelling (accompanied by beer drinking) during the rainy season, asked their visitor to tell a story. She chose Shakespeare's *Hamlet,* believing that its universality would make it comprehensible, even in a culture very different from the one in which it was originally conceived. This assumption turned out to be quite wrong.

Just before I left Oxford for the Tiv in West Africa, conversation turned to   1
the season at Stratford. "You Americans," said a friend, "often have difficulty with Shakespeare. He was, after all, a very English poet, and one can easily misinterpret the universal by misunderstanding the particular."

I protested that human nature is pretty much the same the whole   2
world over; at least the general plot and motivation of the greater tragedies would always be clear—everywhere—although some details of custom might have to be explained and difficulties of translation might produce other slight changes. To end an argument we could not conclude, my friend gave me a copy of *Hamlet* to study in the African bush: it would, he hoped, lift my mind above its primitive surroundings, and possibly I might, by prolonged meditation, achieve the grace of correct interpretation.

It was my second field trip to that African tribe, and I thought   3
myself ready to live in one of its remote sections—an area difficult to cross even on foot. I eventually settled on the hillock of a very knowledgeable old man, the head of a homestead of some hundred and forty people, all of whom were either his close relatives or their wives

and children. Like the other elders of the vicinity, the old man spent most of his time performing ceremonies seldom seen these days in the more accessible parts of the tribe. I was delighted. Soon there would be three months of enforced isolation and leisure, between the harvest that takes place just before the rising of the swamps and the clearing of new farms when the water goes down. Then, I thought, they would have even more time to perform ceremonies and explain them to me.

I was quite mistaken. Most of the ceremonies demanded the   4 presence of elders from several homesteads. As the swamps rose, the old men found it too difficult to walk from one homestead to the next, and the ceremonies gradually ceased. As the swamps rose even higher, all activities but one came to an end. The women brewed beer from maize and millet. Men, women, and children sat on their hillocks and drank it.

People began to drink at dawn. By midmorning the whole home-   5 stead was singing, dancing, and drumming. When it rained, people had to sit inside their huts: there they drank and sang or they drank and told stories. In any case, by noon or before, I either had to join the party or retire to my own hut and my books. "One does not discuss serious matters when there is beer. Come, drink with us." Since I lacked their capacity for the thick native beer, I spent more and more time with *Hamlet*. Before the end of the second month, grace descended on me. I was quite sure that *Hamlet* had only one possible interpretation, and that one universally obvious.

Early every morning, in the hope of having some serious talk   6 before the beer party, I used to call on the old man at his reception hut—a circle of posts supporting a thatched roof above a low mud wall to keep out wind and rain. One day I crawled through the low doorway and found most of the men of the homestead sitting huddled in their ragged cloths on stools, low plank beds, and reclining chairs, warming themselves against the chill of the rain around a smoky fire. In the center were three pots of beer. The party had started.

The old man greeted me cordially. "Sit down and drink." I accepted   7 a large calabash full of beer, poured some into a small drinking gourd, and tossed it down. Then I poured some more into the same gourd for the man second in seniority to my host before I handed my calabash over to a young man for further distribution. Important people shouldn't ladle beer themselves.

"It is better like this," the old man said, looking at me approvingly   8 and plucking at the thatch that had caught in my hair. "You should sit and drink with us more often. Your servants tell me that when you are not with us, you sit inside your hut looking at a paper."

The old man was acquainted with four kinds of "papers": tax   9 receipts, bride price receipts, court fee receipts, and letters. The messenger who brought him letters from the chief used them mainly as a badge of office, for he always knew what was in them and told the old man. Personal letters for the few who had relatives in the government or mission stations were kept until someone went to a large market where there was a letter writer and reader. Since my arrival, letters were brought to me to be read. A few men also brought me bride price receipts, privately, with requests to change the figures to a higher sum. I found moral arguments were of no avail, since in-laws are fair game, and the technical hazards of forgery difficult to explain to an illiterate people. I did not wish them to think me silly enough to look at any such paper for days on end, and I hastily explained that my "paper" was one of the "things of long ago" of my country.

"Ah," said the old man. "Tell us."   10

I protested that I was not a storyteller. Storytelling is a skilled art   11 among them; their standards are high, and the audiences critical—and vocal in their criticism. I protested in vain. This morning they wanted to hear a story while they drank. They threatened to tell me no more stories until I told them one of mine. Finally, the old man promised that no one would criticize my style "for we know you are struggling with our language." "But," put in one of the elders, "you must explain what we do not understand, as we do when we tell you our stories." Realizing that here was my chance to prove *Hamlet* universally intelligible, I agreed.

The old man handed me some more beer to help me on with my   12 storytelling. Men filled their long wooden pipes and knocked coals from the fire to place in the pipe bowls; then, puffing contentedly, they sat back to listen. I began in the proper style.

"Not yesterday, not yesterday, but long ago, a thing occurred. One   13 night three men were keeping watch outside the homestead of the great chief, when suddenly they saw the former chief approach them."

"Why was he no longer the chief?"   14

"He was dead," I explained. "That is why they were troubled and   15 afraid when they saw him."

"Impossible," began one of the elders, handing his pipe on to his   16 neighbor, who interrupted, "Of course it wasn't the dead chief. It was an omen sent by a witch. Go on."

Slightly shaken, I continued. "One of these three was a man who   17 knew things"—the closest translation for scholar, but unfortunately it also meant witch. The second elder looked triumphantly at the first. "So he spoke to the dead chief saying, 'Tell us what we must do so you may rest in your grave,' but the dead chief did not answer. He vanished, and they could see him no more. Then the man who knew things—his name was Horatio—said this event was the affair of the dead chief's son, Hamlet."

There was a general shaking of heads round the circle. "Had the dead   18 chief no living brothers? Or was this son the chief?"

"No," I replied. "That is, he had one living brother who became the   19
chief when the elder brother died."

The old men muttered: such omens were matters for chiefs and   20
elders, not for youngsters; no good could come of going behind a chief's
back; clearly Horatio was not a man who knew things.

"Yes, he was," I insisted, shooing a chicken away from my beer. "In   21
our country the son is next to the father. The dead chief's younger
brother had become the great chief. He had also married his elder
brother's widow only about a month after the funeral."

"He did well," the old man beamed and announced to the others,   22
"I told you that if we knew more about Europeans, we would find they
really were very like us. In our country also," he added to me, "the
younger brother marries the elder brother's widow and becomes the
father of his children. Now, if your uncle, who married your widowed
mother, is your father's full brother, then he will be a real father to you.
Did Hamlet's father and uncle have one mother?"

His question barely penetrated my mind; I was too upset and   23
thrown too far off balance by having one of the most important elements
of *Hamlet* knocked straight out of the picture. Rather uncertainly I said
that I thought they had the same mother, but I wasn't sure—the story
didn't say. The old man told me severely that these genealogical details
made all the difference and that when I got home I must ask the elders
about it. He shouted out the door to one of his younger wives to bring his
goatskin bag.

Determined to save what I could of the mother motif, I took a deep   24
breath and began again. "The son Hamlet was very sad because his
mother had married again so quickly. There was no need for her to do so,
and it is our custom for a widow not to go to her next husband until she
has mourned for two years."

"Two years is too long," objected the wife, who had appeared with   25
the old man's battered goatskin bag. "Who will hoe your farms for you
while you have no husband?"

"Hamlet," I retorted without thinking, "was old enough to hoe his   26
mother's farms himself. There was no need for her to remarry." No one
looked convinced. I gave up. "His mother and the great chief told Hamlet
not to be sad, for the great chief himself would be a father to Hamlet.
Furthermore, Hamlet would be the next chief: therefore he must stay to
learn the things of a chief. Hamlet agreed to remain, and all the rest went
off to drink beer."

While I paused, perplexed at how to render Hamlet's disgusted   27
soliloquy to an audience convinced that Claudius and Gertrude had
behaved in the best possible manner, one of the younger men asked me
who had married the other wives of the dead chief.

"He had no other wives," I told him.   28

"But a chief must have many wives! How else can he brew beer and   29
prepare food for all his guests?"

I said firmly that in our country even chiefs had only one wife, that   30
they had servants to do their work, and that they paid them from tax
money.

It was better, they returned, for a chief to have many wives and   31
sons who would help him hoe his farms and feed his people; then
everyone loved the chief who gave much and took nothing—taxes were
a bad thing.

I agreed with the last comment, but for the rest fell back on their   32
favorite way of fobbing off my questions: "That is the way it is done, so
that is how we do it."

I decided to skip the soliloquy. Even if Claudius was here thought   33
quite right to marry his brother's widow, there remained the poison
motif, and I knew they would disapprove of fratricide. More hopefully I
resumed, "That night Hamlet kept watch with the three who had seen his
dead father. The dead chief again appeared, and although the others
were afraid, Hamlet followed his dead father off to one side. When they
were alone, Hamlet's dead father spoke."

"Omens can't talk!" The old man was emphatic.   34

"Hamlet's dead father wasn't an omen. Seeing him might have been   35
an omen, but he was not." My audience looked as confused as I sounded.
"It *was* Hamlet's dead father. It was a thing we call a 'ghost.' " I had to use
the English word, for unlike many of the neighboring tribes, these
people didn't believe in the survival after death of any individuating part
of the personality.

"What is a 'ghost'? An omen?"   36

"No, a 'ghost' is someone who is dead but who walks around and   37
can talk, and people can hear him and see him but not touch him."

They objected. "One can touch zombis."   38

"No, no! It was not a dead body the witches had animated to   39
sacrifice and eat. No one else made Hamlet's dead father walk. He did it
himself."

"Dead men can't walk," protested my audience as one man.   40

I was quite willing to compromise. "A 'ghost' is the dead man's   41
shadow."

But again they objected. "Dead men cast no shadows."   42

"They do in my country," I snapped.   43

The old man quelled the babble of disbelief that arose immediately   44
and told me with that insincere, but courteous, agreement one extends to
the fancies of the young, ignorant, and superstitious, "No doubt in your
country the dead can also walk without being zombis." From the depths
of his bag he produced a withered fragment of kola nut, bit off one end
to show it wasn't poisoned, and handed me the rest as a peace offering.

"Anyhow," I resumed, "Hamlet's dead father said that his own   45
brother, the one who became chief, had poisoned him. He wanted
Hamlet to avenge him. Hamlet believed this in his heart, for he did not
like his father's brother." I took another swallow of beer. "In the country
of the great chief, living in the same homestead, for it was a very large
one, was an important elder who was often with the chief to advise and
help him. His name was Polonius. Hamlet was courting his daughter, but
her father and her brother . . . [I cast hastily about for some tribal analogy]
warned her not to let Hamlet visit her when she was alone on her farm,
for he would be a great chief and so could not marry her."

"Why not?" asked the wife, who had settled down on the edge of   46
the old man's chair. He frowned at her for asking stupid questions and
growled, "They live in the same homestead."

"That was not the reason," I informed them. "Polonius was a   47
stranger who lived in the homestead because he helped the chief, not
because he was a relative."

"Then why couldn't Hamlet marry her?"   48

"He could have," I explained, "But Polonius didn't think he would.   49
After all, Hamlet was a man of great importance who ought to marry a
chief's daughter, for in his country a man could have only one wife.
Polonius was afraid that if Hamlet made love to his daughter, then no one
else would give a high price for her."

"That might be true," remarked one of the shrewder elders, "but a   50
chief's son would give his mistress's father enough presents and patron-
age to more than make up the difference. Polonius sounds like a fool to
me."

"Many people think he was," I agreed. "Meanwhile Polonius sent   51
his son Laertes off to Paris to learn the things of that country, for it was
the homestead of a very great chief indeed. Because he was afraid that
Laertes might waste a lot of money on beer and women and gambling, or
get into trouble by fighting, he sent one of his servants to Paris secretly, to
spy out what Laertes was doing. One day Hamlet came upon Polonius's
daughter Ophelia. He behaved so oddly he frightened her. Indeed"—I
was fumbling for words to express the dubious quality of Hamlet's
madness—"the chief and many others had also noticed that when
Hamlet talked one could understand the words but not what they meant.
Many people thought that he had become mad." My audience suddenly
became much more attentive. "The great chief wanted to know what was
wrong with Hamlet, so he sent for two of Hamlet's age mates [school
friends would have taken long explanation] to talk to Hamlet and find out
what troubled his heart. Hamlet, seeing that they had been bribed by the
chief to betray him, told them nothing. Polonius, however, insisted that
Hamlet was mad because he had been forbidden to see Ophelia, whom
he loved."

"Why," inquired a bewildered voice, "should anyone bewitch   52
Hamlet on that account?"

"Bewitch him?"   53

"Yes, only witchcraft can make anyone mad, unless, of course, one   54
sees the beings that lurk in the forest."

I stopped being a storyteller, took out my notebook and demanded   55
to be told more about these two causes of madness. Even while they
spoke and I jotted notes, I tried to calculate the effect of this new factor
on the plot. Hamlet had not been exposed to the beings that lurk in the
forests. Only his relatives in the male line could bewitch him. Barring
relatives not mentioned by Shakespeare, it had to be Claudius who was
attempting to harm him. And, of course, it was.

For the moment I staved off questions by saying that the great chief   56
also refused to believe that Hamlet was mad for the love of Ophelia and
nothing else. "He was sure that something much more important was
troubling Hamlet's heart."

"Now Hamlet's age mates," I continued, "had brought with them a   57
famous storyteller. Hamlet decided to have this man tell the chief and all
his homestead a story about a man who had poisoned his brother
because he desired his brother's wife and wished to be chief himself.
Hamlet was sure the great chief could not hear the story without making
a sign if he was indeed guilty, and then he would discover whether his
dead father had told him the truth."

The old man interrupted, with deep cunning, "Why should a father   58
lie to his son?" he asked.

I hedged: "Hamlet wasn't sure that it really was his dead father." It was   59
impossible to say anything, in that language, about devil-inspired visions.

"You mean," he said, "it actually was an omen, and he knew   60
witches sometimes send false ones. Hamlet was a fool not to go to one
skilled in reading omens and divining the truth in the first place. A
man-who-sees-the-truth could have told him how his father died, if he
really had been poisoned, and if there was witchcraft in it; then Hamlet
could have called the elders to settle the matter."

The shrewd elder ventured to disagree. "Because his father's   61
brother was a great chief, one-who-sees-the-truth might therefore have
been afraid to tell it. I think it was for that reason that a friend of Hamlet's
father—a witch and an elder—sent an omen so his friend's son would
know. Was the omen true?"

"Yes," I said, abandoning ghosts and the devil; a witch-sent omen it   62
would have to be. "It was true, for when the storyteller was telling his
tale before all the homestead, the great chief rose in fear. Afraid that
Hamlet knew his secret he planned to have him killed."

The stage set of the next bit presented some difficulties of transla-   63
tion. I began cautiously. "The great chief told Hamlet's mother to find out

from her son what he knew. But because a woman's children are always first in her heart, he had the important elder Polonius hide behind a cloth that hung against the wall of Hamlet's mother's sleeping hut. Hamlet started to scold his mother for what she had done."

There was a shocked murmur from everyone. A man should never   64
scold his mother.

"She called out in fear, and Polonius moved behind the cloth.   65
Shouting, 'A rat!' Hamlet took his machete and slashed through the cloth." I paused for dramatic effect. "He had killed Polonius!"

The old men looked at each other in supreme disgust. "That   66
Polonius truly was a fool and a man who knew nothing! What child would not know enough to shout, 'It's me!' " With a pang, I remembered that these people are ardent hunters, always armed with bow, arrow, and machete; at the first rustle in the grass an arrow is aimed and ready, and the hunter shouts "Game!" If no human voice answers immediately, the arrow speeds on its way. Like a good hunter Hamlet had shouted, "A rat!"

I rushed in to save Polonius's reputation. "Polonius did speak.   67
Hamlet heard him. But he thought it was the chief and wished to kill him to avenge his father. He had meant to kill him earlier that evening. . . ." I broke down, unable to describe to these pagans, who had no belief in individual afterlife, the difference between dying at one's prayers and dying "unhousell'd, disappointed, unaneled."

This time I had shocked my audience seriously. "For a man to raise   68
his hand against his father's brother and the one who had become his father—that is a terrible thing. The elders ought to let such a man be bewitched."

I nibbled at my kola nut in some perplexity, then pointed out that   69
after all the man had killed Hamlet's father.

"No," pronounced the old man, speaking less to me than to the   70
young men sitting behind the elders. "If your father's brother has killed your father, you must appeal to your father's age mates; *they* may avenge him. No man may use violence against his senior relatives." Another thought struck him. "But if his father's brother had indeed been wicked enough to bewitch Hamlet and make him mad that would be a good story indeed, for it would be his fault that Hamlet, being mad, no longer had any sense and thus was ready to kill his father's brother."

There was a murmur of applause. *Hamlet* was again a good story to   71
them, but it no longer seemed quite the same story to me. As I thought over the coming complications of plot and motive, I lost courage and decided to skim over dangerous ground quickly.

"The great chief," I went on, "was not sorry that Hamlet had killed   72
Polonius. It gave him a reason to send Hamlet away, with his two treacherous age mates, with letters to a chief of a far country, saying that

Hamlet should be killed. But Hamlet changed the writing on their papers, so that the chief killed his age mates instead." I encountered a reproachful glare from one of the men whom I had told undetectable forgery was not merely immoral but beyond human skill. I looked the other way.

"Before Hamlet could return, Laertes came back for his father's 73 funeral. The great chief told him Hamlet had killed Polonius. Laertes swore to kill Hamlet because of this, and because his sister Ophelia, hearing her father had been killed by the man she loved, went mad and drowned in the river."

"Have you already forgotten what we told you?" The old man was 74 reproachful. "One cannot take vengeance on a madman; Hamlet killed Polonius in his madness. As for the girl, she not only went mad, she was drowned. Only witches can make people drown. Water itself can't hurt anything. It is merely something one drinks and bathes in."

I began to get cross. "If you don't like the story, I'll stop." 75

The old man made soothing noises and himself poured me some 76 more beer. "You tell the story well, and we are listening. But it is clear that the elders of your country have never told you what the story really means. No, don't interrupt! We believe you when you say your marriage customs are different, or your clothes and weapons. But people are the same everywhere; therefore, there are always witches and it is we, the elders, who know how witches work. We told you it was the great chief who wished to kill Hamlet, and now your own words have proved us right. Who were Ophelia's male relatives?"

"There were only her father and her brother." Hamlet was clearly 77 out of my hands.

"There must have been many more; this also you must ask of your 78 elders when you get back to your country. From what you tell us, since Polonius was dead, it must have been Laertes who killed Ophelia, although I do not see the reason for it."

We had emptied one pot of beer, and the old men argued the point 79 with slightly tipsy interest. Finally one of them demanded of me, "What did the servant of Polonius say on his return?"

With difficulty I recollected Reynaldo and his mission. "I don't think 80 he did return before Polonius was killed."

"Listen," said the elder, "and I will tell you how it was and how your 81 story will go, then you may tell me if I am right. Polonius knew his son would get into trouble, and so he did. He had many fines to pay for fighting, and debts from gambling. But he had only two ways of getting money quickly. One was to marry off his sister at once, but it is difficult to find a man who will marry a woman desired by the son of a chief. For if the chief's heir commits adultery with your wife, what can you do? Only a fool calls a case against a man who will someday be his judge. Therefore Laertes had to take the second way: he killed his sister by witchcraft, drowning her so he could secretly sell her body to the witches."

I raised an objection. "They found her body and buried it. Indeed   82 Laertes jumped into the grave to see his sister once more—so, you see, the body was truly there. Hamlet, who had just come back, jumped in after him."

"What did I tell you?" The elder appealed to the others. "Laertes   83 was up to no good with his sister's body. Hamlet prevented him, because the chief's heir, like a chief, does not wish any other man to grow rich and powerful. Laertes would be angry, because he would have killed his sister without benefit to himself. In our country he would try to kill Hamlet for that reason. Is this not what happened?"

"More or less," I admitted. "When the great chief found Hamlet was   84 still alive, he encouraged Laertes to try to kill Hamlet and arranged a fight with machetes between them. In the fight both the young men were wounded to death. Hamlet's mother drank the poisoned beer that the chief meant for Hamlet in case he won the fight. When he saw his mother die of poison, Hamlet, dying, managed to kill his father's brother with his machete."

"You see, I was right!" exclaimed the elder.   85

"That was a very good story," added the old man, "and you told it   86 with very few mistakes. There was just one more error, at the very end. The poison Hamlet's mother drank was obviously meant for the survivor of the fight, whichever it was. If Laertes had won, the great chief would have poisoned him, for no one would know that he arranged Hamlet's death. Then, too, he need not fear Laertes' witchcraft; it takes a strong heart to kill one's only sister by witchcraft.

"Sometime," concluded the old man, gathering his ragged toga about   87 him, "you must tell us some more stories of your country. We, who are elders, will instruct you in their true meaning, so that when you return to your own land your elders will see that you have not been sitting in the bush, but among those who know things and who have taught you wisdom."

Exercises

Some Important Words

meditation (paragraph 2), homesteads (4), calabash (7), gourd (7), bride price (9), no avail (9), intelligible (11), omen (16), genealogical (23), motif (24), retorted (26), soliloquy (27), fobbing off (32), fratricide (33), quelled (44), babble (44), dubious (51), cunning (58), hedged (59), unhousell'd (67), unaneled (67), toga (87).

Some of the Issues

1. In paragraphs 1 and 2 Bohannan and a friend discuss human nature in relation to Shakespeare's *Hamlet*. What are their opinions?
2. Read paragraphs 3-6. What were Bohannan's expectations for her second field trip to the Tiv, and why were they mistaken? How do her plans change?
3. What is the significance of the discussion about "papers" in paragraphs 8 and 9? How does it foretell that the Tiv's interpretation of *Hamlet* may differ from Bohannan's (and ours)?
4. In a number of instances, Bohannan shows that she is knowledgeable about the social customs of the Tiv and is trying to conform to them. Give some specific instances.
5. In paragraphs 24-32 two differences between the Tiv and the West are made clear: they relate to the period of mourning for the dead and to the number of wives a chief may have. In what way does the Tiv's view on these matters differ from Western views? Does their view have any advantages for their culture?
6. The Tiv elders are shocked—morally upset—at several parts of the story of *Hamlet*. What specific instances can you cite? Do their moral perceptions differ from ours in those instances?
7. Bohannan makes several efforts to make *Hamlet* more intelligible or acceptable to the Tiv. What are some of these? Does she succeed?
8. Both Bohannan (paragraph 2) and the chief (paragraph 76) say that human nature is much the same everywhere. What evidence do you find in the essay to support or contradict these assertions?

The Way We Are Told

9. Why does Bohannan begin her essay with the conversation with a friend at Oxford?
10. Several times in her essay Bohannan expresses surprise at the Tiv's reaction to her story. Is it possible that she was in reality not as surprised as she indicates?

Some Subjects for Writing

11. Bohannan does her best to adapt the story of Hamlet to the experiences, customs, and feelings of the Tiv. Have you ever had the experience of having to adapt yourself in some way to a situation in which the rules and assumptions differed greatly from your own? Tell the story.
12. Practice writing short, accurate summaries of stories, plays, movies, or television shows you know.

13. Describe a particular American event or activity to someone who has never experienced it. Topics might be Thanksgiving, a rock concert, a commencement exercise.

*14. Read "A Modest Proposal" by Jonathan Swift. In an essay demonstrate that both Bohannan and Swift adopt poses in order to make their arguments effectively.

LIFE ON THE GLOBAL ASSEMBLY LINE

Barbara Ehrenreich and Annette Fuentes

Barbara Ehrenreich, born in 1941, is a journalist writing for *The New York Times,* among other publications. She is the coauthor of *For Her Own Good: 150 Years of the Experts' Advice to Women* (1979), *The American Health Empire* (1970), and *Witches, Midwives and Nurses: A History of Women Healers* (1972), and the author of *Re-Making Love: The Feminization of Sex* (1986), *Fear of Falling* (1989), and *The Worst Years of Our Lives* (1991). Annette Fuentes, also a journalist, is the coauthor, with Barbara Ehrenreich, of *Women in the Global Factory* (1983).

This selection, which first appeared in *Ms.* magazine in January 1981, traces the consequences of large corporations shifting their production to Third World countries to take advantage of cheaper labor. Many of their new employees are women, lured by a promise of higher salaries and relative independence. The reality of these jobs for most Third World women is different from the promise. They perform tedious, often health-destroying tasks, at wages too low to accumulate savings. If the company moves, or a woman has exhausted her health, she is unlikely to find another job and is often unable to reintegrate herself into the traditional society she had left.

In Ciudad Juárez, Mexico, Anna M. rises at 5 A.M. to feed her son before 1
starting on the two-hour bus trip to the maquiladora (factory). He will spend the day along with four other children in a neighbor's one-room home. Anna's husband, frustrated by being unable to find work for himself, left for the United States six months ago. She wonders, as she carefully applies her new lip gloss, whether she ought to consider herself still married. It might be good to take a night course, become a secretary. But she seldom gets home before eight at night, and the factory, where she stitches brassieres that will be sold in the United States through J.C. Penney, pays only $48 a week.

346

In Penang, Malaysia, Julie K. is up before the three other young   2
women with whom she shares a room, and starts heating the leftover rice
from last night's supper. She looks good in the company's green-trimmed
uniform, and she's proud to work in a modern, American-owned factory.
Only not quite so proud as when she started working three years ago—she
thinks as she squints out the door at a passing group of women. Her job
involves peering all day through a microscope, bonding hair-thin gold
wires to a silicon chip destined to end up inside a pocket calculator, and
at 21, she is afraid she can no longer see very clearly.

Every morning, between four and seven, thousands of women like Anna   3
and Julie head out for the day shift. In Ciudad Juárez, they crowd into
ruteras (run-down vans) for the trip from the slum neighborhoods to the
industrial parks on the outskirts of the city. In Penang they squeeze, 60 or
more at a time, into buses for the trip from the village to the low, modern
factory buildings of the Bayan Lepas free trade zone. In Taiwan, they
walk from the dormitories—where the night shift is already asleep in the
still-warm beds—through the checkpoints in the high fence surrounding
the factory zone.

This is the world's new industrial proletariat: young, female, Third   4
World. Viewed from the "first world," they are still faceless, genderless
"cheap labor," signaling their existence only through a label or tiny
imprint—"made in Hong Kong," or Taiwan, Korea, the Dominican
Republic, Mexico, the Philippines. But they may be one of the most
strategic blocs of womanpower in the world of the 1980s. Conservatively,
there are 2 million Third World female industrial workers employed now,
millions more looking for work, and their numbers are rising every year.
Anyone whose image of Third World women features picturesque
peasants with babies slung on their backs should be prepared to update
it. Just in the last decade, Third World women have become a critical
element in the global economy and a key "resource" for expanding
multinational corporations.

It doesn't take more than second-grade arithmetic to understand   5
what's happening. In the United States, an assembly-line worker is likely
to earn, depending on her length of employment, between $3.10 and $5
an hour. In many Third World countries, a woman doing the same work
will earn $3 to $5 a *day*. According to the magazine *Business Asia,* in
1976 the average hourly wage for unskilled work (male or female) was
55 cents in Hong Kong, 52 cents in South Korea, 32 cents in the
Philippines, and 17 cents in Indonesia. The logic of the situation is
compelling: why pay someone in Massachusetts $5 an hour to do what
someone in Manila will do for $2.50 a day? Or, as a corollary, why pay a
male worker anywhere to do what a female worker will do for 40 to 60
percent less?

And so, almost everything that can be packed up is being moved   6
out to the Third World; not heavy industry, but just about anything light
enough to travel—garment manufacture, textiles, toys, footwear, pharmaceuticals, wigs, appliance parts, tape decks, computer components,
plastic goods. In some industries, like garment and textile, American jobs
are lost in the process, and the biggest losers are women, often black and
Hispanic. But what's going on is much more than a matter of runaway
shops. Economists are talking about a "new international division of
labor," in which the process of production is broken down and the
fragments are dispersed to different parts of the world. In general, the
low-skilled jobs are farmed out to the Third World, where labor costs are
minuscule, while control over the overall process and technology remains safely at company headquarters in "first world" countries like the
United States and Japan.

The American electronics industry provides a classic example: 7
circuits are printed on silicon wafers and tested in California; then the
wafers are shipped to Asia for the labor-intensive process by which they
are cut into tiny chips and bonded to circuit boards; final assembly into
products such as calculators or military equipment usually takes place in
the United States. Garment manufacture too is often broken into geographically separated steps, with the most repetitive, labor-intensive jobs
going to the poor countries of the southern hemisphere. Most Third
World countries welcome whatever jobs come their way in the new
division of labor, and the major international development agencies—like
the World Bank and the United States Agency for International Development (AID)—encourage them to take what they can get.

So much any economist could tell you. What is less often noted is   8
the *gender* breakdown of the emerging international division of labor.
Eighty to 90 percent of the low-skilled assembly jobs that go to the
Third World are performed by women—in a remarkable switch from
earlier patterns of foreign-dominated industrialization. Until now,
"development" under the aegis of foreign corporations has usually
meant more jobs for men and—compared to traditional agricultural
society—a diminished economic status for women. But multinational
corporations and Third World governments alike consider assembly-
line work—whether the product is Barbie dolls or missile parts—to be
"women's work."

One reason is that women can, in many countries, still be legally   9
paid less than men. But the sheer tedium of the jobs adds to the
multinationals' preference for women workers—a preference made clear,
for example, by this ad from a Mexican newspaper: *We need female
workers; older than 17, younger than 30; single and without children:
minimum education primary school, maximum education one year of
preparatory school (high school): available for all shifts.*

It's an article of faith with management that only women can do, or   10
will do, the monotonous, painstaking work that American business is
exporting to the Third World. Bill Mitchell, whose job is to attract United
States businesses to the Bermudez Industrial Park in Ciudad Juárez told
us with a certain macho pride: "A man just won't stay in this tedious kind
of work. He'd walk out in a couple of hours." The personnel manager of
a light assembly plant in Taiwan told anthropologist Linda Gail Arrigo:
"Young male workers are too restless and impatient to do monotonous
work with no career value. If displeased, they sabotage the machines and
even threaten the foreman. But girls? At most, they cry a little."

In fact, the American businessmen we talked to claimed that Third   11
World women genuinely enjoy doing the very things that would drive a
man to assault and sabotage. "You should watch these kids going into
work," Bill Mitchell told us. "You don't have any sullenness here. They
smile." A top-level management consultant who specializes in advising
American companies on where to relocate their factories gave us this
global generalization: "The [factory] girls genuinely enjoy themselves.
They're away from their families. They have spending money. They can
buy motorbikes, whatever. Of course it's a regulated experience too—
with dormitories to live in—so its a healthful experience."

What is the real experience of the women in the emerging Third   12
World industrial work force? The conventional Western stereotypes leap
to mind: You can't really compare, the standards are so different. . . .
Everything's easier in warm countries. . . . They really don't have any
alternatives. . . . Commenting on the low wages his company pays its
women workers in Singapore, a Hewlett-Packard vice-president said,
"They live much differently here than we do. . . ." But the differences are
ultimately very simple. To start with, they have less money.

The great majority of the women in the new Third World work   13
force live at or near the subsistence level for one person, whether they
work for a multinational corporation or a locally owned factory. In the
Philippines, for example, starting wages in U.S.-owned electronics plants
are between $34 to $46 a month, compared to a cost of living of $37 a
month; in Indonesia the starting wages are actually about $7 a month less
than the cost of living. "Living," in these cases, should be interpreted
minimally: a diet of rice, dried fish, and water—a Coke might cost a
half-day's wages—lodging in a room occupied by four or more other
people. Rachael Grossman, a researcher with the Southeast Asia Resource Center, found women employees of U.S. multinational firms in
Malaysia and the Philippines living four to eight in a room in boarding-
houses, or squeezing into tiny extensions built onto squatter huts near
the factory. Where companies do provide dormitories for their employees, they are not of the "healthful," collegiate variety implied by our
corporate informant. Staff from the American Friends Service Committee

report that dormitory space is "likely to be crowded, with bed rotation paralleling shift rotation—while one shift works, another sleeps, as many as twenty to a room." In one case in Thailand, they found the dormitory "filthy," with workers forced to find their own place to sleep among "splintered floorboards, rusting sheets of metal, and scraps of dirty cloth."

Wages do increase with seniority, but the money does not go to pay   14
for studio apartments or, very likely, motorbikes. A 1970 study of young women factory workers in Hong Kong found that 88 percent of them were turning more than half their earnings over to their parents. In areas that are still largely agricultural (such as parts of the Philippines and Malaysia), or places where male unemployment runs high (such as northern Mexico), a woman factory worker may be the sole source of cash income for an entire extended family.

But wages on a par with what an 11-year-old American could earn on   15
a paper route, and living conditions resembling what Engels found in 19th-century Manchester are only part of the story. The rest begins at the factory gate. The work that multinational corporations export to the Third World is not only the most tedious, but often the most hazardous part of the production process. The countries they go to are, for the most part, those that will guarantee no interference from health and safety inspectors, trade unions, or even free-lance reformers. As a result, most Third World factory women work under conditions that already have broken or will break their health—or their nerves—within a few years, and often before they've worked long enough to earn any more than a subsistence wage.

Consider first the electronics industry, which is generally thought to   16
be the safest and cleanest of the exported industries. The factory buildings are low and modern, like those one might find in a suburban American industrial park. Inside, rows of young women, neatly dressed in the company uniform or T-shirt, work quietly at their stations. There is air conditioning (not for the women's comfort, but to protect the delicate semiconductor parts they work with), and high-volume piped-in Bee Gees hits (not so much for entertainment, as to prevent talking).

For many Third World women, electronics is a prestige occupation,   17
at least compared to other kinds of factory work. They are unlikely to know that in the United States the National Institute on Occupational Safety and Health (NIOSH) has placed electronics on its select list of "high health-risk industries using the greatest number of toxic substances." If electronics assembly work is risky here, it is doubly so in countries where there is no equivalent of NIOSH to even issue warnings. In many plants toxic chemicals and solvents sit in open containers, filling the work area with fumes that can literally knock you out. "We have been told of cases where ten to twelve women passed out at once," an AFSC field worker in northern Mexico told us, "and the newspapers report this as 'mass hysteria.'"

In one stage of the electronics assembly process, the workers have   18
to dip the circuits into open vats of acid. According to Irene Johnson and
Carol Bragg, who toured the National Semiconductor plant in Penang,
Malaysia, the women who do the dipping "wear rubber gloves and
boots, but these sometimes leak, and burns are common." Occasionally,
whole fingers are lost. Most commonly, what electronics workers lose is
the 20/20 vision they are required to have when they are hired. Most
electronics workers spend seven to nine hours a day peering through
microscopes, straining to meet their quotas.

One study in South Korea found that most electronics assembly   19
workers developed severe eye problems after only one year of
employment; 88 percent had chronic conjunctivitis; 44 percent became
nearsighted, and 19 percent developed astigmatism. A manager for
Hewlett-Packard's Malaysia plant, in an interview with Rachael
Grossman, denied that there were any eye problems. "These girls are
used to working with scopes. We've found no eye problems. But it sure
makes me dizzy to look through those things."

Electronics, recall, is the "cleanest" of the exported industries.   20
Conditions in the garment and textile industry rival those of any
19th-century (or 20th—see below) sweatshop. The firms, generally local
subcontractors to large American chains such as J.C. Penney and Sears, as
well as smaller manufacturers, are usually even more indifferent to the
health of their employees than the multinationals. Some of the worst
conditions have been documented in South Korea, where the garment
and textile industries have helped spark that country's "economic miracle." Workers are packed into poorly lit rooms, where summer temperatures rise above 100 degrees. Textile dust, which can cause permanent
lung damage, fills the air. When there are rush orders, management may
require forced overtime of as much as 48 hours at a stretch, and if that
seems to go beyond the limits of human endurance, pep pills and
amphetamine injections are thoughtfully provided. In her diary (originally published in a magazine now banned by the South Korean government) Min Chong Suk, 30, a sewing-machine operator, wrote of working
from 7 A.M. to 11:30 P.M. in a garment factory. "When [the apprentices]
shake the waste threads from the clothes, the whole room fills with dust,
and it is hard to breathe. Since we've been working in such dusty air,
there have been increasing numbers of people getting tuberculosis,
bronchitis, and eye diseases. Since we are women, it makes us so sad
when we have pale, unhealthy, wrinkled faces like dried-up spinach. . . .
It seems to me that no one knows our blood dissolves into the threads
and seams, with sighs and sorrow."

In all the exported industries, the most invidious, inescapable   21
health hazard is stress. On their home ground United States corporations
are not likely to sacrifice productivity for human comfort. On someone

else's home ground, however, anything goes. Lunch breaks may be barely long enough for a woman to stand in line at the canteen or hawkers' stalls. Visits to the bathroom are treated as privilege; in some cases, workers must raise their hands for permission to use the toilet, and waits up to a half hour are common. Rotating shifts—the day shift one week, the night shift the next—wreak havoc with sleep patterns. Because inaccuracies or failure to meet production quotas can mean substantial pay losses, the pressures are quickly internalized; stomach ailments and nervous problems are not unusual in the multinationals' Third World female work force. In some situations, good work is as likely to be punished as slow or shoddy work. Correspondent Michael Flannery, writing for the AFL-CIO's *American Federationist,* tells the story of 23-year-old Basilia Altagracia, a seamstress who stitched collars onto ladies' blouses in the La Romana (Dominican Republic) free trade zone (a heavily guarded industrial zone owned by Gulf & Western Industries, Inc.):

"A nimble veteran seamstress, Miss Altagracia eventually began to earn as much as $5.75 a day. . . . 'I was exceeding my piecework quota by a lot. . . .' But then, Altagracia said, her plant supervisor, a Cuban emigré, called her into his office. 'He said I was doing a fine job, but that I and some other of the women were making too much money, and he was being forced to lower what we earned for each piece we sewed.' On the best days, she now can clear barely $3, she said. 'I was earning less, so I started working six and seven days a week. But I was tired and I could not work as fast as before.' " Within a few months, she was too ill to work at all.   22

As if poor health and the stress of factory life weren't enough to drive women into early retirement, management actually encourages a high turnover in many industries. "As you know, when seniority rises, wages rise," the management consultant to U.S. multinationals told us. He explained that it's cheaper to train a fresh supply of teenagers than to pay experienced women higher wages. "Older women, aged 23 or 24, are likely to be laid off and not rehired.   23

We estimate, based on fragmentary data from several sources, that the multinational corporations may already have used up (cast off) as many as 6 million Third World workers—women who are too ill, too old (30 is over the hill in most industries), or too exhausted to be useful any more. Few "retire" with any transferable skills or savings. The lucky ones find husbands.   24

The unlucky ones find themselves at the margins of society—as bar girls, "hostesses," or prostitutes.   25

At 21, Julie's greatest fear is that she will never be able to find a husband. She knows that just being a "factory girl" is enough to give anyone   26 *a bad reputation. When she first started working at the electronics company, her father refused to speak to her for three months. Now, every time she leaves Penang to go back to visit her home village she has to put up with a lecture on morality from her older brother—not to mention a barrage of lewd remarks from men outside her family. If they knew that she had actually gone out on a few dates, that she had been to a discotheque, that she had once kissed a young man who said he was a student. . . . Julie's stomach tightens as she imagines her family's reaction. She tries to concentrate on the kind of man she would like to marry: an engineer or technician of some sort, someone who had been to California, where the company headquarters are located and where even the grandmothers wear tight pants and lipstick—someone who had a good attitude about women. But if she ends up having to wear glasses, like her cousin who worked three years at the "scopes," she might as well forget about finding anyone to marry her.*

One of the most serious occupational hazards that Julie and millions of   27
women like her may face is the lifelong stigma of having been a "factory girl." Most of the cultures favored by multinational corporations in their search for cheap labor are patriarchal in the grand old style: any young woman who is not under the wing of a father, husband, or older brother must be "loose." High levels of unemployment among men, as in Mexico, contribute to male resentment of working women. (Ironically, in some places the multinationals have increased male unemployment—for example, by paving over fishing and farming villages to make way for industrial parks.) Add to all this the fact that certain companies—American electronics firms are in the lead—actively promote Western-style sexual objectification as a means of insuring employee loyalty: there are company-sponsored cosmetics classes, "guess whose legs these are" contests, and swimsuit-style beauty contests where the prize might be a free night *for two* in a fancy hotel. Corporate-promoted Westernization only heightens the hostility many men feel toward any independent working women—having a job is bad enough, wearing jeans and mascara to work is going too far.

Anthropologist Patricia Fernandez, who has worked in a *maquila-*   28
dora herself, believes that the stigmatization of working women serves, indirectly, to keep them in line. "You have to think of the kind of socialization that girls experience in a very Catholic—or, for that matter, Muslim—society. The fear of having a 'reputation' is enough to make a lot of women bend over backward to be 'respectable' and ladylike, which is just what management wants." She points out that in northern Mexico, the tabloids delight in playing up stories of alleged vice in the *maquiladoras*—indiscriminate sex on the job, epidemics of venereal disease, fetuses found in factory rest rooms. "I worry about this because

there are those who treat you differently as soon as they know you have a job at a *maquiladora,*" one woman told Fernandez, "Maybe they think that if you have to work, there is a chance you're a whore."

And there is always a chance you'll wind up as one. Probably only   29
a small minority of Third World factory workers turn to prostitution when their working days come to an end. But it is, as for women everywhere, the employment of last resort, the only thing to do when the factories don't need you and traditional society won't—or, for economic reasons, can't—take you back. In the Philippines, the brothel business is expanding as fast as the factory system. If they can't use you one way, they can use you another.

Exercises

Some Important Words

proletariat (paragraph 4), Third World (4), genderless (4), imprint (4), picturesque (4), multinational (4), compelling (5), corollary (5), pharmaceuticals (6), farmed-out (6), minuscule (6), silicon wafers (7), labor-intensive (7), emerging (8), under the aegis of (8), tedium (9), article of faith (10), painstaking (10), macho (10), sabotage (10), sullenness (11), stereotypes (12), subsistence (13), collegiate (13), seniority (14), sole (14), extended family (14), tedious (15), toxic (17), solvents (17), chronic (19), astigmatism (19), sweatshop (20), amphetamine (20), tuberculosis (20), bronchitis (20), invidious (21), inescapable (21), wreak havoc (21), hawker (21), internalized (21), emigré (22), lewd (26), stigma (27), patriarchal (27), ironically (27), objectification (27), Westernization (27), hostility (27), stigmatization (28), socialization (28), tabloids (28), alleged (28), indiscriminate (28).

Some of the Issues

1. In paragraph 5, the authors discuss the wage differential between the First and Third World. What are its consequences? Who loses jobs as a result (paragraph 6)?
2. What do economists mean when they speak of a "new international division of labor"? How does this concept differ from the traditional meaning of the term "division of labor"?
3. How does the American electronics industry exemplify both that new division of labor and the consequences of wage differentials (paragraph 7)?
4. In paragraph 8 the authors begin to discuss in detail the "gender breakdown" of the new division of labor. What do they refer to?

What are the reasons for the fact that 80-90 percent of the assembly line jobs go to women?

5. What do the authors believe are the contradictions between the "conventional Western stereotypes" (paragraph 12) and the realities of women's work (paragraphs 13-14)?
6. In paragraphs 16-19 the authors describe the differences between appearance and reality in the electronics industry. What are the various hazards workers risk?
7. On what grounds do the authors assert that the garment industry is even worse than the electronics industry (paragraphs 20-22)?
8. What additional risks do women run when they rise in seniority?
9. Describe the conflicts that may arise in traditional societies between the young women who work in factories and their families.
10. What is "the employment of last resort" (paragraph 29) and how are women driven to it?

The Way We Are Told

11. Three paragraphs of this essay (1, 2, and 26) are set in italics. What do you think is the reason?
12. The authors base the essay on different kinds of research. Cite examples of each kind and evaluate their effectiveness.
13. In a number of instances (paragraphs 11 and 12, for example) the authors cite what people in the First World assume to be the case, and compare that view to reality. Cite some other instances and examine the effectiveness of the comparison.

Some Subjects for Writing

14. If you have any work experience, describe it. How did its reality differ from your expectations before starting?
15. Ehrenreich and Fuentes describe the hardships of women workers in the Third World. Compare and contrast the situations the authors describe with the situation of women workers in industrialized societies. Give supporting evidence gained from library research.
16. Write an essay documenting discrimination in the workplace against one of the following groups: women, a racial or religious minority, the handicapped, the young worker, the older worker, or any other group of workers you believe is treated unjustly. Support your argument with evidence gained from library research.

A MODEST PROPOSAL

Jonathan Swift

Jonathan Swift (1667–1745) is the author of *Gulliver's Travels* (1726). Born in Dublin of a Protestant family in a Catholic country, he was educated at Trinity College, Dublin, and Oxford University. He took orders in the Anglican Church and eventually became Dean of St. Patrick's Cathedral in Dublin. One of the great satirists of English literature, he attacked religious as well as social and educational corruption in his books *A Tale of a Tub* and *Gulliver's Travels*. In his "Modest Proposal" Swift addresses himself to the English absentee rulers of Ireland.

"This great town" in the first paragraph refers to Dublin. The last sentence of paragraph 1 refers to the practice of poor people committing themselves, usually for a fixed number of years, to service in a military enterprise or in a colony (including the American colonies).

A MODEST PROPOSAL

For Preventing the Children of Poor People in Ireland from Being a Burden to Their Parents or Country, and for Making Them Beneficial to the Public

It is a melancholy object to those who walk through this great town or travel in the country, when they see the streets, the roads, and cabin doors, crowded with beggars of the female sex, followed by three, four, or six children, all in rags and importuning every passenger for an alms. These mothers, instead of being able to work for their honest livelihood, are forced to employ all their time in strolling to beg sustenance for their helpless infants, who, as they grow up, either turn thieves for want of work, or leave their dear native country to fight for the Pretender in Spain, or sell themselves to the Barbadoes. 1

I think it is agreed by all parties that this prodigious number of children in the arms, or on the backs, or at the heels of their mothers, and frequently of their fathers, is in the present deplorable state of the kingdom a very great additional grievance; and therefore whoever could 2

356

find out a fair, cheap, and easy method of making these children sound, useful members of the commonwealth would deserve so well of the public as to have his statue set up for a preserver of the nation.

But my intention is very far from being confined to provide only for 3 the children of professed beggars; it is of a much greater extent, and shall take in the whole number of infants at a certain age who are born of parents in effect as little able to support them as those who demand our charity in the streets.

As to my own part, having turned my thoughts for many years upon 4 this important subject, and maturely weighed the several schemes of other projectors, I have always found them grossly mistaken in their computation. It is true, a child just dropped from its dam may be supported by her milk for a solar year, with little other nourishment; at most not above the value of two shillings, which the mother may certainly get, or the value in scraps, by her lawful occupation of begging; and it is exactly at one year old that I propose to provide for them in such a manner as instead of being a charge upon their parents or the parish, or wanting food and raiment for the rest of their lives, they shall on the contrary contribute to the feeding, and partly to the clothing, of many thousands.

There is likewise another great advantage in my scheme, that it will 5 prevent those voluntary abortions, and that horrid practice of women murdering their bastard children, alas, too frequent among us, sacrificing the poor innocent babes, I doubt, more to avoid the expense than the shame, which would move tears and pity in the most savage and inhuman breast.

The number of souls in this kingdom being usually reckoned one 6 million and a half, of these I calculate there may be about two hundred thousand couples whose wives are breeders; from which number I subtract thirty thousand couples who are able to maintain their own children, although I apprehend there cannot be so many under the present distress of the kingdom; but this being granted, there will remain an hundred and seventy thousand breeders. I again subtract fifty thousand for those women who miscarry, or whose children die by accident or disease within the year. There only remain an hundred and twenty thousand children of poor parents annually born. The question therefore is, how this number shall be reared and provided for, which, as I have already said, under the present situation of affairs, is utterly impossible by all the methods hitherto proposed. For we can neither employ them in handicraft nor agriculture; we neither build houses (I mean in the country) nor cultivate land. They can very seldom pick up a livelihood by stealing till they arrive at six years old, except where they are of towardly parts; although I confess they learn the rudiments much earlier, during which time they can however be looked upon only as probationers, as I have been informed by a principal gentleman in the country of

Cavan, who protested to me that he never knew above one or two instances under the age of six, even in a part of the kingdom so renowned for the quickest proficiency in that art.

I am assured by our merchants that a boy or a girl before twelve years old is no salable commodity; and even when they come to this age, they will not yield above three pounds, or three pounds and half a crown at most on the Exchange; which cannot turn to account either to the parents or the kingdom, the charge of nutriment and rags having been at least four times that value.   7

I shall now therefore humbly propose my own thoughts, which I hope will not be liable to the least objection.   8

I have been assured by a very knowing American of my acquaintance in London, that a young healthy child well nursed is at a year old a most delicious, nourishing, and wholesome food, whether stewed, roasted, baked, or boiled; and I make not doubt that it will equally serve in a fricassee or a ragout.   9

I do therefore humbly offer it to public consideration that of the hundred and twenty thousand children, already computed, twenty thousand may be reserved for breed, whereof only one fourth part to be males, which is more than we allow to sheep, black cattle, or swine; and my reason is that these children are seldom the fruits of marriage, a circumstance not much regarded by our savages, therefore one male will be sufficient to serve four females. That the remaining hundred thousand may at a year old be offered in sale to the persons of quality and fortune through the kingdom, always advising the mother to let them suck plentifully in the last month, so as to render them plump and fat for a good table. A child will make two dishes at an entertainment for friends; and when the family dines alone, the fore or hind quarter will make a reasonable dish, and seasoned with a little pepper or salt will be very good boiled on the fourth day, especially in winter.   10

I have reckoned upon a medium that a child just born will weigh twelve pounds, and in a solar year if tolerably nursed increaseth to twenty-eight pounds.   11

I grant this food will be somewhat dear, and therefore very proper for landlords, who, as they have already devoured most of the parents, seem to have the best title to the children.   12

Infant's flesh will be in season throughout the year, but more plentiful in March, and a little before and after. For we are told by a grave author, an eminent French physician, that fish being a prolific diet, there are more children born in Roman Catholic countries about nine months after Lent, than at any other season; therefore, reckoning a year after Lent, the markets will be more glutted than usual, because the number of popish infants is at least three to one in this kingdom; and therefore it will have one other collateral advantage, by lessening the number of Papists among us.   13

I have already computed the charge of nursing a beggar's child (in   14
which list I reckon all cottagers, laborers, and four fifths of the farmers) to
be about two shillings per annum, rags included; and I believe no
gentleman would repine to give ten shillings for the carcass of a good fat
child, which, as I have said, will make four dishes of excellent nutritive
meat, when he hath only some particular friend or his own family to dine
with him. Thus the squire will learn to be a good landlord, and grow
popular among the tenants; the mother will have eight shillings net
profit, and be fit for work till she produces another child.

Those who are more thrifty (as I must confess the times require)   15
may flay the carcass; the skin of which artificially dressed will make
admirable gloves for ladies, and summer boots for fine gentlemen.

As to our city of Dublin, shambles may be appointed for this purpose   16
in the most convenient parts of it, and butchers we may be assured will
not be wanting; although I rather recommend buying the children alive,
and dressing them hot from the knife as we do roasting pigs.

A very worthy person, a true lover of this country, and whose   17
virtues I highly esteem, was lately pleased in discoursing on this matter to
offer a refinement upon my scheme. He said that many gentlemen of his
kingdom, having of late destroyed their deer, he conceived that the want
of venison might be well supplied by the bodies of young lads and
maidens, not exceeding fourteen years of age nor under twelve, so great
a number of both sexes in every county being now ready to starve for
want of work and service; and these to be disposed of by their parents,
if alive, or otherwise by their nearest relations. But with due deference to
so excellent a friend and so deserving a patriot, I cannot be altogether in
his sentiments; for as to the males, my American acquaintance assured
me from frequent experience that their flesh was generally tough and
lean, like that of our schoolboys, by continual exercise, and their taste
disagreeable; and to fatten them would not answer the charge. Then as
to the females, it would, I think with humble submission, be a loss to the
public, because they soon would become breeders themselves; and
besides, it is not improbable that some scrupulous people might be apt to
censure such a practice (although indeed very unjustly) as a little
bordering upon cruelty; which, I confess, hath always been with me the
strongest objection against any project, how well soever intended.

But in order to justify my friend, he confessed that this expedient   18
was put into his head by the famous Psalmanazar, a native of the island
Formosa, who came from thence to London above twenty years ago, and
in conversation told my friend that in his country when any young
person happened to be put to death, the executioner sold the carcass to
the persons of quality as a prime dainty; and that in his time the body of
a plump girl of fifteen, who was crucified for an attempt to poison the
emperor, was sold to his Imperial Majesty's prime minister of state, and

other great mandarins of the court, in joints from the gibbet, at four hundred crowns. Neither indeed can I deny that if the same use were made of several plump young girls in this town, who without one single groat to their fortunes cannot stir abroad without a chair, and appear at the playhouse and assemblies in foreign fineries which they never will pay for, the kingdom would not be the worse.

Some persons of a desponding spirit are in great concern about that vast number of poor people who are aged, diseased, or maimed, and I have been desired to employ my thoughts what course may be taken to ease the nation of so grievous an encumbrance. But I am not in the least pain upon that matter, because it is very well known that they are every day dying and rotting by cold and famine, and filth and vermin, as fast as can be reasonably expected. And as to the younger laborers, they are now in almost as hopeful a condition. They cannot get work, and consequently pine away for want of nourishment to a degree that if any time they are accidentally hired to common labor, they have not strength to perform it; and thus the country and themselves are happily delivered from the evils to come.   19

I have too long digressed, and therefore shall return to my subject. I think the advantages by the proposal which I have made are obvious and many, as well as of the highest importance.   20

For first, as I have already observed, it would greatly lessen the number of Papists, with whom we are yearly overrun, being the principal breeders of the nation as well as our most dangerous enemies; and who stay at home on purpose to deliver the kingdom to the Pretender, hoping to take their advantage by the absence of so many good Protestants, who have chosen rather to leave their country than to stay at home and pay tithes against their conscience to an Episcopal curate.   21

Secondly, the poorer tenants will have something valuable of their own, which by law may be made liable to distress, and help to pay their landlord's rent, their corn and cattle being already seized and money a thing unknown.   22

Thirdly, whereas the maintenance of an hundred thousand children, from two years old and upwards, cannot be computed at less than ten shillings a pierce per annum, the nation's stock will be thereby increased fifty thousand pounds per annum, besides the profit of a new dish introduced to the tables of all gentlemen of fortune in the kingdom who have any refinement in taste. And the money will circulate among ourselves, the goods being entirely of our own growth and manufacture.   23

Fourthly, the constant breeders, besides the gain of eight shillings sterling per annum by the sale of their children, will be rid of the charge for maintaining them after the first year.   24

Fifthly, this food would likewise bring great custom to taverns, where the vintners will certainly be so prudent as to procure the best   25 receipts for dressing it to perfection, and consequently have their houses frequented by all the fine gentlemen, who justly value themselves upon their knowledge in good eating; and a skillful cook, who understands how to oblige his guests, will contrive to make it as expensive as they please.

Sixthly, this would be a great inducement to marriage, which all wise nations have either encouraged by rewards or enforced by laws and penalties. It would increase the care and tenderness of mothers toward their children, when they were sure of a settlement for life to the poor babes, provided in some sort by the public, to their annual profit instead of expense. We should see an honest emulation among the married women, which of them could bring the fattest child to the market. Men would become as fond of their wives during the time of their pregnancy as they are now of their mares in foal, their cows in calf, or sows when they are ready to farrow; nor offer to beat or kick them (as is too frequent a practice) for fear of a miscarriage.   26

Many other advantages might be enumerated. For instance, the addition of some thousand carcasses in our exportation of barreled beef, the propagation of swine's flesh, and improvements in the art of making good bacon, so much wanted among us by the great destruction of pigs, too frequent at our tables, which are no way comparable in taste or magnificence to a well-grown, fat, yearling child, which roasted whole will make a considerable figure at a lord mayor's feast or any other public entertainment. But this and many others I omit, being studious of brevity.   27

Supposing that one thousand families in this city would be constant customers for infants' flesh, besides others who might have it at merry meetings, particularly weddings and christenings, I compute that Dublin would take off annually about twenty thousand carcasses, and the rest of the kingdom (where probably they will be sold somewhat cheaper) the remaining eighty thousand.   28

I can think of no one objection that will possibly be raised against this proposal, unless it should be urged that the number of people will be thereby much lessened in the kingdom. This I freely own, and it was indeed one principal design in offering it to the world. I desire the reader will observe, and I calculate my remedy for this one individual kingdom of Ireland and for no other that ever was, is, or I think ever can be upon earth. Therefore, let no man talk to me of other expedients: of taxing our absentees at five shillings a pound: of using neither clothes nor household furniture except what is of our own growth and manufacture: of utterly rejecting the materials and instruments that promote foreign luxury: of curing the expensiveness of pride, vanity, idleness, and gaming in our women: of introducing a vein of parsimony, prudence, and temperance: of learning to love our country, in the want of which we differ even from Laplanders and the inhabitants of Topinamboo: of   29 quitting our animosities and factions, nor acting any longer like the Jews, who were murdering one another at the very moment their city was taken: of being a little cautious not to sell our country and conscience for nothing: of teaching landlords to have at least one degree of mercy toward their tenants: lastly, of putting a spirit of honesty, industry, and skill into our shopkeepers; who, if a resolution could not be taken to buy only our native goods, would immediately unite to cheat and exact upon us in the price, the measure, and the goodness, nor could every yet be brought to make one fair proposal of just dealing, though often and earnestly invited to it.

Therefore, I repeat, let no man talk to me of these and the like expedients, til he hath at least some glimpse of hope that there will ever be some hearty and sincere attempt to put them in practice.

But as to myself, having been wearied out for many years with offering vain, idle, visionary thoughts, and at length utterly despairing of success, I fortunately fell upon this proposal, which, as it is wholly new, so it hath something solid and real, of no expense and little trouble, full in our own power, and whereby we can incur no danger in disobliging England. For this kind of commodity will not bear exportation, the flesh being of too tender a consistence to admit a long continuance in salt, although perhaps I could name a country which would be glad to eat up our whole nation without it.

After all, I am not so violently bent upon my own opinion as to reject any offer proposed by wise men, which shall be found equally innocent, cheap, easy, and effectual. But before something of that kind shall be advanced in contradiction to my scheme, and offering a better, I desire the author or authors will be pleased maturely to consider two points. First, as things now stand, how they will be able to find food and raiment for an hundred thousand useless mouths and backs. And secondly, there being a round million of creatures in human figure throughout this kingdom, whose sole subsistence put into a common stock would leave them in debt two millions of pounds sterling, adding those who are beggars by profession to the bulk of farmers, cottagers, and laborers, with their wives and children who are beggars in effect; I desire those politicians who dislike my overture, and may perhaps be so bold to attempt an answer, that they will first ask the parents of these mortals whether they would not at this day think it a great happiness to have been sold for food at a year old in this manner I prescribe, and thereby have avoided such a perpetual scene of misfortunes as they have since gone through by the oppression of landlords, the impossibility of paying rent without money or trade, the want of common sustenance, with neither house nor clothes to cover them from the inclemencies of the weather, and the most inevitable prospect of entailing the like or greater miseries upon their breed forever.

I profess, in the sincerity of my heart, that I have not the least 33
personal interest in endeavoring to promote this necessary work, having
no other motive than the public good of my country, by advancing our
trade, providing for infants, relieving the poor, and giving some pleasure
to the rich. I have no children by which I can propose to get a single
penny; the youngest being nine years old, and my wife past childbearing.

Exercises

Some Important Words

object (paragraph 1), importuning (1), alms (1), sustenance (1), Pretender
(1), prodigious (2), dam (4), raiment (4), towardly parts (6), rudiments (6),
probationer (6), commodity (7), nutriment (7), fricassee (9), ragout (9),
quality (10), fortune (10), popish (13), collateral (13), Papist (13), repine
(14), shambles (16), deference (17), scrupulous (17), censure (17), expedient (18), gibbet (18), groat (18), assemblies (18), desponding (19), maimed
(19), encumbrance (19), vermin (19), digressed (20), prudent (25), receipts
(25), propagation (27), gaming (29), parsimony (29), inclemencies (32).

Some of the Issues

1. Paragraphs 1–6 are an introduction. What is the main point the
   author wants to make?
2. Paragraph 7 is a transition. Before you have read the rest, what might
   it foretell?
3. The short paragraph 8 is the beginning of the real proposal; and
   paragraph 9, its central idea. Explain that idea.
4. Paragraph 10 expands the proposal in 9. It relates in particular to
   paragraph 6. Why are all these statistical calculations important?
   What do they contribute to the impact of the essay?
5. Look back to paragraph 5. What hints of the idea to come do you
   now find in it?
6. Paragraphs 15 through 17 offer refinements on the main theme.
   What are they?
7. Examine the logic of each of the advantages of the proposal, as listed
   in paragraphs 21 through 26. Why is the lessening of the number of
   Papists a particular advantage?
8. In paragraph 29, when the essay turns to possible objections, which
   are the ones that are omitted completely? Why? Why does the
   narrator so vehemently concentrate on Ireland in this paragraph?
9. In paragraph 29 other remedies are also proposed for solving the
   plight of Ireland. What distinguishes them from the one the narrator
   is advocating?

The Way We Are Told

10. Readers of this essay will for a time take Swift's observations at face value. At what point in the essay are they likely to change their minds?

11. Swift creates a narrator whose modest proposal this is. Try to imagine him: what kind of person might he be? What might be his profession? Consider some of the phrases he uses, his obsession with statistics and the financial aspects of the problem, and his attention to detail.

12. In paragraph 4, in the narrator's choice of words, you find the first hint of what is to come. Locate it. Do you find an echo in paragraph 6?

13. Having made his proposal boldly in paragraph 9, the narrator develops it in paragraphs 10 through 14. Paragraphs 15 through 17 heighten the effect. Consider the choice of images in these paragraphs.

Some Subjects for Writing

14. Do you have any modest proposals as to what to do with teachers, younger brothers or sisters, former boyfriends or girlfriends, or anyone else?

LIVING IN A
JAPANESE HOME

John David Morley

John David Morley was born in Singapore in 1948, of British parents, and educated at Oxford University. His earliest job was as tutor to the children of Elizabeth Taylor and Richard Burton when they were filming in Mexico. His interest in the theater led him to Japanese theater and eventually to Japanese culture in general. He taught himself Japanese, studied at the Language Research Institute at Waseda University in Tokyo, and then went to work for Japanese Television as liaison officer, interpreter, and researcher, stationed in Munich, Germany. In 1985 he published a novel, *Pictures from the Water Trade: Adventures of a Westerner in Japan,* from which the present selection is taken. The novel is based on some of his own experiences.

The Japanese island empire successfully managed to isolate itself from foreign influences until the middle of the nineteenth century. Once that isolation had been breached, however, Japan moved rapidly to catch up with the Western world, not only by industrializing but also by following the major powers' expansionist policies. Japan fought a successful war with Russia (1905), occupied and eventually annexed Korea (1910), and in the 1930s, occupied Manchuria and large parts of China. After its surprise attack on Pearl Harbor (December 7, 1941), Japan had spectacular initial successes in World War II, occupying the Philippines, Indochina, Indonesia, Burma, and Singapore. Defeated and virtually destroyed in the later phases of the war, Japan was occupied by the U.S. Army under General Douglas MacArthur, whose administration of the islands is primarily responsible for converting Japan into a constitutional monarchy with a parliamentary government. Japan's economic recovery has been spectacular—today the country is the second most powerful industrial nation in the world. Japan's success is all the more remarkable when one considers that the country has almost no natural resources of its own on its crowded islands. With its size smaller than California, it has 122 million inhabitants, half as many as the United States. Japanese society is highly homogeneous, has a very low crime rate, a very high level of literacy, and is considered very hard-working.

The introduction was arranged through a mutual acquaintance, Yoshida,   1
at the private university where Boon was taking language courses and
where Sugama was employed on the administrative staff. They met one
afternoon in the office of their acquaintance and inspected each other
warily for ten minutes.

"Nice weather," said Boon facetiously as he shook hands with   2
Sugama. Outside it was pouring with rain.

"Nice weather?" repeated Sugama doubtfully, glancing out of the   3
window. "But it's raining."

It was not a good start.   4

Sugama had just moved into a new apartment. It was large enough   5
for two, he said, but he was looking for someone to share the expenses.
This straightforward information arrived laboriously, in bits and pieces,
sandwiched between snippets of Sugama's personal history and vague
professions of friendship, irritating to Boon, because at the time he felt
they sounded merely sententious. All this passed back and forth between
Sugama and Boon through the mouth of their mutual friend, as Boon
understood almost no Japanese and Sugama's English, though well-
intentioned, was for the most part impenetrable.

It made no odds to Boon where he lived or with whom. All he wanted   6
was a Japanese-speaking environment in order to absorb the language as
quickly as possible. He had asked for a family, but none was available.

One windy afternoon in mid-October the three of them met outside   7
the gates of the university and set off to have a look at Sugama's new
apartment. It was explained to Boon that cheap apartments in Tokyo
were very hard to come by, the only reasonable accommodation available being confined to housing estates subsidised by the government.
Boon wondered how a relatively prosperous bachelor like Sugama
managed to qualify for government-subsidised housing. Sugama admitted that this was in fact only possible because his grandfather would also
be living there. It was the first Boon had heard of the matter and he was
rather taken aback.

It turned out, however, that the grandfather would "very seldom"   8
be there—in fact, that he wouldn't live there at all. He would only be
there on paper, he and his grandson constituting a "family." That was the
point. "You must *say* he is there," said Sugama emphatically.

The grandfather lived a couple of hundred miles away, and   9
although he never once during the next two years set foot in the
apartment he still managed to be the bane of Boon's life. A constant
stream of representatives from charities, government agencies and old
people's clubs, on average one or two a month, came knocking on the
door, asking to speak to grandfather. At first grandfather was simply "not
in" or had "gone for a walk," but as time passed and the flow of visitors
never faltered, Boon found himself having to resort to more drastic

measures. Grandfather began to make long visits to his home in the country; he had not yet returned because he didn't feel up to making the journey; his health gradually deteriorated. Finally Boon decided to have him invalided, and for a long time his condition remained "grave." On grandfather's behalf Boon received the condolences of all these visitors, and occasionally even presents.

Two years later grandfather did in fact die. Boon was thus exonerated, but in the meantime he had got to know grandfather well and had become rather fond of him. He attended his funeral with mixed feelings.   10

Sugama had acquired tenure of his government-subsidised apartment by a stroke of luck. He had won a ticket in a lottery. These apartments were much sought after, and in true Japanese style their distribution among hundreds of thousands of applicants was discreetly left to fate. The typical tenant was a young couple with one or two children, who would occupy the apartment for ten or fifteen years, often under conditions of bleak frugality, in order to save money to buy a house. Although the rent was not immoderate, prices generally in Tokyo were high, and it was a mystery to Boon how such people managed to live at all. Among the lottery winners there were inevitably also those people for whom the acquisition of an apartment was just a prize, an unexpected bonus, to be exploited as a financial investment. It was no problem for these nominal tenants to sub-let their apartments at prices well above the going rate.   11

Boon had never lived on a housing estate and his first view of the tall concrete compound where over fifty thousand people lived did little to reassure him. Thousands of winner families were accommodated in about a dozen rectangular blocks, each between ten and fifteen stories high, apparently in no way different (which disappointed Boon most of all) from similar housing compounds in Birmingham or Berlin. He had naively expected Japanese concrete to be different, to have a different colour, perhaps, or a more exotic shape.   12

But when Sugama let them into the apartment and Boon saw the interior he immediately took heart: this was unmistakably Japanese. Taking off their shoes in the tiny box-like hall, the three of them padded reverently through the kitchen into the *tatami* rooms.   13

"Smell of fresh *tatami*," prounouced Sugama, wrinkling his nose.   14

Boon was ecstatic. Over the close-woven pale gold straw matting lay a very faint greenish shimmer, sometimes perceptible and sometimes not, apparently in response to infinitesimal shifts in the texture of the falling light. The *tatami* was quite unlike a carpet or any other form of floor-covering he had ever seen. It seemed to be alive, humming with colours he could sense rather than see, like a greening tree in the brief interval between winter and spring. He stepped on to it and felt the fibres recoil, sinking under the weight of his feet, slowly and softly.   15

"You can see green?" asked Sugama, squatting down.   16

"Yes indeed."   17

"Fresh *tatami*. Smell of grass, green colour. But not for long, few   18
weeks only."

"What exactly is it?"   19

"Yes."   20

Boon turned to Yoshida and repeated the question, who in turn   21
asked Sugama and conferred with him at length.

"*Tatami* comes from *oritatamu,* which means to fold up. So it's a   22
kind of matting you can fold up."

"Made of straw."   23

"Yes."   24

"How long does it last?"   25

Long consultation.   26

"He says this is not so good quality. Last maybe four, five years."   27

"And then what?"   28

"New *tatami*. Quite expensive, you see. But very practical."   29

The three *tatami* rooms were divided by a series of *fusuma,* sliding   30
screens made of paper and light wood. These screens were decorated at
the base with simple grass and flower motifs; a natural extension, it
occurred to Boon, of the grass-like *tatami* laid out in-between. Sugama
explained that the *fusuma* were usually kept closed in winter, and in
summer, in order to have "nice breeze," they could be removed altogether. He also showed Boon the *shoji,* a type of sliding screen similar to
the *fusuma* but more simple: an open wooden grid covered on one side
with semi-transparent paper, primitive but rather beautiful. There was
only one small section of *shoji* in the whole apartment; almost as a token,
thought Boon, and he wondered why.

With the exception of a few one- and two-room apartments every   31
house that Boon ever visited in Japan was designed to incorporate these
three common elements: *tatami, fusuma* and *shoji.* In the houses of rich
people the *tatami* might last longer, the *fusuma* decorations might be
more costly, but the basic concept was the same. The interior design of
all houses being much the same, it was not surprising to find certain
similarities in the behavior and attitudes of the people who lived in them.

The most striking feature of the Japanese house was lack of   32
privacy; the lack of individual, inviolable space. In winter, when the
fusuma were kept closed, any sound above a whisper was clearly
audible on the other side, and of course in summer they were usually
removed altogether. It is impossible to live under such conditions for
very long without a common household identity emerging which naturally takes precedence over individual wishes. This enforced family unity
was still held up to Boon as an ideal, but in practice it was ambivalent, as
much a yoke as a bond.

There was no such thing as the individual's private room, no   33
bedroom, dining- or sitting-room as such, since in the traditional Japanese house there was no furniture determining that a room should be
reserved for any particular function. A person slept in a room, for
example, without thinking of it as a bedroom or as his room. In the
morning his bedding would be rolled up and stored away in a cupboard;
a small table known as the *kotatsu,* which could also be plugged into the
mains to provide heating, was moved back into the centre of the room
and here the family ate, drank, worked and relaxed for the rest of the
day. Although it was becoming standard practice in modern Japan for
children to have their own rooms, many middle-aged and nearly all older
Japanese still lived this way. They regarded themselves as "one flesh,"
their property as common to all; the *uchi* (household, home) was
constituted according to a principle of indivisibility. The system of
moveable screens meant that the rooms could be used by all the family
and for all purposes: walls were built round the *uchi,* not inside it.

Boon later discovered analogies between this concept of house and   34
the Japanese concept of self. The Japanese carried his house around in
his mouth and produced it in everyday conversation, using the word
uchi to mean "I," the representative of my house in the world outside.
His self-awareness was naturally expressed as corporate individuality,
hazy about quite what that included, very clear about what it did not.

Ittaikan, the traditional view of the corporate *uchi* as one flesh, had   35
unmistakably passed into decline in modern Japan. A watery sentiment
remained, lacking the conviction that had once made the communal *uchi*
as self-evident in practice as it was in principle. This was probably why
people had become acutely aware of the problem of space, although
they did not necessarily have less space now than they had had before.
A tendency to restrict the spatial requirements of daily life quite volun-
tarily had been evident in Japan long before land became scarce. When
the tea-room was first introduced during the Muromachi period (early
fourteenth to late sixteenth century) the specification of its size was four
and a half mats, but in the course of time this was reduced to one mat
(two square metres). The reasons for this kind of scaling down were
purely aesthetic. It was believed that only within a space as modest as
this could the spirit of *wabi,* a taste for the simple and quiet, be truly
cultivated.

The almost wearying sameness about all the homes which Boon   36
visited, despite differences in the wealth and status of their owners,
prompted a rather unexpected conclusion: the classlessness of the
Japanese house. The widespread use of traditional materials, the preservation of traditional structures, even if in such contracted forms as to have
become merely symbolic, suggested a consensus about the basic requirements of daily life which was very remarkable, and which presumably

held implications for Japanese society as a whole. Boon's insight into
that society was acquired very slowly, after he had spent a great deal of
time sitting on the *tatami* mats and looking through the sliding *fusuma*
doors which had struck him as no more than pleasing curiosities on his
first visit to a Japanese-style home.

Exercises

Some Important Words

warily (paragraph 1), facetiously (2), laboriously (5), snippets (5), professions of friendship (5), sententious (5), impenetrable (5), prosperous (7),
bane (9), faltered (9), deteriorated (9), invalided (9), condolences
(9), exonerated (10), tenure (11), bleak frugality (11), exploited (11),
nominal (12), naively (12), exotic (12), *tatami*—woven straw matting
used as floor covering in Japanese homes (13), ecstatic (15), perceptible
(15), infinitesimal (15), recoil (15), token (30), inviolable (32), audible
(32), precedence (32), ambivalent (32), yoke (32), analogies (34), corporate individuality (34), consensus (36).

Some of the Issues

1. Describe the first meeting of Boon and Sugama. Why did Boon
   consider it "not a good start"?
2. Describe the selection process for government-subsidized housing in
   Japan—very different from Western practices. Can you find a ratio-
   nale for the Japanese system?
3. On entering the new apartment Sugama wrinkles his nose while
   Boon is ecstatic. What accounts for their difference in attitude?
4. What are the key elements of the Japanese home? What are the
   advantages of this mode of living? What disadvantages does it have?
5. How does the arrangement condition the lives of the people who
   live in it? How does it reflect Japanese values?
6. Morley says that the most striking feature of the Japanese house is
   lack of privacy. Later he speaks of the classlessness of the Japanese
   home. How does he illustrate his two points?
*7. Read Marcus Mabry's "Living in Two Worlds." Both Morley (through
   Boon) and Mabry are concerned with privacy, Boon when he joins
   Sugama and Mabry when he goes home to New Jersey. How and why
   are their attitudes different?

The Way We are Told

8. The author does not at any time refer to Western conditions and
   attitudes; yet they are constantly implied in his discussion of events,

contacts with people, and descriptions of living conditions. Give some examples.

9. What does the author achieve by his gradual revelation of the truth about Sugama's grandfather?

10. The story is told by Boon, a fictional British visitor, but the experiences presumably reflect Morley's own. What does the author gain by creating Boon to tell his story?

Some Subjects for Writing

11. Compare and contrast the Western or American concept of privacy to the Japanese view as described by Morley. How does the physical environment of the Japanese home support Japanese notions of privacy? In describing the American living space, you might think of the "ideal" American family home, a bedroom for each child, preferably with a private bath, and a kitchen and family room as places for the family to gather.

12. How important is privacy to you? How did the physical environment in which you grew up shape your attitudes?

THEY CLAPPED

Nikki Giovanni

Nikki Giovanni (1943–) is a graduate of Fisk College. She has published a number of volumes of poetry, including *Black Feeling/ Black Talk/Black Judgment* (1970), *The Women and the Men* (1975), and *My House* (1972), from which the following poem is taken. She has also written an autobiography, *Gemini* (1971).

Giovanni's poem is a comment on a people's search for their roots, in this case the search of African-Americans traveling to Africa, excited at the prospect and confident of finding the meaning they were searching for. Giovanni's wry humor only partly hides the hurt and disappointment, summed up in the line: "when they finally realized they were strangers all over." Yet, as the final lines indicate, there may be hope.

they clapped when we landed
thinking Africa was just an extension
of the black world
they smiled as we taxied home to be met
black to black face not understanding africans lack
color prejudice
they rushed to declare
cigarettes, money, allegiance to the mother land
not knowing despite having read fanon and davenport
hearing all of j.h. clarke's lectures, supporting
nkrumah in ghana and nigeria in the war that there was once
a tribe called afro-americans that populated the whole
of africa
they stopped running when they learned the packages
on the women's heads were heavy and that babies didn't
cry and disease is uncomfortable and that villages are fun
only because you knew the feel of good leather on good
pavement
they cried when they saw mercedes benz were as common
in lagos as volkswagens are in berlin
they shook their heads when they understood there was no

difference between the french and the english and the americans
and the afro-americans or the tribe next door or the country
across the border
they were exasperated when they heard sly and the family stone
in francophone africa and they finally smiled when little boys
who spoke no western tongue said "james brown" with reverence
they brought out their cameras and bought out africa's drums
when they finally realized they are strangers all over
and love is only and always about the lover not the beloved
they marveled at the beauty of the people and the richness
of the land knowing they could never possess either

they clapped when they took off
for home despite the dead
dream they saw a free future

PART EIGHT

Communicating

How do we communicate? The first answer that is likely to come to most people's minds is through language: we speak, we listen, we read, we write. When we think further, we become increasingly aware that we also communicate in nonverbal ways, through gestures and other visual images. Increasingly, advances in technology—videos, faxes, e-mail, car phones, answering machines, etc.—have relieved us from the necessity of personal, physical contact and, in so doing, have changed the ways in which our messages are relayed. In addition to altering the medium of the message, technology may in fact shape both form and content of the message in subtle ways. For example, in responding to an e-mail message, we may dispense with preliminary common courtesies, necessary in face-to-face interactions. Or, in viewing music videos, we may be presented with fleeting, split-second successions of patriotic images that we are not even aware of, but that leave us feeling proud nonetheless.

When we turn to communication across cultural and social groups, the complexities and subtleties multiply. Language is again the most obvious example. If you speak only English and the person you wish to talk to speaks only Japanese, communication will be limited—although you might be able to understand to some extent by means of gestures. With speakers of the same language, problems may be the result of dialectal or intracultural differences, that is, language distinctions between subgroups. Gloria Naylor, in the first selection, alerts the reader to one such example concerning the use of an incendiary word that takes on different meanings within the African-American community.

The next two essays are about gender and social bias in language. William Hines cites the case of doctors who address women patients they have never met before by their first names while expecting to be addressed by their proper titles. Robin Lakoff in her essay demonstrates that English usage provides ample opportunity to view women unequally.

The three essays that follow give some indication of the extent to which the media influence our thinking and our communication. Jack G. Shaheen analyzes the media's hostile and one-sided view of Arabs, which he feels might shape a negative stereotype of all Middle Easterners. Myrna Knepler examines the emotional, as distinct from the informational, impact of language: American advertisers use French words to enhance the appeal of their products, just as French advertisers use English for the same purpose. Donna Woolfolk Cross describes the social impact of the American soap opera in fostering the American dream.

The next selections are concerned with issues involved in speaking, or being educated in, more than one dialect or language. Richard Rodriguez compares the way he felt about English as a child to the way he felt about his "private" language, Spanish. Ngugi wa Thiong'o, a Kenyan writer who grew up speaking two East African languages but had most of his education in English, draws attention to the problem of many authors in his position. Should he write in his native language and thereby restrict his audience, or in English, which will in the end never fully be his language? In his short story, Bernard Malamud describes the loss of language—the inability to express in a second language one's most subtle thoughts. In the beginning stages of language learning, one can manage to communicate, but "just to communicate was frustrating."

Finally, in Alan Devenish's poem "After the Beep," a recorded telephone message speaks ironically to the failure of true communication, despite our era's mastery of telecommunication.

THE MEANING OF
A WORD

Gloria Naylor

Gloria Naylor, a native of New York City, was born in 1950 and educated at Brooklyn College and Yale, She has taught at George Washington, New York, and Boston universities. Her first novel, *The Women of Brewster Place* (1982), won an American Book Award. Since then she has written *Linden Hills* (1985), *Mama Day* (1988), and *Bailey's Cafe* (1992). The essay included here appeared in the *New York Times* on February 20, 1986.

The word whose meaning Naylor learned was *nigger*. She explains that she had heard it used quite comfortably by friends and relatives, but the way it was uttered to her by a white child in school was so different that she at first did not realize that it was the same word.

Language is the subject. It is the written form with which I've managed to keep the wolf away from the door and, in diaries, to keep my sanity. In spite of this, I consider the written word inferior to the spoken, and much of the frustration experienced by novelists is the awareness that whatever we manage to capture in even the most transcendent passages falls far short of the richness of life. Dialogue achieves its power in the dynamics of a fleeting moment of sight, sound, smell and touch. 1

I'm not going to enter the debate here about whether it is language that shapes reality or vice versa. That battle is doomed to be waged whenever we seek intermittent reprieve from the chicken and egg dispute. I will simply take the position that the spoken word, like the written word, amounts to a nonsensical arrangement of sounds or letters without a consensus that assigns "meaning." And building from the meanings of what we hear, we order reality. Words themselves are innocuous; it is the consensus that gives them true power. 2

I remember the first time I heard the word nigger. In my third-grade class, our math tests were being passed down the rows, and as I handed the papers to a little boy in back of me, I remarked that once again he 3 had received a much lower mark than I did. He snatched his test from me and spit out that word. Had he called me a nymphomaniac or a necrophiliac, I couldn't have been more puzzled. I didn't know what a nigger was, but I knew that whatever it meant, it was something he shouldn't have called me. This was verified when I raised my hand, and in a loud voice repeated what he had said and watched the teacher scold him for using a "bad" word. I was later to go home and ask the inevitable question that every black parent must face—"Mommy, what does 'nigger' mean?"

And what exactly did it mean? Thinking back, I realize that this   4
could not have been the first time the word was used in my presence. I was part of a large extended family that had migrated from the rural South after World War II and formed a close-knit network that gravitated around my maternal grandparents. Their ground-floor apartment in one of the buildings they owned in Harlem was a weekend mecca for my immediate family, along with countless aunts, uncles and cousins who brought along assorted friends. It was a bustling and open house with assorted neighbors and tenants popping in and out to exchange bits of gossip, pick up an old quarrel or referee the ongoing checkers game in which my grandmother cheated shamelessly. They were all there to let down their hair and put up their feet after a week of labor in the factories, laundries and shipyards of New York.

Amid the clamor, which could reach deafening proportions—two   5
or three conversations going on simultaneously, punctuated by the sound of a baby's crying somewhere in the back rooms or out on the street—there was still a rigid set of rules about what was said and how. Older children were sent out of the living room when it was time to get into the juicy details about "you-know-who" up on the third floor who had gone and gotten herself "p-r-e-g-n-a-n-t!" But my parents, knowing that I could spell well beyond my years, always demanded that I follow the others out to play. Beyond sexual misconduct and death, everything else was considered harmless for our young ears. And so among the anecdotes of the triumphs and disappointments in the various workings of their lives, the word nigger was used in my presence, but it was set within contexts and inflections that caused it to register in my mind as something else.

In the singular, the word was always applied to a man who had   6
distinguished himself in some situation that brought their approval for his strength, intelligence or drive:

"Did Johnny *really* do that?"   7

"I'm telling you, that nigger pulled in $6,000 of overtime last year.   8
Said he got enough for a down payment on a house."

When used with a possessive adjective by a woman—"my   9
nigger"—it became a term of endearment for husband or boyfriend. But it could be more than just a term applied to a man. In their mouths it

became the pure essence of manhood—a disembodied force that channeled their past history of struggle and present survival against the odds
into a victorious statement of being: "Yeah, that old foreman found out
quick enough—you don't mess with a nigger."

In the plural, it became a description of some group within the   10
community that have overstepped the bounds of decency as my family
defined it: Parents who neglected their children, a drunken couple who
fought in public, people who simply refused to look for work, those with
excessively dirty mouths or unkempt households were all "trifling
niggers." This particular circle could forgive hard times, unemployment,
the occasional bout of depression—they had gone through all of that
themselves—but the unforgivable sin was a lack of self-respect.

A woman could never be a "nigger" in the singular, with its   11
connotation of confirming worth. The noun girl was its closest equivalent
in that sense, but only when used in direct address and regardless of the
gender doing the addressing. "Girl" was a token of respect for a woman.
The one-syllable word was drawn out to sound like three in recognition
of the extra ounce of wit, nerve or daring that the woman had shown in
the situation under discussion.

"G-i-r-l, stop. You mean you said that to his face?"   12

But if the word was used in a third-person reference or shortened   13
so that it almost snapped out of my mouth, it always involved some
element of communal disapproval. And age became an important factor
in these exchanges. It was only between individuals of the same
generation, or from an older person to a younger (but never the other
way around), that "girl" would be considered a compliment.

I don't agree with the argument that use of the word nigger at this social   14
stratum of the black community was an internalization of racism. The
dynamics were the exact opposite: the people in my grandmother's
living room took a word that whites used to signify worthlessness or
degradation and rendered it impotent. Gathering there together, they
transformed "nigger" to signify the varied and complex human beings
they knew themselves to be. If the word was to disappear totally from
the mouths of even the most liberal of white society, no one in that room
was naïve enough to believe it would disappear from white minds.
Meeting the word head-on, they proved it had absolutely nothing to do
with the way they were determined to live their lives.

So there must have been dozens of times that the word "nigger"   15
was spoken in front of me before I reached the third grade. But I didn't
"hear" it until it was said by a small pair of lips that had already learned
it could be a way to humiliate me. That was the word I went home and
asked my mother about. And since she knew that I had to grow up in
America, she took me in her lap and explained.

Exercises

Some Important Words

transcendent (paragraph 1), intermittent (2), reprieve (2), consensus (2), innocuous (2), nymphomaniac (3), necrophiliac (3), extended family (4), gravitated (4), mecca (4), possessive (9), essence (9), disembodied (9), unkempt (10), trifling (10), connotation (11), communal (13), social stratum (14), internalization (14), degradation (14), naïve (14).

Some of the Issues

1. What reasons does Naylor give for considering the spoken word superior to the written?
2. Reread paragraph 2. What, according to Naylor, gives meaning to words?
3. In paragraph 3 the author tells a story from her experience as a child. How does it relate to the general statement on language that she made in the first two paragraphs? What is it that made Naylor think that she had been called a "bad" word?
4. At the end of paragraph 5 and in the examples that follow Naylor demonstrates that she had heard the word "nigger" before the boy in her class used it. Why did the previous uses register with her as something different?

The Way We Are Told

5. Naylor starts with a general statement—"language is the subject"— which she then expands on in paragraphs 1 and 2. What focus does this beginning give her essay? How would the focus differ if she started with the anecdote in paragraph 3?
6. Naylor asserts that "the written word is inferior to the spoken." What devices does she use to help the reader *hear* the dialogue?
7. The essay consists of three parts: paragraphs 1 and 2, 3–13, and 14 and 15. The first is a general statement and the second an anecdote followed by records of conversations. How does the third part relate to the preceding two?

Some Subjects for Writing

8. Many words differ in their meaning depending on the circumstances in which they are used. Write a brief essay on the different words applied to a particular nationality or ethnic group and explain their impact.

9. "Sticks and stones may break my bones but words can never hurt me." Do you have any experiences that would either confirm or deny the truth of that saying?

*10. Read Countee Cullen's poem "Incident." The subject is the same as Naylor's, but the way we are told is of course different. Try to analyze the difference in two respects: as a poem compared to a prose essay, and as to the actual circumstances of the two events they describe.

HELLO, JUDY.
I'M DR. SMITH

William Hines

William Hines is a reporter for the *Chicago Sun-Times,* in which this article appeared on June 2, 1983. Here he concerns himself with a habit that reflects the attitudes of medical practitioners, usually male, toward women: at first meeting they often address female patients by their first names while, of course, expecting to be respectfully addressed by their titles and last names.

If feminine reaction to one aspect of the doctor-patient relationship is any indication, it's high time for some consciousness-raising in the medical profession. 1

Many women, not solely of the feminist persuasion, object to being first-named by a physician they hardly know—especially when the man in the white coat makes it clear that he, in turn, expects to be addressed as "Doctor." 2

The opening bell for another round in this battle of the sexes sounded early this year when Elizabeth Babbott Conant of Buffalo, N.Y., wrote the New England Journal of Medicine laying out her objections to doctors addressing patients by their first names. 3

"It is a bogus, unearned familiarity," said Conant, who sports a doctor's degree of her own, in biology, which she teaches at Canisius College. It causes "a loss of confidence, of dignity and of one's sense of individuality," she added. 4

More than just demeaning to a person who doesn't like familiarity from every Tom, Dick and Harry, Conant contended that the practice also may defeat the purpose of treatment. 5

"The physician's role includes the task of enlisting the patient's own healing powers," Conant wrote. "Any procedure that increases confidence and inner energy will be important; any procedure that disempowers or diminishes the sense of self may impede the patient's progress." 6

"An insidious effect of the automatic use of the first name is to make the patient a child again. By reinforcing dependency and passivity, you"—directly addressing the Journal's medical readership—"have stolen power from your potential ally." 7

Conant's letter evoked a reply published in the most recent issue of   8
the Journal. Dr. Marc E. Heller of the Mary Imogene Bassett Hospital at
Cooperstown, N.Y., said a survey of obstetrics-gynecology patients there
disclosed that "78 percent wished to be called by their first name" and
only 2 percent specifically objected.

This drew a hearty snort the other day from a leading feminist with   9
A-1 scientific credentials and medical connections.

"Very interesting," said Professor Estelle Ramey, a physiologist at   10
the Georgetown University school of medicine here. "Ob-Gyn people
did it. That questionnaire would never be done by anyone who dealt
with a practice that included men. Men would be absolutely astonished
even to be asked such a thing."

The 78 percent who endorsed first-name use, Ramey opined, "were   11
answering what they thought the doctor wanted them to answer."

Ramey reserved most of her feminist scorn for specialists in   12
childbirth and women's diseases, but in point of fact it was not Ob-Gyns
at all that prompted Conant's letter; it was radiologists. Not only the
doctors, but also technicians first-named the patients at this clinic, she
said.

Doctors in general seem to treat their female patients with more   13
familiarity and what is taken as condescension than they exhibit in
dealing with male patients. Belita Cowan, head of the Washington-based
National Women's Health Network, said the medical literature contains
evidence of this.

Cowan cited a study reported in the New England Journal in 1973   14
showing that when men and women go to a doctor complaining of
identical symptoms the doctor is far more likely to ascribe the problem to
psychological factors when the patient is female.

The authors of the study, physicians Jean and John Lennane, said   15
the tendency to brush off women's complaints as psychogenic leads to
"inadequate and even derisive treatments for patients."

Many women who said they detest first-naming by doctors they   16
don't really know are reluctant to object. "He's like God," one normally
hard-bitten Washington career woman said.

Ellen Warren, a member of the Sun-Times Washington bureau, said   17
she gets "livid" when her male gynecologist calls her "Ellen." She is
diffident about calling him "Don" and is "damned if I'll call him Doctor,"
so the upshot is that Warren calls her physician nothing.

Ramey acknowledged that it's difficult to brace a doctor about   18
first-naming. She said it's "like that terrible TV ad where the woman in
the dental chair says, 'Oh, by the way, you've got bad breath.' "

"If you did that you'd have to have rocks in your head," Ramey   19
said. "He'd put the drill right through the top of your skull."

How do doctors feel about this? Official doctrine is that the patient's   20
dignity should be preserved at all times. Formal discourse between

patient and physician is to be preferred, both the American College of Obstetricians and Gynecologists and the Association of American Medical Colleges say. But when the doctor is out there in private practice, it's dealer's choice.

Dr. Vicki Seltzer, director of Ob-Gyn at Queens Hospital Center, 21 said she prefers to be on a "Mrs. So-and-so—Dr. Seltzer" basis with her patient until she really knows them well, after which mutual first-naming is appropriate.

A patient who objects to being first-named should say so, Seltzer 22 said, "not hostilely but factually: 'I'd prefer it if you'd call me Mrs. Whatever.' " If she basically doesn't like the doctor's style, Seltzer added, she should get a new one.

Dr. August Swanson, director of academic affairs for AAMC, a 23 national association representing more than 100 U.S. medical schools, blames the way doctors are trained for some of the traits that come through as insensitivity toward patients. The association is reviewing medical curricula, and human relations is one of the areas under study, he said.

The old rule still applies, however: A gentleman never unintention- 24 ally offends—and on this score many a female patient thinks her physician is no gentleman.

Exercises

Some Important Words

consciousness-raising (paragraph 1), bogus (4), demeaning (5), disempower (6), impede (6), insidious (7), dependency (7), passivity (7), potential (7), obstetrics-gynecology (Ob-Gyn) (8), snort (9), physiologist (10), endorsed (11), radiologists (12), condescension (13), psychogenic (15), derisive (15), reluctant (16), livid (17), diffident (17), brace (18), doctrine (20), formal discourse (20), dealer's choice (20).

Some of the Issues

1. In paragraphs 5–7 Hines cites an argument against the casual use of first names. What is it?
2. What is the argument in favor of using first names in paragraph 8, and how is it countered in paragraphs 9 and 10?
3. In paragraph 10 Hines cites a study; how do the results of that study relate to the overall topic of the essay?
4. Why are women who do not like doctors to call them by their first names hesitant to object?

5. Does the article propose any solutions to the problem? What are they? Are they likely to be effective?

The Way We Are Told

6. In paragraph 3 Hines uses the term "opening bell"; what does he refer to?
7. Hines quotes a number of people throughout the article. What is their claim to authority?
8. As a feature article in a daily newspaper, the selection is designed to draw and hold the casual reader's attention. How well does the author succeed in doing this?

Some Subjects for Writing

9. The essay presents an argument; it raises objections to a current practice and proposes changes. Write an essay carefully explaining what Hines argues for, and how he supports his argument.
10. Choose a subject for which you are able to collect evidence from friends or acquaintances as authorities. For example, if you have friends who are parents of young children, interview them on their opinions on child rearing; or if you have friends interested in music, interview them about their tastes and attitudes. Write an essay quoting your authorities and generalizing on what you have found out.

YOU ARE WHAT
YOU SAY

Robin Lakoff

Robin Lakoff (1942–) is a professor of linguistics at the University of
California, Berkeley. She was educated at Radcliffe, the University of
Indiana, and Harvard, and is the author of *Language and Women's
Place* (1975) and *Talking Power: The Politics of Language* (1990), and
coauthor of *Face Value: The Politics of Beauty* (1984). In the
following essay (*Ms.* magazine, July 1974) Lakoff discusses language
used by, about, and toward women. She demonstrates in detail how
the English language contributes extensively to put-downs of
women.

"Women's language" is that pleasant (dainty?), euphemistic, never-   1
aggressive way of talking we learned as little girls. Cultural bias was built
into the language we were allowed to speak, the subjects we were
allowed to speak about, and the ways we were spoken of. Having
learned our linguistic lesson well, we go out in the world, only to
discover that we are communicative cripples—damned if we do, and
damned if we don't.

If we refuse to talk "like a lady," we are ridiculed and criticized for   2
being unfeminine. ("She thinks like a man" is, at best, a left-handed
compliment.) If we do learn all the fuzzy-headed, unassertive language
of our sex, we are ridiculed for being unable to think clearly, unable to
take part in a serious discussion, and therefore unfit to hold a position of
power.

It doesn't take much of this for a woman to begin feeling she   3
deserves such treatment because of inadequacies in her own intelligence
and education.

"Women's language" shows up in all levels of English. For example,   4
women are encouraged and allowed to make far more precise discriminations in naming colors than men do. Words like *mauve, beige, ecru,
aquamarine, lavender,* and so on, are unremarkable in a woman's active
vocabulary, but largely absent from that of most men. I know of no
evidence suggesting that women actually *see* a wider range of colors than

men do. It is simply that fine discriminations of this sort are relevant to women's vocabularies, but not to men's; to men, who control most of the interesting affairs of the world, such distinctions are trivial—irrelevant.

In the area of syntax, we find similar gender-related peculiarities of speech. There is one construction, in particular, that women use conversationally far more than men: the tag question. A tag is midway between an outright statement and a yes-no question; it is less assertive than the former, but more confident than the later.

A *flat statement* indicates confidence in the speaker's knowledge and is fairly certain to be believed; a *question* indicates a lack of knowledge on some point and implies that the gap in the speaker's knowledge can and will be remedied by an answer. For example, if, at a Little League game, I have had my glasses off, I can legitimately ask someone else: "Was the player out at third?" A *tag question,* being intermediate between statement and question, is used when the speaker is stating a claim, but lacks full confidence in the truth of that claim. So if I say, "Is Joan here?" I will probably not be surprised if my respondent answers "no"; but if I say, "Joan is here, isn't she?" instead, chances are I am already biased in favor of a positive answer, wanting only confirmation. I still want a response, but I have enough knowledge (or think I have) to predict that response. A tag question, then, might be thought of as a statement that doesn't demand to be believed by anyone but the speaker, a way of giving leeway, of not forcing the addressee to go along with the views of the speaker.

Another common use of the tag question is in small talk when the speaker is trying to elicit conversation: "Sure is hot here, isn't it?"

But in discussing personal feelings or opinions, only the speaker normally has any way of knowing the correct answer. Sentences such as "I have a headache, don't I?" are clearly ridiculous. But there are other examples where it is the speaker's opinions, rather than perceptions, for which corroboration is sought, as in "The situation in Southeast Asia is terrible, isn't it?"

While there are, of course, other possible interpretations of a sentence like this, one possibility is that the speaker has a particular answer in mind—"yes" or "no"—but is reluctant to state it baldly. This sort of tag question is much more apt to be used by women than by men in conversation. Why is this the case?

The tag question allows a speaker to avoid commitment, and thereby avoid conflict with the addressee. The problem is that, by so doing, speakers may also give the impression of not really being sure of themselves, or looking to the addressee for confirmation of their views. This uncertainty is reinforced in more subliminal ways, too. There is a peculiar sentence intonation pattern, used almost exclusively by women, as far as I know, which changes a declarative answer into a question. The effect of using the rising inflection typical of a yes-no question is to imply that the speaker is seeking confirmation, even though the speaker is clearly the only one who has the requisite information, which is why the question was put to her in the first place:

> (Q) When will dinner be ready?
> (A) Oh . . . around six o'clock . . .?

It is as though the second speaker were saying, "Six o'clock—if that's okay with you, if you agree." The person being addressed is put in the position of having to provide confirmation. One likely consequence of this sort of speech-pattern in a woman is that, often unbeknownst to herself, the speaker builds a reputation of tentativeness, and others will refrain from taking her seriously or trusting her with any real responsibilities, since she "can't make up her mind," and "isn't sure of herself."

Such idiosyncrasies may explain why women's language sounds much more "polite" than men's. It is polite to leave a decision open, not impose your mind, or views, or claims, on anyone else. So a tag question is a kind of polite statement, in that it does not force agreement or belief on the addressee. In the same way a request is a polite command, in that it does not force obedience on the addressee, but rather suggests something be done as a favor to the speaker. A clearly stated order implies a threat of certain consequences if it is not followed, and—even more impolite—implies that the speaker is in a superior position and able to enforce the order. By couching wishes in the form of a request, on the other hand, a speaker implies that if the request is not carried out, only the speaker will suffer; noncompliance cannot harm the addressee. So the decision is really left up to the addressee. The distinction becomes clear in these examples:

> Close the door.
> Please close the door.
> Will you close the door?
> Will you please close the door?
> Won't you close the door?

In the same ways as words and speech patterns used *by* women undermine her image, those used *to describe* women make matters even worse. Often a word may be used of both men and women (and perhaps of things as well); but when it is applied to women, it assumes a special meaning that, by implication rather than outright assertion, is derogatory to women as a group.

The use of euphemisms has this effect. A euphemism is a substitute for a word that has acquired a bad connotation by association with something unpleasant or embarrassing. But almost as soon as the new word comes into common usage, it takes on the same old bad connotations, since feelings about the things or people referred to are not altered by a change of name; thus new euphemisms must be constantly found.

There is one euphemism for *woman* still very much alive. The word, of course, is *lady*. *Lady* has a masculine counterpart, namely *gentleman*, occasionally shortened to *gent*. But for some reason *lady* is very much commoner than *gent* (*leman*).   14

The decision to use *lady* rather than *woman*, or vice versa, may considerably alter the sense of a sentence, as the following examples show: 15

> (a) A woman (lady) I know is a dean at Berkeley.
> (b) A woman (lady) I know makes amazing things out of shoelaces and old boxes.

The use of *lady* in (a) imparts a frivolous, or nonserious, tone to the sentence: the matter under discussion is not one of great moment. Similarly, in (b), using *lady* here would suggest that the speaker considered the "amazing things" not to be serious art, but merely a hobby or an aberration. If *woman* is used, she might be a serious sculptor. To say *lady doctor* is very condescending, since no one ever says *gentleman doctor* or even *man doctor*. For example, mention in the San Francisco *Chronicle* of January 31, 1972, of Madalyn Murray O'Hair as the *lady atheist* reduces her position to that of scatter-brained eccentric. Even *woman atheist* is scarcely defensible: sex is irrelevant to her philosophical position.   16

Many women argue that, on the other hand, *lady* carries with it overtones recalling the age of chivalry: conferring exalted stature on the person so referred to. This makes the term seem polite at first, but we must also remember that these implications are perilous: they suggest that a "lady" is helpless, and cannot do things by herself.   17

Lady can also be used to infer frivolousness, as in titles of organizations. Those that have a serious purpose (not merely that of enabling "the ladies" to spend time with one another) cannot use the word *lady* in their titles, but less serious ones may. Compare the *Ladies' Auxiliary* of a men's group, or the *Thursday Evening Ladies' Browning and Garden Society* with *Ladies' Liberation* or *Ladies' Strike for Peace*.   18

What is curious about this split is that *lady* is in origin a euphemism—a substitute that puts a better face on something people find uncomfortable—for *woman*. What kind of euphemism is it that subtly denigrates the people to whom it refers? Perhaps *lady* functions as a euphemism for *woman* because it does not contain the sexual implications present in *woman;* it is not "embarrassing" in that way. If   19 this is so, we may expect that, in the future, *lady* will replace woman as the primary word for the human female, since *woman* will have become too blatantly sexual. That this distinction is already made in some contexts at least is shown in the following examples, where you can try replacing *woman* with *lady:*

(a) She's only twelve, but she's already a woman.
(b) After ten years in jail, Harry wanted to find a woman.
(c) She's my woman, see, so don't mess around with her.

Another common substitute for *woman* is *girl.* One seldom hears a   20
man past the age of adolescence referred to as a boy, save in expressions like "going out with the boys," which are meant to suggest an air of adolescent frivolity and irresponsibility. But women of all ages are "girls": one can have a man—not a boy—Friday, but only a girl—never a woman or even a lady—Friday; women have girlfriends, but men do not—in a nonsexual sense—have boyfriends. It may be that this use of *girl* is euphemistic in the same way the use of *lady* is: in stressing the idea of immaturity, it removes the sexual connotations lurking in *woman. Girl* brings to mind irresponsibility: you don't send a girl to do a woman's errand (or even, for that matter, a boy's errand). She is a person who is both too immature and too far from real life to be entrusted with responsibilities or with decisions of any serious or important nature.

Now let's take a pair of words which, in terms of the possible   21
relationships in an earlier society, were simple male-female equivalents, analogous to *bull: cow.* Suppose we find that, for independent reasons, society has changed in such a way that the original meanings now are irrelevant. Yet the words have not been discarded, but have acquired new meanings, metaphorically related to their original senses. But suppose these new metaphorical uses are no longer parallel to each other. By seeing where the parallelism breaks down, we discover something about the different roles played by men and women in this culture. One good example of such a divergence through time is found in the pair, *master: mistress.* Once used with reference to one's power over servants, these words have become unusable today in their original master-servant sense as the relationship has become less prevalent in our society. But the words are still common.

Unless used with reference to animals, *master* now generally refers   22
to a man who has acquired consummate ability in some field, normally nonsexual. But its feminine counterpart cannot be used this way. It is practically restricted to its sexual sense of "paramour." We start out with two terms, both roughly paraphrasable as "one who has power over another." But the masculine form, once one person is no longer able to have absolute power over another, becomes usable metaphorically in the

sense of "having power over *something*." *Master* requires as its object only the name of some activity, something inanimate and abstract. But *mistress* requires a masculine noun in the possessive to precede it. One cannot say: "Rhonda is a mistress." One must be *someone's* mistress. A man is defined by what he does, a woman by her sexuality, that is, in terms of one particular aspect of her relationship to men. It is one thing to be an *old master* like Hans Holbein, and another to be an *old mistress*.

The same is true of the words *spinster* and *bachelor*—gender words   23
for "one who is not married." The resemblance ends with the definition. While *bachelor* is a neuter term, often used as a compliment, *spinster* normally is used pejoratively, with connotations of prissiness, fussiness, and so on. To be a bachelor implies that one has the choice of marrying or not, and this is what makes the idea of a bachelor existence attractive in the popular literature. He has been pursued and has successfully eluded his pursuers. But a spinster is one who has not been pursued, or at least not seriously. She is old, unwanted goods. The metaphorical connotations of *bachelor* generally suggest sexual freedom; of *spinster,* puritanism or celibacy.

These examples could be multiplied. It is generally considered a   24
faux pas, in society, to congratulate a woman on her engagement, while it is correct to congratulate her fiancé. Why is this? The reason seems to be that it is impolite to remind people of things that may be uncomfortable to them. To congratulate a woman on her engagement is really to say, "Thank goodness! You had a close call!" For the man, on the other hand, there was no such danger. His choosing to marry is viewed as a good thing, but not something essential.

The linguistic double standard holds throughout the life of the   25
relationship. After marriage, bachelor and spinster become man and wife, not man and woman. The woman whose husband dies remains "John's widow"; John, however, is never "Mary's widower."

Finally, why is it that salesclerks and others are so quick to call   26
women customers "dear," "honey," and other terms of endearment they really have no business using? A male customer would never put up with it. But women, like children, are supposed to enjoy these endearments, rather than being offended by them.

In more ways than one, it's time to speak up.   27

Exercises

Some Important Words

euphemistic (paragraph 1), bias (1), linguistic (1), left-handed compliment (2), unassertive (2), syntax (5), gender-related (5), confirmation (6), leeway (6), small talk (7), elicit (7), corroboration (8), baldly (9), subliminal (10), intonation pattern (10), declarative (10), inflection (10), requisite (10), idiosyncrasies (11), couching (11), noncompliance (11), implication (12), derogatory (12), frivolous (16), moment (16), aberration (16), condescending (16), atheist (16), overtones (17), chivalry (17), exalted (17), perilous (17), denigrates (19), blatantly (19), connotations (20), lurking (20), analogous (21), metaphorically (21), consummate (22), paramour (22), paraphrasable (22), neuter (23), pejoratively (23), eluded (23), puritanism (23), celibacy (23), *faux pas*—misstep (24), double standard (25).

Some of the Issues

1. In paragraph 1 Lakoff says, "[we are] damned if we do, and damned if we don't." What does she refer to?
2. In paragraph 2 Lakoff refers to a "left-handed compliment." Why "left-handed"? What is implied in this phrase?
3. Paragraphs 5–10 are devoted to tag questions. Why, according to Lakoff, are such questions characteristic of women's speech?
4. What does Lakoff mean in paragraph 11 when she says that women's language is more "polite" than men's language? Is politeness considered a virtue here?
5. Paragraphs 1–11 deal with the way women talk and paragraphs 12–15 with the way women are talked about. Sum up the major parts of the argument in each of these sections.
6. In paragraphs 21–23 Lakoff discusses pairs of male-female terms of which the female term has acquired additional (often derogatory) meanings. Can you add further examples to that list?
7. Cite examples of the ways, in recent times, we have tried to avoid male-female stereotyping, for example, by replacing "mailman" with "letter carrier."

The Way We Are Told

8. Examine the first two paragraphs and show how Lakoff uses words with strong connotations (emotional impact) to reinforce her argument.
9. Who is Lakoff's audience? Is it one that needs convincing or one that looks for reinforcement? Cite reasons for your answer.
10. Who is the "we" in the first two paragraphs?

Some Subjects for Writing

11. Search for examples of language used by groups other than women: minorities, certain occupations. Select one such group and write an essay describing what you have found.

12. Keep a notebook for two weeks in which you record examples of women's language and men's language. At the end of that period look over your notes, try to classify them, and write an analytical paper about the results.

THE MEDIA'S IMAGE
OF ARABS

Jack G. Shaheen

Jack G. Shaheen, born in 1935, teaches mass communications at Southern Illinois University in Edwardsville. He has also taught at the American University in Beirut and the University of Jordan in Amman. He is the author of *The TV Arab* (1984).

Lebanon, where Shaheen's family came from, is a small country at the eastern end of the Mediterranean, bordering on Israel to the south and Syria to the east and north. Its capital, Beirut, was once known as the Paris of the Middle East, a lively, sophisticated city that was also the financial center of the region. In recent years Lebanon has been in a state of civil war that has ravaged much of the country and led at times to the occupation of parts of it by its two neighbors.

The following selection first appeared in the "My Turn" section of *Newsweek* on February 29, 1988. The media's image of Arabs, Shaheen asserts, is almost invariably hostile and one-sided. It contributes to, perhaps is even responsible for, the negative stereotype Americans have of Arabs.

American's bogeyman is the Arab. Until the nightly news brought us TV pictures of Palestinian boys being punched and beaten, almost all portraits of Arabs seen in America were dangerously threatening. Arabs were either billionaires or bombers—rarely victims. They were hardly ever seen as ordinary people practicing law, driving taxis, singing lullabies or healing the sick. Though TV news may portray them more sympathetically now, the absence of positive media images nurtures suspicion and stereotype. As an Arab-American, I have found that ugly caricatures have had an enduring impact on my family.

I was sheltered from prejudicial portraits at first. My parents came from Lebanon in the 1920s; they met and married in America. Our home in the steel city of Clairton, Pa., was a center for ethnic sharing—black, white, Jew and gentile. There was only one major source of media images then, at the State movie theater where I was lucky enough to get a part-time job as an usher. But in the late 1940s, Westerns and war movies were popular, not Middle Eastern dramas. Memories of World War II were fresh, and the screen heavies were the Japanese and the Germans. True to the cliché of the times, the only good Indian was a dead Indian. But when I mimicked or mocked the bad guys, my mother cautioned me. She explained that stereotypes blur our vision and corrupt the imagination. "Have compassion for all people, Jackie," she said. "This way, you'll learn to experience the joy of accepting people as they are, and not as they appear in films. Stereotypes hurt."

Mother was right. I can remember the Saturday afternoon when my   3 son, Michael, who was seven, and my daughter, Michele, six, suddenly called out: "Daddy, Daddy, they've got some bad Arabs on TV." They were watching that great American morality play, TV wrestling. Akbar the Great, who liked to hear the cracking of bones, and Abdullah the Butcher, a dirty fighter who liked to inflict pain, were pinning their foes with "camel locks." From that day on, I knew I had to try to neutralize the media caricatures.

It hasn't been easy. With my children, I have watched animated   4 heroes Heckle and Jeckle pull the rug from under "Ali Boo-Boo, the Desert Rat," and Laverne and Shirley stop "Sheik Ha-Mean-Ie" from conquering "the U.S. and the world." I have read comic books like the "Fantastic Four" and "G.I. Combat" whose characters have sketched Arabs as "lowlifes" and "human hyenas." Negative stereotypes were everywhere. A dictionary informed my youngsters that an Arab is a "vagabond, drifter, hobo and vagrant." Whatever happened, my wife wondered, to Aladdin's good genie?

To a child, the world is simple: good versus evil. But my children   5 and others with Arab roots grew up without ever having seen a humane Arab on the silver screen, someone to pattern their lives after. Is it easier for a camel to go through the eye of a needle than for a screen Arab to appear as a genuine human being?

Hollywood producers must have an instant Ali Baba kit that   6 contains scimitars, veils, sunglasses and such Arab clothing as *chadors* and *kufiyahs*. In the mythical "Ay-rabland," oil wells, tents, mosques, goats and shepherds prevail. Between the sand dunes, the camera focuses on a mock-up of a palace from "Arabian Nights"—or a military air base. Recent movies suggest that Americans are at war with Arabs, forgetting the fact that out of 21 Arab nations, America is friendly with 19 of them. And in "Wanted Dead or Alive," a movie that starred Gene Simmons, the leader of the rock group Kiss, the war comes home when an Arab terrorist comes to the United States dressed as a rabbi and, among other things, conspires with Arab-Americans to poison the people of Los Angeles. The movie was released last year.

The Arab remains American culture's favorite whipping boy. In his   7
memoirs, Terrel Bell, Ronald Reagan's first secretary of education, writes
about an "apparent bias among mid-level, right-wing staffers at the White
House" who dismissed Arabs as "sand niggers." Sadly, the racial slurs
continue. At a recent teacher's conference, I met a woman from Sioux
Falls, S.D., who told me about the persistence of discrimination. She was
in the process of adopting a baby when an agency staffer warned her that
the infant had a problem. When she asked whether the child was
mentally ill, or physically handicapped, there was silence. Finally, the
worker said: "The baby is Jordanian."

To me, the Arab demon of today is much like the Jewish demon of   8
yesterday. We deplore the false portrait of Jews as a swarthy menace. Yet
a similar portrait has been accepted and transferred to another group of
Semites—the Arabs. Print and broadcast journalists have started to
challenge this stereotype. They are now revealing more humane images
of Palestinian Arabs, a people who traditionally suffered from the myth
that Palestinian equals terrorist. Others could follow that lead and retire
the stereotypical Arab to a media Valhalla.

It would be a step in the right direction if movie and TV producers   9
developed characters modeled after real-life Arab-Americans. We could
then see a White House correspondent like Helen Thomas, whose father
came from Lebanon, in "The Golden Girls," a heart surgeon patterned
after Dr. Michael DeBakey on "St. Elsewhere," or a Syrian-American
playing tournament chess like Yasser Seirawan, the Seattle grandmaster.

Politicians, too should speak out against the cardboard caricatures.   10
They should refer to Arabs as friends, not just as moderates. And religious
leaders could state that Islam like Christianity and Judaism maintains that
all mankind is one family in the care of God. When all imagemakers
rightfully begin to treat Arabs and all other minorities with respect and
dignity, we may begin to unlearn our prejudices.

Exercises

Some Important Words

bogeyman (paragraph 1), positive media images (1), stereotype (1),
enduring (1), prejudicial (2), ethnic (2), gentile (2), heavies (2), cliché (2),
morality play (3), neutralize (3), caricatures (3), animated (4), vagabond
(4), drifter (4), hobo (4), vagrant (4), Aladdin's genie (4), humane (5),
scimitars (6), *chadors* (6), *kufiyahs* (6), mythical (6), prevail (6), mock-up
(6), bias (7), slurs (7), demon (8), swarthy (8), Semite (8), Valhalla (8),
moderates (10).

Some of the Issues

1. What, according to the author, is the standard image of the Arab in the American media? Why is he concerned that Arabs are hardly ever portrayed as ordinary people?
2. When did Shaheen first become aware of stereotypes? Why was he not conscious of them earlier?
3. Shaheen is especially concerned about the influence of the media on his children. Why does he believe that children are particularly vulnerable to stereotypes?
4. Shaheen states that the image of Arabs in the media is changing somewhat (paragraphs 8 and 9). To what does he attribute that shift? What further changes does he advocate?

The Way We Are Told

5. Cite several instances in which Shaheen supports a general assertion with specific examples drawn from his own experience.
6. Shaheen's essay concentrates on the media's treatment of Arabs, yet he mentions unfair treatment of other groups as well. What does his argument gain from this expansion?

Some Subjects for Writing

7. If you have encountered stereotyping, describe the circumstances in an essay.
*8. Read Maya Angelou's "Graduation." Analyze the event she describes as an example of stereotyping.
9. Describe a character in a film or a TV program who is represented as a stereotype, either negatively or positively.

SOLD AT FINE STORES EVERYWHERE, NATURELLEMENT

Myrna Knepler

Myrna Knepler, born in 1934, is a professor of linguistics at North-eastern Illinois University and the author of textbooks in English as a second language. The following selection is reprinted from the February 1978 issue of *Verbatim,* a magazine about language. It describes a particular gambit in the language of advertising—the use of the snob appeal French has for some Americans, as well as the opposite, the use of English to enhance the sales appeal of some products to the French.

Why is it that a high priced condominium is advertised in American 1 newspapers as a *de luxe* apartment while French magazines try to sell their more affluent readers *appartements de grand standing*? Madison Avenue, when constructing ads for high priced non-necessary items, may use French phrases to suggest to readers that they are identified as super-sophisticated, subtly sexy, and privy to the secrets of old world charm and tradition. In recent years French magazines aimed at an increasingly affluent public have made equally canny use of borrowed English words to sell their wares.

The advertising pages of the *New Yorker* and the more elegant 2 fashion and home decorating magazines often depend on blatant flattery of the reader's sense of exclusiveness. Time and time again the reader is told "only *you* are elegant, sophisticated, discriminating and rich enough to use this product." Of course the "you" must encompass a large enough group to insure adequate sales. Foreign words, particularly prestigious French words, may be used to reinforce this selling message.

French magazines often use English words in their advertising to 3 suggest to potential consumers a slightly different but equally flattering self-image. The reader is pictured as someone in touch with new ideas from home and abroad who has not forgotten the traditional French arts of living, but is modern enough to approach them in a completely up-to-date and casual manner.

Of course, each language has borrowed words from the other   4
which have, over the course of time, been completely assimilated. It is not these that the advertiser exploits but rather words that are foreign enough to evoke appealing images of an exotic culture. When the French reader is urged to try "Schweppes, le 'drink' des gens raffinés" or an American consumer is told that a certain manufacturer has "the *savoir faire* to design *la crème de la crème* of luxurious silky knits," the foreign words do not say anything that could not be as easily said by native ones. What they do convey is something else. They invite the reader to share in the prestige of the foreign language and the power of the images associated with that language's country of origin.

In each country a knowledge of the other's language is an   5
important sign of cultivation. Today, English is the language studied by an overwhelming majority of French students, and the ability to speak it well is increasingly valued as a symbol of prestige as well as a marketable skill. Despite the decrease in foreign language study in the United States, French has maintained its reputation as a language people ought to know. Adding a few obvious foreign words from the prestige language not only increases the prestige of the product itself but also flatters the reader by reminding him that he has enough linguistic talent to understand what is being said. As in the "only-*you*-are-elegant, -sophisticated, -discriminating-and-rich enough" appeal, the advertiser must be careful not to exclude too many potential customers, and the foreign expressions are usually transparent cognates or easily understood words. A French reader may be urged to buy cigarettes by being told that "partout dans le monde c'est YES à Benson and Hedges" while the *New Yorker* reader can consider a vacation on "an island [off the coast of South Carolina] where change hasn't meant commercialism, and tranquility still comes *au naturelle.*"

Even monolinguals are not excluded from this flattery. The word   6
can be given in the foreign language and then translated; the reader is still in on the secret: " 'goût' is the French word for taste and Christofle is the universal word for taste in vases."

The prestige of a foreign term and its possible ambiguity for the   7
reader may serve to disguise a negative fact about the product. A necklace of *Perle de Mer* advertised in an American magazine is not composed of real pearls made by nature in the seas but of simulated pearls produced by a large American manufacturer. By the same token, when a French advertisement for a packaged tour offers "aller et retour en classe coach" the prestige of the English word *coach* disguises the fact that it is the less luxurious form of airline transportation that is being offered.

But the most important function of borrowed words in advertising   8
is to project an image of their country of origin in order to create for the
reader the illusion that the product, and by implication its user, will share
in the good things suggested by that image. French names like *Grand
Prix, Coupe De Ville,* and *Monte Carlo* attached to American car models
help the advertiser to get across the message that the car is luxurious,
sophisticated, and elegantly appointed and that driving such an automobile reflects positively on the taste of its potential owner. In almost all
cases French names are reserved for the more expensive models while
American words are favored for small meat-and-potatoes cars like
Charger, Maverick, Pinto and *Bronco.* Similarly, the French reader is
likely to encounter a large number of American technical terms in ads for
appliances, radio and television equipment, cameras, and "gadgets de
luxe," since the manufacturer benefits by associating American mechanical skills with his products. An advertisement for French-made hi-fi
equipment appearing in a French magazine spoke of the product's
"push-pull ultra linéaire, 6 haut-parleurs, 2 elliptiques et 4 tweeters . . .
montés sur baffle."

Images, which are used again and again, are often based on myths   9
of the other country's culture. Words like *tomahawk* and *trading posts*
are used in French advertisements to evoke images of a western-movie
America of naturalness, freedom, and adventure in order to sell products
like "Chemise de 'cow girl,' " "bottes Far West," and vests in the style of
"Arizona Bill," irrespective of the real West that is or was. The name
Monte Carlo attached to an American-made car trades on the American
consumer's image of a once-exclusive vacation spot, now available as
part of low-cost travel packages. Thus the name *Monte Carlo* can convey
to an automobile a prestige that the real trip to Monte Carlo has long
since lost.

These images that are not completely mythic are usually gross   10
stereotypes of the other country's culture. Few Americans would recognize the image of American life presented in French advertising—a new
world filled with eternally youthful, glamorously casual, up-to-date men
and women devoted to consuming the products of their advanced
technology. Similarly, few French men and women would recognize the
nation of elegant and knowing consumers of food, wine, and sophisticated sex pictured in American ads.

The image of France as a nation of lovers, bold yet unusually subtle   11
in their relations with the opposite sex, is often called upon to sell
perfume and cosmetics, sometimes of French origin but packaged and
advertised specifically for the American market. An ad which appeared
several years ago in the *New Yorker* showed a bottle of perfume labeled
"voulez-vous" implanted next to a closeup of a sexy and elegant woman,
her face shadowed by a male hand lighting her cigarette. The text: "The

spark that starts the fire. Voulez-vous a new perfume." *Audace, Robe d'un Soir,* and *Je Reviens* are other perfumes advertised in American magazines with pictures and copy that reinforce the sexual suggestiveness of the prominently featured French name on the label.

It may be surprising for Americans to learn that English names are given to perfumes sold in France to enhance their romantic image. *My Love, Partner* and *Shocking* are some examples. Advertisements for French-made men's cosmetics in French magazines may refer to products such as *l'after-shave* and *le pre-shave*. Givenchy's *Gentleman* is advertised to Frenchmen as an eau de toilette for the man who dares to appear at business lunches in a turtleneck sweater and has the courage to treat love in a casual manner.   12

The recent swelling of the list of Americanisms used in French advertising and in French speech has pained many Frenchmen and has even caused the government to take action. For a number of years the leader in this "war against anglicisms" has been René Etiemble, a professor at the Sorbonne. Etiemble, through magazine articles, radio and television appearances and his widely read book, *Parlez-vous franglais?*, struggles vehemently against what he most often refers to as an "invasion" of American terms. He does little to disguise his strong anti-American sentiments. American words are rejected as agents of a vulgar American culture and both are seen as threats to the French way of life. According to Etiemble "[the] heritage of words [is the] heritage of ideas: with *le twist* and *la ségrégation, la civilisation cocolcoolique,* the American manner of not living will disturb and contaminate all that remains of your cuisine, wines, love and free thought." It would be difficult to find a stronger believer in the power of words than Etiemble.   13

In response to the concerns of Etiemble and others, a series of committees composed of highly placed French scientists and language experts were charged with the task of finding Gallic equivalents for such popular terms as *le meeting, le marketing, le management,* and *le know-how.* The recommended replacements are: *la réunion, la commercialisation, la direction,* and, of course, *le savoir faire.* The replacements do not seem to have taken root.   14

At the end of 1975 a more radical step was taken. The French National Assembly passed a law banning the use of all foreign words in advertising in those cases in which a native alternative has been officially suggested, and instituting a fine against violators.   15

Both Etiemble and the government purists rely strongly on the "logical" argument that most loan words are not needed because there already exists a native equivalent with exactly the same meaning. Yet a look at the advertising pages of French and American magazines will show that borrowed words are used again and again when there are obvious native equivalents. Certainly the English words in "c'est YES à   16

Benson and Hedges" and "Le 'drink' des gens raffinés" could be translated without loss of literal meaning—but they are not.

It is precisely because of the connotations associated with the   17
culture of its country of origin, not its denotations, that advertisers find the borrowed word attractive.

Exercises

Some Important Words

affluent (paragraph 1), Madison Avenue (1), privy (1), blatant (2), potential (3), assimilated (4), exploits (4), *raffinés*—refined (4), *savoir faire*—sophistication, literally know-how (4), *crème de la crème*—the very best (4), discriminating (5), cognates (5), *partout dans le monde*—throughout the whole world (5), monolinguals (6), ambiguity (7), *Perle de Mer*—Pearls of the Sea (7), *aller et retour*—round trip (7), elegantly appointed (8), *haut-parleurs*—loudspeakers (8), *montés sur*—mounted on (8), *chemise*—shirt (9), *bottes*—boots (9), mythic (10), *Voulez-vous*—Are you willing? (11), *Audace*—Boldness (11), *Robe d'un Soir*—Evening wrap (11), *Je Reviens*—I will return (11), anglicisms (13), *Parlez-vous franglais?*—Do you speak franglais? (13), vehemently (13), Gallic (14), connotations (17), denotations (17).

Some of the Issues

1. According to Knepler, what classes of people are addressed through the use of French words in American advertising, and vice versa? How do her examples substantiate her argument?
2. Advertisers use foreign words to provide a sense of exclusivity for the reader; at the same time, they want to make sure their message comes across. How is this done? Cite some examples.
3. What kinds of products are likely to be sold in America with the use of French words? What kinds of products will use English to enhance sales appeal in France?
4. Paragraph 7 presents cases in which the foreign language disguises negative information. Explain the examples.
5. What kind of stereotype of America does French advertising play upon?

The Way We Are Told

6. Consider the first three paragraphs. Why does paragraph 1 begin with a question? Is it answered? How do paragraphs 2 and 3 relate to the first paragraph?

7. In paragraphs 9–11 Knepler discusses the myths the Americans and the French believe about each other's culture. What means does Knepler use to make the reader believe in the unreality of these respective views?

Some Subjects for Writing

8. Examine several magazine advertisements for a particular kind of product, for example, automobiles, clothes, liquor. What flattering images of the potential consumer are used to sell the product? Explain the effect in detail.
9. Write an essay comparing and contrasting the reality of a specific place, type of person, or institution you know with the myth or stereotype about it.

SIN, SUFFER
AND REPENT

Donna Woolfolk Cross

Donna Woolfolk Cross was born in New York City in 1947 and teaches English at Onondaga Community College. Her books are concerned with the uses and abuses of language, especially in advertising and the media: *Speaking of Words* (1977, with James MacKillup), *Word Abuse: How the Words We Use Abuse Us* (1979), and *Mediaspeak* (1981), from which the following selection is taken. It describes and analyzes an American cultural phenomenon that has spread across the globe: the soap opera.

    Although Cross may refer to some programs no longer aired, the article is still valuable as a springboard for discussing the relationship between the media and the world it represents.

Soap operas reverse Tolstoy's famous assertion in *Anna Karenina* that "Happy families are all alike; every unhappy family is unhappy in its own way." On soaps, *every* family is unhappy, and each is unhappy in more or less the same way.

—Marjory Perloff

It is the hope of every advertiser to habituate the housewife to an engrossing narrative whose optimum length is forever and at the same time to saturate all levels of her consciousness with the miracle of a given product, so she will be aware of it all the days of her life and mutter its name in her sleep.

—James Thurber

In July 1969, when the entire nation was glued to television sets watching 1
the first man walk on the moon, an irate woman called a Wausau, Wisconsin, TV station to complain that her favorite soap opera was not being shown that day and why was that. The station manager replied, "This is probably the most important news story of the century, some-

thing you may never again see the equal of." Unimpressed, the lady replied, "Well, I hope they crash."

One can hardly blame her. For weeks, she had been worrying that 2 Audrey might be going blind, that Alice would marry that scoundrel Michael, and that Dr. Hardy might not discover his patient Peter to be his long-lost natural son before the boy died of a brain tumor. Suddenly, in the heat of all these crises, she was cut off from all information about these people and forced to watch the comings and goings of men in rubber suits whom she had never met. It was enough to unhinge anybody.

Dedicated watchers of soap operas often confuse fact with fiction.* 3 Sometimes this can be endearing, sometimes ludicrous. During the Senate Watergate hearings (which were broadcast on daytime television), viewers whose favorite soap operas were preempted simply adopted the hearings as substitute soaps. Daniel Shorr reports that the listeners began "telephoning the networks to criticize slow-moving sequences, suggesting script changes and asking for the return of favorite witnesses, like 'that nice John Dean.' "

Stars of soap operas tell hair-raising stories of their encounters with 4 fans suffering from this affliction. Susan Lucci, who plays the promiscuous Erica Kane on "All My Children," tells of a time she was riding in a parade: "We were in a crowd of about 250,000, traveling in an antique open car moving ver-r-ry slowly. At that time in the series I was involved with a character named Nick. Some man broke through, came right up to the car and said to me, 'Why don't you give *me* a little bit of what you've been giving Nick?' " The man hung onto the car, menacingly, until she was rescued by the police. Another time, when she was in church, the reverent silence was broken by a woman's astonished remark, "Oh, my god, Erica prays!" Margaret Mason, who plays the villainous Lisa Anderson in "Days of Our Lives," was accosted by a woman who poured a carton of milk all over her in the supermarket. And once a woman actually tried to force her car off the Ventura Freeway.

Just as viewers come to confuse the actors with their roles, so too 5 they see the soap opera image of life in America as real. The National Institutes of Mental Health reported that a majority of Americans actually adopt what they see in soap operas to handle their own life problems. The images are not only "true to life"; they are a guide for living.

What, then, is the image of life on soap operas? For one thing, 6 marriage is touted as the *ne plus ultra* of a woman's existence. Living

*Contrary to popular belief, soap operas are not the harmless pastime of lonely housewives only. Recent surveys show that many high school and college students, as well as many working and professional people, are addicted to soaps. A sizable chunk of the audience is men. Such well-known people as Sammy Davis, Jr., Van Cliburn, John Connally, and Supreme Court Justice Thurgood Marshall admit to being fans of one or more soap operas.

together is not a respectable condition and is tolerated only as long as one of the partners (usually the woman) is bucking for eventual marriage. Casual sex is out; only the most despicable villains engage in it: "Diane has no respect for marriage or any of the values we were brought up with. She's a vicious, immoral woman." Occasionally, a woman will speak out against marriage, but it's clear that in her heart of hearts she really wants it. Women who are genuinely not interested in marriage do not appear on soap operas except as occasional caricatures, misguided and immature in their thinking. Reporter Martha McGee appeared on "Ryan's Hope" just long enough to titillate the leading man with remarks like, "I don't know if you're my heart's desire, but you're sexy as hell." Punished for this kind of heretical remark, she was last seen sobbing brokenly in a telephone booth.

No, love and marriage still go together like a horse and carriage in 7 soap operas, though many marriages don't last long enough for the couple to put away all the wedding gifts. As Cornell professor Rose Goldsen says, this is a world of "fly-apart marriages, throwaway husbands, throwaway wives." There is rarely any clear logic behind the dissolution of these relationships; indeed, the TV formula seems to be: the happier the marriage, the more perilous the couple's future. A blissful marriage is the kiss of death: "I just can't believe it about Alice and Steve. I mean, they were the *perfect* couple, the absolute *perfect* couple!"

Most marriages are not pulled apart by internal flaws but by 8 external tampering—often by a jealous rival: "C'mon, Peter. Stay for just one more drink. Jan won't mind. And anyway, the night's still young. Isn't it nice to be together all nice and cozy like this?"

Often the wife has willfully brought this state of affairs on herself by 9 committing that most heinous of all offenses: neglecting her man. "NHM" almost always occurs when the woman becomes too wrapped up in her career. Every time Rachel Corey went to New York City for a weekend to further her career as a sculptress, her marriage tottered. At this writing, Ellen Dalton's marriage to Mark appears to be headed for big trouble as a result of her business trip to Chicago:

ERICA: I warned you, Ellen, not to let your job interfere with your marriage.
ELLEN: I have tried to do my best for my marriage *and* my job. . . . Mark had no right to stomp out of here just now.
ERICA: Don't you understand? He just couldn't take anymore.
ELLEN: What do you mean?
ERICA: It's not just the trip to Chicago that Mark resents. It's your putting your job before having a family.
ELLEN: I demand the right to be treated as an equal. I don't have to apologize because I don't agree to have a child the minute my

husband snaps his fingers. I'm going to Chicago like a big girl and I'm going to do the job I was hired to do. (stalks out the door)

ERICA: (musing, to herself) Well, I may be old-fashioned, but that's no way to hold onto your man.

Career women do appear frequently on soap operas, but the ones who are romantically successful treat their careers as a kind of sideline. Female cardiologists devote fifteen years of their lives to advanced medical training, then spend most of their time in the hospital coffee shop. One man remarked to a career woman who was about to leave her job, "Oh, Kate, you'll miss working. Those long lunches, those intimate cocktail hours!" Women residents apparently schedule all their medical emergencies before dinnertime, because if they should have to stay late at the hospital, it's the beginning of the end for their marriages. It's interesting to speculate how they might work this out: 10

NURSE: Oh my God, Dr. Peterson, the patient's hemorrhaging!

DR. PETERSON: Sorry, nurse, it'll just have to wait. If I don't get my meat loaf in by a quarter to six, it'll never be ready before my husband gets home.

Husbands, weak-minded souls, cannot be expected to hold out against the advances of any attractive woman, even one for whom they have contempt, if their wives aren't around. Meatloafless, they are very easily seduced. The clear suggestion is that they could hardly have been expected to do otherwise: 11

"Well, after all, Karen, you weren't around very much during that time. It's not surprising that Michael turned to Pat for a little comfort and understanding."

If, in the brief span of time allotted to them, a couple manage to have intercourse, the woman is certain to become pregnant. Contraception on soap operas is such a sometime thing that even the Pope could scarcely object to it. The birthrate on soaps is eight times as high as the United States birthrate; indeed it's higher than the birthrate of any underdeveloped nation in the world. This rabbitlike reproduction is fraught with peril. One recent study revealed that out of nineteen soap opera pregnancies, eight resulted in miscarriages and three in death for the mother. Rose Goldsen has estimated that the odds are 7 to 10 against any fetus making it to full term, worse if you include getting through the birth canal. Women on soap operas miscarry at the drop of a pin. And, of course, miscarriages are rarely caused by any defect with mother or baby: again, external forces are to blame. Often, miscarriage is brought on by an unappreciative or unfaithful mate. For example, on "Another World," Alice, the heroine,   12 suffered a miscarriage when her husband visited his ex-wife Rachel. One woman lost her baby because her husband came home drunk. This plot twist is no doubt particularly appealing to women viewers because of the instant revenge visited upon the transgressing mate. They can fantasize about similar punishment for husbandly malfeasance in their own lives— and about his inevitable guilt and repentance:

> HUSBAND: (stonily) Jennifer, these potatoes are too gluey. I can't eat this!
>
> WIFE: (clutches her belly) Oh, no!
>
> HUSBAND: What? What is it?
>
> WIFE: It's the baby! Something's wrong—call the doctor!
>
> HUSBAND: Oh my god, what have I done?
>
> *Later, at the hospital:*
>
> DOCTOR: I'm sorry, Mr. Henson, but your wife has lost the baby.
>
> HUSBAND: (brokenly) I didn't know, I didn't know. How could I have attacked her potatoes so viciously with her in such a delicate condition!
>
> DOCTOR: Now, now. You musn't blame yourself. We still don't know exactly what causes miscarriages except that they happen for a complicated set of physical and emotional reasons.
>
> HUSBAND: Oh, thank you, Doctor.
>
> DOCTOR: Of course, carping about the potatoes couldn't have *helped.*

Miscarriage is effective as a punishment because it is one of the very worst things that can happen to a woman on a soap opera. In the world of soaps, the one thing every good and worthwhile woman wants is a baby. Soap operas never depict childless women as admirable. These "real people" do not include women like Katharine Hepburn, who once announced that she never wanted to have children because "the first time the kid said no to me, I'd kill it!" Childless women are either to be pitied, if there are physical reasons that prevent them from getting pregnant, or condemned, if they are childless by choice. 13

Second only to neglecting her man in her hierarchy of female crime is having an abortion. No admirable character *ever* gets an abortion on a soap opera. Occasionally, however, a virtuous woman will consider it, usually for one of two reasons: she doesn't want the man she loves to feel "trapped" into marrying her; or she has been "violated" by her husband's best friend, a member of the underworld, or her delivery boy, who may also be her long-lost half brother. But she always "comes around" in the end, her love for "the new life growing inside me" conquering her misgivings. If the baby should happen to survive the perilous journey through the birth canal (illegitimate babies get miscarried at a far higher rate than legitimate ones), she never has any regrets. 14

Why should she? Babies on soap operas never drool, spit up, or throw scrambled eggs in their mother's faces. Babyhood (and its inevitable counterpart, motherhood) is "sold" to American women as slickly as soap. Kimberly, of "Ryan's Hope," is so distressed when she finds out she is pregnant that she runs away from home. She has the baby, prematurely, while alone and unattended on a deserted houseboat. It is a difficult and dangerous birth. But once the baby is born, Kimberly is all maternal affection. "Where is she?" she shouts. "Why won't they let me see my little girl?" By the end of the day, she announces, "If anything happens to this baby, I don't know what I'll do!"

Under the surface of romantic complications, soap operas sell a vision of morality and American family life, of a society where marriage is the highest good, sex the greatest evil, where babies are worshiped and abortion condemned, where motherhood is exalted and children ignored. It is a vision of a world devoid of social conflict. There are hardly any short-order cooks, bus drivers, mechanics, construction workers, or farmers on soap operas. Blue-collar problems do not enter these immaculate homes. No one suffers from flat feet or derrière spread from the long hours spent at an unrewarding or frustrating job. The upwardly mobile professionals who populate soap operas love their work, probably because they are hardly ever at it—one lawyer clocked in at his office exactly once in three months. Their problems are those of people with time on their hands to covet the neighbor's wife, track down villains, betray friends, and enjoy what one observer has called "the perils of Country Club Place."   15

It is a world largely devoid of black people and black viewpoints. When black characters do appear, they are doctors or lawyers whose problems, ambitions, and anxieties are identical to those of their white colleagues.* Racial discrimination and inequality do not exist, and the black romantic plotlines are indistinguishable from white—though, of course, the two *never* mix. Once, it is true, in a daring departure from the straight and narrow, "All My Children" showed a black-white romance which shocked a lot of viewers. But it wasn't really a romance in the usual sense. At least, it was perfectly clear that black Dr. Nancy Grant had turned to her white boyfriend Owen solely for comfort after the breakup of her marriage to Dr. Frank Grant. They were not—gasp!—sleeping together. Anyway, the whole mess was resolved when Owen considerately died just minutes after marrying Nancy to save her from disgrace   16

---

*"All My Children" has recently introduced a "lower-class" black character—a street-wise teenager named Jesse, who is the despair of his black aunt and uncle, both doctors. It is clear, however, that Jesse's scorn for Establishment values is merely a defense against rejection, and his eventual conversion and admittance to Pine Valley society seems inevitable.

because she was pregnant with black Dr. Frank Grant's baby. Another experiment with a black-white flirtation was abruptly ended when the black family moved to another town. Still another such plotline was resolved when it turned out that the white woman in an interracial relationship was actually a light-skinned black woman who had been "ashamed" of her heritage.

The world of soap operas is without doubt white, upper middle-class—and decidedly small-town. Emerging out of the mists of the American heartland as mysteriously as Brigadoon are towns like Oakdale, Pine Valley, Rosehill. On soap operas, towns never have real-life names like Secaucus or Weedsport. The great American myth of the Good, Clean, Safe Small Town, which some thought had been laid to rest by the likes of Sinclair Lewis and Sherwood Anderson, has been resurrected on the soaps. Only in small towns, the daily message is, can one find true happiness and fulfillment: 17

> CAROL: I've wondered sometimes if you don't get bored living in Oakdale? Living in New York or on the Coast can be so much more exciting.
>
> SANDY: Excitement is one thing. Real feelings are another.

One half expects her to add, "Oh, Auntie Em, there's no place like home!"

Exercises

Some Important Words

Quotations: assertion, habituate, engrossing, optimum, saturate, mutter. irate (paragraph 1), scoundrel (2), natural son (2), unhinge (2), endearing (3), ludicrous (3), Watergate (3), preempted (3), affliction (4), promiscuous (4), villainous (4), accosted (4), touted (6), *ne plus ultra*—highest point (6), bucking (6), despicable (6), caricatures (6), titillate (6), heretical (6), dissolution (7), perilous (7), tampering (8), heinous (9), sculptress (9), tottered (9), cardiologists (10), hemorrhaging (10), allotted (12), contraception (12), underdeveloped (12), fraught (12), fetus (12), transgressing (12), fantasize (12), malfeasance (12), inevitable (12), repentance (12), carping (12), hierarchy (14), misgiving (14), exalted (15), devoid (15), blue-collar (15), immaculate (15), derrière (15), upwardly mobile (15), covet (15), colleagues (16), Establishment (16, footnote), inevitable (16, footnote), Brigadoon (17), Sinclair Lewis (17), Sherwood Anderson (17).

Note: In answering the questions on Donna Woolfolk Cross's article, focus on her contention that the "soaps" give a highly distorted picture of American life. Even though both the world and the programs have changed since the article was published, that contention may still be true.

If you watch soap operas, look for specific instances of their portrayal of the lives of men, women, and minorities to share with your classmates. Together you can determine whether the characters and their stories represent contemporary life as you know it.

Some of the Issues

1. After you have read the essay examine its title: "Sin, Suffer and Repent." Who is it that sins, suffers, and repents?
2. Cross gives several instances of soap viewers confusing soap-opera life with real life. Cite them. What does the confusion consist of? Why is it important for her to convince us that there is confusion?
3. Cross cites several examples of characters who break the moral code of the soaps. What happens to them? Are the consequences different for male characters and female characters?
4. Summarize what the soaps say about working women. What kind of restrictions are they placed under? Are men's jobs portrayed in the same way?
5. What is the attitude toward motherhood expressed in soaps? Toward children? Why do you think there are so many miscarriages?
6. Why are husbands portrayed as "weak-minded souls"? Are men in soaps given more, or less, dignity than women?
7. Why do women in soap operas who carry illegitimate babies miscarry more often?
8. How, according to Cross, do the soaps treat abortion? Is it the worst crime?
9. How are members of minorities treated on soaps according to Cross?

The Way We Are Told

10. In several instances, Cross supports her arguments with citations from authorities. Find the ones in which a specific source is cited, and others which are more vague. How convincing is Cross's use of authorities?
11. Cross uses what are apparently actual excerpts from the soaps, but also makes up her own parodies of soap-opera dialog to convince us. Does she make the difference clear? Is what she does fair?
12. What is the effect of the abbreviation NHM (paragraph 9)?
13. In paragraph 14 several single words are emphasized by putting them in quotation marks. What is the effect of doing so?
14. Cross has a serious purpose in writing this essay. Are her uses of humor, irony, and exaggeration appropriate? Examine some specific examples.

Some Subjects for Writing

15. Write an essay justifying *one* of the following propositions:
    a. Soap operas are a harmless entertainment, and nobody is likely to confuse soap-opera life with real life.
    b. While soap operas may occasionally distort reality, on the whole they do provide an accurate picture of American life.
    c. Soaps have a detrimental effect on their audiences, and steps should be taken to discourage their production.
16. Soap operas are interspersed with commercials. Examine a daytime soap, looking at the picture of life in both the commercial messages and the drama. Can you see ways in which they reinforce each other?
17. Design a questionnaire about the soap-opera viewing habits of your classmates, and summarize and explain your findings in an essay. Include questions that can help you determine whether soap operas have changed in any of their basic values since the time of Cross's essay.

PUBLIC AND PRIVATE LANGUAGE

Richard Rodriguez

Richard Rodriguez was born in California in 1944 to Mexican immigrant parents. He attended Stanford and Columbia universities, and received his doctorate in English literature from the University of California, Berkeley. He is the author of *Days of Obligation: An Argument with My Mexican Father* (1992), which deals with his encounters with contemporary liberalism; *Mexico's Children* (1990), a book about California; and an autobiography, *Hunger of Memory: The Education of Richard Rodriguez* (1981), which describes the contradictions of his growing up bilingual in America.

In this selection from his autobiography, Richard recounts the difficult process of learning his "public" language, English, at a parochial school in Sacramento. He describes how Americans sounded to him as a young Spanish-speaking boy; his embarrassment at his parents attempts to speak English; and the sounds of their "private" language, Spanish.

I remember to start with that day in Sacramento—a California now nearly 1 thirty years past—when I first entered a classroom, able to understand some fifty stray English words.

The third of four children, I had been preceded to a neighborhood 2 Roman Catholic school by an older brother and sister. But neither of them had revealed very much about their classroom experiences. Each afternoon they returned, as they left in the morning, always together, speaking in Spanish as they climbed the five steps of the porch. And their mysterious books, wrapped in shopping-bag paper, remained on the table next to the door, closed firmly behind them.

An accident of geography sent me to a school where all my 3 classmates were white, many the children of doctors and lawyers and business executives. All my classmates certainly must have been uneasy on that first day of school—as most children are uneasy—to find themselves apart from their families in the first institution of their lives. But I was astonished.

413

The nun said, in a friendly but oddly impersonal voice, "Boys and   4
girls, this is Richard Rodriguez." (I heard her sound out: *Rich-heard
Road-ree-guess.*) It was the first time I had heard anyone name me in
English. "Richard," the nun repeated more slowly, writing my name down
in her black leather book. Quickly I turned to see my mother's face
dissolve in a watery blur behind the pebbled glass door.

Many years later there is something called bilingual education—a   5
scheme proposed in the late 1960s by Hispanic-American social activists,
later endorsed by a congressional vote. It is a program that seeks to
permit non-English-speaking children, many from lower-class homes,
to use their family language as the language of school. (Such is the goal
its supporters announce.) I heard them and am forced to say no: It is
not possible for a child—any child—ever to use his family's language
in school. Not to understand this is to misunderstand the public uses
of schooling and to trivialize the nature of intimate life—a family's
"language."

Memory teaches me what I know of these matters; the boy reminds   6
the adult. I was a bilingual child, a certain kind—socially disadvantaged—
the son of working-class parents, both Mexican immigrants.

In the early years of my boyhood, my parents coped very well in   7
America. My father had steady work. My mother managed at home. They
were nobody's victims. Optimism and ambition led them to a house (our
home) many blocks from the Mexican south side of town. We lived
among *gringos* and only a block from the biggest, whitest houses. It
never occurred to my parents that they couldn't live wherever they
chose. Nor was the Sacramento of the fifties bent on teaching them a
contrary lesson. My mother and father were more annoyed than intimidated by those two or three neighbors who tried initially to make us
unwelcome. ("Keep your brats away from my sidewalk!") But despite all
they achieved, perhaps because they had so much to achieve, any deep
feeling of ease, the confidence of "belonging" in public was withheld
from them both. They regarded the people at work, the faces in crowds,
as very distant from us. They were the others, *los gringos.* That term was
interchangeable in their speech with another, even more telling, *los
americanos.*

I grew up in a house where the only regular guests were my   8
relations. For one day, enormous families of relatives would visit and
there would be so many people that the noise and the bodies would spill
out to the backyard and front porch. Then, for weeks, no one came by. (It
was usually a salesman who rang the doorbell.) Our house stood apart. A
gaudy yellow in a row of white bungalows. We were the people with the
noisy dog. The people who raised pigeons and chickens. We were the
foreigners on the block. A few neighbors smiled and waved. We waved

back. But no one in the family knew the names of the old couple who lived next door; until I was seven years old, I did not know the names of the kids who lived across the street.

In public, my father and mother spoke a hesitant, accented, not   9 always grammatical English. And they would have to strain—their bodies tense—to catch the sense of what was rapidly said by *los gringos*. At home they spoke Spanish. The language of their Mexican past sounded in counterpoint to the English of public society. The words would come quickly, with ease. Conveyed through those sounds was the pleasing, soothing, consoling reminder of being at home.

During those years when I was first conscious of hearing, my   10 mother and father addressed me only in Spanish; in Spanish I learned to reply. By contrast, English (*inglés*), rarely heard in the house, was the language I came to associate with *gringos*. I learned my first words of English overhearing my parents speak to strangers. At five years of age, I knew just enough English for my mother to trust me on errands to stores one block away. No more.

I was a listening child, careful to hear the very different sounds of   11 Spanish and English. Wide-eyed with hearing, I'd listen to sounds more than words. First, there were English (*gringo*) sounds. So many words were still unknown that when the butcher or the lady at the drugstore said something to me, exotic polysyllabic sounds would bloom in the midst of their sentences. Often, the speech of people in public seemed to me very loud, booming with confidence. The man behind the counter would literally ask, "What can I do for you?" But by being so firm and so clear, the sound of his voice said that he was a *gringo;* he belonged in public society.

I would also hear then the high nasal notes of middle-class   12 American speech. The air stirred with sound. Sometimes, even now, when I have been traveling abroad for several weeks, I will hear what I heard as a boy. In hotel lobbies or airports, in Turkey or Brazil, some Americans will pass, and suddenly I will hear it again—the high sound of American voices. For a few seconds I will hear it with pleasure, for it is now the sound of *my* society—a reminder of home. But inevitably— already on the flight headed for home—the sound fades with repetition. I will be unable to hear it anymore.

When I was a boy, things were different. The accent of *los gringos*   13 was never pleasing nor was it hard to hear. Crowds at Safeway or at bus stops would be noisy with sound. And I would be forced to edge away from the chirping chatter above me.

I was unable to hear my own sounds, but I knew very well that I   14 spoke English poorly. My words could not stretch far enough to form complete thoughts. And the words I did speak I didn't know well enough to make into distinct sounds. (Listeners would usually lower their heads, better to hear what I was trying to say.) But it was one thing for *me* to speak English with difficulty. It was more troubling for me to hear my parents speak in public: their high-whining vowels and guttural consonants; their sentences that got stuck with "ch" and "ah" sounds; the confused syntax; the hesitant rhythm of sounds so different from the way *gringos* spoke. I'd notice, moreover, that my parents' voices were softer than those of *gringos* we'd meet.

I am tempted now to say that none of this mattered. In adulthood   15
I am embarrassed by childhood fears. And, in a way, it didn't matter very much that my parents could not speak English with ease. Their linguistic difficulties had no serious consequences. My mother and father made themselves understood at the county hospital clinic and at government offices. And yet, in another way, it mattered very much—it was unsettling to hear my parents struggle with English. Hearing them, I'd grow nervous, my clutching trust in their protection and power weakened.

There were many times like the night at a brightly lit gasoline   16
station (a blaring white memory) when I stood uneasily, hearing my father. He was talking to a teenaged attendant. I do not recall what they were saying, but I cannot forget the sounds my father made as he spoke. At one point his words slid together to form one word—sounds as confused as the threads of blue and green oil in the puddle next to my shoes. His voice rushed through what he had left to say. And, toward the end, reached falsetto notes, appealing to his listener's understanding. I looked away to the lights of passing automobiles. I tried not to hear anymore. But I heard only too well the calm, easy tones in the attendant's reply. Shortly afterward, walking toward home with my father, I shivered when he put his hand on my shoulder. The very first chance that I got, I evaded his grasp and ran on ahead into the dark, skipping with feigned boyish exuberance.

But then there was Spanish. *Español:* my family's language. *Es-*   17
pañol: the language that seemed to me a private language. I'd hear strangers on the radio and in the Mexican Catholic church across town speaking in Spanish, but I couldn't really believe that Spanish was a public language, like English. Spanish speakers, rather, seemed related to me, for I sensed that we shared—through our language—the experience of feeling apart from *los gringos*. It was thus a ghetto Spanish that I heard and I spoke. Like those whose lives are bound by a barrio, I was reminded by Spanish of my separateness from *los otros, los gringos* in power. But more intensely than for most barrio children—because I did not live in a barrio—Spanish seemed to me the language of home. (Most days it was only at home that I'd hear it.) It became the language of joyful return.

A family member would say something to me and I would feel   18
myself specially recognized. My parents would say something to me and

I would feel embraced by the sounds of their words. Those sounds said: *I am speaking with ease in Spanish. I am addressing you in words I never use with los gringos. I recognize you as someone special, close, like no one outside. You belong with us. In the family.*

(*Ricardo.*)   19

At the age of five, six, well past the time when most other children   20
no longer easily notice the difference between sounds uttered at home
and words spoken in public, I had a different experience. I lived in a
world magically compounded of sounds. I remained a child longer than
most; I lingered too long, poised at the edge of language—often
frightened by the sounds of *los gringos,* delighted by the sounds of
Spanish at home. I shared with my family a language that was startlingly
different from that used in the great city around us.

For me there were none of the gradations between public and   21
private society so normal to a maturing child. Outside the house was
public society; inside the house was private. Just opening or closing the
screen door behind me was an important experience. I'd rarely leave
home all alone or without reluctance. Walking down the sidewalk, under
the canopy of tall trees, I'd warily notice the—suddenly—silent neighborhood kids who stood warily watching me. Nervously, I'd arrive at the
grocery store to hear there the sounds of the *gringo*—foreign to
me—reminding me that in this world so big, I was a foreigner. But then
I'd return. Walking back toward our house, climbing the steps from the
sidewalk, when the front door was open in summer, I'd hear voices
beyond the screen door talking in Spanish. For a second or two, I'd stay,
linger there, listening. Smiling, I'd hear my mother call out, saying in
Spanish (words): "Is that you, Richard?" All the while her sounds would
assure me: *You are home now; come closer; inside. With us.*

"*Sí,*" I'd reply.   22

Once more inside the house I would resume (assume) my place in   23
the family. The sounds would dim, grow harder to hear. Once more at
home, I would grow less aware of that fact. It required, however, no more
than the blurt of the doorbell to alert me to listen to sounds all over
again. The house would turn instantly still while my mother went to the
door. I'd hear her hard English sounds. I'd wait to hear her voice return to
soft-sounding Spanish, which assured me, as surely as did the clicking
tongue of the lock on the door, that the stranger was gone.

Plainly, it is not healthy to hear such sounds so often. It is not   24
healthy to distinguish public words from private sounds so easily. I
remained cloistered by sounds, timid and shy in public, too dependent
on voices at home. And yet it needs to be emphasized: I was an
extremely happy child at home. I remember many nights when my father
would come back from work, and I'd hear him call out to my mother in
Spanish, sounding relieved. In Spanish, he'd sound light and free notes

he never could manage in English. Some nights I'd jump up just at hearing his voice. With *mis hermanos* I would come running into the room where he was with my mother. Our laughing (so deep was the pleasure!) became screaming. Like others who know the pain of public alienation, we transformed the knowledge of our public separateness and made it consoling— the reminder of intimacy. *We are speaking now the way we never speak out in public. We are alone—together,* voices sounded, surrounded to tell me. Some nights, no one seemed willing to loosen the hold sounds had on us. At dinner, we invented new words. (Ours sounded Spanish, but made sense only to us). We pieced together new words by taking, say, an English verb and giving it Spanish endings. My mother's instructions at bedtime would be lacquered with mock-urgent tones. Or a word like *sí* would become, in several notes, able to convey added measures of feeling. Tongues explored the edges of words, especially the fat vowels. And we happily sounded that military drum roll, the twirling roar of the Spanish *r.* Family language: my family's sounds. The voices of my parents and sisters and brother. Their voices insisting: *You belong here. We are family members. Related. Special to one another. Listen!* Voices singing and sighing, rising, straining, then surging, teeming with pleasure that burst syllables into fragments of laughter. At times it seemed there was steady quiet only when, from another room, the rustling whispers of my parents faded and I moved closer to sleep.

Exercises

Some Important Words

bilingual education (paragraph 5), trivialize (5), disadvantaged (6), *gringos* (7), counterpoint (9), exotic (11), polysyllabic (11), nasal (12), chirping (13), guttural (14), syntax (14), linguistic (15), falsetto (16), evaded (16), feigned (16), exuberance (16), ghetto (17), barrio (17), *los otros*—the others (17), lingered (20), poised (20), gradations (21), canopy (21), warily (21), cloistered (24), *mis hermanos*—my brothers and sisters (24), alienation (24), lacquered (24), mock-urgent (24).

Some of the Issues

1. In paragraph 3 Rodriguez claims that on the first day of school most other children were uneasy but he was astonished. What accounts for his astonishment?
2. In paragraph 5 and throughout the essay, Rodriguez makes a distinction between family language and public language. What does he say about each?

3. What effect did his parents' limited fluency with English have on Rodriguez as a boy?
4. In paragraph 11 Rodriguez describes himself as "a listening child." To what aspects of language is he particularly sensitive and why?
5. In paragraph 20 he says he remained a child longer than most children. What reason does he give?
6. Describe Rodriguez's ambivalent feelings (i.e., positive and negative) about his use of Spanish.

The Way We Are Told

7. On the first day of school, Rodriguez turns to watch his mother's face "dissolve in a watery blur behind the pebbled glass door." In what way is this image symbolic? Find another instance of the door image in the story and explain its significance.
8. Rodriguez uses some Spanish words. Analyze where and why he chooses to include them.
9. Find specific words and phrases that Rodriguez uses to characterize the strong contrasts between the sounds of English and Spanish.

Some Subjects for Writing

10. Has anyone ever mispronounced, accented differently, or simply made a mistake with your name? If not, have you ever mispronounced or confused another person's name? Recall that experience and, in a short narrative essay, recapture your feelings at the time.
11. If you grew up with two languages, compare and contrast your experience with Rodriguez's.
12. Have you ever been in a place where your own language or regional accent was not easily understood? Describe your efforts at communicating and compare your experience with that of Rodriguez's parents.
*13. Read Ngugi wa Thiong'o's "The Politics of Language." In speaking of Gĩkũyũ, his first language, and English, which displaced it in his later education, Ngugi can be said to refer to a concept of a private and a public language similar to Rodriguez's. Describe Ngugi's and Rodriguez's concepts, noting in particular the differences in the points of view of the two writers.

THE POLITICS
OF LANGUAGE

Ngugi wa Thiong'o

Ngugi wa Thiong'o was born in Limuru, Kenya, in 1938. He is considered one of Africa's most important contemporary writers. He was educated at Makerere University in Uganda and taught briefly in the United States. From 1972 until his detention in 1978 he served as head of the English Department at the University of Nairobi in Kenya. Since his release he has devoted himself to his writing. His earlier works were written in English and include the novels *Weep Not, Child, The River Between,* and *Petals of Blood,* as well as the plays *The Black Hermit* and *The Trial of Dedan Kimathi.*

    Decolonizing the Mind, from which this selection is taken, was originally given as a series of lectures at Auckland University in New Zealand. In an introductory statement, Ngugi says: "This book . . . is my farewell to English as a vehicle of any of my writings. From now on it is Gĩkũyũ and Kiswahili all the way."

    What language to write in—for writers in many cultures that is a serious and thorny question. It is a particularly difficult one for African writers. Until the 1960s almost all of Africa was ruled as colonies by European powers, most notably and extensively by Britain and France. Education beyond the elementary level was largely provided only for a select few, and in the language of the ruling power, so much so that one usually referred to various countries as Anglophone or Francophone, respectively, depending on whether they had been British or French (or Belgian) colonies before independence. Major African authors Chinua Achebe and Wole Soyinka, who both are Nigerians, write in English; and Leopold Senghor and Ousmane Sembene, both Senegalese, write in French.

    In his essay Ngugi first describes his own experience: how, working in the fields during the day, and around the fireside in the evening, stories were told; how such stories, well told, had power beyond the meaning of the words; how, "through images and symbols, [language] gave us a view of the world." Then he relates how "this harmony was broken" when his education shifted to the language of the colonizers, English, and relates the pressures on the children to abandon their native language. Ngugi then turns to a more general consideration of language, which he sees as consisting of two major divisions: language as communication and language as a carrier of culture. The imposition of a colonial language and its literature, he says, produces a sense of alienation from his environment for the African child and may diminish his feeling of self-worth.

You may want to relate Ngugi's ideas to Richard Rodriguez's "Public and Private Language."

I was born into a large peasant family: father, four wives and about twenty-eight children. I also belonged, as we all did in those days, to a wider extended family and to the community as a whole.

We spoke Gĩkũyũ as we worked in the fields. We spoke Gĩkũyũ in and outside the home. I can vividly recall those evenings of story-telling around the fireside. It was mostly the grown-ups telling the children but everybody was interested and involved. We children would re-tell the stories the following day to other children who worked in the fields picking the pyrethrum flowers, tea-leaves or coffee beans of our European and African landlords.

The stories, with mostly animals as the main characters, were all told in Gĩkũyũ. Hare, being small, weak but full of innovative wit and cunning, was our hero. We identified with him as he struggled against the brutes of prey like lion, leopard, hyena. His victories were our victories and we learnt that the apparently weak can outwit the strong. We followed the animals in their struggle against hostile nature— drought, rain, sun, wind—a confrontation often forcing them to search for forms of co-operation. But we were also interested in their struggles amongst themselves, and particularly between the beasts and the victims of prey. These twin struggles, against nature and other animals, reflected real-life struggles in the human world.

Not that we neglected stories with human beings as the main characters. There were two types of characters in such human-centered narratives: the species of truly human beings with qualities of courage, kindness, mercy, hatred of evil, concern for others; and a man-eat-man two-mouthed species with qualities of greed, selfishness, individualism and hatred of what was good for the larger co-operative community. Co-operation as the ultimate good in a community was a constant theme. It could unite human beings with animals against ogres and beasts of prey, as in the story of how dove, after being fed with castor-oil seeds, was sent to fetch a smith working far away from home and whose pregnant wife was being threatened by these man-eating two-mouthed ogres.

There were good and bad story-tellers. A good one could tell the same story over and over again, and it would always be fresh to us, the listeners. He or she could tell a story told by someone else and make it more alive and dramatic. The differences really were in the use of words and images and the inflexion of voices to effect different tones.

We therefore learnt to value words for their meaning and nuances.   6
Language was not a mere string of words. It had a suggestive power well beyond the immediate and lexical meaning. Our appreciation of the suggestive magical power of language was reinforced by the games we played with words through riddles, proverbs, transpositions of syllables, or through nonsensical but musically arranged words. So we learnt the music of our language on top of the content. The language, through images and symbols, gave us a view of the world, but it had a beauty of its own. The home and the field were then our pre-primary school but what is important, for this discussion, is that the language of our evening teach-ins, and the language of our immediate and wider community, and the language of our work in the fields were one.

And then I went to school, a colonial school, and this harmony was   7
broken. The language of my education was no longer the language of my culture. I first went to Kamaandura, missionary run, and then to another called Maanguuũ run by nationalists grouped around the Gĩkũyũ Independent and Karinga Schools Association. Our language of education was still Gĩkũyũ. The very first time I was ever given an ovation for my writing was over a composition in Gĩkũyũ. So for my first four years there was still harmony between the language of my formal education and that of the Limuru peasant community.

It was after the declaration of a state of emergency over Kenya in   8
1952 that all the schools run by patriotic nationalists were taken over by the colonial regime and were placed under District Education Boards chaired by Englishmen. English became the language of my formal education. In Kenya, English became more than a language: it was *the* language, and all the others had to bow before it in deference.

Thus one of the most humiliating experiences was to be caught   9
speaking Gĩkũyũ in the vicinity of the school. The culprit was given corporal punishment—three to five strokes of the cane on bare buttocks—or was made to carry a metal plate around the neck with inscriptions such as I AM STUPID or I AM A DONKEY. Sometimes the culprits were fined money they could hardly afford. And how did the teachers catch the culprits? A button was initially given to one pupil who was supposed to hand it over to whoever was caught speaking his mother tongue. Whoever had the button at the end of the day would sing who had given it to him and the ensuing process would bring out all the culprits of the day. Thus children were turned into witch-hunters and in the process were being taught the lucrative value of being a traitor to one's immediate community.

The attitude to English was the exact opposite: any achievement in   10
spoken or written English was highly rewarded: prizes, prestige, ap-

plause; the ticket to higher realms. English became the measure of intelligence and ability in the arts, the sciences, and all the other branches of learning. English became *the* main determinant of a child's progress up the ladder of formal education.

As you may know, the colonial system of education in addition to its 11 apartheid racial demarcation had the structure of a pyramid: a broad primary base, a narrowing secondary middle, and an even narrower university apex. Selections from primary into secondary were through an examination, in my time called Kenya African Preliminary Examination, in which one had to pass six subjects ranging from Maths to Nature Study and Kiswahili. All the papers were written in English. Nobody could pass the exam who failed the English language paper no matter how brilliantly he had done in the other subjects. I remember one boy in my class of 1954 who had distinctions in all subjects except English, which he had failed. He was made to fail the entire exam. He went on to become a turn boy in a bus company. I who had only passes but a credit in English got a place at the Alliance High School, one of the most elitist institutions for Africans in colonial Kenya. The requirements for a place at the University, Makerere University College, were broadly the same: nobody could go on to wear the undergraduate red gown, no matter how brilliantly they had performed in all the other subjects unless they had a credit—not even a simple pass!—in English. Thus the most coveted place in the pyramid and in the system was only available to the holder of an English language credit card. English was the official vehicle and the magic formula to colonial elitedom.

Literary education was now determined by the dominant language 12 while also reinforcing that dominance. Orature (oral literature) in Kenyan languages stopped. In primary school I now read simplified Dickens and Stevenson alongside Rider Haggard. Jim Hawkins, Oliver Twist, Tom Brown—not Hare, Leopard and Lion—were now my daily companions in the world of imagination. In secondary school, Scott and G. B. Shaw vied with more Rider Haggard, John Buchan, Alan Paton, Captain W. E. Johns. At Makerere I read English: from Chaucer to T. S. Eliot with a touch of Graham Greene.

Thus language and literature were taking us further and further 13 from ourselves to other selves, from our world to other worlds.

What was the colonial system doing to us Kenyan children? What 14 were the consequences of, on the other hand, this systematic suppression of our languages and the literature they carried, and on the other the elevation of English and the literature it carried? To answer those questions, let me first examine the relationship of language to human experience, human culture, and the human perception of reality.

Language, any language, has a dual character: it is both a means of 15 communication and a carrier of culture. Take English. It is spoken in

Britain and in Sweden and Denmark. But for Swedish and Danish people English is only a means of communication with non-Scandinavians. It is not a carrier of their culture. For the British, and particularly the English, it is additionally, and inseparably from its use as a tool of communication, a carrier of their culture and history. Or take Swahili in East and Central Africa. It is widely used as a means of communication across many nationalities. But it is not the carrier of a culture and history of many of those nationalities. However in parts of Kenya and Tanzania, and particularly in Zanzibar, Swahili is inseparably both a means of communication and a carrier of the culture of those people to whom it is a mother-tongue.

Language as communication has three aspects or elements. There is first what Karl Marx once called the language of real life, the element basic to the whole notion of language, its origins and development: that is, the relations people enter into with one another in the labour process, the links they necessarily establish among themselves in the act of a people, a community of human beings, producing wealth or means of life like food, clothing, houses. A human community really starts its historical being as a community of co-operation in production through the division of labour; the simplest is between man, woman and child within a household; the more complex divisions are between branches of production such as those who are sole hunters, sole gatherers of fruits or sole workers in metal. Then there are the most complex divisions such as those in modern factories where a single product, say a shirt or a shoe, is the result of many hands and minds. Production is co-operation, is communication, is language, is expression of a relaxation between human beings and it is specifically human.   16

The second aspect of language as communication is speech and it imitates the language of real life, that is communication in production. The verbal signposts both reflect and aid communication or the relations established between human beings in the production of their means of life. Language as a system of verbal signposts makes that production possible. The spoken word is to relations between human begins what the hand is to the relations between human beings and nature. The hand through tools mediates between human beings and nature and forms the language of real life: spoken words mediate between human beings and form the language of speech.   17

The third aspect is the written signs. The written word imitates the spoken. Where the first two aspects of language as communication through the hand and the spoken word historically evolved more or less simultaneously, the written aspect is a much later historical development. Writing is representation of sounds with visual symbols, from the simplest knot among shepherds to tell the number in a herd or the hieroglyphics among the Agĩkũyũ gicaandi singers and poets of Kenya, to the most   18 complicated and different letter and picture writing systems of the world today.

In most societies the written and the spoken languages are the same, in that they represent each other: what is on paper can be read to another person and be received as that language which the recipient has grown up speaking. In such a society there is broad harmony for a child between the three aspects of language as communication. His interaction with nature and with other men is expressed in written and spoken symbols or signs which are both a result of that double interaction and a reflection of it. The association of the child's sensibility is with the language of his experience of life.   19

But there is more to it: communication between human beings is also the basis and process of evolving culture. In doing similar kinds of things and actions over and over again under similar circumstances, similar even in their mutability, certain patterns, moves, rhythms, habits, attitudes, experiences and knowledge emerge. Those experiences are handed over to the next generation and become the inherited basis for their further actions on nature and on themselves. There is a gradual accumulation of values which in time become almost self-evident truths governing their conception of what is right and wrong, good and bad, beautiful and ugly, courageous and cowardly, generous and mean in their internal and external relations. Over a time this becomes a way of life distinguishable from other ways of life. They develop a distinctive culture and history. Culture embodies those moral, ethical and aesthetic values, the set of spiritual eyeglasses, through which they come to view themselves and their place in the universe. Values are the basis of a people's identity, their sense of particularity as members of the human race. All this is carried by language. Language as culture is the collective memory bank of a people's experience in history. Culture is almost indistinguishable from the language that makes possible its genesis, growth, banking, articulation and indeed its transmission from one generation to the next.   20

Language as culture also has three important aspects. Culture is a product of the history which it in turn reflects. Culture in other words is a product and a reflection of human beings communicating with one another in the very struggle to create wealth and to control it. But culture does not merely reflect that history, or rather it does so by actually forming images or pictures of the world of nature and nurture. Thus the second aspect of language as culture is as an image-forming agent in the mind of a child. Our whole conception of ourselves as a people, individually and collectively, is based on those pictures and images which may or may not correctly correspond to the actual reality of the struggles with nature and nurture which produced them in the first place. But our capacity to confront the world creatively is dependent on how those   21

The Politics of Language

images correspond or not to that reality, how they distort or clarify the reality of our struggles. Language as culture is thus mediating between me and my own self; between my own self and other selves; between me and nature. Language is mediating in my very being. And this brings us to the third aspect of language as culture. Culture transmits or imparts those images of the world and reality through the spoken and the written language, that is through a specific language. In other words, the capacity to speak, the capacity to order sounds in a manner that makes for mutual comprehension between human beings is universal. This is the universality of language, a quality specific to human beings. It corresponds to the universality of the struggle against nature and that between human beings. But the particularity of the sounds, the words, the word order into phrases and sentences, and the specific manner, or laws, of their ordering is what distinguishes one language from another. Thus a specific culture is not transmitted through language in its universality but in its particularity as the language of a specific community with a specific history. Written literature and orature are the main means by which a particular language transmits the images of the world contained in the culture it carries.

Language as communication and as culture are then products of   22
each other. Communication creates culture: culture is a means of communication. Language carries culture, and culture carries, particularly through orature and literature, the entire body of values by which we come to perceive ourselves and our place in the world. How people perceive themselves affects how they look at their culture, at their politics and at the social production of wealth, at their entire relationship to nature and to other beings. Language is thus inseparable from ourselves as a community of human beings with a specific form and character, a specific history, a specific relationship to the world.

So what was the colonialist imposition of a foreign language doing to us   23
children?

The real aim of colonialism was to control the people's wealth: what   24
they produced, how they produced it, and how it was distributed; to control, in other words, the entire realm of the language of real life. Colonialism imposed its control of the social production of wealth through military conquest and subsequent political dictatorship. But its most important area of domination was the mental universe of the colonised, the control, through culture, of how people perceived themselves and their relationship to the world. Economic and political control can never be complete or effective without mental control. To control a people's culture is to control their tools of self-definition in relationship to others.

For colonialism this involved two aspects of the same process: the   25
destruction or the deliberate undervaluing of a people's culture, their art,

dances, religions, history, geography, education, orature and literature, and the conscious elevation of the language of the coloniser. The domination of a people's language by the languages of the colonising nations was crucial to the domination of the mental universe of the colonised.

Take language as communication. Imposing a foreign language, 26 and suppressing the native languages as spoken and written, were already breaking the harmony previously existing between the African child and the three aspects of language. Since the new language as a means of communication was a product of and was reflecting the "real language of life" elsewhere, it could never as spoken or written properly reflect or imitate the real life of that community. This may in part explain why technology always appears to us as slightly external, *their* product and not *ours*. The word "missile" used to hold an alien faraway sound until I recently learnt its equivalent in Gĩkũyũ, *ngurukuhi,* and it made me apprehend it differently. Learning, for a colonial child, became a cerebral activity and not an emotionally felt experience.

But since the new, imposed languages could never completely 27 break the native languages as spoken, their most effective area of domination was the third aspect of language as communication, the written. The language of an African child's formal education was foreign. The language of the books he read was foreign. The language of his conceptualisation was foreign. Thought, in him, took the visible form of a foreign language. So the written language of a child's upbringing in the school (even his spoken language within the school compound) became divorced from his spoken language at home. There was often not the slightest relationship between the child's written world, which was also the language of his schooling, and the world of his immediate environment in the family and the community. For a colonial child, the harmony existing between the three aspects of language as communication was irrevocably broken. This resulted in the disassociation of the sensibility of that child from his natural and social environment, what we might call colonial alienation. The alienation became reinforced in the teaching of history, geography, music, where bourgeois Europe was always the centre of the universe.

This disassociation, divorce, or alienation from the immediate 28 environment becomes clearer when you look at colonial language as a carrier of culture.

Since culture is a product of the history of a people which it in turn 29 reflects, the child was now being exposed exclusively to a culture that was a product of a world external to himself. He was being made to stand outside himself to look at himself.

Since culture does not just reflect the world in images but actually, 30 through those very images, conditions a child to see that world in a certain way, the colonial child was made to see the world and where he stands in it as seen and defined by or reflected in the culture of the language of imposition.

And since those images are mostly passed on through orature and literature it meant the child would now only see the world as seen in the literature of his language of adoption. From the point of view of alienation, that is of seeing oneself from outside oneself as if one was another self, it does not matter that the imported literature carried the great humanist tradition of the best in Shakespeare, Goethe, Balzac, Tolstoy, Gorky, Brecht, Sholokhov, Dickens. The location of this great mirror of imagination was necessarily Europe and its history and culture and the rest of the universe was seen from that centre.   31

But obviously it was worse when the colonial child was exposed to images of his world as mirrored in the written languages of his coloniser. Where his own native languages were associated in his impressionable mind with low status, humiliation, corporal punishment, slow-footed intelligence and ability or downright stupidity, non-intelligibility and barbarism, this was reinforced by the world he met in the works of such geniuses of racism as a Rider Haggard or a Nicholas Monsarrat; not to mention the pronouncement of some of the giants of western intellectual and political establishment, such as Hume (". . . the negro is naturally inferior to the whites . . ."), Thomas Jefferson (". . . the blacks . . . are inferior to the whites on the endowments of both body and mind . . ."), or Hegel with his Africa comparable to a land of childhood still enveloped in the dark mantle of the night as far as the development of self-conscious history was concerned. Hegel's statement that there was nothing harmonious with humanity to be found in the African character is representative of the racist images of Africans and Africa such a colonial child was bound to encounter in the literature of the colonial languages. The results could be disastrous.   32

Exercises

Some Important Words

extended family (paragraph 1), innovative (3), cunning (3), prey (3), outwit (3), hostile (3), drought (3), ogres (4), inflection (5), nuances (6), lexical (6), deference (8), corporal punishment (9), lucrative (9), apartheid (11), demarcation (11), apex (11), elitist (11), coveted (11), orature (12), vied (12), Karl Marx (16), sole (16), hieroglyphics (18), sensibility (19), evolving (20), mutability (20), mean (20), embodies (20), aesthetic (20), particularity (20), collective memory bank (20), genesis (20), nurture (21), mediating (21), universality (21), cerebral (26), conceptualization (27), irrevocably (27), disassociation (27), alienation (27), bourgeois (27), imposition (30), impressionable (32), non-intelligibility (32), barbarism (32).

Some of the Issues

1. Examine the animal stories Ngugi tells about in paragraph 3. With whom do the storytellers and their listeners identify? What are the lessons the listeners are likely to learn?
2. Do you know any similar animal stories or fairytales? Do they differ in their message from the Gĩkũyũ stories?
3. What are the themes of the stories about humans that Ngugi describes in paragraph 4?
4. In paragraph 6 Ngugi repeatedly refers to the "suggestive magical power" of language. What is the place of language in his early life?
5. How was the use of English enforced in the school system?
6. What is the "dual character" of language (paragraph 15)? For whom is it merely a means of communication? For whom also a carrier of culture?
7. Among the "three aspects or elements" of language as communication that Ngugi cites in paragraph 16, the first he calls, after Karl Marx, "the language of real life." What does that phrase mean? Does it mean something we ordinarily would call language?
8. How does Ngugi define culture and cultural values in paragraph 20? How are they related to language and communication?
9. How does Ngugi sum up the reciprocal relationship of language as culture and as communication?
10. What, according to Ngugi, was "the real aim of colonialism" (paragraph 24)?
11. What role did the colonizer's language play in establishing control (paragraphs 24 – 26)?

The Way We Are Told

12. Ngugi's essay is concerned with language. Yet the first paragraph does not introduce that topic but speaks of family and community. Why is that relevant?
13. In the essay two paragraphs— 13 and 23 —stand out because each of them consists of only one short sentence. What is the function of each?

Some Subjects for Writing

14. In a statement prefacing his book *Decolonizing the Mind,* Ngugi says that it will be his last work in English and that his future writing will

be in Gĩkũyũ and Kiswahili. Examine the advantages and disadvantages in this step he intends to take.

*15. Read Richard Rodriguez's "Public and Private Language." Ngugi, in discussing the divorce between the language of home and school (paragraph 27), makes the same distinction as Rodriguez. However, each of them comes to a different conclusion as to the meaning of that split. In an essay present their respective conclusions and explain how and why they reach them.

THE GERMAN REFUGEE

Bernard Malamud

Bernard Malamud (1914–86) was born in Brooklyn, New York, and educated at City College of New York and Columbia University. In the 1940s he was an evening instructor of English and a clerk for the Bureau of the Census. From 1949–61, he taught writing at Oregon State University, where he began publishing his short stories and novels. From 1961 until his death in 1986 he was a professor at Bennington College in Vermont. His numerous honors include two National Book Awards and a Pulitzer Prize. Among his best known works are *The Natural* (1952), *The Assistant* (1957), *The Magic Barrel* (1958), *The Fixer* (1966), *Dubin's Lives* (1979), and *God's Grace* (1982).

    Much of Malamud's work draws from life on New York's Lower East Side, where his Russian Jewish immigrant parents worked in their store 16 hours a day. The short story "The German Refugee," taken from a collection entitled *Idiots First* (1963), portrays the agonizing displacement, sense of alienation, and despair of the German Jews who fled the Nazi occupation.

Oskar Gassner sits in his cotton-mesh undershirt and summer bathrobe at the window of his stuffy, hot, dark hotel room on West Tenth Street as I cautiously knock. Outside, across the sky, a late-June green twilight fades in darkness. The refugee fumbles for the light and stares at me, hiding despair but not pain. 1

I was in those days a poor student and would brashly attempt to teach anybody anything for a buck an hour, although I have since learned better. Mostly I gave English lessons to recently arrived refugees. The college sent me, I had acquired a little experience. Already a few of my students were trying their broken English, theirs and mine, in the American marketplace. I was then just twenty, on my way into my senior year in college, a skinny, life-hungry kid, eating himself waiting for the next world war to start. It was a miserable cheat. Here I was panting to get going, and across the ocean Adolf Hitler, in black boots and a square mustache, was tearing up and spitting at all the flowers. Will I ever forget what went on with Danzig that summer? 2

Times were still hard from the Depression but I made a little living   3
from the poor refugees. They were all over uptown Broadway in 1939. I
had four I tutored—Karl Otto Alp, the former film star; Wolfgang Novak,
once a brilliant economist; Friedrich Wilhelm Wolff, who had taught
medieval history at Heidelberg; and after the night I met him in his
disordered cheap hotel room, Oskar Gassner, the Berlin critic and
journalist, at one time on the *Acht Uhr Abendblatt.* They were accomplished men. I had my nerve associating with them, but that's what a
world crisis does for people, they get educated.

Oskar was maybe fifty, his thick hair turning gray. He had a big face   4
and heavy hands. His shoulders sagged. His eyes, too, were heavy, a
clouded blue; and as he stared at me after I had identified myself, doubt
spread in them like underwater currents. It was as if, on seeing me, he
had again been defeated. I had to wait until he came to. I stayed at the
door in silence. In such cases I would rather be elsewhere, but I had to
make a living. Finally he opened the door and I entered. Rather, he
released it and I was in. "Bitte"—he offered me a seat and didn't know
where to sit himself. He would attempt to say something and then stop,
as though it could not possibly be said. The room was cluttered with
clothing, boxes of books he had managed to get out of Germany, and
some paintings. Oskar sat on a box and attempted to fan himself with his
meaty hand. "Zis heat," he muttered, forcing his mind to the deed.
"Impozzible. I do not know such heat." It was bad enough for me but
terrible for him. He had difficulty breathing. He tried to speak, lifted a
hand, and let it drop. He breathed as though he was fighting a war; and
maybe he won because after ten minutes we sat and slowly talked.

Like most educated Germans Oskar had at one time studied   5
English. Although he was certain he couldn't say a word he managed to
put together a fairly decent, if sometimes comical English sentence. He
misplaced consonants, mixed up nouns and verbs, and mangled idioms,
yet we were able at once to communicate. We conversed in English, with
an occasional assist by me in pidgin-German or Yiddish, what he called
"Jiddish." He had been to America before, last year for a short visit. He
had come a month before Kristallnacht, when the Nazis shattered the
Jewish store windows and burnt all the synagogues, to see if he could
find a job for himself; he had no relatives in America and getting a job
would permit him quickly to enter the country. He had been promised
something, not in journalism, but with the help of a foundation, as a
lecturer. Then he returned to Berlin, and after a frightening delay of six
months was permitted to emigrate. He had sold whatever he could,
managed to get some paintings, gifts of Bauhaus friends, and some boxes
of books out by bribing two Dutch border guards; he had said goodbye
to his wife and left the accursed country. He gazed at me with cloudy
eyes. "We parted amicably," he said in German, "my wife was gentile. Her

mother was an appalling anti-Semite. They returned to live in Stettin." I
asked no questions. Gentile is gentile, Germany is Germany.

His new job was in the Institute for Public Studies, in New York. He   6
was to give a lecture a week in the fall term and during next spring, a
course, in English translation, in "The Literature of the Weimar Republic."
He had never taught before and was afraid to. He was in that way to be
introduced to the public, but the thought of giving the lecture in English
just about paralyzed him. He didn't see how he could do it. "How is it
pozzible? I cannot say two words. I cannot pronounziate. I will make a
fool of myself." His melancholy deepened. Already in the two months
since his arrival, and a round of diminishingly expensive hotel rooms, he
had had two English tutors, and I was the third. The others had given
him up, he said, because his progress was so poor, and he thought he
also depressed them. He asked me whether I felt I could do something
for him, or should he go to a speech specialist, someone, say, who
charged five dollars an hour, and beg his assistance? "You could try him,"
I said, "and then come back to me." In those days I figured what I knew,
I knew. At that he managed a smile. Still, I wanted him to make up his
mind or it would be no confidence down the line. He said, after a while,
he would stay with me. If he went to the five-dollar professor it might
help his tongue but not his appetite. He would have no money left to eat
with. The Institute had paid him in advance for the summer, but it was
only three hundred dollars and all he had.

He looked at me dully. "Ich weiss nicht, wie ich weiter machen   7
soll."

I figured it was time to move past the first step. Either we did that   8
quickly or it would be like drilling rock for a long time.

"Let's stand at the mirror," I said.   9

He rose with a sigh and stood there beside me, I thin, elongated,   10
red-headed, praying for success, his and mine; Oskar uneasy, fearful,
finding it hard to face either of us in the faded round glass above his
dresser.

"Please," I said to him, "could you say 'right'?"   11
"Ghight," he gargled.   12
"No—right. You put your tongue here." I showed him where as he   13
tensely watched the mirror. I tensely watched him. "The tip of it curls
behind the ridge on top, like this."

He placed his tongue where I showed him.   14
"Please," I said, "now say right."   15
Oskar's tongue fluttered. "Rright."   16
"That's good. Now say 'treasure'—that's harder."   17
"Tgheasure."   18
"The tongue goes up in front, not in the back of the mouth. Look."   19
He tried, his brow wet, eyes straining, "Trreasure."   20

"That's it."   21

"A miracle," Oskar murmured.   22

I said if he had done that he could do the rest.   23

We went for a bus ride up Fifth Avenue and then walked for a while   24
around Central Park Lake. He had put on his German hat, with its
hatband bow at the back, a broad-lapeled wool suit, a necktie twice as
wide as the one I was wearing, and walked with a small-footed waddle.
The night wasn't bad, it had got a bit cooler. There were a few large stars
in the sky and they made me sad.

"Do you sink I will succezz?"   25

"Why not?" I asked.   26

Later he bought me a bottle of beer.   27

To many of these people, articulate as they were, the great loss was the   28
loss of language—that they could not say what was in them to say. You
have some subtle thought and it comes out like a piece of broken bottle.
They could, of course, manage to communicate, but just to communicate
was frustrating. As Karl Otto Alp, the ex-film star who became a buyer for
Macy's, put it years later, "I felt like a child, or worse, often like a moron.
I am left with myself unexpressed. What I know, indeed, what I am,
becomes to me a burden. My tongue hangs useless." The same with
Oskar it figures. There was a terrible sense of useless tongue, and I think
the reason for his trouble with his other tutors was that to keep from
drowning in things unsaid he wanted to swallow the ocean in a gulp:
today he would learn English and tomorrow wow them with an impeccable Fourth of July speech, followed by a successful lecture at the
Institute for Public Studies.

We performed our lessons slowly, step by step, everything in its   29
place. After Oskar moved to a two-room apartment in a house on West
Eighty-fifth Street, near the Drive, we met three times a week at
four-thirty, worked an hour and a half, then, since it was too hot to cook,
had supper at the Seventy-second Street Automat and conversed on my
time. The lessons we divided into three parts: diction exercises and
reading aloud; then grammar, because Oskar felt the necessity of it, and
composition correction; with conversation, as I said, thrown in at supper.
So far as I could see he was coming along. None of these exercises was
giving him as much trouble as they apparently had in the past. He
seemed to be learning and his mood lightened. There were moments of
elation as he heard his accent flying off. For instance when sink became
think. He stopped calling himself "hopelezz," and I became his "bezt
teacher," a little joke I liked.

Neither of us said much about the lecture he had to give early in   30
October, and I kept my fingers crossed. It was somehow to come out of
what we were doing daily, I think I felt, but exactly how, I had no idea;

and to tell the truth, though I didn't say so to Oskar, the lecture frightened me. That and the ten more to follow during the fall term. Later, when I learned that he had been attempting, with the help of the dictionary, to write in English and had produced "a complete disahster," I suggested maybe he ought to stick to German and we could afterwards both try to put it into passable English. I was cheating when I said that because my German is meager, enough to read simple stuff but certainly not good enough for serious translation; anyway, the idea was to get Oskar into production and worry about translating later. He sweated with it, from enervating morning to exhausted night, but no matter what language he tried, though he had been a professional writer for a generation and knew his subject cold, the lecture refused to move past page one.

It was a sticky, hot July, and the heat didn't help at all.   31

I had met Oskar at the end of June, and by the seventeenth of July we   32
were no longer doing lessons. They had foundered on the "impozzible" lecture. He had worked on it each day in frenzy and growing despair. After writing more than a hundred opening pages he furiously flung his pen against the wall, shouting he could not longer write in that filthy tongue. He cursed the German language. He hated the damned country and the damned people. After that, what was bad became worse. When he gave up attempting to write the lecture, he stopped making progress in English. He seemed to forget what he already knew. His tongue thickened and the accent returned in all its fruitiness. The little he had to say was in handcuffed and tortured English. The only German I heard him speak was in a whisper to himself. I doubt he knew he was talking it. That ended our formal work together, though I did drop in every other day or so to sit with him. For hours he sat motionless in a large green velour armchair, hot enough to broil in, and through tall windows stared at the colorless sky above Eighty-fifth Street with a wet depressed eye.

Then once he said to me, "If I do not this legture prepare, I will take   33
my life."

"Let's begin, Oskar," I said. "You dictate and I'll write. The ideas   34
count, not the spelling."

He didn't answer so I stopped talking.   35

He had plunged into an involved melancholy. We sat for hours,   36
often in profound silence. This was alarming to me, though I had already had some experience with such depression. Wolfgang Novak, the economist, though English came more easily to him, was another. His problems arose mainly, I think, from physical illness. And he felt a greater sense of the lost country than Oskar. Sometimes in the early evening I persuaded Oskar to come with me for a short walk on the Drive. The tail end of sunsets over the Palisades seemed to appeal to him. At least he

looked. He would put on full regalia—hat, suit coat, tie, no matter how hot or what I suggested—and we went slowly down the stairs, I wondering whether he would make it to the bottom.

We walked slowly uptown, stopping to sit on a bench and watch night rise above the Hudson. When we returned to his room, if I sensed he had loosened up a bit, we listened to music on the radio; but if I tried to sneak in a news broadcast, he said to me, "Please, I cannot more stand of world misery." I shut off the radio. He was right, it was a time of no good news. I squeezed my brain. What could I tell him? Was it good news to be alive? Who could argue the point? Sometimes I read aloud to him—I remember he liked the first part of *Life on the Mississippi*. We still went to the Automat once or twice a week, he perhaps out of habit, because he didn't feel like going anywhere—I to get him out of his room. Oskar ate little, he toyed with a spoon. His eyes looked as though they had been squirted with a dark dye.   37

Once after a momentary cooling rainstorm we sat on newspapers on a wet bench overlooking the river and Oskar at last began to talk. In tormented English he conveyed his intense and everlasting hatred of the Nazis for destroying his career, uprooting his life, and flinging him like a piece of bleeding meat to the hawks. He cursed them thickly, the German nation, an inhuman, conscienceless, merciless people. "They are pigs mazquerading as peacogs," he said. "I feel certain that my wife, in her heart, was a Jew hater." It was a terrible bitterness, and eloquence beyond the words he spoke. He became silent again. I wanted to hear more about his wife but decided not to ask.   38

Afterwards in the dark, Oskar confessed that he had attempted suicide during his first week in America. He was living, at the end of May, in a small hotel, and had one night filled himself with barbiturates; but his phone had fallen off the table and the hotel operator had sent up the elevator boy, who found him unconscious and called the police. He was revived in the hospital.   39

"I did not mean to do it," he said, "it was a mistage."   40

"Don't ever think of it," I said, "it's total defeat."   41

"I don't," he said wearily, "because it is so arduouz to come bag to life."   42

"Please, for any reason whatever."   43

Afterwards when we were walking, he surprised me by saying, "Maybe we ought to try now the legture onze more."   44

We trudged back to the house and he sat at his hot desk, I trying to read as he slowly began to reconstruct the first page of his lecture. He wrote, of course, in German.   45

He got nowhere. We were back to sitting in silence in the heat. Sometimes, after a few minutes, I had to take off before his mood   46 overcame mine. One afternoon I came unwillingly up the stairs—there were times I felt momentary surges of irritation with him—and was frightened to find Oskar's door ajar. When I knocked no one answered. As I stood there, chilled down the spine, I realized I was thinking about the possibility of his attempting suicide again. "Oskar?" I went into the apartment, looked into both rooms and the bathroom, but he wasn't there. I thought he might have drifted out to get something from a store and took the opportunity to look quickly around. There was nothing startling in the medicine chest, no pills but aspirin, no iodine. Thinking, for some reason, of a gun, I searched his desk drawer. In it I found a thin-paper airmail letter from Germany. Even if I had wanted to, I couldn't read the handwriting, but as I held it in my hand I did make out a sentence: "Ich bin dir siebenundzwanzig Jahre treu gewesen." There was no gun in the drawer. I shut it and stopped looking. It had occurred to me if you want to kill yourself all you need is a straight pin. When Oskar returned he said he had been sitting in the public library, unable to read.

Now we are once more enacting the changeless scene, curtain   47
rising on two speechless characters in a furnished apartment, I in a straight-back chair, Oskar in the velour armchair that smothered rather than supported him, his flesh gray, the big gray face unfocused, sagging. I reached over to switch on the radio but he barely looked at me in a way that begged no. I then got up to leave but Oskar, clearing his throat, thickly asked me to stay. I stayed, thinking, was there more to this than I could see into? His problems, God knows, were real enough, but could there be something more than a refugee's displacement, alienation, financial insecurity, being in a strange land without friends or a speakable tongue? My speculation was the old one: not all drown in this ocean, why does he? After a while I shaped the thought and asked him was there something below the surface, invisible? I was full of this thing from college, and wondered if there mightn't be some unknown quantity in his depression that a psychiatrist maybe might help him with, enough to get him started on his lecture.

He meditated on this and after a few minutes haltingly said he had   48
been psychoanalyzed in Vienna as a young man. "Just the jusual drek," he said, "fears and fantazies that afterwaards no longer bothered me."

"They don't now?"   49

"Not."   50

"You've written many articles and lectures before," I said. "What I   51
can't understand, though I know how hard the situation is, is why you can never get past page one."

He half lifted his hand. "It is a paralyzis of my will. The whole   52
legture is clear in my mind, but the minute I write down a single word—in English or in German—I have a terrible fear I will not be

able to write the negst. As though someone has thrown a stone at a window and the whole house—the whole idea zmashes. This repeats, until I am dezperate."

He said the fear grew as he worked that he would die before he completed the lecture, or if not that, he would write it so disgracefully he would wish for death. The fear immobilized him. 53

"I have lozt faith. I do not—not longer possezz my former value of myself. In my life there has been too much illusion." 54

I tried to believe what I was saying: "Have confidence, the feeling will pass." 55

"Confidenze I have not. For this and alzo whatever elze I have lozt I thank the Nazis." 56

It was by then mid-August and things were growing steadily worse wherever one looked. The Poles were mobilizing for war. Oskar hardly moved. I was full of worries though I pretended calm weather. 57

He sat in his massive armchair, breathing like a wounded animal. 58

"Who can write aboud Walt Whitman in such terrible times?" 59

"Why don't you change the subject?" 60

"It mages no differenze what is the subject. It is all uzelezz." 61

I came every day, as a friend, neglecting my other students and therefore my livelihood. I had a panicky feeling that if things went on as they were going they would end in Oskar's suicide; and I felt a frenzied desire to prevent that. What's more, I was sometimes afraid I was myself becoming melancholy, a new talent, call it, of taking less pleasure in my little pleasures. And the heat continued, oppressive, relentless. We thought of escape into the country, but neither of us had the money. One day I bought Oskar a secondhand electric fan—wondering why we hadn't thought of that before—and he sat in the breeze for hours each day, until after a week, shortly after the Soviet-Nazi non-aggression pact was signed, the motor gave out. He could not sleep at night and sat at his desk with a wet towel on his head, still attempting to write the lecture. He wrote reams on a treadmill, it came out nothing. When he slept in exhaustion he had fantastic frightening dreams of the Nazis inflicting torture, sometimes forcing him to look upon the corpses of those they had slain. In one dream he told me about he had gone back to Germany to visit his wife. She wasn't home and he had been directed to a cemetery. There, though the tombstone read another name, her blood seeped out of the earth above her shallow grave. He groaned aloud at the memory. 62

Afterwards he told me something about her. They had met as students, lived together, and were married at twenty-three. It wasn't a very happy marriage. She had turned into a sickly woman, unable to have children. "Something was wrong with her interior strugture." 63

Though I asked no questions, Oskar said, "I offered her to come with me here, but she refused this." 64

"For what reason?"   65

"She did not think I wished her to come."   66

"Did you?" I asked.   67

"Not," he said.   68

He explained he had lived with her for almost twenty-seven years   69
under difficult circumstances. She had been ambivalent about their
Jewish friends and his relatives, though outwardly she seemed not a
prejudiced person. But her mother was always a dreadful anti-Semite.

"I have nothing to blame myzelf," Oskar said.   70

He took to his bed. I took to the New York Public Library. I read   71
some of the German poets he was trying to write about, in English
translation. Then I read *Leaves of Grass* and wrote down what I thought
one or two of them had got from Whitman. One day, toward the end of
August, I brought Oskar what I had written. It was in good part guessing,
but my idea wasn't to do the lecture for him. He lay on his back,
motionless, and listened sadly to what I had written. Then he said, no, it
wasn't the love of death they had got from Whitman—that ran through
German poetry—but it was most of all his feeling for Brudermensch, his
humanity.

"But this does not grow long on German earth," he said, "and is   72
soon deztroyed."

I said I was sorry I had got it wrong, but he thanked me anyway.   73

I left, defeated, and as I was going down the stairs, heard the sound 74
of sobbing. I will quit this, I thought, it has got to be too much for me. I
can't drown with him.

I stayed home the next day, tasting a new kind of private misery too 75
old for somebody my age, but that same night Oskar called me on the
phone, blessing me wildly for having read those notes to him. He had got
up to write me a letter to say what I had missed, and it ended in his
having written half the lecture. He had slept all day and tonight intended
to finish it up.

"I thank you," he said, "for much, alzo including your faith in me."   76

"Thank God," I said, not telling him I had just about lost it.   77

Oskar completed his lecture—wrote and rewrote it—during the first   78
week in September. The Nazis had invaded Poland, and though we were
greatly troubled, there was some sense of release; maybe the brave Poles
would beat them. It took another week to translate the lecture, but here
we had the assistance of Friedrich Wilhelm Wolff, the historian, a gentle,
erudite man, who liked translating and promised his help with future
lectures. We then had about two weeks to work on Oskar's delivery. The
weather had changed, and so, slowly, had he. He had awakened from
defeat, battered, after a weary battle. He had lost close to twenty pounds.
His complexion was still gray; when I looked at his face I expected to see
scars, but it had lost its flabby unfocused quality. His blue eyes had

returned to life and he walked with quick steps, as though to pick up a few for all the steps he hadn't taken during those long hot days he had lain in his room.

We went back to our former routine, meeting three late afternoons   79
a week for diction, grammar, and the other exercises. I taught him the phonetic alphabet and transcribed lists of words he was mispronouncing. He worked many hours trying to fit each sound in place, holding a matchstick between his teeth to keep his jaws apart as he exercised his tongue. All this can be a dreadfully boring business unless you think you have a future. Looking at him, I realized what's meant when somebody is called "another man."

The lecture, which I now knew by heart, went off well. The director   80
of the Institute had invited a number of prominent people. Oskar was the first refugee they had employed, and there was a move to make the public cognizant of what was then a new ingredient in American life. Two reporters had come with a lady photographer. The auditorium of the Institute was crowded. I sat in the last row, promising to put up my hand if he couldn't be heard, but it wasn't necessary. Oskar, in a blue suit, his hair cut, was of course nervous, but you couldn't see it unless you studied him. When he stepped up to the lectern, spread out his manuscript, and spoke his first English sentence in public, my heart hesitated; only he and I, of everybody there, had any idea of the anguish he had been through. His enunciation wasn't at all bad—a few *s*'s for *th*'s, and he once said bag for back, but otherwise he did all right. He read poetry well—in both languages—and though Walt Whitman, in his mouth, sounded a little as though he had come to the shores of Long Island as a German immigrant, still the poetry read as poetry:

> *And I know the Spirit of God is the brother of my own,*
> *And that all the men ever born are also my brothers,*
> *and the women my sisters and lovers,*
> *And that the kelson of creation is love . . .*

Oskar read it as though he believed it. Warsaw had fallen, but the verses were somehow protective. I sat back conscious of two things: how easy it is to hide the deepest wounds; and the pride I felt in the job I had done.

Two days later I came up the stairs into Oskar's apartment to find a crowd   81
there. The refugee, his face beet-red, lips bluish, a trace of froth in the corners of his mouth, lay on the floor in his limp pajamas, two firemen on their knees working over him with an inhalator. The windows were open and the air stank.

A policemen asked me who I was and I couldn't answer.   82
"No, oh no."   83

I said no but it was unchangeably yes. He had taken his life—gas—I   84
hadn't even thought of the stove in the kitchen.

"Why?" I asked myself. "Why did he do it?" Maybe it was the fate of   85
Poland on top of everything else, but the only answer anyone could
come up with was Oskar's scribbled note that he wasn't well, and had
left Martin Goldberg all his possessions. I am Martin Goldberg.

I was sick for a week, had no desire either to inherit or investigate,   86
but I thought I ought to look through his things before the court
impounded them, so I spent a morning sitting in the depths of Oskar's
armchair, trying to read his correspondence. I had found in the top
drawer a thin packet of letters from his wife and an airmail letter of recent
date from his mother-in-law.

She writes in a tight script it takes me hours to decipher, that her   87
daughter, after Oskar abandons her, against her own mother's fervent
pleas and anguish, is converted to Judaism by a vengeful rabbi. One
night the Brown Shirts appear, and though the mother wildly waves her
bronze crucifix in their faces, they drag Frau Gassner, together with the
other Jews, out of the apartment house, and transport them in lorries to
a small border town in conquered Poland. There, it is rumored, she is
shot in the head and topples into an open ditch with the naked Jewish
men, their wives and children, some Polish soldiers, and a handful of
gypsies.

Exercises

Some Important Words

brashly (paragraph 2), refugees (2), Adolf Hitler (2), Danzig (2), *Acht Uhr Abendblatt*—The Eight O'Clock Evening Paper (3), *Bitte*—Please (4), idioms (5), Yiddish (5), Kristallnacht (5), Bauhaus (5), gentile (5), Weimar Republic (6), *Ich weiss nicht, wie ich weiter machen soll*—I do not know how to go further with this (7), elongated (10), articulate (28), impeccable (28), elation (29), enervating (30), foundered (32), *Life on the Mississippi* (37), *Ich bin dir siebenundzwanzig Jahre treu gewesen*—I was faithful to you for twenty-seven years (46), displacement (47), speculation (47), *drek*—crap, junk (48), Nazis (56), Walt Whitman (59), ambivalent (69), *Leaves of Grass* (71), *Brudermensch*—humanity (71), erudite (78), cognizant (80), kelson (80, poem), Brown Shirts (87).

Some of the Issues

1. How did Martin Goldberg feel about being an English language tutor?
2. In paragraph 6, what reasons does Oskar Gassner give for his failure with his previous language tutors?

3. Why do you suppose Martin didn't "give him up" as the other tutors had?

4. In paragraphs 51–56, Oskar explains his inability to write the impossible lecture. What reasons does he give?

5. Reread paragraphs 71–77. What is the turning point that enables Oskar to break through his writing block?

6. What is the theme of his lecture at the Institute for Public Studies (paragraphs 71 and 80)?

7. What role does Martin Goldberg play in Oskar's success?

8. Why does Oskar commit suicide? Do you think there is something "below the surface" that may have been the catalyst?

9. In paragraphs 63–70, how does Oskar characterize his relationship with his wife? Did he love her?

10. Why do you think Frau Gassner converted to Judaism (paragraph 87)? From her actions, what can you infer about her feelings toward her husband and their marriage?

11. "Gentile is gentile, Germany is Germany." Explain the significance of Martin's sentiment in paragraph 5 to the story as a whole.

The Way We Are Told

12. What details does Malamud include to create an oppressive atmosphere for the reader as well as for his characters?

13. Malamud illustrates Oskar's German utterances and his English mispronunciations in the story. What effect do you think he wants to achieve?

14. In paragraph 46, what narrative purpose does the apartment scene have in relation to the entire story?

Some Subjects For Writing

15. How does this story confirm the importance of the ability to communicate? Describe how Oskar's inability to express himself had tragic consequences in his marriage, his friendships, and his profession.

* 16. Read Ngugi wa Thiong'o's "The Politics of Language," in particular, the section on the dual character of language as a means of communication and as a carrier of culture. Show how Ngugi's views might explain Oskar's paralysis in writing and in speaking in German.

AFTER THE BEEP

Alan Devenish

Alan Devenish, poet and college professor of writing, was born in Brooklyn, New York, in 1947. As faculty associate at the Institute for Writing and Thinking at Bard College, he has led creative writing and poetry workshops for teachers, administrators, college students, and elementary school children. The workshops focus on writing as a creative, communal process of inquiry and exploration.

His poetry, which has been published in numerous literary magazines, including *Gargoyle, Manhattan Poetry Review, The Little Magazine,* and *The Washington Review,* often relies on humor to delight, to amuse, and to probe serious aspects of human relationships. In this poem, he takes an ironic glimpse at modern technology and its impact on communication.

Hello. this is the Preston residence
and this is she speaking.
Sorry I'm not broadcasting live but do leave a message
and I or my machine will get back to you
or your machine.

Please wait
until the cannonade from Tchaikovsky's 1812 Overture
completes its third volley and the strains
of the Marseillaise stir faintly in the background
before starting your message.

Kindly repress the urge to be cute or cryptic.
On the other hand don't make it ten years long either.
I would also ask that you refrain
from rhetorical questions and long subordinate clauses.
Just be yourself, keeping in mind
this is the late twentieth century
and literary flourishes tend to disgust.

Now, if you're the guy I met out jogging, I'm sorry but
forget it. It was all a mistake and anyway
I'm into squash now.

If however this is about an appointment
or interview which could advance my career
please speak distinctly and don't make any decisions
until I can process your message.

Lastly, if you've gotten my number
from any other source except me personally
you'd better have a good story.

So, until I get back to you, have a nice day
or should I decide to ignore your call,
a nice rest of your life.

ACKNOWLEDGMENTS

Agueros, Jack. "Halfway to Dick and Jane" by Jack Agueros, copyright © 1971 by Doubleday, a division of Bantam Doubleday Dell Publishing Group, Inc. From *The Immigrant Experience* by Thomas Wheeler. Used by permission of the publisher.

Angelou, Maya. "Graduation" from *I Know Why the Caged Bird Sings* by Maya Angelou. Copyright © 1969 by Maya Angelou. Reprinted by permission of Random House Inc.

Anonymous. "Recapture the Flag: 34 Reasons to Love America." *City Pages* (Minneapolis, MN), July 3, 1991. Reprinted by permission of the publisher.

Atwood, Margaret. "Canadians: What Do They Want?" by Margaret Atwood. Reprinted with permission from *Mother Jones* magazine. Copyright © 1982, Foundation for National Progress.

Bohannon, Laura. "Shakespeare in the Bush" from *Natural History,* August/September, 1966, Vol. 75, No. 7, by Dr. Laura Bohannon. Reprinted by permission of the author.

Brooks, Gwendolyn. "We Real Cool" by Gwendolyn Brooks. Taken from *Blacks,* copyright 1987. Published by The David Co., Chicago. Reprinted by permission of the author.

Bruchac, Joseph. "Ellis Island" by Joseph Bruchac from *The Remembered Earth,* Ed. Geary Hobson. Albuquerque: Red Earth Press, 1979. Reprinted by permission of the author.

Buruma, Ian. "Work as a Form of Beauty" by Ian Buruma. Excerpt from *Tokyo: Form and Spirit* by Ian Buruma. Reprinted by permission of the author.

Campa, Arthur L. "Anglo vs. Chicano: Why?" in *Western Review,* 1972. Copyright © 1972. Reprinted by permission of Mrs. Arthur L. Campa.

Chase, Lincoln. "From Such a Night" by Lincoln Chase. Published by Shelby Singleton Music, Inc., Nashville, TN. Reprinted by permission.

Chira, Susan. "The Good Mother: Searching for an Ideal" by Susan Chira. Reprinted from "New Realities Fight Old Images of Mother." *The New York Times,* August 23, 1992, Section 4, pg. 2. Copyright © 1992 by The New York Times Company. Reprinted by permission.

Cisneros, Sandra. "Barbie-Q" by Sandra Cisneros. From *Woman Hollering Creek.* Copyright © by Sandra Cisneros 1991. Published in the United States by Vintage Books, a division of Random House, Inc., New York and distributed in Canada by Random House of Canada Limited, Toronto, 1991. Originally published in somewhat different form by Arte Publico Press in 1984, revised in 1989. Reprinted by permission of Susan Bergholz Literary Services, New York.

445

Columbus, Christopher. From the book *The Voyage of Christopher Columbus,* translated by John Cummings. Copyright © 1992. Reprinted with permission from St. Martin's Press, Inc., New York, NY.

Cooke, Alistair. "The Huddled Masses." From *Alistair Cooke's America* by Alistair Cooke. Copyright © 1973 by Alistair Cooke. Reprinted by permission of Alfred A. Knopf, Inc.

Cross, Donna Woolfolk. "Sin, Suffer and Repent." Reprinted by permission of the Putnam Publishing Group from *Media Speak: How Television Makes Up Your Mind* by Donna Woolfolk Cross. Copyright © 1983 by Donna Woolfolk Cross.

Cullen, Countee. "Incident," from the book *Color* by Countee Cullen. Reprinted by permission of GRM Associates, Inc., agents for the Estate of Ida M. Cullen. Copyright © 1925 by Harper & Brothers; copyright renewed 1953 by Ida M. Cullen.

Devenish, Alan. "After the Beep," by Alan Devenish. Reprinted from *College English,* vol. 49, no. 7, November 1987. First published in *College English,* November 1987. Reprinted with permission.

Dorris, Michael. "For the Indians, No Thanksgiving." Copyright © Michael Dorris 1989. From the *Chicago Tribune,* November 24, 1988. Reprinted with permission.

Early, Gerald. "Their Malcolm, My Problem," by Gerald Early. Copyright © 1992 by *Harper's Magazine.* All rights reserved. Reprinted from the December issue by special permission.

Ehrenreich, Barbara and Annette Fuentes. "Life on the Global Assembly Line." Reprinted from *Ms.* magazine, June, 1981. Barbara Ehrenreich is a freelance writer based in New York.

Gates, David. "Who Was Columbus?" From *Newsweek* [Special Issue f/w 1991]. Copyright © 1991, Newsweek, Inc. All rights reserved. Reprinted by permission.

Giovanni, Nikki. "They Clapped." From *My House* by Nikki Giovanni. Copyright © 1972 by Nikki Giovanni. Reprinted by permission of William Morrow & Co.

Hall, Edward T. "Private Space." Excerpts from *The Hidden Dimension* by Edward T. Hall, copyright © 1966 by Edward T. Hall. Used by permission of Doubleday, a division of Bantam, Doubleday, Dell Publishing Group, Inc.

Hines, William. "Hello, Judy. I'm Dr. Smith." Reprinted with permission from *Chicago Sun Times/1990.*

Hoffman, Eva. "Lost in Translation," by Eva Hoffman. From *Lost in Translation.* Copyright © 1989 by Eva Hoffman. Used by permission of the publisher, Dutton, an imprint of New American Library, a division of Penguin Books USA Inc.

Houston, Jeanne Wakatsuki and James D. Houston. "Shikata Ga Nai" from *Farewell to Manzanar* by Jeanne Wakatsuki Houston and James D. Houston. Copyright © 1973 by James D. Houston. Reprinted by permission of Houghton Mifflin Company.

Howard, Jane. "Families," by Jane Howard. Copyright © 1978 by Jane Howard. Reprinted by permission of Simon & Schuster, Inc.

Illich, Ivan. "Effects of Development." Reprinted with permission from *The New York Review of Books.* Copyright © 1969 Nyrev, Inc.

Johnson, James Weldon, J. Rosamund Johnson. "Lift Ev'ry Voice and Sing," song in Maya Angelou, *I Know Why the Caged Birds Sing*. Used by permission of Edward B. Marks Music Company.

Kazin, Alfred. Excerpt from "The Kitchen" in *A Walker in the City,* copyright 1951 and renewed 1979 by Alfred Kazin, reprinted by permission of Harcourt Brace Jovanovich, Inc.

Kingston, Maxine Hong. "Girlhood Among Ghosts." From *The Woman Warrior: Memoirs of a Girlhood Among Ghosts* by Maxine Hong Kingston. Copyright © 1975, 1976 by Maxine Hong Kingston. Reprinted by permission of Alfred A. Knopf, Inc.

Knepler, Myrna. "Sold at Fine Stores, Naturellement," in *Verbatim,* February, 1978. Copyright © 1978 by *Verbatim,* Vol. 4, The Language Quarterly, 1978. Used by permission.

Lakoff, Robin. "You Are What You Say." From *Ms.* magazine, July 1974. Reprinted by permission.

Lord, Bette Bao. "Walking in Lucky Shoes." *Newsweek* (July 6, 1992). Reprinted by permission of the author.

Mabry, Marcus. "Living in Two Worlds." From *Newsweek on Campus,* April, 1988. Copyright © 1988, Newsweek, Inc. All rights reserved. Reprinted by permission.

Malamud, Bernard. "The German Refugee" from *Idiots First* by Bernard Malamud. Copyright © 1963 by Bernard Malamud. Copyright renewed © 1991 by Ann Malamud. Reprinted by permission of Farrar, Straus and Giroux, Inc.

Malcolm X. "Hair." From *The Autobiography of Malcolm X* by Malcolm X, with the assistance of Alex Haley. Copyright © 1964 by Alex Haley and Malcolm X. Copyright © 1965 by Alex Haley and Betty Shabazz. Reprinted by permission of Random House, Inc.

Morley, John David. "Living in a Japanese Home." From the book, *Pictures from the Water Trade,* copyright © 1985 by John David Morley. Used by permission of the Atlantic Monthly Press.

Morrison, Toni. "A Slow Walk of Trees." From *The New York Times Magazine,* July 4, 1975. Copyright © 1976 by The New York Times Company. Reprinted by permission.

Muñiz, Maria L. "Back, but Not Home." From the *New York Times,* July 13, 1979. Copyright © 1979/85 by The New York Times Company. Reprinted by permission.

Naylor, Gloria. "The Meaning of a Word," by Gloria Naylor. Reprinted by permission of Sterling Lord Literistic, Inc. Copyright © 1986 by Gloria Naylor.

Novak, Michael. "In Ethnic America." Reprinted with permission of Macmillan Publishing Company from *The Rise of the Unmeltable Ethnics* by Michael Novak. Copyright © 1971 Michael Novak.

Okita, Dwight. "In Response to Executive Order 9066: All Americans of Japanese Descent Must Report to Relocation Centers" by Dwight Okita. From Dwight Okita's new first book of poems, *Crossing with the Light,* published by Tia Chucha Press in Chicago. Copyright © 1992 Dwight Okita.

Orwell, George. "Shooting an Elephant" from *Shooting an Elephant and Other Essays* by George Orwell, copyright 1950 by Sonia Brownell Orwell and renewed 1978 by Sonia Pitt-Rivers. Reprinted by permission of Harcourt Brace Jovanovich, Inc.

Paley, Grace. "The Loudest Voice" from *The Little Disturbances of Man* by Grace Paley. Copyright 1956, 1957, 1958, 1959, renewed © 1984 by Grace Paley. Reprinted by permission of Viking Penguin Inc.
Park, Sun. "Don't Expect Me to Be Perfect" from Special Edition for Teens, 1984, *Newsweek.*
Petrakis, Harry Mark. "Barba Nikos" from *Reflections: A Writer's Life—A Writer's Work.* Lake View Press, Chicago, copyright by Harry Mark Petrakis.
Podhoretz, Norman. "The Brutal Bargain." Excerpt from *The Brutal Bargain* by Norman Podhoretz. Copyright © 1967 by Norman Podhoretz. Reprinted by permission of Georges Borchardt, Inc. for the author.

Rodriguez, Richard. "Public and Private Language," by Richard Rodriguez. From *Hunger of Memory* by Richard Rodriguez. Copyright © 1982 by Richard Rodriguez. Reprinted by permission of David R. Godine, Publisher.
Roethke, Theodore. "My Papa's Waltz," copyright 1942 by Hearst Magazines, Inc. From *The Collected Poems of Theodore Roethke* by Theodore Roethke. Used by permission of Doubleday, a division of Bantam, Doubleday, Dell Publishing Group, Inc.
Rose, Mike. "I Just Wanna Be Average." Reprinted with the permission of The Free Press, a Division of Macmillan, Inc., from *Lives on the Boundary: The Struggles and Achievements of America's Underprepared* by Mike Rose. Copyright © 1989 by Mike Rose.
Rose, Wendy. "Three Thousand Dollar Death Song," by Wendy Rose. From *Lost Copper.* Copyright © 1980, Malki Museum, Inc.

Salzman, Mark. "Teacher Mark." From *Iron and Silk,* by Mark Salzman. Copyright © 1986 by Mark Salzman. Reprinted by permission of Random House, Inc.
Shaheen, Jack. "The Media's Image of Arabs," by Jack Shaheen. From *Newsweek,* February 29, 1988. Reprinted by permission of the author.
Shammas, Anton. "Amérka, Amérka," by Anton Shammas. Copyright © 1991 by *Harper's Magazine.* All rights reserved. Reprinted from the February issue by special permission.
Skolnick, Arlene. "The Paradox of Perfection," by Arlene Skolnick. From *Wilson Quarterly,* Summer, 1980. Reprinted by permission of the author.
Staples, Brent. "The Language of Fear," by Brent Staples. From *Ms.* magazine, September, 1986. Reprinted by permission of the author.

Tan, Amy. "Two Kinds." Reprinted by permission of The Putnam Publishing Group from *The Joy Luck Club* by Amy Tan. Copyright © 1989 by Amy Tan.
Tarkov, John. "Fitting In," by John Tarkov from the *New York Times* (About Men column), July 7, 1985. Reprinted by permission of the *New York Times.*
Thiong'o, Ngugi Wa. "The Politics of Language," by Ngugi Wa Thiong'o. From *Decolonizing the Mind.* Published by James Currey Publishers, London. Reprinted by permission of the publisher.

Thomas, Piri. "Alien Turf." From *Down These Mean Streets* by Piri Thomas. Copyright © 1967 by Piri Thomas. Reprinted by permission of Alfred A. Knopf, Inc.

Van Gelder, Lindsy. "The Importance of Being Eleven: Carol Gilligan Takes on Adolescence." Published in *Ms.* magazine, July–August, 1990. Reprinted by permission of the author.

White, Walter. "I Learn What I Am." From *A Man Called White* (Arno Press, 1948). Reprinted by permission of Jane White Viazzi.
Wong, Elizabeth. "The Struggle to Be an All-American Girl," by Elizabeth Wong. Reprinted by permission of the author.

Yezierska, Anzia. "Soap and Water" by Anzia Yezierska from *How I Found America: Collected Stories of Anzia Yezierska.* Copyright © 1991 by Louise Levitas Henriksen. Reprinted by permission of Persea Books, Inc.

Photo Credits: © Martha Cooper (p. 208); © Lawrence Migdale (p. 209); © Bob Daemmrich/The Image Works (p. 211); © Katrina Thomas (p. 212); © Julie Markes/AP/Wide World (p. 213)

AUTHOR/TITLE INDEX

After the Beep, 443
Agueros, Jack, 25
Alien, Turf, 240
*Amérka, Amérka: A Palestinian
        Abroad in the Land of the
        Free,* 96
Angelou, Maya, 7
Anglo vs. Chicano: Why?, 90
Arrival at Manzanar, 229
Atwood, Margaret, 312

Back, but Not Home, 167
Barba, Nikos, 106
Barbie-Q, 203
Bohannan, Laura, 334
Brooks, Gwendolyn, 206
Bruchac, Joseph, 299
Brutal Bargain, The, 177
Buruma, Ian, 326

Campa, Arthur L., 90
Canadians: What Do They Want?,
        312
Chira, Susan, 129
Cisneros, Sandra, 203
Columbus, Christopher, 261
Conformity and Individuality in
        Japan, 326
Cooke, Alistair, 277
Crèvecoeur, Michel Guillaume St.
        Jean de, 271
Cross, Donna Woolfolk, 404
Cullen, Countee, 68

Devenish, Alan, 443
Don't Expect Me to Be Perfect, 116
Dorris, Michael, 236

Early, Gerald, 190
Ehrenreich, Barbara, 346
Ellis Island, 299

Families, 123
Fitting In, 71
For the Indians, No Thanksgiving,
        236
Fuentes, Annette, 346

Gates, David, 266
German Refugee, The, 431
Giovanni, Nikki, 372
Girlhood Among Ghosts, 19
Good Mother: Searching for an
        Ideal, The, 129
Graduation, 7

Hair, 187
Halfway to Dick and Jane: A Puerto
        Rican Pilgrimage, 25
Hello, Judy, I'm Dr. Smith, 382
Hines, William, 382
Hoffman, Eva, 171
Houston, James D., 229
Houston, Jeanne Wakatsuki, 229
Howard, Jane, 123
Huddled Masses, The, 277

I Just Wanna Be Average, 45
I Learn What I Am, 222
Importance of Being Eleven: Carol
        Gilligan Takes on
        Adolescence, The, 39
Incident, 68
In Ethnic America, 82
In Response to Executive Order
        9066: All Americans of
        Japanese Descent Must Report
        to Relocation Centers, 252

Journal of Discovery, October 10th
        to 12th, 1492, 261

Kazin, Alfred, 119

Kingston, Maxine Hong, 19
Kitchen, The, 119
Knepler, Myrna, 398

Lakoff, Robin, 386
Life on the Global Assembly Line,
    346
Living in a Japanese Home, 365
Living in Two Worlds, 163
Lord, Betty Bao, 257
Lost in Translation, 171
Loudest Voice, The, 60

Mabry, Marcus, 163
Malamud, Bernard, 431
Malcolm X, 187
Meaning of a Word, The, 377
Media's Image of Arabs, The, 394
Modest Proposal, A, 356
Morley, John David, 365
Morrison, Toni, 76
Muñiz, Maria L., 167
My Papa's Waltz, 160

Naylor, Gloria, 377
Ngugi wa Thiong'o, 420
Night Walker, 217
Novak, Michael, 82

Okita, Dwight, 252
Orwell, George, 318

Paley, Grace, 60
Paradox of Perfection, The, 139
Park, Sun, 116
Petrakis, Harry Mark, 106
Podhoretz, Norman, 177
Politics of Language, The, 420
Public and Private Language, 413

Recapture the Flag: 34 Reasons to
    Love America, 287
Rites of Passage in America (Photo
    Essay), 207

Rodriguez, Richard, 413
Roethke, Theodore, 160
Rose, Mike, 45
Rose, Wendy, 112

Salzman, Mark, 303
Shaheen, Jack G., 394
Shakespeare in the Bush, 334
Shammas, Anton, 96
Shooting an Elephant, 318
Sin, Suffer and Repent, 404
Skolnick, Arlene, 139
Slow Walk of Trees, A, 76
Soap and Water, 291
Sold at Fine Stores Everywhere,
    Naturellement, 398
Staples, Brent, 217
Struggle to Be an All-American Girl,
    The, 3
Swift, Jonathan, 356

Tan, Amy, 148
Tarkov, John, 71
Teacher Mark, 303
Their Malcolm, My Problem, 190
They Clapped, 372
Thomas, Piri, 240
Three Thousand Dollar Death Song,
    112
Two Kinds, 148

Van Gelder, Lindsy, 39

Walking in Lucky Shoes, 257
We Real Cool, 206
What Is an American?, 271
Who Was Columbus?, 266
White, Walter, 222
Wong, Elizabeth, 3

Yezierska, Anzia, 291
You Are What You Say, 386